... AND
WHAT
DO
YOU
DO?

"They are the pinnacle of privilege, leading enviably gilded lives, but how much do we really know of the royal family's cosy, taxpayer-funded existence? Norman Baker goes behind palace walls to shine a much-needed light on this most secretive of institutions and expose the greed, hypocrisy and – yes – disregard for public money which keep it afloat. Filled with fascinating detail and insight, … *And What Do You Do?* is an essential primer for understanding the myth of modern royalty."

RICHARD KAY, ROYAL WRITER FOR THE *DAILY MAIL*

"With our democracy in turmoil, it's right to be asking questions about constitutional reform, and that includes the role of the royal family. Norman Baker tackles the subject with his trademark energy and in forensic detail, looking at the facts beyond the headlines. An important book for anyone serious about questioning how our country is run."

CAROLINE LUCAS MP

"Norman Baker brilliantly exposes how a Ruritanian farce is ripping us off. Vive la British revolution!"

KEVIN MAGUIRE, *DAILY MIRROR*

"Norman Baker is a fiercely independent writer and former Lib Dem MP and government minister who speaks his mind and goes where others fear to tread. After probing the mysterious death of Dr Kelly after the Iraq War, he now turns his attention to the public costs of the royal family, based on careful research and facts rather than sentiments or prejudice."

SIR VINCE CABLE MP

"… *And What Do You Do?* is a clear-eyed assessment of our royal family, looking at its strengths, weaknesses and eccentricities. Parts of Norman Baker's well-researched book will make for uncomfortable reading for some die-hard royal fans, but it should become an important text for anyone who cares about our monarchy and wants to see it reform and evolve to face head on the challenges of the twenty-first century."

CHRISTOPHER HOPE, CHIEF POLITICAL CORRESPONDENT AND ASSISTANT EDITOR, *DAILY TELEGRAPH*

... AND WHAT DO YOU DO?

WHAT THE ROYAL FAMILY DON'T WANT YOU TO KNOW

NORMAN BAKER

Biteback Publishing

ISBN 978-1-78590-621-3

10 9 8 7 6 5 4 3 2 1

A CIP catalogue record for this book is available from the British Library.

Set in Minion Pro by Adrian McLaughlin

Printed and bound in Great Britain by
CPI Group (UK) Ltd, Croydon CR0 4YY

'At any given moment, there is a sort of pervading orthodoxy, a general tacit agreement, not to discuss large and uncomfortable facts.'

– GEORGE ORWELL

'No institution – city, monarchy, whatever – should expect to be free from the scrutiny of those who give it their loyalty.'

– QUEEN ELIZABETH II, NOVEMBER 1992

Contents

Introduction

The royal family is the original *Coronation Street*, a long-running soap opera with the occasional real coronation thrown in. Its members have become celebrities, like up-market versions of film stars and footballers. The mainstream media coverage treats them accordingly. So, for the most part, we are fed a constant diet of sickeningly sycophantic coverage which reports their activities with breathless and uncritical awe. The Queen looked marvellous. The crowd that lined the streets was hugely enthusiastic. For Mrs Miggins, just to be within 100 yards of Harry made it a day she will never forget as long as she lives.

Alternatively, the family is subject to trivial voyeurism into what are genuinely their private lives, unconnected with their public roles. Who was that very distant relative of the Queen snorting coke at some Chelsea party? Are Andrew and Sarah going to remarry? Didn't Kate wear that same dress four months ago?

Whether infantile infatuation or intolerable intrusion, the British public deserves better than this puerile diet.

The monarchy is an important part of our constitution and exercises considerable influence on the kind of nation we are. Yet you will struggle to find very much in the way of proper journalism that examines the monarchy in the way that their position and influence merit in a mature democracy.

This book sets out to correct this. It is a serious book about a serious subject. It is most definitely not slavishly sycophantic, but nor does it seek to paint the royals in a deliberately unflattering light. It simply aims to establish and present the facts.

When the American author Kitty Kelley was researching for *The Royals*, her book on the monarchy which was published about twenty years ago, she was scolded by Lady Rothschild: 'We don't need a book by an objective American. You're not supposed to be objective about royalty,' adding for good measure: 'We have to protect our royal family from themselves.'

I disagree. This is the twenty-first century, and the time for fantasies is over. Let us instead have the facts.

And What Do You Do?

We all arrived much too early. I was to learn that the arrival time given to guests for royal visits was always much too early, even where the royal personage in question was so far down the pecking order that nobody really had very much idea who they were.

The reason, I discovered, was to prevent the apparently appalling possibility of someone arriving after the royal in question. On this occasion, the visitor was to be none other than the Queen herself, accompanied by the garrulous Prince Philip, so the delay between arrival and anything happening was even longer than normal.

It was 1999 and the unlikely setting was The Triangle, the new leisure centre in Burgess Hill, which the Queen was officially to open. A large crowd filled the main area of the leisure centre. Here and there bird tables had sprung up, offering various unappetising canapés and sorry-looking biscuits. There were no seats anywhere and a few of the elderly guests were clearly finding it something of an ordeal to be on their feet so long.

One elderly woman looked to be finding the wait particularly difficult and was leaning rather heavily on one of the bird tables.

I spotted one of the Palace flunkeys nearby, part of the forward party that was milling around.

'Is there a seat we can get for this lady?' I asked, pointing to the woman in question.

'Nobody is allowed to sit down in the presence of the Queen,' he told me grandly, and walked away, leaving me agape and the old woman still clinging to the bird table. Presumably she would have been allowed to fall down, if necessary. I discovered later that this archaic etiquette was not simply enforced for the Queen. Her sister, Princess Margaret, who demanded curtseys and head bows from those whose presence she graced, decreed that nobody was allowed to sit without her permission, and no one was allowed to leave before her.

Although Burgess Hill was not in my Lewes constituency, it was only just outside, and I had been invited along for the occasion by Ken Blanshard, the then Lib Dem leader of Mid Sussex District Council whose new leisure centre it was. To pass the time, Ken showed me around the centre, but when we got to the balcony overlooking the main area where everyone had congregated, our way was barred by another Palace flunkey.

'You can't come along here, sir,' he said firmly.

'What do you mean?' I challenged, and pointed to Ken. 'It's his leisure centre.'

'I'm sorry, sir, nobody can look down on the Queen.'

The Queen of course was not even there, and would not be for some time. It occurred to me afterwards that he, the flunkey, would be looking down on the Queen, but perhaps that did not count. I began to wonder how many centuries these royal rules of etiquette had existed and, more to the point, why they had not withered on the vine, like bear baiting and sending children up chimneys.

A similar thought had occurred to me a few years earlier when, as then leader of Lewes District Council, I had attended an event in my council ward at Middle Farm in Firle, a village just outside Lewes. Middle Farm is a rather splendid farm shop offering a great range of local produce, including wines and ciders, much of it organic. It is now a tourist attraction in its own right. The royal guest on that occasion was Prince Charles. Again, everyone had been required to arrive much too early, and we were ushered into a rather too small room, naturally without anywhere to sit. People were beginning to grumble about it when the door opened and some sort of equerry, who gave a fair impression of John Inman in *Are You Being Served?*, clapped his hands, and the conversations died away.

The purpose of the interruption was to tell us that Prince Charles would be with us shortly, and, to make him feel at ease, could we all give him a round of applause upon his entry. It was more of an instruction than a request. When the Prince entered shortly afterwards, the guests, or at least most of them, dutifully did as they had been bidden, and a polite ripple went round the room.

However, far from putting Charles at his ease, as his equerry had suggested, a pained grimace crossed his countenance when the applause began. He seemed almost shy, in a rather endearing sort of way.

I wondered, and still do, whether Charles is aware of these sorts of instructions from his servants, or has perhaps even initiated them, seeing them as a necessary intervention to ensure the majesty of the crown is upheld, or whether he has gone through life oblivious to these actions, believing that the welcoming applause from his audiences is a genuine and spontaneous expression of support.

Having been refused entry to the leisure centre balcony, I made my way back downstairs and mingled with the crowds. Eventually the royal guests arrived, and before long Prince Philip was working the room and soon came to join our small huddle of about seven. Under the

3

imperial rules of the British monarchy, the royal personage has to initiate any conversation. A standard opening gambit is to ask: 'And what do you do?'

It is safe, gives nothing away, and allows the royal personage to select an item of the reply to pursue. If the reply does not offer a suitable line, then the second standard question may follow: 'Have you come far?'

These genteel questions can take on a rougher edge when Prince Philip is the questioner. 'Who are you?' he barked at me.

'I'm a local MP,' I replied.

'Oh! I thought it was that fat chap.'

I smiled, and explained that Nicholas Soames was indeed the MP for Burgess Hill, but I was just across the border. He grunted.

He was actually rather good at making meaningless conversation sound quite interesting. I suppose he had had plenty of practice. One particular technique he deployed was elegant, effective and impressive. When he decided it was time to move on from one group to the next, he would laugh uproariously at something not particularly funny while simultaneously walking backwards and then turning round, ensuring nobody had the chance to detain him further.

Eventually the Queen appeared from behind a curtain somewhere at the back of the room. She walked along the raised walkway that ran along one of the walls and was perhaps five feet above the main floor area. At the end she turned to begin walking along the raised second side of the square until she reached the centre. There she stood for a moment, her back to the audience, before pulling back the curtain to reveal the plaque specially prepared to commemorate the opening.

As the curtains opened, a sycophantic round of applause filled the room as she wordlessly read the plaque to herself. Then without a word, or once looking at those who had gathered for the occasion, she retraced her steps and disappeared once more.

I was taken aback, and I was not alone. All she had to do was smile, thank people for coming, and declare the centre open, but not a word, not even a glance, was offered. Now we all have off days, and if the Queen thought that opening a leisure centre in Burgess Hill was hardly the stuff of monarchs, then that is a viewpoint many, including me, would sympathise with. Indeed her other official activity on that visit, to inspect the town council's Help Point, was doubtless even less riveting.

Nevertheless, had any politician, or indeed almost anyone else, performed the opening ceremony as gracelessly as she had done, there would have been a price to pay: in reputation, popularity, ultimately in votes. Both the public present and any media in attendance would have seen to that.

On this occasion, the papers, of course, carried not a whiff of criticism of, or even made any allusion to, this episode, although there were journalists in the hall. The reports were only factual insofar as they were able to present the royal visit in a good light. Anything else was excised. The papers declared that the visit had been a tremendous success.

Over the years I began to notice the same language cropping up in reports of royal visits. They were always successful, the crowds were always enthusiastic, the royal personage was always in good form – radiant even. Only the names of the royals, the locations, and the weather changed. The pieces that appeared in local papers could safely have been written in advance – perhaps were – with only the pictures slotted in afterwards, in the manner of a theatre critic who writes a review without bothering to see the play in question, only with royal visits there would be rather less risk.

The perceived wisdom is that for a constitutional monarchy to survive and prosper, it needs to be in tune with the citizens of its country, in fact, to be an embodiment of the people. What I had witnessed that day, in terms of preposterous rules of etiquette and the rest, may at a push have embodied the nation at the time of the Queen's accession to the throne, but was way out of line with a country about to enter the twenty-first century. These matters may be small in themselves, but there are many other ways, all too visible, to suggest a disconnect between the royal family and the people of this nation they are supposed to embody.

This disconnect opens up for the royals options simply not available to the public at large, even if some are questionable in benefit. All the Queen's children were privately educated, and today's royal offspring continue to be sent to expensive public schools, nowadays usually Eton. This, I suppose, is progress of a sort, in that it was not very long ago that royal children did not mingle at all, and instead were home educated. None of the central figures in the royal family uses the NHS, that most valued institution that politicians tamper with at their peril. In transport, there is still a preference amongst most members of the family for specially chartered flights, at vast cost to the taxpayer, or helicopter travel, even for short distances, where much cheaper alternatives, in terms of scheduled flights or trains or cars, exist. The Queen herself has never lived in a house without servants. The first thing a royal child is taught by Nanny is how to ring for service.

Then there are the landholdings, extensive and way in excess of what is needed to sustain a constitutional monarchy. The state supports not just Buckingham Palace, but also St James's Palace, the base for the Prince of Wales, Clarence House, Marlborough House Mews, Kensington Palace, Windsor Castle, Frogmore House and Hampton Court Mews, to name but a few. In total, the taxpayer pays for over a hundred buildings, six thousand rooms and twenty acres of roofs.

And of course the Queen owns plenty of private property too, notably Balmoral and Sandringham, both bought with public funds, which also qualify for taxpayer support when they are used for official business.

There are also the unique and highly beneficial tax arrangements from which the royals benefit, the exemptions from inconvenient laws like the Freedom of Information Act and the astonishing ability to object to proposed legislation that affects them personally. Other beneficial practices are the questionable business dealings and friendships, particularly those indulged in by Prince Andrew, that no other section of people on the public payroll – MPs, Lords, councillors, civil servants – could get away with.

A particularly unattractive tendency amongst the monarchy is that of self-congratulation, epitomised by the huge numbers of medals every member of the royal family seems to acquire without in most cases experiencing the sort of military action that would justify the awarding of such medals. Prince Charles alone has a choice of thirty-one from which to choose.

Even their accents seem, indeed are, from another era. It is interesting to listen to clips from the BBC or Pathé News from the 1940s and 1950s, and to hear accents that have in two or three generations vanished almost totally, except in the royal family. Only the Queen now pronounces 'coffee' as if it were 'corfee', and only Prince Charles pronounces the singular of 'mice' as indistinguishable from its plural.

In all these ways, and many more, the royal family operates in, and implicitly advocates, a different world from that occupied by the vast majority of the citizens of the UK, and a world where the rules are skewed to benefit them. And more insidiously, that those with power and influence should use that power rather determinedly to look after their own personal interests.

But just imagine the liberating effect if the royal children had been born in a local NHS hospital, or had instead attended a local state school, or if they were given a name that is not the name of a previous monarch, frequently George. Archie seems likely to be an aberration from a semi-detached section of the royal family rather than the start of a trend.

Perhaps the time will come when members of the royal family will emerge from their rarefied and silkily cushioned bubble, but so far the nearest we have come is Prince Harry choosing to take an easyJet flight. At the moment, however, such displays of normality, humility even, are very much the exception.

Yet the fact remains that the royal family, and the Queen in particular, consistently generate strong popularity ratings, so the disconnect between their actions and those of the great British public appears not to matter. Is this because the real facts are hidden? The blanket exemption from the Freedom of Information Act hides the gluttonous excesses and the breathtaking tax breaks, and the unique ability to seal wills hides the enormous wealth that has been accumulated. A forelock-tugging political Establishment turns a blind eye, and a compliant media, fearful of losing access to the royal photos and press passes, is careful never to go too far in its criticism. Is it that the public do not know just how much the royals bend the rules to look after themselves? Or are we all playing along, complicitly indulging in some comforting fantasy of fairy princes and princesses, Disney castles and *Downton Abbey*, that shuts out the hard reality of Britain's diminished place in the world in 2020?

It is time to turn the tables on the British monarchy and ask them: 'And what do *you* do?'

The Name Game

The two-carriage diesel train slowly made its way along the single track before coming to a halt next to the sad solitary platform at the terminus, Windsor and Eton Central. Beyond the end of the platform, the grand ironwork, the old booking office and all the other remnants of what was clearly once a substantial station remained, though now given over to that modern leisure activity – shopping. Between the rudimentary platform and the shopping complex, inevitably called Windsor Royal Shopping, were the first indications you were in Windsor – a lovingly polished old steam engine called *The Queen*, older than the monarch herself, and a slightly incongruous mosaic of Harry and Meghan.

Windsor is a royal town like no other. Union Jacks hang from the shops, which often bear names like 'King & Queen' (this a gift shop), and 'Ice Queen', where you can buy ice cream, though I did not see many takers on the cold January day I was first there.

The pubs too show their loyalty. There is the Queen Charlotte, then the Prince Harry, and the Duchess of Cambridge, clearly recent name changes. Had they previously been something like the White Hart or the Black Horse, I wondered, or had previous royals been gently eased aside, like waxworks in Madame Tussauds being discreetly replaced?

So royal were the pub names that the Carpenters' Arms seemed almost disloyal.

The town centre generally felt as if it could be a setting for an Agatha Christie mystery. Quaintness abounds, such as the car parking space bearing the sign: 'Reserved for Church Organist'. I was on my way to the Royal Archives in Windsor Castle, a visit that had taken quite some time and a good deal of patience to organise. Inside the castle, the upstairs reading room for researchers is surprisingly small, with space for only six people at a time at most. I am grateful to the archivists who work there, who were all most helpful.

Amongst other matters, I wanted to research the change that had occurred in 1917 when the royal family adopted the name Windsor. Throughout the war, there had been mutterings about the German connections to the royal family, connections which to many hardly seemed patriotic. It was when German planes bombed Britain in June that year, killing 160 people, that the King was finally propelled into action. A month later, on 17 July 1917, a Royal Proclamation announced that the German name of Saxe-Coburg-Gotha was now replaced by Windsor. Here was a simple way of giving a clear signal as to whose side the royal family was on.

It is a tried and tested technique to adopt a name change to imply changes in culture. In reality, it is often merely a superficial act, providing a veneer for the continuation of existing practices beneath. So, similarly, after years of unremitting bad publicity, the nuclear complex at Windscale was renamed Sellafield. Group 4, who at one point were building up an unenviable reputation for losing prisoners they were escorting, became G4S. And in government, the Ministry of War became the Ministry of Defence.

The adoption of a new family name led to Kaiser Wilhelm's acid observation that he intended to go and see *The Merry Wives of Saxe-*

Coburg-Gotha. We were spared any reference to brown Saxe-Coburg-Gotha soup. At the same time, Louis of Battenberg had his name anglicised to Mountbatten, though the eponymous cake survived unchanged. In the extensive Royal Archives are letters that show the decision to adopt the name Windsor was not a straightforward one. One serious objection came from Sir Alfred Scott-Gatty, Garter King of Arms, in a letter to Lord Stamfordham, the King's private secretary. 'I feel it is my duty,' he wrote, 'to point out that the surname Windsor is the family name of Lord Plymouth and other families both gentle and in humble circumstances.' Nicely put.

Instead he suggested Plantagenet, which 'as far as I know is extinct and His Majesty holds the throne of His ancestors through his descent from that family, or again Plantagenet-Tudor-Stuart would embody the principal Royal descents and could not fail to be popular with the two Kingdoms and the Principality.' In other words, England, Scotland and Wales. Plantagenet harked back to the royal dynasty which held the English throne from the accession of Henry II in 1154 until the death of Richard III in 1485.

These suggestions were all knocked back by Lord Stamfordham. 'The King has gone carefully into this question ... Plantagenet is no doubt a grand name but it has become to be considered too theatrical ... Tudor and Stuart are considered inadvisable.' He also countered that Lord Plymouth's family name was actually Windsor-Clive.

Lord Stamfordham was in fact representing the views of Herbert Asquith, who the archives show took a good deal of interest in the matter. Asquith had ended his term as Prime Minister in December 1916, the last leader of a majority Liberal government, but remained as leader of the party. It was Asquith who used the term 'theatrical' to describe the name Plantagenet and observed that 'Tudor' conjured up Henry VIII and Bloody Mary, while one Stuart was beheaded and one driven from

11

the throne. He also knocked back the suggestion of Fitzroy, advanced by Lord Rosebery, but was sympathetic to Guelph as a solution.

The Guelphs were one of the great political factions in late medieval Germany and Italy, and the ancestral family of the reigning British monarch at the time, George V. This hardly seemed to break the German link. Interestingly, there was wide consultation on what name to adopt, not just with the inner circle and with key members of the Lords, but also with Fleet Street, with the editors of a wide range of papers, from *The Times* to the *Daily Sketch*, being invited to comment. Commonwealth countries were also given the opportunity to comment, though only Canada did.

The consensus was that Windsor had a lot to commend it, and little to be said against it, and so was adopted. All in all, it is a curious way to decide one's family name. That, however, was not the end of the matter. The traditional – some might say archaic – arrangements which give prominence to males came into play when the present monarch inherited the crown in 1952.

By this point, Elizabeth Windsor had married Philip Mountbatten – a union of two artificial recently invented surnames.

Philip was of Greek and Danish royal blood and bore the family name Schleswig-Holstein-Sonderburg-Glücksburg. In 1947, he was naturalised as Philip Mountbatten, although he had originally been minded to take the name Oldburgh.

There is in fact a school of thought that this naturalisation was unnecessary, that he was already a British subject by birth, by reference in the Act of Queen Anne as applying to all descendants of Princess Sophia. A House of Lords ruling in 1957 in the case of the Prince of Hanover was to confirm this. Be that as it may, because male trumped female, the implicit position was that when Elizabeth ascended the throne in 1952, the House of Mountbatten replaced the House of Windsor.

Papers in the National Archives at Kew reveal that this consequence was deeply unpopular with the then Prime Minister, Winston Churchill, who was appalled at the idea of the House of Mountbatten becoming the ruling dynasty. He seemed to believe that the Duke of Edinburgh's uncle, Dickie Mountbatten, had unnecessarily sacrificed India.

Accordingly, on Churchill's advice, the Privy Council, with the agreement of the Queen, resolved on 9 April 1952 that 'She and Her children shall be styled and known as the House and Family of Windsor, and that her descendants, other than female descendants, and their descendants, shall bear the name of Windsor.'

The House of Mountbatten had lasted from 6 February to 9 April 1952. Prince Philip had objected to the change back to Windsor but lost out. The existence of a family name, as opposed to a House name designating territory, had in fact been rather intermittent, not to say haphazard. Tudor and Stuart were well-established surnames, but then the practice died out, until resurrected by George V in 1917, as part of the process of anglicising the family, in order to ensure that not all legitimate descendants of the sovereign could style themselves as princes or princesses. The matter was further amended by George VI in 1948 to the effect that Elizabeth's children would not have a surname, so in due course we got HRH Prince Charles and HRH Princess Anne. Henceforth the implied surname of Mountbatten would be hidden.

On to 1959 and enter Edward Frank Iwi, an English lawyer and something of an amateur constitutional expert. He was also a vibrant campaigner, collecting, for instance, a petition of some 50,000 signatures in 1947 calling for women to be able to sit in the House of Lords. The Lords was to vote in favour of this two years later, although it did not take full effect until 1963.

Five months before the Queen's third child was due, he wrote to the Prime Minister, Harold Macmillan, to suggest that whereas Charles and Anne had been born before Elizabeth became Queen and so bore the surname Mountbatten, the forthcoming birth would be the first after the official change of family name back to Windsor in 1952 and that therefore the new child, being given his mother's maiden name, would bear 'the Badge of Bastardy'.

The Establishment kicked in with its all too usual response when it came to royal matters. Referring to Iwi's letter, the Lord Chancellor told the Prime Minister: 'This is in very bad taste. Iwi must be silenced … he might go quietly.'

But Mr Iwi would not be silenced, maintaining that it would be unfair on any child to leave the position unchanged. He was to find a vocal ally in the Bishop of Carlisle, who commented on the issue in public, saying that he did not like to think of any child born in wedlock being deprived of his father's family name. 'We in this country are accustomed to have respect for titles, but a family name transcends these and stirs deeper and more powerful emotions in the family circle,' he suggested.

The bishop's comments were regarded with even more hostility than those of Mr Iwi. As *The Guardian* editorialised on 14 December 1959: 'The remarks of the Bishop of Carlisle about the Royal Family's surname seem to have accorded the kind of stony reception given to a courageous traveller who lets down the window in a stuffy railway carriage.'

The irony was that the action taken by George VI in 1948 meant that the child would have no overt surname anyway, and indeed he duly became HRH Prince Andrew. But there was a consequence two generations down the line when the ability simply to be styled Prince or Princess would no longer apply, as a result of the 1917 changes.

The solution landed upon was to create yet another new name, Mountbatten-Windsor, for those who in due course would need a surname. This was given effect by another royal declaration, on 8 February 1960, just eleven days before Andrew's birth.

As Cyril Hankinson, the then editor of *Debrett's*, noted after the declaration: 'It seems to me that this has been announced now so that the new baby will be born with the surname of Mountbatten-Windsor, which of course it will not use.' This new name, one civil servant wrote dryly, should not be confused with the Browne-Windsors.

Not everybody approved of the outcome. On 11 February, a Mr Kendall wrote to the Speaker, who as it happens was his MP.

> Surely for the Queen to change the surname of the Royal Family is a public, and not a private matter? Would it not be in keeping with the position and responsibility of Monarchy to have the question debated in the House, to give an opportunity for public opinion to be gauged? There is, I believe, strong antagonism throughout the country to Lord Louis Mountbatten, to the Battenberg family, and no desire to strengthen ties with Germany. Is not the English name of Windsor good enough?

The messy upshot of all this was:

- that the Queen, although she had acquired the name Mountbatten upon her marriage, now retained the surname Windsor that she held before her marriage and again since 1952;
- that Philip retained his assumed name of Mountbatten;
- that their children would have no surnames, except that Mountbatten-Windsor would be latent and would apply to their grandchildren;
- that the hidden surname of Mountbatten-Windsor would apply retrospectively to Prince Charles and Princess Anne;

- that the surname of the grandchildren of the Duke of Gloucester, the Duke of Kent, and of Prince Michael of Kent would be Windsor.

The conclusion that can be drawn from this saga is the same as applies to other matters affecting the royals, such as wills. It is that tradition is valued and defended, except when it is inconvenient, whereupon it is jettisoned, and new rules are made up as they go along to fashion the desired outcome.

Much of the problem from 1952 arose from the long-established practice of institutionalising male rights above female ones. As well as the complications referred to above, further oddities arise. For example, the pre-eminence of the male line means female members of the royal household are required to take the name of their husbands. So we have had Princess Michael of Kent, and before that Princess Arthur of Connaught, who sounds more like a character Graham Chapman might have played in a *Monty Python's Flying Circus* sketch.

It also means when a female succeeds to the throne, her husband is only a consort, but when a male succeeds, his wife is a queen. Well, normally. We have yet to see whether Camilla will be queen. Clearly that is an outcome both she and Charles want, but public opinion after Diana's death was strongly opposed to the idea, and Charles, under pressure, indicated that she would not take on the mantle of queen. The Clarence House website in 2005 announced that Camilla would become Princess Consort, rather than Queen, when Charles succeeded to the throne. That particular entry has now disappeared from the website. Charles may hope that the passage of time has mollified public opinion. We will see.

This bias towards the male is not unique to the royal family. In councils up and down the land, male mayors have mayoresses, while female mayors have only consorts. Is it not time, well into the twenty-first century, that we got rid of this antiquated gender bias? The optimum solution is that a monarch or a mayor, irrespective of gender, should always just have a consort. The other method of equalisation would be to say that if a king can create a queen through marriage, then a queen ought to be able to create a king.

At least, and at last, the question of equal rights of succession to the throne has been sorted. The law was changed on 26 March 2015 to mean that the order of succession is no longer skewed by gender. The first consequence of this is to keep William and Kate's daughter Charlotte ahead of Louis. Under the old arrangements, she would have been moved down the order. This happened to Victoria's daughter, also called Victoria, who, as a consequence, lost out on taking the throne to Edward VII.

Another change related to the terms of the Treason Act 1351, one of the oldest pieces of legislation still on the statute book. Indeed, it is so old, it was written originally in Norman French. Under this law, it constituted high treason to violate the wife of the King's eldest son, which suggests a number of prosecutions could have taken place in respect of the consensual arrangements Princess Diana engaged in. The penalty until 1814 was death by hanging, drawing and quartering, thereafter reduced to death by hanging. The last prosecution under the Act for high treason, though not in respect of the violation of a royal personage, was of the traitor William Joyce, unpopularly known as Lord Haw-Haw, who was found guilty and hanged in 1945.

As so often, modernisation in British law occurs at a snail's pace. The Succession to the Crown Act 2013, which updated these matters, retained the crime of violating the wife of the King's eldest son, but now only if he were heir apparent. It also remains an offence under the Act to violate the King's eldest daughter if unmarried, though not a crime, it seems, if she has wed. Equally, it is an offence to violate the companion of a male monarch, whether male or female, but not that of a female monarch, whether male or female.

Another important modernisation took place at the same time, which was to end the debarment of individuals from the order of succession simply because of marriage to a Catholic. However, it is still the case that no Catholic can sit on the throne. I took this matter up with Prime Minister Tony Blair back in 2000, when I pressed him to amend the Act of Settlement 1701 that introduced this prohibition. He replied, 'The Government has always stood firm against discrimination in all its forms and will continue to do so. We have no immediate plans to legislate in this area.' Standing firm, but doing nothing.

The reasoning is that the monarch is also Defender of the Faith, head of the Protestant Church of England. But suppose the person that the roll of the dice throws up as monarch is not a Protestant, but a Catholic or a Buddhist, or a Muslim or indeed an atheist. Should they be barred from the throne simply because of their religious beliefs or lack of them? Or should they simply pretend to be Protestant to get past go, and take an oath as part of their coronation which they do not really ascribe to, just as dissenting MPs pretend to pledge allegiance to the Crown in order to take up the seats in the Commons to which they have been democratically elected?

It must be wrong to bar someone from the throne on account of their personal view on religion, and arguably even more wrong to require them to lie to get over this hurdle. Prince Charles clearly feels conflicted and has expressed a wish to be 'Defender of Faiths' rather than any particular one. And why should he not be allowed to do that if he wants? The logic of all this, of course, is that the Church should be disestablished.

As well as the convulsions with surnames and the name of the royal House referred to above, first names have been far from sacrosanct either. King Edward VII was actually Albert Edward by birth, named predictably after Victoria's husband. Edward VIII was Edward, but had always been called David by his family. He was christened Edward Albert Christian George Andrew Patrick David. And George VI was Albert Frederick Arthur George, known as Bertie. So, curiously, all three used their last forename.

In the case of George VI, he already had a brother of that name, namely the Duke of Kent, which must have confused matters even more. The question then arises: what will Charles choose to call himself when he becomes king? We cannot automatically assume he will be Charles III, even if that is widely taken for granted. The Queen certainly showed no doubt when she was asked, within minutes of learning of her father's death, what name she wanted to adopt. 'My own name, of course,' she replied, surprised. 'Elizabeth. What else?'

The birth names she gave to her son are Charles Philip Arthur George, so if he too goes for the last in the list, we could end up with George VII, and indeed there have been mutterings over the years to suggest he has at least been considering this. The public would for certain regard it as weird that someone they have known as Charles for over seventy years would suddenly adopt a name that is not obviously his, but then the royal family does not always behave as ordinary mortals do.

Opinion polls have consistently shown that there is a high percentage of the population who want to skip a generation from the Queen to Prince William. HuffPost in early 2019 put the figure at 46 per cent, all of which is a bit hard on Charles, who has been heir to the throne longer than anyone else in history. There is of course zero chance that Charles will simply stand aside and pass the baton meekly on. The public, who admire the Queen, nevertheless want someone more modern to replace her, and a septuagenarian hardly fits the bill. Charles changing his name in some sort of bizarre royal throwback is only likely to reinforce that view.

Yet the Prince of Wales is undoubtedly conscious of the fate that befell his predecessors. Charles I had his head cut off, while his son, Charles II, was associated with the Great Plague of 1665 and the Great Fire of London in 1666. His nickname, the 'merry monarch', seemed particularly ill-judged. After allowing the matter to fester, or to enable public opinion to be judged, depending on your point of view, Clarence House let it be known in 2018 that the Prince will definitely not supplant Charles with George, so that would appear to settle the issue. Is the royal name game finally over?

Germany Calling

' Dix mille sur le noir.' The society playboy that was the Duke of Windsor was hitting the gaming tables hard. It was 1940, and the Duke, still officially a serving military officer, was rather more interested in the black of the roulette wheel in glamorous Lisbon than in the blackouts that had fallen like a shroud over grime-filled London.

In London, the black that had interested him was elsewhere. It was to be found in the nasty British fascist organisation that was set up to mirror the German Nazi party, the Blackshirts, with its leader Oswald Mosley, a sort of bargain basement version of Adolf Hitler.

Edward VIII, before, during and after his short reign of 325 days, revealed himself as not just a Nazi sympathiser, but as someone who was a source of much useful information for the Axis powers. Had he been an ordinary mortal rather than a member of the royal family, it would not have been surprising to have seen him charged with treason in the trials that followed the end of the Second World War.

The Duke of Windsor, as he became upon abdication, was politically far to the right, but also far from the only member of the royal family in the 1930s to express pro-German sentiments, to have a grudging admiration for Hitler and to espouse appeasement in the face of Nazi aggression across Europe. He was merely an extreme expression of that tendency.

That the British royal family should be sympathetic to Germany should shock nobody. After all, they are a German royal line. Queen Victoria even died in the arms of the German emperor, her grandson, on the Isle of Wight in 1901. Referring to that episode, the Kaiser wrote thus to George V in 1911: 'Those sacred hours have riveted my heart firmly to your house and family, of which I am proud to feel myself a member.' He signed the letter, 'Your affectionate cousin and friend, Willy.'

So close were the family connections between the British and German royal families that, when the First World War began, the Kaiser still held the rank of Commander-in-Chief of the Royal Dragoons, while the German crown prince was Colonel of the 11th Hussars. The Kaiser also held the rank of Field Marshal.

The matter was raised by the King's private secretary, Lord Stamfordham, with the War Office on 9 August 1914. Replying, Sir Reginald Brade wrote: 'Personally I would have disposed of the issue by not raising it.' George V, even some weeks into the war, refused to act. Stamfordham wrote on 12 August: 'The King has decided that the names of the German Emperor and the Crown Prince of Germany shall remain on the Army List as heretofore.'

The same view was taken of the fact that the Kaiser and Prince Harry of Prussia bore the rank of Admirals of the Fleet in the Navy List. Two days later Stamfordham wrote to Lord Roberts, the highly respected soldier who had for years before been warning of the militarisation of Germany, about the honours bestowed on the Kaiser and his family: 'His Majesty [George V] is strongly against the return of Decorations. It would be impossible for instance to send back their Garters or for the King to return the Black Eagle.'

But the issue would not go away, and finally came to a head that October. On the first of the month, Stamfordham received a note from the War Office pointing out that the Austrian Emperor was Chief of the 1st Dragoon Guards, and that the Duke of Albany was serving in the German Army while being Chief (actually Colonel) of the Seaforth Highlanders. The following day, the King finally agreed to remove names, but, in an attempt to bury the issue, made it clear he 'does not wish any order promulgated to this effect, and nothing to be done beyond omitting these names', as Stamfordham put it in a letter to Winston Churchill, then First Lord of the Admiralty. The reluctance of the King to take any action on this front could very well be explained by the fact that the British and German royal families were heavily intertwined.

Until the end of the First World War, it was standard practice for members of the British royal family to marry only other royals, the continuation of a practice that had cemented political alliances for centuries past. The British Empire under Queen Victoria and the German Empire under Kaiser Wilhelm II were, along with the Romanovs in Russia and the Habsburgs in Austria, the great imperial monarchies of Europe, so it is hardly surprising that there was a great deal of intermarriage between Britain and Germany. It might even be termed incestuous.

The military positions in the British armed forces held by the German and Austrian emperors may have finally been disposed of some months into the war, but other matters took even longer to deal with. One running sore was the presence of Garter flags honouring the Kaiser and other German relatives which hung in St George's Chapel in Windsor. The fact that it was standard practice to pray twice a day for all Knights, including, therefore, the German Kaiser and Austrian Emperor, only exacerbated matters.

On 12 May 1915, the Dean of St George's Chapel received a letter from a Mr Arnold White, described by Stamfordham as 'a somewhat prominent pressman'. The letter warned:

> I have reason to believe an attack will shortly be made upon St
> George's Chapel and an effort will be made to remove the eight
> peccant [offensive] banners by physical force ... the only way to
> avoid a collision between the authorities and the people is the
> removal of the German banners.

The Dean notified the Palace, telling Stamfordham that 'it would be most unfortunate if anything like a riot or a disturbance were to take place in the Chapel'. The next day Stamfordham told the Dean that the banners would be removed and added, 'If I might suggest, would it not be better to take no notice of Mr. Arnold White's letter.' Notwithstanding that we were at war with Germany and Austria, the removal of the banners was not undertaken with exuberance but reluctance. The King in fact made clear that 'none of the <u>Plates</u> of the said Knights are to be removed' from the chapel. These were to all intents and purposes hidden from view, which is doubtless why they were allowed to remain.

An even bigger issue remained to be dealt with – the family name of the British royal family was a German one: Saxe-Coburg-Gotha. This survived well into the First World War until in 1917 George V decided, in the light of public mutterings and his fears for his own throne, on a rebranding exercise, and, abracadabra, the House of Windsor was born.

At the same time, in Parliament, the Titles Deprivation Act 1917 removed German relatives from the succession line to the British throne. Name change or not, the German sympathies of the royal family continued, and how could it be otherwise when the people remained the same? Most pertinently in 1917, George V's wife Mary was German. She had been Mary of Teck, a German princess. The majority of family members spoke excellent German. George V was actually the first monarch since 1714 not to be a fluent speaker of the language. By contrast, his predecessor, Edward VII, had never learnt to speak English without a German accent. It is perhaps fortuitous that there were no regal radio or television broadcasts possible in those days.

The present Duke of Edinburgh, Prince Philip, is directly descended from Victoria's daughter, Princess Alice, the Grand Duchess of Hesse-Darmstadt. Both he and the present Queen are German speakers. Edward VIII was therefore mainstream in his tilting towards Germany. As Prince of Wales he had spent his summers up to 1913 at Kaiser Wilhelm's Bernstorff Palace. Unsurprisingly, therefore, he spoke fluent German, and indeed was somewhat irritated when, on meeting Hitler many years later, the Führer insisted on using an interpreter. 'Every drop of blood in my veins is German,' he was to assert to Diana Mitford. Hitler's ambassador to Britain, Joachim von Ribbentrop, called him 'half-German'. The German influence is still felt to this day. The British royal family celebrates Christmas as it always has – the German way – with presents opened after afternoon tea on Christmas Eve.

Amongst the royals in the 1930s, there was some alarm at what had befallen monarchies across Europe. Even before the First World War, a discernible trend away from monarchy had appeared, with abolition in Portugal and China. The war would accelerate this, with monarchies falling like diamond-encrusted dominoes. It was not just the Kaiser who lost his throne. The centuries-old Habsburg Empire in Austria-Hungary also came to an end, as did the Greek monarchy in 1924 (although it was recreated later before being finally abolished in 1973).

Most dramatic were the events that unfolded in Russia. Here too there were family connections, with Tsar Nicholas a cousin of George V, and also a holder of high honorary ranks in the British armed forces. Indeed the King wrote to the Tsar in December 1915 to say he was 'anxious' to appoint him 'a Field Marshal in my army as a mark of my affection for you'. The Tsar accepted the offer the following month. The Russian Tsar and the British King kept up a friendly, almost intimate, correspondence during the war, and when the Tsar was forced to abdicate in 1917, the King immediately sent him a personal message: 'I shall always remain your true and devoted friend as you know I have been in the past.' But the affection of the King went only so far. The new Russian government was keen to get the Tsar out of the country and to England as soon as possible, a suggestion the British government agreed to. The King, however, was hesitant. His private secretary, Lord Stamfordham, wrote to the foreign secretary, Arthur Balfour on 30 March 1917:

> As you are doubtless aware the King has a strong personal regard for the Emperor, and therefore would be glad to do anything to help him in this crisis. But His Majesty cannot help doubting, not only on account of the dangers of the voyage, but on general grounds of expediency, whether it is advisable that the Imperial Family should take up their residence in this country.

Balfour replied two days later: 'His Majesty's Government thought it preferable, the initiative having come from the Russian Government, that the Imperial Family should come to England.' But the King would not let go, and he sought to persuade the government to withdraw the offer of sanctuary. Three further letters winged their way to Balfour. The first, on 3 April, had reluctantly conceded that constitutionally the

King had to accept the advice of his ministers, but by 6 April, he had changed his mind. The second stated: 'Every day the King is becoming more concerned about the question of the Emperor and Empress of Russia coming to this country.' The third, with the King now agitated, followed later the very same day:

> He must beg you to represent to the Prime Minister that from all he hears and reads in the Press, the residence in this Country of the Ex-Emperor and Empress would be strongly resented by the public, and would undoubtedly compromise the position of the King and Queen from whom it is generally already supposed the invitation has emanated … we must be allowed to withdraw from the consent previously given to the Russian Government's proposal.

Shortly afterwards, Balfour received a lurid letter from a privy counsellor, the Rt Hon. E. G. Russell: 'If the Ex-Czar and Czarina come to live here we shall have a Revolution, and remember that I warned you.' The pressure worked and Balfour buckled. A telegram, headed 'Personal and most confidential', was sent to the British ambassador in Petrograd:

> There are indications that a considerable anti-monarchical movement is developing here including personal attacks upon the King. Part of the ground of the attacks is that he has supported the ex-Emperor and King Constantine of Greece. It is thought if the Emperor comes here it may dangerously increase this movement…

The ambassador in his reply of 15 April acknowledged this point, but added, 'If there was any indication of counter-revolution His Majesty's life [that is, the Tsar's] would be in serious danger.' But the

King prevailed and the Tsar was kept out of England, and in fact out of any country, for the delay proved fatal for the Tsar and his family. They were rounded up, taken to the countryside and executed by firing squad. If George V, the Tsar's 'true and devoted friend', had immediately agreed the Russian royal family could come to England, they would very likely have been able to escape before the net closed in.

Britain was thus the home of the last great imperial monarchy left standing, and the royal family experienced a new vulnerability, no longer being able to take the permanence of monarchy for granted. Nerves were further jangled by the transformation in 1931 of Spain into a republic. This feeling of vulnerability was heightened by the social changes that were sweeping Europe, most notably by what was seen as the Bolshevik threat from Russia, and at home the arrival in 1924 of the first ever Labour government.

The response from the British royal family, always a conservative institution, was to embrace those who could head off social revolution, while also seeking to dull the radicals by coaxing them inside the tent where possible. The British royals, through their relatives, were painfully aware of the chaos that existed in the Weimar republic in Germany, and came to see Hitler and the Nazis both as a stabilising influence in that country, as well as one that could head off any further leftward drift. Nazi Germany represented a useful bulwark against Bolshevism. As the 1930s wore on, another consideration came into play: the threat of another major European conflict. The British royal family, with 1918 still fresh in their minds, were fearful that another war would prove fatal for the Empire, and constitute a grave threat to the future of the monarchy itself.

Their fears were well grounded. The Second World War, when it came, generated a further loss of monarchies in Europe, with those in Yugoslavia, Romania, Bulgaria and Albania being consigned to history.

And the war did indeed deliver a body blow to the British Empire. Atlases which not long before had shown a quarter of the world painted pink were horribly out of date within twenty years. The empire had all but shrivelled to nothing.

Then there were the family ties that abhorred the notion that Britain and Germany could once again be in conflict. These ties were astutely reinforced by Hitler, who used royal relatives to seduce key members of the family. He even deployed Friedrich William, the son of the last Kaiser, to act as an emissary. As well as proving effective in opening Palace doors, these German relatives gave a cloak of respectability to the thuggish Nazi regime. One key emissary was Carl Eduard, Queen Victoria's grandson and Duke of Saxe-Coburg and Gotha (but not Windsor). An openly strong supporter of Hitler, he spent Christmas 1933 at Sandringham with George V and his German wife, Mary, and was a regular visitor to Buckingham Palace throughout the 1930s. The fact that he had become a 'traitor peer' as a result of the 1917 Act seemed not to weigh with his British hosts. George V's body was barely cold when Carl Eduard went to see his cousin, now Edward VIII. He would sit on Edward's table for the dinner that followed his father's funeral, having followed the coffin dressed in his Nazi uniform.

And it was Carl Eduard who was to host the Duke of Windsor's controversial visit to Germany in 1937, a visit that included a nice friendly tête-à-tête with Adolf and which was overall a huge propaganda success for the Nazis. A month after the visit, Carl Eduard was invited round to tea by Queen Mary. He was also received by the King, by then George VI, and regularly dined with the Prime Minister, Neville Chamberlain. For his efforts to keep the royal diplomacy going, he was paid 4,000 Reichsmarks monthly by Hitler, the equivalent of about £16,000 today. After the war ended, Carl Eduard was arrested by the Americans, to whom he made the astonishing assertion that

'No German is guilty of any war crimes.' He was eventually allowed to go free following pressure from Buckingham Palace.

Queen Mary believed fervently in the aristocratic code of loyalty to one's roots, which, in her eyes, meant trying to patch up the divisions between the German and British branches of the family that the Great War had created. Her main complaint about Hitler was that he spoke German badly. George V himself also felt strong ties to his German relations, and a good many attended his silver jubilee celebrations in 1935. It seems they needed little pushing to attend, and the British royals little persuasion to welcome them. The King was not unsympathetic to German demands for revisions to the Treaty of Versailles and other concessions consistent with appeasement. He was not, however, enamoured of Hitler, whom he regarded as common, a tad absurd and yet also dangerous. He found his 'Jew-baiting' distasteful.

Generally, the old right in Germany was only too keen to embrace Nazism. According to Jonathan Petropoulos in his book *Royals and the Reich*, between a third and a half of Germany's princely families, around 270 in number, joined the Nazi party, a higher percentage than for any other grouping in society. And the historian Stephan Malinowski counted 3,592 members of 312 old aristocratic families who enlisted, more than a quarter of them doing so before 1933. A number of these Nazi aristocrats were related to the British royal family. For example, of the four sisters of the present Duke of Edinburgh, all had married German princes, and three of those became leading Nazis. One served as an SS Colonel on Himmler's personal staff. The Duke even attended the funeral of one sister, Cecile, in Nazi Germany in 1937, when he was sixteen. He was captured for posterity with other relatives who were dressed in SS and brownshirt uniforms. Another sister, Sophie, had a son, Karl Adolf, named in praise of the Führer. Meanwhile, an uncle, Prince Christoph of Hesse, headed up Göring's telephone-tapping operation that was to become the Gestapo.

None of these German relatives would make the invitation list for Philip's wedding to Elizabeth in 1947. Also excluded were the Duke and Duchess of Windsor. The inconvenient past, much of it quite recent, was to be airbrushed out. Philip's mother was invited – she could hardly not be – but it helped that her hands were clean. She was deeply religious and during the war had hidden a Jewish family in her Athens home.

I wonder what went through Philip's mind when, many decades later, his grandson Prince Harry was photographed wearing Nazi regalia, apparently for a laugh. The photos appeared in the press just before a commemoration service was held for the more than one million people who were killed at Auschwitz. Together, these considerations – the family ties, the fear of Communism, the grudging admiration for the order Hitler had brought to Germany, and the desire to avoid another war with the threat that posed for the survival of both the royal family and the empire – led to a markedly pro-German, and so by definition a pro-Nazi, attitude across the royal family and strong support for the concept of appeasement.

It was the predominant royal view that there should be an accommodation reached with Hitler that encouraged the Germans to channel their aggression and desire for *Lebensraum* eastwards, and that Britain should stay out of any conflict in return for Hitler agreeing to leave the British Empire untouched. They may not have all shared Edward's enthusiasm for Hitler, but when it came to a choice between the German dictator and the Bolsheviks, they were in no doubt that Hitler was the lesser of two evils. The lead from the royals in turn influenced a great many occupying positions of power and influence in this country. Kim Philby, already spying for the Soviets, compiled a list of Establishment figures in government and elsewhere who were sympathetic to the

Nazis. It ran to several pages. Notable amongst the cheerleaders were the Fleet Street magnates Lords Rothermere, Beaverbrook and Kemsley, proprietors respectively of the *Mail*, *Express* and *Telegraph*.

While the Duke of Coburg concentrated on his royal relatives, a German princess, Stephanie von Hohenlohe, was deputed to maintain good relations with Lord Rothermere. It was time well spent. When Germany occupied the Sudetenland in 1938, Rothermere sent Hitler a personal note of congratulations, calling him 'Adolf the Great'. The *Daily Mail* followed the Nazi line like a panting dog following its master. Rothermere even paid to secure access to Hitler. Goebbels called him 'our most reliable press magnate'. The *Mail* did break with the anti-Jew purism of the Nazis in one regard, however. They were prepared to accept money from Jewish advertisers.

It was to Beaverbrook in 1940 that the Duke of Windsor turned when he wanted help to kick-start a peace process with the Germans, hoping Beaverbrook could enlist City support. He was not alone in wanting to pursue this line. It was a view shared with, amongst others, Lord Halifax and Rab Butler. Nevertheless, with Britain by now at war with Germany, to seek to take steps to actively undermine and con-tradict the official position of the British government was little short of treason, even if the desire for peace was well intentioned. The initiative ran into the sand. As Karina Urbach reveals in her comprehensive work, *Go-Betweens for Hitler*, Lord Kemsley was sent to Germany in the summer of 1939 by Prime Minister Neville Chamberlain, and without Cabinet knowledge or approval. His task was to reassure Hitler that the talks then underway between Britain and the USSR into which Chamberlain had been forced were only for show and not genuine. It probably helped the mission that Lady Kemsley, who accompanied her husband, told her German hosts that 'only the Jews wanted to bring about a war between Germany and England'. Meanwhile, Hitler's plans for further conquests were well advanced, and, within weeks, Britain and Germany would be at war.

So the consistent line that came from Buckingham Palace throughout the 1930s was one in favour of appeasement. It was a view shared by George V and his wife Mary, and his four sons: Edward VIII, the Duke of Kent, the Duke of Gloucester and George VI. There was no prominent member of the British royal family advocating the sort of robust line being advanced by Winston Churchill. Of the royals, Edward VIII was in a class of his own. His position was not merely to support appeasement, but to embrace to a large degree the vile philosophy of Nazism. His enthusiasm began early. *The Sun* in 2015 secured and published stills from a ciné film taken at Balmoral that the royal family would have much preferred never to have seen the light of day. Under the sardonic headline *Their Royal Heilnesses*, the stills, dating from 1933, show the future Edward VIII encouraging the young Princesses Elizabeth and Margaret to give a Nazi salute, and indeed the future Elizabeth II, then aged just seven, is shown doing just that. Now, nobody can possibly blame the young princesses for innocently following the cajoling of their uncle. Indeed we can feel angry on their behalf. We can, however, look critically at Edward, who was clearly already enamoured of the Nazis, and critically at the future Queen Mother, also pictured giving a Nazi salute. She would not have wanted to look the East End in the face with that image. Already Prince of Wales, it was clear both that Edward was not just supportive of the Nazi regime, but that he felt he had the right to speak out, whether or not what he said was in agreement with the official government line. He publicly suggested that Britain should extend the hand of friendship to the Nazi regime, and was strongly told off by his father, George V, for his unconstitutional behaviour. The admonishment was wasted.

In January 1936 as he was ascending the throne, he told an American diplomat, James Clement Dunn, that he intended to diverge from his father's policy of blindly following Cabinet decisions. On the contrary, it was his duty to intervene when the Cabinet adopted a course of action which he believed was against British interests. Those who favour the hereditary principle of monarchy have to accept that the roll of the dice can turn up someone entirely inappropriate, dangerous even, like Edward VIII, just as easily as someone steady and diligent like George V. Here, over the course of one year, was a violent transition from a conscientious constitutional monarch to an unpleasantly right-wing loose cannon with little respect for constitutional niceties.

Anthony Eden tartly observed that while George V knew much but interfered little, Edward VIII knew little but interfered much. 'Who is king? Baldwin or I?' Edward is reported as having said to the Duke of Coburg, who was enquiring about the views of the Prime Minister. And the new king added: 'I myself wish to talk to Hitler and will do so here or in Germany.' In the event, he met him the next year, but only after his abdication. He had indicated a wish to attend the Berlin Olympics, which took place during his short reign, but presumably was arm-twisted out of this. Plenty of British aristocrats sympathetic to Hitler did go, though.

Edward even went as far as to threaten abdication if Baldwin instigated military action in response to the illegal German occupation of the demilitarised Rhineland that year. Actually, it is doubtful that Britain would have intervened in any case, though historians now recognise that Hitler was taking a big gamble and if Britain and France had stood up to him here, he would almost certainly have had to withdraw, and that would have changed the dynamic in Berlin markedly. Edward thought that the Blackshirt movement was 'a good thing', and he and Wallis Simpson were close friends with the Mosleys. Mrs Simpson, who was even keener on the Nazis than Edward, sent a congratulatory message to the couple on the occasion of their wedding in Berlin, held at the home of Joseph Goebbels and in the presence of Hitler. The friendship worked both ways. Mosley's fascist January Club was in March 1935 renamed the Windsor Club. And after the King's abdication broadcast, 500 Blackshirts congregated outside Buckingham Palace, where they gave the Nazi salute and shouted, 'We want Edward'. The friendship between the Windsors and the Mosleys was to become even stronger after the war ended.

Edward's short reign was a worrying one for the government. Apart from the King's dangerously pro-Nazi leanings and his disregard for long-established constitutional conventions, he was simply not prepared to knuckle down and carry out his duties properly. He had been asked to open what would be the new Royal Infirmary in Aberdeen, where, incidentally, my mother later worked as a nurse and where I was born. The King, however, had cried off, saying he was still in mourning for his late father, an unlikely justification at any point, given how they disliked each other. The excuse was shot to pieces when, on the day he had been due to undertake the opening, he was spotted at nearby Ballater Station to meet Wallis off the train and escort her to Balmoral. It was a public relations disaster.

His red boxes, delivered to him daily at his residence at Fort Belvedere in Windsor Great Park and containing the most sensitive government information, were often left open and lying around at home for any guest to inspect, if they were minded to. This carelessness extended to conversations too, and he seemed to regard any information he had come across, no matter how sensitive, as suitable for dinner table talk. This might have mattered less if he had not had as his milieu a coterie of dubious Nazi sympathisers. And nobody was more central to this coterie than Wallis Simpson. Moreover, she bore no love for the royal family, who had made plain their disapproval of her from the start. Not only was she a divorcee, but she was American. How unpleasantly and distastefully nouveau. She had also spent a colourful period in China, detailed in a dossier put together for Baldwin, which unsurprisingly has now vanished without trace.

According to the royal author Kenneth Rose, George V regarded her as 'unsuitable as a friend, disreputable as a mistress, and unthinkable as a queen'. His private secretary went further, describing her as a witch and a vampire. Wallis undoubtedly had a close friendship with von Ribbentrop, which many believe was of a sexual nature. Her physical appearance was not in fact dissimilar to that of Ribbentrop's wife back home. Andrew Morton's book *17 Carnations* is so named after the flowers that the German is alleged to have sent to the duchess every day, believed to represent one flower for every time they had made love. Other historians dispute this, however. She was also having an affair with a married car salesman called Guy Trundle. And of course Wallis herself was still married to husband Ernest until not long before her wedding to Edward, only filing for divorce in October 1936. It might be seen as a consolation prize that Edward managed to get Ernest accepted into his masonic lodge.

Edward's reign ended with a syrupy broadcast, telling the nation that he could not continue as king without the woman he loved at his side. While that was indeed how he felt, the more interesting question is whether the Prime Minister in 1936, Stanley Baldwin, took advantage of Edward's determination to marry Wallis to make sure his abdication took place, believing Edward to be a serious security risk, and ensuring it occurred before the coronation, after which it would have been much more difficult. Von Ribbentrop certainly believed he had been made to abdicate because of his political views. Andrew Morton cites in his book a 1940 FBI report in the name of J. Edgar Hoover to President Roosevelt:

> For some time the British government has known that the Duchess
> of Windsor was exceedingly pro-German in her sympathies and
> connections and there is strong reason to believe that this is
> the reason why she was considered so obnoxious to the British
> Government that they refused to permit Edward to marry her and
> maintain the throne.

Baldwin had consulted Commonwealth leaders to sound them out
about the possible marriage of the King to Wallis Simpson, and found
hostility to the idea, but it might just have been possible for him to
have swung a morganatic marriage between the two. In this situation,
neither Mrs Simpson nor any issue they produced would have had
any claim to the titles or possessions of the King. The fact that Baldwin
was not keen to pursue this option, although it had been mooted, may
well relate to his political concerns about the King. In 1937, eight years
after they had first met, Edward and Wallis got married in France. It
was a wedding that was boycotted by the rest of the royal family. The
ceremony itself took place at the home of their friend Charles Bedaux,
a Frenchman who had spied for the Germans in the First World War.
Bedaux also kept a property at Berchtesgaden, the spiritual home of
Nazism and close to Hitler's residence. Hitler sent them a wedding
present of an inscribed gold box.

After their wedding, the couple visited Italy, then under the control
of the fascist Mussolini. Edward delighted the crowds by repeatedly
giving the fascist salute. And that salute was in evidence again when
he visited Germany later that year. The hundreds who greeted him
upon his arrival at the railway station responded by crying out 'Heil
Edward' and 'Heil Windsor', which was certainly snappier than 'Heil
Saxe-Coburg-Gotha' would have been. During his trip, Edward met
all the leading Nazis and he and Wallis were treated with, in his view,

the dignity and respect that was their due and that had been lacking in England. He was particularly incensed that Wallis was barred from using the title Her Royal Highness. In 1940, when the two were sitting with Claire Luce, an American journalist, listening on the radio to the news of bombs falling on London, Edward is reported as saying: 'I can't say I feel sorry for them. A whole nation against a lone woman.'

This story, if true, is breathtaking in its egotistical horror. Ordinary Londoners deserve to get bombed as a punishment for the way Wallis Simpson was treated? And 'them'? This was his country. Or was it? From the archives of other countries, Karina Urbach has uncovered evidence that Edward had volunteered the view that 'if one bombed England effectively this could bring peace' – which would have meant a forced negotiation on German terms. This opinion was expressed on 25 June 1940 to a Spanish diplomat, Don Javier Bermejillo, and passed on to the Germans. The sustained bombing of Britain began on 10 July 1940. Claire Luce's anecdote was regaled in Martin Allen's book, *Hidden Agenda*, which is a very readable account of the activities of the Windsors. Unfortunately, it transpired that a number of key documents upon which the author relied for his more sensational revelations turned out to be forgeries. The documents he had discovered in the National Archives had been smuggled in, and then found by him in his researches. That this came to light is only due to diligent detective work by the journalist Ben Fenton. The National Archives have now put in place measures to check what is coming in as well as what is going out. It is a pity that Martin Allen's book had its credibility damaged in this way, for the case he makes against Edward stands up perfectly well without the icing on the cake.

Edward's fascist sympathies had caused the British government to take the unprecedented step of subjecting him to secret surveillance. The Channel 4 documentary *Spying on the Royals* confirmed that

George V had assented to this. It began with physical surveillance and was then stepped up to intercepted phone calls. This surveillance continued after his father died and he had succeeded to the throne, and indeed after he abdicated. It was constitutionally a questionable proposition that the Prime Minister of the day, with support from his Home Secretary, could decide to subject the King to surveillance and tap his phone, and it caused consternation at MI5 who had to carry this out. The director general referred it to the board of the organisation, who convinced him that the surveillance was necessary. History has more than justified Baldwin's actions. Rudolf Hess, who had met Edward and Wallis in Paris just prior to their trip to Germany, recorded: 'The Duke is proud of his German blood, says he is more German than British … There is no need to lose a single German life in invading Britain. The Duke and his clever wife will deliver the goods.' Hess's note implies a faith in Edward's ability to produce an official British government position in favour of a deal between the two countries, regarded by the Germans in 1937 as not a wholly unrealistic proposition, given the support for appeasement in the upper echelons of society in Britain at that time.

Edward was seen as a solid and reliable figure for the Nazis, and even after war broke out they harboured the idea of reinstating him on the throne, as a puppet like Pétain or Quisling. This is reinforced by Soviet intelligence records from 1940 which reveal a belief, or at least a fear, that Edward was conducting negotiations with Germany on a peace treaty, a new British government, and a military alliance against the USSR. Having Edward on the throne would have been a smart move. For one thing, he retained a great deal of public support at home amongst ordinary people, support probably only heightened by his decision to give up his throne for love. For another, the armed forces all take a personal oath to the monarch, and if he instructed them all to lay down their arms, they may well have done so – whatever Churchill or anyone else said. Physical surveillance of Edward continued after George VI ascended the throne – with the King's support. Indeed, there is evidence, according to the Nottingham historian Dr Rory Cormac, that the new monarch paid for some of it. When the war finally broke out, Edward was still in exile. He offered his services to Britain, but this was received with lukewarm enthusiasm. He was eventually allocated to the British Military Mission in France from where he was sent on a tour to boost the morale of the French troops dug into their defensive positions. For the British, this was also an opportunity to nail down exactly what the French were doing, which was information they had been reluctant to share in its entirety with the British. Edward therefore made detailed notes of everything he saw, including the potential weaknesses in the French lines.

One key weakness he identified was the vulnerability of the potential route for the Germans through the Ardennes forest, a route the French had concluded would be too challenging for the Germans to attempt. This turned out to be exactly the route they would take, leading to the capitulation of the French in just six weeks. It seems certain that the Germans must have had knowledge of the French positions or they would have been most unlikely to want to go through the forest. The question is whether they gained that information from Edward or a source connected to him, or from a different direction. The general view amongst historians appears to be that the intelligence may well have come from someone in Edward's circle, gleaned from him blabbing irresponsibly.

No such benefit of doubt can be given to the Duke on another occasion when sensitive information reached the Axis powers, as recounted in Andrew Morton's book. At a dinner, Edward learnt from the American ambassador of the derailment in Austria of a train heading from Germany to Italy. This revealed that the cargo consisted of naval shells on their way to an Italian port, clearly implying that the Germans were gearing up for a naval war. As soon as he could, Edward took an Italian diplomat present at the dinner to one side and told him of the find. Unsurprisingly, it was not long before the authorities in Rome and Berlin were aware they had been rumbled.

The Duke of Windsor continued to be a major headache for the British government as the war unfolded and there was a genuine concern that while in Franco's Spain, he might succumb to German courting, including the offer of a crude financial bribe. In the end, Churchill had to threaten to court-martial him if he failed to follow instructions to leave for the Bahamas, where he was to take up post as governor-general. The Bahamas was chosen for him to sit out the war to ensure that he would be as far as possible from Britain, and as far as possible from the Nazis.

Edward still smarted from this appointment years later. In an otherwise friendly letter to his brother George VI in October 1945, he included this barbed comment: 'I am satisfied that the job I undertook as your representative in a third-class British colony was fulfilled to the best of my ability.' Yet even in the Bahamas he had continued to undermine the British war effort, attempting to persuade the Americans not to join in the fray. In a meeting in December 1940 with the writer (and undercover FBI agent) Fulton Oursler, he volunteered the view that it would be 'a tragic thing for the world if Hitler were to be overthrown'. Hitler, he added, was 'a very great man'.

Meanwhile he lounged around, much to the annoyance of Scotland Yard, who, not unreasonably, felt that the police officer deputed to guard him would be better deployed back in Britain. I was able as part of the research for this book to access hitherto closed papers of Walter Monckton, who acted as Edward VIII's lawyer. Monckton was a significant figure in Edward's circle, acting as a go-between between him and the government, and even helping to draft the famous abdication speech. He was the first person knighted after Edward ascended to the throne in 1936. The papers, held at Balliol College, Oxford, question why the officer, a Detective Sergeant Harold Holder, was still with the Duke, almost a year after he had accompanied him to the Bahamas. In a letter dated 7 May 1941 from Christopher Eastwood, the private secretary to the Secretary of State for the Colonies, to H. A. Strutt at the Home Office, he noted that the reason a police officer had accompanied him to the Bahamas at all 'was a rumour of some plot against his life, which turned out eventually to be a mare's nest ... It was not, I think, intended that he should necessarily stay in the Bahamas for as long as the Duke is there.' A Mr W. Bolland of Scotland Yard, who had been copied in, also wrote with feeling to the Home Office:

> The Commissioner was reluctant to allow Holder to go in the first place, but had to agree when told that the Duke would not go without a police officer. He feels that in his present job Holder is almost certainly wasting his time. The Duke and Duchess are probably in no danger whatsoever. If they were, one police officer could not look after them efficiently. Probably Holder spends most of his time fetching and carrying for the Duchess or wandering round golf links behind the Duke ... If the Colonial Officer or anyone else can persuade the Duke to give Holder up, the Commissioner would be very grateful to have him back again.

The Home Office batted the whole thing back to Christopher Eastwood at the Colonial Office. Edward would continue to be closely monitored throughout the war, including by the Americans, and information helpful to the Germans would continue to reach them from his base.

He did, however, strongly disapprove of the Japanese attack on Pearl Harbor, although this was at least in part driven by his racist views of the Japanese.

So, was Edward a traitor? The charge sheet is bleak. He was pro-Hitler; he surrounded himself with Nazis and Nazi sympathisers; he encouraged the bombing of London; he tried to persuade the United States to keep out of the war; and variously deliberately and carelessly, he passed on highly sensitive intelligence to Britain's enemies. On the other hand, with magnificent self-delusion, he probably really did believe he was acting in the best interests of Britain, and his absurd sense of self-importance probably clouded his judgement as to the consequences of his actions.

So he will not have seen himself as a German asset or spy, even if that was what he was. Whether that would have been enough for him to have been found not guilty of a charge of treason, had it been brought, is however doubtful. Others certainly suffered the ultimate penalty for their expression of pro-Nazi sentiments, including William Joyce, and for whom there could be no defence of good intentions. His was the fake soft upper-class voice that regularly broadcast Nazi propaganda to the British, his reports beginning with the sinister 'Germany calling, Germany calling.' After the war, he was hanged for treason, even though he was actually American by birth.

Edward, of course, escaped any official censure and continued to live a life of comfort and opulence until his death in 1972. Wallis Simpson continued to live in their Paris house until she died in 1986. The villa had been home to Louis Renault, the car manufacturer, who was deemed to have collaborated with the Germans, although some revisionists dispute this. In any case, his house was seized and nationalised. In another of those interesting quirks of fate, after the duchess's demise, the house was then taken over by Mohamed Al-Fayed, whose link to the royal family came about through the relationship between his son Dodi and Princess Diana, which came to the violent end in a Paris road tunnel that shocked the world in the summer of 1997. Mr Al-Fayed still lives there.

It is generally believed that with Edward out of the way and his brother George VI on the throne, it was back to business as usual. So it was in the sense that the new King was a fundamentally decent person who was wholly committed to doing the right thing for Britain. Nevertheless, he shared an ambivalent approach to Hitler along with others in the royal family. He recognised the dangers Hitler posed for Germany's neighbours and disliked the crude antisemitism he peddled. Yet there was grudging admiration for the economic progress and order the Nazis had brought to Germany, and he shared the view that Britain should seek to appease Hitler and, after the war started, attempt to secure a negotiated peace.

Karina Urbach quotes in her book a pre-war confidential note from a German observer to von Ribbentrop in Berlin, which recorded that George VI 'has great sympathies for the Third Reich'. While this may be a tad exaggerated, and while it is without doubt that they would have preferred Edward to have remained on the throne, it does accurately capture the King's overall pro-German sentiments. He was very much in Chamberlain's camp, and even wanted to meet his plane at the airport as it touched down, bringing the Prime Minister back from Munich, waving his piece of paper which purported to demonstrate 'the desire of our two peoples never to go to war with one another again'. He was dissuaded from this, so instead invited Chamberlain up on to the balcony at Buckingham Palace to give royal endorsement to this seemingly magnificent achievement.

This act on the part of the King was unwise, and pulled him into the politics of the time. He was implicitly endorsing the Conservative

Prime Minister Neville Chamberlain and his policy of appeasement, which, by 1938, was far from universally held to be the correct approach. As for Chamberlain, before war broke out he was obsessed with monitoring and seeking to influence the various factions, even to the extent that he had Churchill's activities reported to him. On 23 October 1938, three weeks after Chamberlain's return from Germany, George VI wrote to his brother, the recently abdicated Edward:

> I was so glad that the Prime Minister decided to see Hitler. I was always very anxious that he should make 'personal contact' with him and speak to him face to face. I am sure his policy is the right one in this case and let us hope this will be the turning point in our relations with Hitler in the future.

Edward replied: 'I agree with you wholeheartedly that the Prime Minister's personal contact with Hitler was the only thing that saved the World from war last month … I am in the front rank for taking my hat off to him.' George VI, like his brother Edward before him, held the view that kings and queens still had a hands-on role to play when it came to foreign policy, and not necessarily one in line with the elected government. It was, according to the historian Tom MacDonnell, 'as if nothing had happened to the map of Europe since 1914 when the Continent had been the private domain of royal cousins'. George VI repeatedly suggested he make a personal appeal to Hitler, something which would have been both inappropriate and ineffective. He suggested that his cousin, and uncompromising Nazi, Prince Philipp of Hesse could be used as a conduit to Hitler. When that did not find favour, he sent his brother, the Duke of Kent, to speak to his cousin anyway. Royal weddings and funerals provided ideal cover for such meetings. The present Duke of Edinburgh told the historian Jonathan

Petropoulos in 2004 that there had been 'a tremendous amount of contact between the two.'

As the war unfolded, George VI encouraged Lord Halifax to use the metaphorical back door at Buckingham Palace to keep him briefed. Halifax, with the support of the King, continued to pursue appeasement well into the summer of 1940, even attempting to enlist the help of Mussolini to secure it. Naturally George VI much preferred the idea of the appeaser Halifax as Prime Minister rather than Churchill, though as time went on, his opposition to the Nazis did harden. As an aside, had the King succeeded in having Halifax as Prime Minister, he would have managed to wind the clock back. It had become standard practice for the Prime Minister of the day to sit in the Commons, not the Lords. That remains the case today. The last PM who sat in the upper house was Lord Salisbury, up to 1902.

What is perplexing is that anyone would think, after a string of betrayals and broken promises throughout the previous decade, that any agreement reached with Hitler would be honoured. The royals may have thought that there was a special relationship with Germany, and that Hitler's alleged soft spot for Britain would make him amenable to a deal, but the evidence to date was that any pact or promise to respect neutrality lasted only as long as it suited Hitler politically and militarily.

One strange and much discussed event of the war was the flight to Britain by Hitler's deputy Rudolf Hess on 10 May 1941. What is not in dispute is that he emerged from his twin-engined fighter bomber near the village of Eaglesham in Scotland, and when confronted by the local Home Guard, gave his name as Alfred Horn and asked to see the Duke of Hamilton. The Duke had been personally appointed by George VI in 1940 to the important court position of Lord Steward of the Household, the first dignitary of the court. The King had in fact sacked his predecessor, the Duke of Buccleuch, who had served from 1937, on account of his embarrassingly overt pro-Nazi views – the Duke had even attended Hitler's birthday party in 1939.

After he was unmasked, Hess stated that the purpose of his visit was to seek peace between Germany and Britain. He would be detained here until 1946 when he was convicted for crimes against peace in the Nuremberg trials and thereafter held in Spandau prison until he died in 1987, aged ninety-three. What is in dispute is why he made the flight at all. After his capture, Hitler issued a statement suggesting Hess was mentally ill, but that smacks more of a deniability strategy than a serious suggestion. Numerous theories have been put forward, of which there are perhaps two credible front-runners. One is that he was deliberately lured here by the British in a sort of sting operation, holding out the false prospect of peace negotiations. If that were the case, we might have expected the authorities to have been prepared and to have whisked him away quite quickly upon arrival. As it was, he was left in a scout hut for four hours under the control of members of the Home Guard. The more likely explanation is that this was a genuine attempt by some on the British side to secure peace, and that the Nazis had received from key individuals in this country signals of sufficient weight to believe that it was worth Hess making the trip. After all, Britain was in poor shape by May 1941, and by any objective account was losing the war. That the country might want to come to some accommodation with Germany may well have seemed credible to the Nazis.

Interestingly, the then Lord Provost of Glasgow, Sir Patrick Dollan, seemed to know a good deal about the trip. He was reported in a Scottish newspaper shortly after Hess's arrival saying that the leading Nazi believed he could remain in Scotland for two days, discuss peace terms, and then be given petrol and maps to return to Germany. It has also been suggested that there was a welcoming committee for Hess at the Duke of Hamilton's residence at Dungavel House, and that that party included the King's brother, the Duke of Kent. We shall never know what would have happened if Hess had not landed eleven miles away from where it seems he was expected.

It would certainly have required someone of sufficient importance to convince Hess, and probably Hitler too, that the flight was worth making. The Duke of Hamilton, who had worked for British Intelligence in the mid-1930s, was a known appeaser, and had even attended the Berlin Olympics in 1936. But he would surely not have been regarded on his own as that significant. The only people of sufficient clout would have been a senior politician like Lord Halifax. Or the Duke of Kent. Or George VI himself. Churchill seemed to give some credibility to the appeasement theory when he addressed the Commons on 27 January 1942:

> When Rudolf Hess flew over here some months ago, he firmly believed that he had only to gain access to certain circles in this country for what he described as the Churchill clique to be thrown out of power and for a government to be set up with which Hitler could negotiate a magnanimous peace.

This statement from Churchill, nearly nine months after Hess landed, was the first public one he had made on the incident – an extraordinary gap in time.

The other interesting timing is that 10 May 1941, the day Hess landed, was both the night of a devastating air attack on London by 520 bombers, and the last significant air raid on the capital until 1944. It is mere speculation, but one explanation that fits the facts is that with Hess's capture, Hitler concluded that Edward's view that the British

48

could be bombed to the peace table was not going to work. It is perhaps worth noting that Hess's flight occurred shortly before the German invasion of the Soviet Union. It would certainly have helped Germany if their western front could have been neutralised first, and of course, they had for years been receiving recurrent messages from members of the British royal family and others in the upper echelons of society that a solution that left the British Empire intact and Hitler free to tackle what they regarded as the scourge of Bolshevism was a good solution. So the royal family survived the war, not least due to the King himself, whose basic decency and genuineness struck a chord with the public. How different it would all have been if Edward had remained as king.

In 1956, the new German state released some wartime papers which cast a bad light on the motives and actions of the Duke of Windsor. The British government quickly issued a statement by way of response which included the following statement: 'His Royal Highness has never wavered in his loyalty to the British cause.' Sir Alan Lascelles, Edward's private secretary, saw it rather differently. He was to observe: 'He never cared for England or the English … He hated this country.'

L'État, C'est Moi

Before the action comes the formality. The spectators may be itching for the game to start, but first come the obligatory musical diversions – the national anthems of the countries involved in the match.

Most anthems eulogise the country, hence 'O Canada', 'God Bless Fiji', or 'Das Lied der Deutschen' (the Song of the Germans), the latter which has understandably replaced the strident 'Deutschland Uber Alles'. Some celebrate advances towards democracy, such as Greece's 'Hymn To Liberty', or across the channel 'La Marseillaise', born three years after the revolution of 1789 and which has such a fantastic, rousing tune that the words almost take second place. In fact, they are rather bloodthirsty, reflecting their time of origin:

Listen to the sound in the fields
The baying of those fearsome soldiers
They are coming into our midst
To cut the throats of your sons and consorts …
All those tigers who without pity
Ripped out their mothers' wombs.

These anthems, whether hymns to their country, or celebrating significant events in history, can be fairly said to embody the spirit of each
nation. Can the same be said of the British national anthem, which
almost alone refers to an individual, and by implication suggests that
person embodies the nation?

Yet this embodiment, to be accurate, requires both the monarch of
the day to hold the values of the nation as a whole, and assumes that
each subsequent inheritor of the throne will do likewise. But while it
is a reasonably safe assumption that Canadians or Fijians will almost
indefinitely continue to embrace the warm sentiments about their
countries expressed in their anthems, no such certainty can apply to
the public view of the personage who occupies the British throne. This
may not be controversial with Elizabeth II, who is widely regarded as
having shown diligence and done a good job. But God Save George IV,
that wastrel playboy? God Save Edward VIII, the Nazi sympathiser? The
characteristics of a country do not change, or change only slowly.
The characteristics of the monarch can turn 180 degrees with the arrival
of a new incumbent on the throne.

Right from the opening of the anthem, we are asked to accept that the
monarch, whoever he or she may be, is both 'noble' and 'gracious'. As the
quality and characteristics of monarchs vary wildly, just as they will do
down and across the generations in any family, the implication is that
these worthy qualities can be achieved automatically merely by virtue
of accident of birth or position in society. That of course is to imply
that the monarch is always majestic and the nobility is always noble,
which is clearly not the case any more than saying that 'Honourable
Members' of the House of Commons are always honourable, which
they manifestly are not.

By annexing complimentary adjectives to themselves, those in
privileged positions have sought, over the centuries, to justify the

existing order, asserting that somehow the right people are at the top. It is an approach that fossilises society, entrenches advantage based on birth and wealth, and stifles the opportunity for progress based on merit. The inalienable link between the anthem and the monarch of the day is reinforced by the fact that when played in the presence of the Queen (or, after 1960, Prince Philip), others in attendance are supposed to salute them for the duration of the anthem. We are given some relief when the royal personage is Prince Charles, who only merits a salute for the first six bars. Who decides these things? It does not help that the anthem has remained largely unchanged since its creation in 1745, a time when virtually all of Europe was largely run by absolute monarchies, and when it was more natural to see the monarch and the state as indivisible.

'L'état, c'est moi,' was how the Sun King, Louis XIV, had succinctly put it. Of course, this is all history now. Except here in the United Kingdom. We cannot even escape the monarch in the name of our country. Other monarchies, such as Sweden or Belgium, manage quite well without inserting a royal reference into the name of their country.

During the First World War, Russia, allied to Britain in that campaign, began to use 'Rule Britannia' during official events in preference to 'God Save The King'. The reason for this was that the tune of the latter was associated in Russian minds with a German hymn, not the British anthem, and led to hisses when it was played. Files in the Royal Archive show the issue was a thorny one. On 3 February 1916, Sir George Buchanan, our man in the British embassy in Petrograd, told the Tsar's representative:

> The King desires me to say that he trusts that Rule Britannia will never be performed again in Russia as our National Anthem … the King is rather exercised in his mind that during these long months God Save The King should not have been played merely because it

happens to have been cribbed by Germany many years after it was adopted as the National Anthem of this country.

It is an unquestionable fact that the use of the British national anthem is withering on the vine, and that the anthem celebrates and extols one individual rather than our country must surely play a part. To sing the anthem enthusiastically, one has to be proud of Britain, a supporter of monarchy, and a believer in God. While it is likely, notwithstanding the debacle of Brexit, that most Britons still feel pride in their country, we know that there are sizeable numbers who do not subscribe to the second and third criteria. Yet a national anthem should be one that everyone can embrace, not just those who are monarchists or who believe in God.

But times do move on, even if the national anthem does not. When I was a young lad, the anthem used to be played at the end of a film presentation in the cinema, in which capacity it was more effective than a fire alarm in emptying the building at speed. People would literally bustle their way out, in marked contrast to the unremarkable pace you can witness today. The handful of people who stood to attention while others pushed past them defined themselves by their actions as old-fashioned sticks-in-the-mud. They were left standing while the rest of the world moved on. This behaviour is captured beautifully in an episode of *Dad's Army*, suggesting that this hurried exodus was also a feature of wartime Britain. In the end, it all seems to have become just too embarrassing and the curtain fell on this use of the anthem.

And it fell elsewhere as well. BBC TV used to play it at the end of its daily schedule, which at least served to wake up those who had fallen asleep in front of the box. Such individuals, if they woke, would not give a second thought to switching the anthem off in mid-play, if only to avoid the unpleasant and continual high-pitched beep that would invariably follow. The advent of 24-hour television gave the BBC an excuse to drop this play of the anthem in 1997, and it is now only heard daily at about 00.59 a.m. on Radio 4, for those who have lasted through the Shipping Forecast, as the channel gives way to the World Service. It is also played on the *Today Programme* on the occasion of the birthday of a senior royal, and pretty incongruous it sounds too. ITV managed to ditch it rather earlier, in 1980, and it was never introduced on the newer terrestrial channels: BBC2, which began in 1964, Channel 4 or Channel 5.

Buoyed by the EU referendum result, the arch-monarchist Tory MP for Romford, Andrew Rosindell, chair of the All-Party Flags and Heraldry Parliamentary Group, tabled a parliamentary motion on 3 November 2016. This called for the reinstatement of 'God Save The Queen' at the end of each day's transmission on BBC1. *Newsnight* responded by acceding to his request – in a way. They played a clip of the Sex Pistols and their archetypal punk song of the same name: 'God save the Queen', which describes 'A fascist regime'.

This is how it begins, before proceeding to insult the monarch personally. ('She ain't no human being' and so on.) Whatever you think about the Sex Pistols, or indeed the Queen, it was good to see the BBC display a bit of backbone for a change. The fact that they did not cave in over this issue is an interesting commentary on the declining respect for the anthem. The single, when it was originally issued in the year of the Queen's silver jubilee, reached number two in the charts, despite being banned by the BBC and so denied airplay, a ban apparently now lifted, at least on *Newsnight*.

The end of empire and the weakening of ties between Commonwealth countries and the motherland has led to a marked decrease in the use of the anthem around the world, though some countries like New Zealand hold on to it, and others like Australia use it as a 'royal anthem' for special occasions, such as royal visits, while using their own homegrown anthem most of the time. Devolution in the United Kingdom has also lessened its use. On sporting occasions, Northern Ireland holds on to the anthem, but Scotland and Wales now use their own tunes, 'Flower Of Scotland' for the former, and 'Land Of My Fathers' for the latter, which emerged from the grassroots up, particularly at rugby matches, and soon elbowed out the official anthem, 'God Bless The Prince Of Wales'.

In England too, there is pressure for change, not least because the existing national anthem is seen, accurately, to refer to the whole country and not simply England, which has no accepted equivalent to, say, 'Flower Of Scotland'. So 'Jerusalem' has now been adopted for cricketing purposes, and by Team England in the Commonwealth Games, whereas other sporting outfits favour 'Land of Hope and Glory', as had Team England prior to 2010. In fact, in the nearest thing we have had to a vote on the national anthem, Team England innovatively held a poll amongst the public in 2010, offering a choice between three options. 'Jerusalem' came top with 53 per cent, 'Land Of Hope And Glory' had 33 per cent and 'God Save The Queen' was last with just 12 per cent.

The national anthem is dying from its roots up, and its use is increasingly restricted to formal occasions and to events that mirror the societal advantages open to those with wealth and privilege, such as Royal Ascot and the Henley Regatta. The national anthem no longer speaks for the whole country, or at all for some sections of the nation. It therefore fails in its central objective as a unifying anthem for the country. The fact that it is also regarded by many as, musically, something of a dirge, hardly helps.

Back in 2007, Greg Mulholland, then Lib Dem MP for Leeds North West, tabled a motion in Parliament which called for the introduction of an English national anthem. It attracted the support of twenty-four MPs from all three major parties. The Oxford West & Abingdon MP, Evan

Harris, added an amendment, calling for the replacement to have 'a bit more oomph than "God Save The Queen" and should also not involve God'. For those who like the tune, however, they can take some joy from the fact that it is also used for the national anthem of Liechtenstein, 'Oben am jungen Rhein', (Up above the Young Rhein). This led to the bizarre outcome of the tune being played twice in 2004 on the occasion of the football match between England and Liechtenstein, though it is limited to one rendition if England play Northern Ireland. It is also used for the Norwegian royal anthem, and for the American song 'My Country, 'Tis of Thee'.

It is not just the national anthem, however, that seeks to stretch the royal tentacles out into the population. Potentially more insidious is the oath of allegiance that pervades the public sphere in Britain today as it has for centuries. In many walks of life, almost no personal career progress can be made without swearing an oath of allegiance, not just to the monarch, but to his or her heirs and successors as well. Given that any successors may not even exist at the relevant point, this is the constitutional equivalent of buying a pig in a poke. It is to solemnly accept that the hereditary principle will invariably throw up a suitable, nay the most suitable person to sit on the throne – a patent absurdity.

So, parliamentary candidates, who may have gone through an exhausting and rigorous process in their constituency of choice before finally emerging as victor with a democratic mandate from those whom they have sought to persuade, find, when they arrive at the Commons, that they cannot assume their seat until they have sworn an oath of allegiance to an unelected person. This also means that even if a majority of seats in the House of Commons were secured by a party expressly elected on a platform of creating a republic, all those MPs would have to pledge loyalty to the King or Queen before proceeding to legislate for the abolition of the monarchy. Some would doubtless then accuse those who voted this way of treason, which would provide an interesting test case if it ever reached the courts. It is at least arguable that having taken an oath of allegiance and broken it, then legally an act of treason may have been committed. That in turn would mean that no constitutional means could exist for removing or replacing the monarchy, which gives a devastating new meaning to the phrase 'hereditary principle'. Here, then, is a very British catch-22: those elected on a platform to remove the monarch first have to swear allegiance to him or her which then prevents them from carrying through the pledge to which they are committed.

The precise wording of the parliamentary oath comes from the Promissory Oaths Act 1868, though the concept is much older. It dates back, in fact, to Magna Carta of 1215, since when the country has moved on a bit, even if the oath has not. The form of the present oath is not so very different from the feudal version which existed in 1215. Members of Parliament were first required to pledge allegiance by the Act of Supremacy 1558. Doubtless Elizabeth I would be pleased that the requirement remains intact under Elizabeth II. The one concession to those who object to the oath occurred in 1888, when the requirement to swear allegiance before God was removed, which at least means that those forced to take it against their will do not have to lie before God.

The two acceptable forms of oath are therefore these:

> I (name of MP) swear by Almighty God that I will be faithful and bear true allegiance to Her Majesty Queen Elizabeth, her heirs and successors, according to law. So help me God.

and

> I (name of MP) do solemnly, sincerely and truly declare and affirm

that I will be faithful and bear true allegiance to Her Majesty Queen
Elizabeth, her heirs and successors, according to law.

The official parliamentary website explains the oath thus: 'Oaths of
allegiance to the Crown are fairly common in British public life and
are similar to those in other countries where a declaration of loyalty
is made to the state.'

Similar, but completely different. An oath to one individual is a completely different concept from an oath to the country to which you
belong. The Queen herself on her accession took an oath to govern the
country and uphold the rights of bishops. Parliamentarians take an oath
to the Queen. Nobody takes an oath to uphold democracy. Well, almost
nobody. The House of Commons, the House of Lords, the Scottish
Parliament and the Welsh Assembly all have a requirement for oaths
of personal allegiance to the monarch, but not the Northern Ireland
Assembly, doubtless because Sinn Féin would not have stomached it.

Instead, that Assembly has a rather enlightened oath, whereby
members are required to 'discharge in good faith the duties of office',
maintain a 'commitment to non-violence and exclusively democratic
means,' and to 'serve all the people of Northern Ireland equally and act
in accordance with the general obligation on government to promote
equality and prevent discrimination'.

The words have clearly been formulated to deal with the specific
circumstances of Northern Ireland and flow from the peace process.
Nevertheless, the oath that has emerged is far more befitting of a
democracy than the feudal version that most in public office are obliged
to accede to. For it is not just parliamentarians who are required to
pledge allegiance in this way. The requirement also applies to members
of the armed forces, a most unsatisfactory situation in a democracy.
The oath sworn by recruits to the Army, the Air Force and the Royal

Marines, goes even further than that sworn by parliamentarians. As well as the usual formula about bearing true allegiance to the Queen, it adds a pledge to 'faithfully defend Her Majesty, Her Heirs and Successors ... against all enemies, and will observe and obey all orders of Her Majesty, Her Heirs and Successors...'

It may be highly unlikely that such an oath can have serious and immediate consequences, but it is not impossible. Suppose Hitler had successfully invaded England, and suppose Edward VIII, with his Nazi sympathies, were restored to the throne as a sort of puppet, a scenario that certainly existed in Hitler's mind. If the restored King Edward had called on the armed forces to lay down their weapons and accept a sort of Vichy Britain with him at the head, they may well have done so, whatever the elected government may have thought. I know members of the armed forces who take their oath to the Queen very seriously, and for them, this allegiance trumps any democratic considerations. The fact that members of the royal family occupy senior positions right across the military only reinforces this.

Interestingly, Hitler, on assuming power, changed the German loyalty oath from one to the constitution to one to him personally as Führer. Perhaps he took inspiration from the royal family of German descent on the British throne.

But it is not just the military who have to take an oath of allegiance to the person who is the unelected head of state. Judges too have to swear to 'serve our Sovereign Lady Queen Elizabeth the Second', as do magistrates and police officers in England and Wales, though not in Scotland or Northern Ireland. Even eight-year-old beaver scouts and wolf cubs are required to pledge themselves to the Queen before they can join the pack.

And of course those who wish to become British citizens had better mug up on the royal family if they want to pass the 'Life in the UK' test which is a requirement for any successful application. In this test, you may face a question asking you whether the adjective associated with King Henry VIII's daughter Mary was (a) Catholic (b) Scary (c) Bloody, or (d) Killer. Or how about this one? After 1588, Queen Elizabeth I became one of the most popular monarchs in English history: (a) Yes, this is true; or (b) False, she was already popular before 1588. Or you might be asked when the union flag was created. Was it (a) 1506, (b) 1556, (c) 1606 or (d) 1656?

How many indigenous British people would score three out of three with these questions? To be perfectly British, I would suggest you should score one at most. (The answers, by the way, are (c) Bloody, (b) False and (c) 1606.) So why are we requiring those who wish to become British citizens to learn all this royal-tinged historical inconsequential minutiae? How will it help someone looking for a house in Halifax or a job in Jedburgh to become an expert on Henry VIII? Naturally, those applying for citizenship have to take an oath of allegiance in similar terms to that sworn by MPs or they cannot qualify. This requirement was in fact only introduced in 2003 by the then Labour government.

Sporadically, there have been attempts in the House of Commons to challenge the wording of the parliamentary oath. Tony Benn tried twice, in 1988 and 1998, but his Bill, changing the terms of the oath to one that pledged allegiance to the country and to democratic values, did not even get off the starting blocks. The Labour MP Kevin McNamara made a little more progress, introducing Bills in both 1998 and 2000, managing to secure a slot for a ten-minute speech, to ask the House for permission to introduce a Bill to change the oath. In his speech to the Commons on 14 November 2000, he argued: 'The present oath of allegiance has no reference whatever to the people who send us here and no reference to our duties and obligations to ... all our constituents, whether they voted for us or not.' He suggested an alternative form of words, whereby an

MP would pledge 'to the best of my ability, discharge the responsibilities required of me by virtue of my membership of the House of Commons and faithfully serve those whom I represent here'.

Challenging Kevin McNamara, the Tory MP Gerald Howarth argued that the oath was 'part of our traditions, going back centuries'. He clearly saw that as a reason for no change, whereas others drew the opposite conclusion. The Tory went on to argue that the change proposed would 'extend inclusivity to fifth columnists and traitors'. The answer was to require MPs to swear an oath of allegiance to the Head of State. I am not familiar with the mindset of fifth columnists or traitors, but I somehow doubt they would be dissuaded from their nefarious activities by the requirement to swear an oath. Kevin McNamara only narrowly lost the 1998 vote by 151 to 137, and the 2000 vote by 148 to 129, which at the very least suggested a sizeable proportion of the Commons, including me, favoured a change. The 129 was made up of Labour, Lib Dem and Nationalist MPs, but not a single Conservative.

So those opposed to the oath therefore still have to swear it in order to pass go, and collect their seat. Faced with this, a variety of wheezes have been developed. Tony Benn would preface his oath-taking with 'as a committed republican' or similar phrases. The Labour MP Tony Banks was seen to be crossing his fingers while taking the oath. For my part, I solemnly swore an oath of my own creation before a startled Speaker, promising to serve my constituents to the best of my ability and to uphold democracy, before then garbling through the official oath in as monotonous and disinterested fashion as I could muster.

When the following day I checked Hansard, the official record of all that is said in Parliament, I noted wryly that my own oath was not recorded for posterity, only the official one. The waters had opened up and swallowed it. Even the official record of Parliament, it seems, has to be perverted to uphold the dignity of the monarchy.

Heralds Triumph

The history of Britain over the last few hundred years has been a momentous one. We went through a huge industrial revolution, at one point being responsible for 45 per cent of the world's industrial output. We gained and then lost the biggest empire the world has ever seen, with at its zenith a quarter of the world painted pink. We endured two highly destructive world wars. We immersed ourselves in the European project and then set about withdrawing from it. And through all that, we gave the world a bewildering array of wonderful creations, from the spinning jenny to television, the hovercraft to the internet, while culturally we have produced such unsurpassable icons as the BBC and the Beatles.

This rollercoaster ride, this fantastic journey, leaves Britain unrecognisable from the pre-industrial country it was. Yet in the hidden crannies of our country, the old ways live on, unscathed by the relentless tick of time, fossilised but somehow still breathing. Many of these living fossils survive in the safe shadow of monarchy, without which their inherent absurdity would be all too painfully apparent.

One such is the College of Heralds, sometimes called the College of Arms. This royal corporation was founded in 1484 by Richard III, and while other heraldic authorities across Europe have been consigned to history books of the medieval period, here in Britain the College creaks on, oblivious to the outside world. The heralds of the college are appointed by the Queen and exercise power on her behalf. Naturally the pool from which heralds are selected is a traditional and rarefied one. You will struggle to find any normal, down-to-earth wage-earners in their ranks. There are thirteen heralds in total, all male, white and elderly, and all from privileged backgrounds. The thirteen is made up of three Kings of Arms, six Heralds of Arms and four Pursuivants of Arms. There are also seven officers extraordinary (though many would regard the whole thing as extraordinary). The college even has its own little hereditary arrangements, being headed today as it always has been by the Duke of Norfolk, currently the eighteenth incarnation, Edward Fitzalan-Howard, here given the title of Earl Marshal.

The Garter Principal King of Arms, an office that has existed since 1415, is presently occupied by someone with a suitably Tudor-sounding name, one Thomas Woodcock CVO DL FSA, sometimes simply known as Garter. This OE (Old Etonian) has progressed through the heraldic ranks, from Rouge Croix Pursuivant in 1978, to Somerset Herald (not a newspaper but an archaic office) in 1982, to Norroy and Ulster in 1997 and finally appointed Garter on April Fools' Day 2010. He is responsible to the Earl Marshal for the running of the College, and is the principal advisor to the Queen on ceremonial and heraldic matters.

The college's authority covers England, Wales and Northern Ireland. Scotland's parallel is the Court of the Lord Lyon. This Lyon King is an office that dates from the fourteenth century, so even older than Garter. He handles ceremonial occasions north of the border, and is invariably accompanied by Her Majesty's Officers of Arms, all of whom are members of the Royal Household. Well, I suppose it gives them something to do.

The Lyon King retains the duty to prosecute as a criminal offence anyone using unauthorised arms under an Act of the pre-union Scottish Parliament passed in 1592. The right to bear arms in Scotland is a rather more esoteric and prosaic matter than its counterpart in the United States constitution. The College of Arms itself can be found in London's Queen Victoria Street, where it has been based since 1555. The building is also home to the Earl Marshal's own court, the High Court of Chivalry, though on the last occasion it sat, on 21 December 1954, this venue was deemed too small and proceedings were transferred to the Royal Courts of Justice instead.

At issue then was a case brought by Manchester Corporation, then the local government body for the city, against Manchester Palace of Varieties, alleging that the latter was using the city's arms and common seal without permission. As they had been using these for some sixty years, it might be thought that the corporation was a tad slow off the mark in bringing the action. Perhaps they were hesitant, given that the Court of Chivalry had not met for over 200 years. Proceedings began in a farcical Lewis Carroll fashion with arguments about whether the Court actually existed and even if it did, whether it had any powers. A Mr Squibb, acting for the Corporation, argued not only that it certainly had powers to grant the equivalent of an injunction, as requested by the public authority, but also had the power to fine, and even imprison.

There was also a rather arcane dispute about whether the Earl Marshal was competent to sit alone without the Hereditary Constable, a post which ceased being hereditary with the execution of the Earl of Buckingham in 1521. That was followed by one contesting whether using arms ceremonially was the same as bearing arms, that being the protected activity. In the end, Lord Goddard, the surrogate acting for the Duke of Norfolk, came down on the side of the Corporation, who were awarded costs of £300. But he also ruled that merely displaying arms was not in itself sufficient to generate a successful complaint by those whose arms were being displayed. It came down to usage and, although he did not use this phrase, the trading standards concept of 'passing off'.

This matter has a modern parallel in the use of the crown symbol which of late has been subject to some controversy. Officially anyone wishing to use certain designated royal symbols or terms is supposed to secure permission first from the Cabinet Office. This especially refers to the use of the term royal, but also covers the words king, queen, duke, duchess, prince, princess and Windsor. The Cabinet Office is, however, reasonably sanguine about incongruous uses of protected terms, provided permission has been sought. Near Victoria, for example, you can find the Queen Mother Sports Centre. Whatever the qualities that particular royal might have had, exuberant attraction to physical sports was not one of them. It is difficult to imagine the Queen Mother working up a sweat on the rowing machine, or lifting weights – other than a brim-filled tumbler of gin and tonic.

A parliamentary question from the Lib Dem MP Norman Lamb in January 2019 elicited the information that 908 applications to use protected words were received in 2018, of which fourteen were approved, 107 were objected to, and 703 were 'issued a non-objection'. The rest were still under consideration.

The prefix 'royal' is much sought after by towns and cities and sparingly allowed. One notable designation, in 2011, was Wootton Bassett, in recognition of the town's honouring of our military dead. Other reasonably recent additions include Greenwich and Kensington. Newmarket is amongst the latest to seek the prefix, doubtless hopeful because of their racing connection, but their application was complicated by the fact that the then relevant minister, the Paymaster General Matt Hancock, was also the local MP. Unlike in many other countries, ministers tend to be hampered in what they can do for their own patch.

I asked the Cabinet Office to publish a list of the requests received over a three-year period for the use of the word 'royal', and to indicate which had been approved and which rejected. Not only would they not release the information, but they even used the formula deployed by MI5 in respect of requests received by them for information: 'We neither confirm nor deny whether we hold information you have requested under Section37(1)(b) [of the Freedom of Information Act 2000]'. It seems information about the use of the word 'royal' is to be treated as a state secret on a par with highly sensitive information about impending terrorist plots. Given that applications on the use of protected royal terms are submitted to the royal names team at the Cabinet Office's premises at 1 Horse Guards Road, the use of 'neither confirm nor deny' is particularly absurd. Incidentally, not that I think it should, but the fact that I am a privy counsellor seemed to make no difference whatsoever. The arbitrary advantages of Establishment appointments only go so far, it seems.

The Cabinet Office finally admitted that they are the body that arbitrates on sensitive words as provided for by the Companies Act, including the word 'royal'. This admission, in a letter to me dated 30 January 2020, followed a query I had raised with the Cabinet Secretary, Mark Sedwill, about the exploitation for profit of the word 'royal' by those with royal connections themselves.

This in turn followed the revelation that Princess Anne's son had appeared in two adverts on Chinese television, promoting Jersey Cattle Fresh Milk. Described as 'British Royal Family member Peter Phillips' and dressed in a bow tie and dinner jacket, he enthusiastically claimed he had been raised on Jersey milk from the herd at Windsor. This seems unlikely, as the royal dairy did not deliver to the Gatcombe Park estate in Gloucestershire where he grew up, as former royal chef Darren McGrady noted when the news broke.

To add to the royal feel, one of the adverts featured a replica of the Queen's state coach and a liveried footman. A grand building is used as a backdrop, which Chinese viewers are invited to assume is a royal palace. Actually, it was Longleat, and its inclusion occurred without the permission of the owners.

Not to be outdone, Lady Kitty Spencer, Princess Diana's niece and a cousin to William and Harry, could also be found on Chinese television promoting Satine, a rival brand. 'The day of the royal family usually begins with a cup of milk or a cup of tea,' she gushed. 'Jersey milk has a close relationship with the royal family.'

Neither Peter Phillips nor Lady Kitty Spencer are officially members of the royal family so are not entitled to imply that they are. Neither the Palace nor the Cabinet Office have seemed very keen to do much about it, however.

This all turned out to be a warm-up for the main act, namely the clear wish of Harry and Meghan to continue to use the registered label 'Sussex Royal' even after they had decided to discontinue their royal duties and move across the Atlantic. This was one step too far for the Palace, which normally likes to smudge everything over, and the couple were told that the use of Sussex Royal would have to end.

Whereas the system to protect certain words seems to work effectively, except perhaps in the case of those with royal connections and an eye for easy money, the same cannot be said for royal symbols. Oddly there is legislation that protects the primary symbols of other countries from misuse, but none to protect our own. The Trade Descriptions Act 1968, which enacted the terms of the Paris Convention in this regard, unaccountably failed to deal with the St Edward's crown symbol that adorns official documents and proclamations, let alone others which imply royal approval, such as the Tudor Crown. This omission only really came to light when complaints began to be received about the use of the St Edward's crown symbol by the unpleasant far-right organisation endorsed by Donald Trump, Britain First, after its formation in 2011.

It then became apparent that, rather embarrassingly, there was no obvious way to stop this use. Even copyright protection could not be invoked, for the design dated from 1952, and the appropriately named crown copyright had lapsed in 2002. Consideration was then given as to whether action could be taken under Royal Prerogative powers, but the foundations for this looked decidedly shaky. Accordingly the then Deputy Prime Minister Nick Clegg, to whom this matter fell, instead referred the case to the police, without direct effect, though in January 2015, their actions did lead to the organisation's leader, Paul Golding, being found guilty on the obscure charge of wearing a political uniform, in this case a Britain First members' jacket. He was fined £100. The offence had been introduced in the Public Order Act 1936 to deal with Oswald Mosley's Blackshirts, but was never invoked until recently. There have only been three successful prosecutions of this offence within the last ten years. Tory MPs wearing blue ties and Labour MPs sporting red roses would, however, appear to be exempt.

The Advertising Standards Authority took up the case of Britain First's use of the crown, and asked for the symbol to be removed from the organisation's website, but this request was contemptuously dismissed. Eventually, in March 2015, the ASA published a ruling upholding complaints about the use of the crown symbol, largely because it falsely implied goods marketed with the symbol were British-made.

Meanwhile, in 2014, the Cabinet Office had written to Britain First ordering them to remove the image from their merchandise, though on what legal basis is unclear. In any case, its use does appear to have been discontinued.

The Britain First website states at the very top that it is 'loyal to Queen and country'. I am not sure that either the Queen or the country would see it that way, but that is presumably why they decided to commandeer the crown symbol. Incidentally, on the day I looked at the website, a full-size pop-up screen appeared asking whether St George's Day should be a public holiday. Website visitors were offered two choices: yes, or close. It appears no was not an option they were prepared to countenance.

Also much sought after is Royal Warrant status, this being a public manifestation of some sort of royal endorsement, which in turn adds status and so a commercial edge to the receiving body. The system that handles Royal Warrants goes back to medieval times and is overseen by the Lord Chamberlain, just as it was in the fifteenth century. To be in the running, a business has to have supplied goods to either the Queen, the Duke of Edinburgh or the Prince of Wales for five years within the last seven. Naturally, warrant status is regarded as a cachet that brings status and a commercial advantage, but who decides which commercial organisations should benefit and what checks are in place to ensure fairness and consistency is applied?

One safeguard would be for the process to be open and transparent, but of course it is not. The official website states: 'As a matter dealt with under the Royal Prerogative, information about any criteria which may exist and the reasons for the grant or refusal of an application are not disclosed.' It goes on: 'The grant of the titles is not, and never has been, a right which can be claimed by a body fulfilling certain conditions.' So not only is the whole process secret, but there is an open admission that a level playing field does not apply. The opportunity for favouritism, or worse, is clear.

What we do know is that between them, the Queen, the Duke of Edinburgh and Prince Charles are associated with around 900 warrants, covering about 800 companies or individuals. The goods and services provided are not necessarily the best on the market, simply those preferred by the royals. So the list includes Ainsworths Homeopathic Pharmacy, Aston Martin Lagonda Ltd, Game and Country Ltd, Jeeves of Belgravia, and no fewer than eight different suppliers of champagne. Up to forty Royal Warrants are cancelled each year, which in some cases will be due to the individual to whom the Warrant has been granted retiring, though presumably some may be removed for malpractice. This reduction is offset by the award of new warrants.

The Royal Warrant Holders Association maintains that business between warrant holders and members of the royal family is 'conducted on a commercial basis'. That implies that the royals do not put any pressure on the warrant holders to supply goods at a discount or even free of charge. Yet *The Observer* reported that Prince Charles receives free supplies of his preferred toothpaste from GlaxoSmithKline, with the Prince of Wales's three-feather emblem appearing annually on the side of twenty-eight million packs of Macleans.

Given that goods and services are officially supplied on a commercial basis, I asked the Lord Chamberlain in 2017 whether those provided, solicited or unsolicited, to individual members of the royal family are kept or returned, and if kept whether there is a register of such occurrences. Answer came there none.

Holders are however required to have in place an acceptable environmental and sustainability policy, which is a helpful and positive condition. It is interesting to see that modern requirement attached to an ancient and largely unchanged mechanism, a bit like adding a satnav to a Ford Model T.

Heralds of course are far from the only archaic hangover to populate the royal circle. *Whitaker's Almanack* contains four-and-a-half pages of closely typed print listing all those in the royal household. They say time marches on, but this particular clock seems to have stopped several centuries ago. So we still have Gold Stick-in-Waiting, and Silver Stick-in-Waiting, bodyguard positions in the royal household, Aides-de-Camp aplenty, a Crown Equerry, a bevy of other Equerries, extra Equerries and Temporary Equerries, a Master of the Queen's Music to play a merry tune, Gentlemen Ushers and, of course, Extra Gentlemen Ushers, nine surgeons, five apothecaries, a couple of Clerks of the Cheque and Adjutant (two who bear the title Ensign), someone else called 'Exons', an Astronomer, a Hereditary Carver, a Sculptor in Ordinary, the Warden of the Queen's Swans, the Royal Bargemaster and enough chaplains to organise a football knock-out competition.

The Crown Equerry, Colonel Toby Browne, handles the monarch's road transport on land, including maintaining the Gold State Coach with its top speed of three miles per hour. He heads a team including the Horsebox Driver of Windsor, the Rough Rider, and the intriguingly named Daily Ladies of London. For his troubles, he gets a free three-storey house just inside the gates to the Royal Mews as a perk.

There is the Mistress of the Robes, who is generally a duchess, and the Ladies of the Bedchamber. In earlier times, these used to change to reflect the political complexion of the government of the day, so alternating between Whig and Tory, but nowadays they are nearly always peeresses and almost invariably Tories. So much for the political independence of the monarchy. As if that was not enough, there are also two extra Ladies of the Bedchamber, who naturally are also titled.

It is clear that to make it through the gates into the Palace of Patronage, you almost invariably need to be white, from an upper-class background, and Conservative in your politics.

I could not find a Keeper of the Belfry or the Lord High Astrologer, but perhaps there were there, hidden somewhere in this ludicrous list of puffed-up piffle. Still at least we have lost the Keeper of the Lions in the Tower, the Laundress of the Body Linen, and the Yeoman of the Mouth, as the royal family moves seamlessly into the eighteenth century. At the top of this medieval mountain of absurdity is the Lord Chamberlain, an office that has existed since 1399. His roles extended outside the royal court, and, until as late as 1968, he had the power to prohibit the staging of plays where he was of the view that it was 'fitting for the preservation of good manners, decorum or of the public peace so to do'. The first performance of *Hair* had to wait for this power to be removed from him.

Before 1968, the restrictions were tightly drawn, often absurdly so. In 1959, the Lionel Bart musical *Fings Ain't Wot They Used T'Be* drew the following admonishment from the unelected Lord Chamberlain: 'The builder's labourer is not to carry the plank of wood in the erotic place and at the erotic angle that he does and the Lord Chamberlain wishes to be informed of the manner in which the plank is in the future to be carried.'

Successive Lords Chamberlain were particularly keen to prevent any criticism, indeed even any mention of the royal family. In 1934, a prosecution was initiated merely because a play had included a harmless portrayal of Queen Victoria. Even as the daylight of modernity was finally allowed in, consideration was given as to whether the restrictions on royal content should be carried over. Fortunately, common sense prevailed. Another no-go area related to friendly foreign powers, which seems to have been any with whom we were not at war. Throughout the 1930s, plays which criticised the Nazi regime in Germany – such as Terence Rattigan's 1938 farce *Follow My Leader*, which poked fun at Hitler and Mussolini – were banned, with authors told to set the location of the plays in a fictional country, to 'Ruritanianise' them.

Out in the country, we still have a phalanx of ninety-eight Lord Lieutenants. These individuals, unelected of course, are the monarch's representatives in the shires. They attend events where it is felt there should be a royal presence but there is either no royal available or the event is deemed too minor to justify their presence. Of the ninety-eight, only seven are under sixty years of age, and none is under fifty. Males outnumber females by two to one. Information on ethnicity is not made available on the basis that it would allegedly contravene the Data Protection Act 1998, though how that can be the case if individuals are not identified is difficult to understand. However you would be hard pressed to find anyone who is not white. Interestingly, back in 2000, the government was prepared to provide an answer to this question: none. Of the forty-seven then in post in England, there were, however, nineteen who had been to Eton, and fourteen to other public schools. Twenty were former military officers, and twenty members of exclusive London private clubs such as White's.

These Lord Lieutenants each has a team of Deputy Lieutenants, also naturally all unelected, to assist them, and to attend those functions too dull for even their bosses. In 2000 I asked a series of parliamentary questions to establish the cost to the public purse of the Lord Lieutenants network. The reply I received showed that for England, costs had shot up from £249,529 in 1990 to £686,173 in 2000. Costs in Scotland had trebled, and almost doubled in Northern Ireland, but seemed to have held steady in Wales. In 2017 I requested updated figures. I was told they were not collected centrally. The clang from the gates of secrecy closing firmly shut is unmistakeable.

Doing the Honours

The year 1348 was a pretty terrible one for England. It saw the arrival of the Black Death, which resulted in one-and-a-half million deaths out of a population of four million. Up to half of London's population succumbed. When the King, Edward III, complained about the lack of street sweepers in the capital, he was told they had all died. Still, at least the King was able to find time for other matters that year, such as creating the first order of chivalry, the Most Noble Order of the Garter. Here was a cheap method of showing royal approval. It also helped to create hierarchies and made sure, of course, that the King was at the top of the tree and, indeed, in charge of dispensing the honours.

Fortunately, the Black Death is long gone, but the Order of the Garter is still with us, along with a bewildering array of other archaic and surreal titles. The Most Ancient and Noble Order of the Thistle, the Most Honourable Order of the Bath, the Most Distinguished Order of Saint Michael and Saint George, and so on. Over the years we have lost a few, but only those relating to territories outside Britain when the tide of history has swept over them. The Order of St Patrick was discontinued shortly after Britain departed from most of Ireland.

The motto of the Order, founded in 1783, was '*Quis Separabit?*' ('Who will separate us?') The answer turned out to be those who helped create the Irish Free State in 1922.

We have also seen the back of the Most Exalted Order of the Star of India, the Most Eminent Order of the Indian Empire, the Imperial Order of the Crown of India and the Order of Burma. This is all distant history, but a cursory examination of the various Orders shows that they have only been abandoned when there was really no alternative, when the withdrawal from empire left them behind. None of the domestic Orders, however archaic or absurd, has disappeared.

These Orders bear little connection with any actions that merit reward. They are simply used, as they were almost 700 years ago, to maintain a medieval top-down hierarchy in society, to reward court favourites, and are fundamentally undemocratic. Even the Orders themselves have their own internal hierarchies. The Order of Wear, revised as recently as 2015, goes into huge details as to which decoration outranks which other. So a Knight Grand Cross precedes a Knight Commander. Knights Bachelor come before those with the rank of Commander. For those of equal rank, members of the higher-ranked Order take precedence. And so on, interminably. Woe betide anyone who inadvertently sins against this elaborate and convoluted guff. Compared to all this, passing the port the wrong way must seem a minor indiscretion.

At the top of the tree is the monarch, who remains 'the fount of honour', and is personally responsible for deciding the recipients of various classes, including the Order of the Garter, the Order of the Thistle, the Royal Victorian Order, the Order of Merit, and the Royal Family Order, the latter unashamedly used to give out honours to members of her own family. The Queen has been particularly keen to shower members of her family with decorations, and they seem to have been particularly keen to receive them.

Prince Charles, for instance, was no doubt delighted in 2006 when he achieved four-star rank in each of the armed services: a General in the Army, an Admiral in the Navy, and an Air Chief Marshal in the RAF, the latter award generously ignoring the episode in 1994 when he crashed a plane in the Hebrides. Charles had last seen active service some twenty years earlier when he captained a coastal minesweeper, HMS *Bronington*. His elevation meant he now had thirty-one decorations he could wear, including of course the Most Noble Order of the Garter, and the Maltese Cross in his capacity as Grand Master and Principal Knight of the Most Honourable Order of the Bath.

It must only be members of the royal family who have to pick and choose which medals to wear on which occasion. Clearly if he were to wear all thirty-one he would look somewhat lop-sided, and possibly it might also lead people to question what unparalleled acts of bravery he had shown – what stupendous contribution he had made to society – to deserve that huge number.

Then there is the Order of Merit, regarded by many as the most prestigious honour there is, possibly because it does generally reflect merit rather than hierarchy or favouritism. There are only twenty-four members of the Order at any one time so it is a matter of dead man's shoes for those who might qualify. Decisions on who merits inclusion are solely a matter for the monarch. Established by Edward VII in 1902, the Order's stated purpose is to reward those who have given 'exceptionally meritorious service towards the advancement of art, literature and science'. This is surely a good concept. Thus the present membership includes such deserving types as Sir Tim Berners-Lee, originator of the world wide web, the artist David Hockney, and the playwright Sir Tom Stoppard.

But wait, it also includes amongst its twenty-four that intellectual giant the Duke of Edinburgh, and for good measure, Prince Charles as well. While the Queen's husband and eldest son seem quite comfortable to have their efforts bracketed with the best and the brightest in society, others over the years have refused an invitation to join. These include Rudyard Kipling and George Bernard Shaw. It would be churlish not to accept that both Prince Philip and Prince Charles have contributed much to British society over their lives, but even the most ardent royalist would have difficulty in suggesting they meet the criteria for inclusion in this Order. To include them in this most select twenty-four is actually to undermine the concept of merit that the Order purportedly celebrates. And of course it means that when Prince Charles succeeds to the throne, he will have himself as one of the exclusive twenty-four in the Order.

The membership is faulty in other ways too. There are currently only two women – former Speaker Betty Boothroyd, and mechanical engineer Dame Ann Dowling. And there are only two below retirement age. Medals can understandably mean a lot to people, as witnessed by the long campaign to secure recognition for those who served in Arctic convoys in the Second World War. This dangerous but important wartime service was finally allocated its own medal, the Arctic Star, only in 2012, more than sixty-seven years after the end of the war, by which time most potential recipients were dead.

There has been within government a decades-long resistance to creating new medals for military service, and a limitation placed on how many one individual could qualify for. Nobody could qualify for more than six Second World War campaign stars, with a maximum limit of one clasp for any one campaign star. I wonder what the recipients of the Arctic Star would have felt if they were aware that the members of the royal family have more than a hundred military medals and decorations between them, almost enough to sink one of those Arctic ships.

To be fair, a smattering of those do actually reflect active military service. The Duke of Edinburgh, for instance, served in the Navy in the Second World War. But does that justify him becoming an Admiral of the Fleet in 1953, and Lord High Admiral in 2011? He also holds thirty-eight other military positions. Similarly, Prince Andrew served as a helicopter pilot in the Falklands War, acting as a decoy for Argentine Exocet missiles. Nobody can deny that he has earned his South Atlantic Campaign Medal. But what about the rest of the bulging array on his chest? Most controversially, he was invested by his mother with the insignia of a Knight Grand Cross of the Royal Victorian Order (highest rank) in 2011, controversial because at the time he was the subject of unflattering articles in the media about his relationship with a convicted paedophile, questions about his role as UK trade ambassador and his close engagement with tyrannical and unsavoury foreign regimes. It seems neither the absence of merit nor the force of public opinion was going to stop the Queen giving a nice fifty-first birthday present to her son. He is also Commander-in-Chief of the Fleet Air Arm, Admiral of the Sea Cadets Corps, and Colonel-in-Chief of the Royal Lancers, of the Yorkshire Regiment, of the Royal Irish Regiment, of the Small Arms School Corps, of the Royal Highland Fusiliers, and Honorary Air Commodore of RAF Lossiemouth.

And still the wagon rolls. In March 2018, his appointment as Colonel of the Grenadier Guards was honoured with an elaborate event at Windsor Castle. I may have missed a few positions out. It is hard to keep track.

Then there is Prince Edward, or the Earl of Wessex, to use the grandiose title he has acquired. He holds nine military appointments, including that of Royal Honorary Colonel of the Royal Wessex

Yeomanry. This is despite the fact he has never taken part in active military service, and was unable even to complete his Royal Marines commando course. As a fifty-fifth birthday present, his mother decreed that henceforth he will also be known as the Earl of Forfar, though his connections with the Scottish town appear to be tenuous at best. Following the announcement, the Forfar Action Network wrote to ask him to open the town's annual Gala Day some six months on, but the Earl declined. It seems his connections are to remain tenuous.

Meanwhile, the public has been softened up to expect that when Philip finally leaves us, his title of Duke of Edinburgh will be bestowed upon Edward, who, unlike his ducal brothers, is a mere earl. Apparently these things matter to the royals.

The younger royals are busy catching up now. In early 2020, the Queen designated William as Lord High Commissioner to the General Assembly of the Church of Scotland, a post created in 1707 but not one that William had hitherto demonstrated any connection with or interest in. William is also now Commodore-in-Chief of the submarine service, but perhaps in this case he has drawn the short straw. In April 2019, he turned up at Westminster Abbey wearing medals for a service to mark fifty years of the Navy's nuclear submarines. He was booed as he went in. Kate Hudson, the CND general secretary, called the service 'morally repugnant ... It says that here in Britain we celebrate weapons, in a place of worship, that can kill millions of people.' Like the endorsement by the Queen Mother of the statue to Bomber Harris, the royals often demonstrate a tin ear on such matters.

I wonder if any members of the royal family have ever thought about refusing any of these decorations on the basis that they have done nothing to deserve them? In late 2016, the government gave its backing to a Private Member's Bill that would make it an offence to wear a medal without justification. Presumably the royal family is exempt from its provisions. Even Princess Anne holds twenty-four senior military positions, which at least means the Queen is gender neutral in the way she sprinkles honours and titles on her children.

Indeed there is also the Royal Family Order, for which you qualify simply if you are a female member of the royal family. Nor is this just limited to Princess Anne. All sorts of distant royals get in on the act, such as Katharine and Birgitte, respectively the Duchess of Kent and the Duchess of Gloucester, and both wives of cousins of the Queen. I mention this in case you have never heard of them. Camilla was added to the list in 2007, signifying her full acceptance into the royal family, ten years after Diana's death. Camilla is now getting in on the act herself. In January 2020, it emerged that in her capacity as Chancellor of Aberdeen University (what did she do to justify that appointment?), she handed an honorary degree to her sister-in-law Princess Anne, who is now a Doctor of Law. Can we expect Anne, who is Chancellor of the University of Edinburgh, to reciprocate?

To be fair, the handing out of titles to female members of the royal family for no reason other than that they exist can be found elsewhere in the world. In Tonga, to be precise. Is it any wonder that this naked nepotism and bestowing of honours based on accident of birth and position in society cascades down the honours tree?

So we see for lesser mortals than the royal favourites a swathe of equally archaically named and often dubiously justified honours being doled out. The titles hail from the same historical palette as ancient London street names such as Poultry, Pudding Lane, and Plough Court in today's City, except that where those names can be regarded as quaintly incongruous, the continuation of the Order of the British Empire or the Medal of the British Empire, and perhaps especially the Commander of the Order of the British Empire – what do they command? – is frankly absurd, or self-delusional, or both.

The sun set on the empire a long time ago, before most of us were born. What is left of this empire? Rockall, was Ronnie Barker's pithy suggestion, and that in itself was about forty years ago.

And the example set by the royal honours is mirrored in another altogether more insidious way. As above, so below. Just as the monarch will have court favourites, so the Establishment has its favourites too. In neither case do the honours awarded to individuals necessarily reflect merit or exceptional contribution to society. For every lollipop lady who is awarded an MBE for fifty years' voluntary work in all weathers on the crossing outside the village school, there are many more civil servants whose gong simply comes up with the rations.

And for every ordinary citizen who receives a CBE for an outstanding effort in their field of activity, so there are many more whose gong can be traced directly to a donation to party funds, or some other partisan favour done for a politician. So we saw Will Straw, son of Jack, awarded a CBE in 2016 for services to the unsuccessful EU Remain campaign, presumably as some sort of consolation prize, the grown-up equivalent of a *Crackerjack!* pencil. At least, we assume that was the reason. Will Straw himself seemed not to be very sure when questioned on the matter by a parliamentary committee.

Now, by all accounts, he is an affable and well-intentioned person, but there are many millions of those in Britain who do not receive a CBE for such personal qualities. That the system is corrupt was formally recognised almost a century ago, after Prime Minister David Lloyd George was found to be selling honours. Roll up, roll up. A knighthood? That'll be £10,000. A baronetcy? £30,000. A peerage? £50,000 or more.

This all led to the impressive sounding Honours (Prevention of Abuses) Act 1925, which made it an offence to sell honours. Yet since that time there has been but one successful prosecution – that of Lloyd

George's own honours broker, Maundy Gregory, in 1933. Mr Gregory, if he were alive today, would doubtless consider himself rather unlucky. It is stretching credulity to breaking point to believe no further offences have been committed in the eighty-plus years since his conviction.

In 1976, there was Harold Wilson's famous, and infamous, Lavender List of honours, so named because it was allegedly drawn up by his secretary Marcia Williams on lavender paper, on the occasion of his resignation as Prime Minister. All Prime Ministers can take it upon themselves to create a resignation honours list, and all in recent times have done so, with the curious and unlikely exception of Tony Blair.

The Lavender List is in fact unexceptional, at least when compared to other resignation lists, but the allegation about her involvement, made by Joe Haines, Wilson's press secretary, damaged the retiring PM's reputation. Marcia Williams was herself honoured in 1970 by being made a CBE, and then in 1974 elevated to the peerage, as Baroness Falkender. She was the longest serving Labour member of the Lords, having clocked up forty-three years in the upper house, yet in all that time never made a speech. She attended regularly, though, which of course qualified her to claim a generous attendance allowance.

In 2006 an analysis by the *Sunday Times* revealed that every person who had donated £1 million or more to the Labour Party since its election in 1997 had been given a knighthood. Twelve out of fourteen donors who had given in excess of £200,000 had received honours, as had seventeen out of twenty-two who had coughed up in excess of £100,000. This all looks rather similar to Lloyd George's price list, allowing for inflation, except that in this case no criminal charges followed.

Most recently, there has been David Cameron's 2016 resignation honours list. Like many such lists before, this was heavily criticised at the time, with frothy calls for reform erupting forth, but as always, the deed was done, and so the fuss died down until the next time.

In his valedictory list, David Cameron nonchalantly doled out fifty-nine honours and titles to various Tory ministers, political advisors, Tory Party fundraisers and former aides, dubbed by the press as the 'chumocracy'.

Amongst them was an OBE for Isabel Spearman, the woman who helped his wife choose her dresses, and an OBE for Thea Rogers, who had been charged with giving George Osborne an image makeover to make him more popular, which admittedly, must have been a challenging task. The party fundraisers who benefited included Andrew Cook, a former Tory Party treasurer, who himself had donated £1 million to the cause. He was given a knighthood 'for political services', while another treasurer, Andrew Fraser, was elevated to the House of Lords.

Other countries have long ago modernised their honours system, greatly simplifying the range of awards made and ensuring that their allocation is based on merit. It is the fossilised royal patronage, dating from 1348, that prevents the mould being broken in Britain, despite the clear need to do so. The majority of honours are of course not allocated by the monarch, but by the Prime Minister of the day, but the royal practices have established legitimacy for patronage and provided cover for those politicians who seek to use and abuse it.

John Major, when he was Prime Minister in the 1990s, did actually try to introduce reforms to move honours away from social rank and towards merit, as part of his drive for a 'classless society'. His efforts on this front somewhat ran into the sand. Apart from the distractions of numerous problems relating to Europe which all Conservative Prime Ministers have to endure, there was predictable resistance to the concept he was trying to promote, not least from those who might expect to benefit from the system as was, including the civil service and many of his parliamentary colleagues. After all, he was seeking to replace a hierarchical structure that had survived centuries with one based on merit, and to have to win support from those most likely to lose out from such a change.

A system based on merit may not sound like a revolutionary concept, but if taken to its logical conclusion would cut off from future honours those who would be given them only because of birthright and their place in society, including of course members of the royal family. Earn an honour? A shocking concept for some, no doubt. In the end, just about all John Major achieved was to end the distinction between the British Empire Medal, hitherto used for the lower classes, and the MBE, used for the more rarefied socially. The award of the medal was accordingly discontinued in 1993, but was reinstated by David Cameron for the Queen's golden jubilee in 2012, so even that paltry modernisation has failed to take root.

So the faulty honours system sails on, despite its glaring shortcomings. These are thrown into particularly sharp relief when the actions of some of the recipients becomes so toxic that the honours given have to be withdrawn by a sort of emergency surgery body called the Honours Forfeiture Committee.

At that point, the public might reasonably ask, even without the benefit of hindsight, why some of these individuals were ever honoured in the first place. Amongst those who have had their honours removed are Germany's Kaiser Wilhelm II, with whom we went to war in 1914, Anthony Blunt, who betrayed us to the Russians, the brutal Romanian dictator Nicolae Ceaușescu, Zimbabwe's awful President Robert Mugabe, who almost destroyed his country single-handedly, and Fred Goodwin, who as chief executive of the Royal Bank of Scotland played a leading role in the financial catastrophe of 2008/09. Oh, and Rolf Harris.

Hubert Chesshyre, an expert on heraldry and genealogy and holder of a number of senior positions in the royal household, was naturally well placed to receive an honour, certainly better placed than the life-time lollipop lady in Leamington Spa, out in all weathers day in and day out to keep our children safe. In fact, he accumulated the Queen's Silver and Golden Jubilee medals, and became a Commander of the Royal Victorian Order, the latter for personal service to the monarch. But in 2015 a jury concluded he had sexually abused a choirboy in the 1990s. His victim duly wrote to the senior Palace official, Sir Alan Reid, to call for his honour to be forfeited. He refused, and it was not until the victim's MP became involved that the honour was finally forfeited, some three years later.

However, according to *The Guardian*, the revelations did not cause him to be removed from his position as a Freeman of the City of London, or from that of vice-president of the Institute of Heraldic and Genealogical Studies, which continued to list him as Hubert Chesshyre CVO. One wonders if the same tolerance would have been offered to our lollipop lady if she had been found guilty of sexually abusing a child.

There is now an Honours Scrutiny Committee, designed to weed out potentially unsuitable candidates, but only on the basis of some dubious past actions, rather than on the basis that they might have done nothing to deserve an honour. Still, that is progress of a sort. The system is overseen by the Cabinet Office Honours and Appointments Secretariat.

None of this is to argue against a process whereby the state can reward those who have contributed to society in a way that merits public recognition. Many recipients of honours have had their names suggested by members of the public. They are, in a real sense, widely acclaimed, and to receive an honour is rightly something they really value. Indeed for some, it can be the high point of their life. Doubt-less many welcome the opportunity to attend Buckingham Palace investitures, and to receive their honour from the Queen, or increasingly

Prince Charles or even Prince William. It is just a pity that the worthy achievements of these good people and the honours they receive are diluted by those who have been given honours without frankly very much in the way of a good reason.

Perhaps this is one reason why, over the years, so many apparently worthy recipients have refused to accept the honours offered to them. These include Aldous Huxley, Francis Bacon, Lucian Freud, L. S. Lowry and Roald Dahl. Overall 277 people refused an honour between 1951 and 1999. And the number of refusals seems to be increasing. In response to a parliamentary question from Baroness Berridge in November 2016, the government revealed that there had been 122 refusals since the New Year's Honours of 2014. However, they refused the Baroness's request to list the reasons for refusals.

Of course we rarely hear of these refusals at the time. That is because each potential recipient is advised a little ahead of the award being made public that they are on the list, and are asked if they would accept it. Those who say no therefore do not appear in the publicly announced list. The misleading impression given, therefore, is that everyone without exception who is up for an honour is only too glad to accept it. In fact, refusals are to be avoided at all costs and if they occur, they are not made public. Willie Hamilton, the republican Labour MP, was informally asked if he would accept an invitation to one of the Queen's 'meet the people' lunches she was hosting back in the 1960s. He replied that he would consider the invitation when it came. It never did.

Some return their honours after they have received them, such as John Lennon, who was protesting either about the Vietnam War, or the failure of his latest single, 'Cold Turkey', to make the top ten, depending on who you believe. It is more likely that he returned his MBE as he just felt uncomfortable with it as he became increasingly radical in his views.

There are even honours for non-British citizens, the majority based on genuine merit, though some eyebrow-raising ones do slip through where foreign policy considerations have played a part. Various American military personnel have been such recipients, as well as Caspar Weinberger, without whose significant help Britain would have had a much tougher challenge in reclaiming the Falkland Islands.

These honours tend not to be handed out by members of the royal family, but by ministers, and in fact I found myself conducting such a ceremony in March 2014 while a Home Office minister. The deserving recipient of the OBE, Professor Marianne Hester, had lived in the UK for decades but had retained her Danish nationality. Denmark, it transpired, does not allow dual nationality. She was quite rightly being rewarded for her sterling work on tackling domestic violence, and was clearly a friendly and genuine person. That made it rather a pity that the room that had been allocated in the Home Office for the ceremony was a rather soulless one, but then they all were. The atmosphere was not helped by the addition of some rather sad-looking sandwiches, but Professor Hester seemed happy enough.

I had a form of words to read out before I formally handed over to her the box with the OBE in it. It was the first time I had seen one close up. I also had to hand her an unattractive brown envelope which apparently provided details of her rights to access St Paul's Cathedral, which struck me as a rather bizarre inclusion, akin to giving her the rights to drive cattle across Tower Bridge. There were also more prosaic instructions as to what to do if her OBE went missing. If only all recipients of honours are as deserving as Professor Hester, but sadly they are not.

This flawed approach to honours is mirrored in elevations to, indeed in the continued existence of, the House of Lords. Here again, birthright and status in society, coupled with a continual flood of naked political appointments, dwarfs the number of those who make it into the upper house based on merit.

The upper house. The very term implies superiority over the elected chamber. Full of people who 'lord' it over 'commoners'. But then the innate pre-eminence of the unelected remains in place. While democratic institutions do not hide their wares, the old unelected power survives, hidden under the surface.

Whitaker's Almanack helpfully lists the nation's Order of Precedence, which tells us that the royal family, including even the Queen's cousins, are first in line for the nuclear bunker, long before even the Prime Minister gets a look-in. There then follows another huge splurge of unelected privileged persons – Dukes, the Earl Marshal, the Lord Great Chamberlain and others that most people have never heard of – before anyone else elected appears. Still, I am sure that Cabinet ministers will understand that they have to wait in line behind the sons of earls and dukes, not to mention bishops.

The essentially medieval construct that is the House of Lords first emerged in the fourteenth century. It has been subject to some reform over the last century or so, but only at a glacial pace.

It used to be the case that Prime Ministers would often originate from the Lords rather than the Commons, but the last to do so was the Marquess of Salisbury, whose term of office ended in 1902.

Gradually, it became the norm that the most important offices of state were filled from the Commons rather than the Lords. Even so, there were exceptions. Margaret Thatcher's Foreign Secretary at the time of the Falklands War, for instance, was Lord Carrington, and as late as 2010, Labour's Transport Secretary could be found on the red rather than the green benches, namely Andrew Adonis.

In many ways, the most important change came back in 1911, in the wake of the then Liberal government's revolutionary 1909 'People's

Budget'. The budget directly challenged the privileges of the Lords, introducing hitherto-unimagined taxes on the rich and a radical social welfare programme. It expressly set out, for the first time, to redistribute wealth. It took two general elections and a threat to create hundreds of new Liberal peers to force through Lloyd George's budget. Faced with this, the peers finally backed down and legislation was introduced to limit the power of the Lords to thwart the Commons, by means of the Parliament Act 1911. Further limitations on what the Lords could do to block the Commons were introduced by the post-war Labour government in the Parliament Act 1949.

Even so, the Lords continued to be populated by individuals who were only there because of the actions of one of their forebears, perhaps pleasing some king or queen centuries earlier.

The Life Peerages Act 1958 meant that from that point on, most new peerages could not be passed on to the next in line, thus for the first time undermining the hereditary principle. Margaret Thatcher, when Prime Minister, tried to undo this. Perhaps aware of the fact that society had moved on, she began tentatively by introducing hereditary peerages for two men without male heirs, namely George Thomas, Speaker of the Commons, and Willie Whitelaw, her ultra-loyal Deputy Prime Minister. These were followed by an earldom for the former Prime Minister Harold Macmillan, a title shortly afterwards inherited by his grandson. She also created a hereditary baronetcy for her husband Denis in 1990, and while a case could be made for some recognition for his public service, you would be hard pressed to argue that this should be inherited, as it has been, by their wayward son, Mark.

But then perhaps, as with the Queen and her children, it is just another example of a mother showing love to her son: an admirable quality, but not one the constitution should be used to give effect to. There have been no further hereditary peerages or baronetcies created by Prime Ministers since 1990, so perhaps the concept of creating new ones has finally been put to bed.

Except that members of the royal family are still given hereditary peerages. Recent beneficiaries of this antiquated arrangement were Prince Edward in 1999, when he was turned into the Earl of Wessex, Prince Harry in 2018, now Duke of Sussex, and Prince William, who became the Duke of Cambridge in 2011 (though this title evaporates if he becomes King). This latter event occurred on the morning of his wedding, though it is a moot point as to whether the creation of a hereditary peerage is not a touch inappropriate as a wedding present.

But then there is no doubt the royal family feel it important to maintain the hereditary principle as much as possible, for fear that people may begin to question the validity of the concept. It may also be part of the reason why the Queen has robustly knocked back any suggestion that she might abdicate in favour of her son, Prince Charles. Hereditary systems expect you to die in the position which you have inherited. Any suggestion that this can be played around with would inevitably make the concept as a whole look less inviolate than those who benefit from it would like. Any variation from unbending rigidity may open the door to reform.

The other side of the coin, perhaps the one with the monarch's head, is that a person cannot be removed from that post, whatever they do. Even when George III lost his mental faculties, he remained the monarch, albeit with a regent in place. The same principle, as a consequence, applies in the House of Lords and indeed extends to life peers. While knighthoods, OBEs and the rest can be withdrawn, a peerage is not technically an 'honour under the crown' so cannot be rescinded. So we have the sleazy situation that a peer who has been sent to prison can resume his seat in the Lords upon release, if he has the neck to do so.

The rules for the unelected who play a part in our constitution are rather laxer than for those who are elected by the people. MPs sent to prison can in theory resume their seats if their sentence is shorter than six months, though in practice the public are unlikely to wear that. In January 2019 the MP for Peterborough, Fiona Onasanya, was jailed for three months for texting and speeding while driving, and then denying that she had been at the wheel. She was then subject to a new process whereby a by-election is triggered if 10 per cent of the electors of the constituency in question demand it. They did, and Peterborough now has a new MP. A second recall was triggered in the Welsh constituency of Brecon & Radnorshire, where the Tory MP Chris Davies was found to have been fiddling his expenses. Undeterred, he put himself forward for re-election in the resultant by-election, to the astonishment of many. He was not re-elected.

The Labour government that came to power in 1997 wanted to end the right of hereditary peers to sit in the Lords, an idea naturally unpopular in the upper house. The 1999 Act that emerged allowed, as a compromise, ninety-two hereditary peers to remain. The intention to remove the hereditaries was of course presaged in the Queen's speech for that session, a speech written for her by the politicians and which sets out the government's legislative programme. Did she perhaps appreciate the irony that she was reading out an intention to weaken the hereditary principle? For delegitimising the hereditary principle in the Lords does leave its continued application to the post of head of state looking rather exposed.

It might be thought that the 1958 Act that made life peerages the norm, and the 1999 Act that abolished most hereditaries, would have succeeded in shrinking the size of the Lords. Not a bit of it. A relentless splurge of new life peerages means the Lords now incredibly has well over 800 members, second in size only to the collection of 2,987 rubber-stamping robots in China's National People's Congress.

David Cameron, while Prime Minister, made a great deal of the cost of democracy, and was determined to force through a big reduction in the numbers of elected MPs, yet at the same time, he was facilitating a huge increase in the number of unelected peers in the Lords.

There is a physical limit to how many peers can be accommodated in what is actually quite a small chamber, a limit already easily surpassed if all 800-plus turned up at the same time. Notwithstanding that the average age of peers is sixty-nine, the bald fact is that new peers are being appointed far faster than old peers are dying out. It is likely, given the prime ministerial propensity for patronage, that this number will continue to grow.

That, however, has not stopped some suggesting the number be increased yet further. David Cameron responded petulantly to a defeat in the Lords which prevented the Chancellor George Osborne from cutting tax credits by £4.4 billion by hinting at further curbs on what the Lords can do, and a new wave of Tory peers to give his party an absolute majority in what is currently a hung house. In other words, he wanted to make the corpulent Lords even larger and at the same time reduce what it could do, while simultaneously cutting the number of MPs, legislators who actually have a legitimate mandate. And in a corrupted echo of the Liberal government's threatened action of 1911, the arch-conservative MP Jacob Rees-Mogg suggested in November 2016 creating a thousand new Tory peers to push through Brexit. He also separately suggested that the Queen should prorogue Parliament to stop MPs voting in a way that he disapproved of – an idea that Boris Johnson clearly found attractive.

All this is patronage writ large. The House of Lords, it seems, is to be populated by people who are 'sound', and who will enact the will of the Prime Minister. Naturally, it suits the government of the day to have an unelected second chamber. Apart from the patronage opportunities this opens up, it also allows the government to argue, when the Lords become difficult, that they are unelected and so can be overruled by the Commons, by which is really meant the Prime Minister, the Cabinet, or the majority party, depending on the dynamics at the time.

If the Conservative government is really exercised about the fact that peers are unelected, and it has regularly pointed this out when it has looked like not getting its way over Brexit and other matters, then it is a pity that the party did not help replace them with an elected body when it had the chance to do so, instead of actively trying to thwart such a development. The move from an all-hereditary house to one which is largely populated by appointed life peers has unfortunately exacerbated the misuse of patronage, and lessened the independence of the Lords. It always was a repository for some former MPs, but is now becoming much more party political, populated by highly tribal types who have gone long past their use-by date. For a great many others, it represents a consolation prize for losing their seats, or a retirement reward for being a party loyalist.

The obvious conclusion is that neither option can really be justified. Nobody deserves an automatic place in a law-making institution simply because of some preferment offered to some family predecessor. But the ascendancy of the life peerage also lacks legitimacy, perhaps even more so. The answer of course is to have a house that is either wholly or substantially elected, and one with far fewer members. Yet there is a great weight of opinion that, while it would find it hard pressed intellectually to defend the present arrangements, is quite content to do nothing to change things. Reform of the Lords really is a case of dead man's handle, the device in the driver's cab of a train that will cause the train to stop unless it is actively pushed forward. This may help to explain why reform of the upper house has so far taken in excess of a hundred years, and we still have hereditary peers and still lack any elected members of the house.

Actually, that is not quite true, for in a deep irony, the ninety-two hereditaries were chosen in an election by all the hereditaries when the 1999 Act took effect. And when one of the ninety-two dies, an election is then held within the relevant party group to elect a replacement hereditary peer from amongst those removed by the 1999 Act.

Thus when a Lib Dem vacancy occurred in early 2016 following the death of Lord Avebury, the former Orpington MP Eric Lubbock, three Lib Dem hereditary peers were called upon to elect a successor. This must make that trio the smallest electorate in the world. In other times it would have been called a rotten borough.

In the election, John Thurso triumphed, winning 100 per cent of the vote, the sort of result even Kim Jong-un would envy. For the Lib Dem, it was a return to the Lords, following an interregnum as MP for Caithness, Sutherland & Easter Ross. And in a nice piece of symmetry, when he began his time in the Commons, his predecessor as MP, Robert Maclennan, was elevated to the Lords, where they therefore both now sit.

But how ironic that the only people who have faced any sort of election to gain access to the Lords are the hereditary peers.

The Powers Behind
the Throne

In autumn 2014, I took a phone call from the Deputy Prime Minister Nick Clegg. An exchange of pleasantries followed while I waited to find out the reason for his call. Then he asked me. Would I like to join the Privy Council? I am afraid I laughed.

This obscure body had largely escaped my attention during my then seventeen years as an MP, but I was aware that membership was eagerly sought after by some as a public recognition of their seniority. Those admitted henceforth could use the prefix Right Honourable, as opposed to the plain ordinary 'Honourable' that all MPs can use. And whereas those who cease to be MPs lose the right to use the Honourable handle, those who are Right Honourable retain that for ever.

This is really more stuff and nonsense of course, as archaically convoluted as the honours system of which it is in effect a part. The public can certainly be forgiven for not knowing the difference between Honourable and Right Honourable, and there are a handful of plaques around the country marking occasions when as an MP or Transport minister, I launched or opened something or other where I was incorrectly etched in as Right Honourable. I suppose my subsequent admission to the Privy Council has retrospectively corrected that.

I was in fact in two minds whether or not to accept or not Nick Clegg's invitation. I was aware that entry would require a further oath of allegiance to the Queen to be taken, or, as it turned out, to be administered to you. I was not keen on this and suspected, rightly, that this would be like the MPs' oath with bells on. On the other hand, I did know, as a minister, the convention that letters from privy counsellors were supposed to elicit replies from secretaries of state as opposed to junior ministers, and that seemed useful. I confess I was also curious as to what admission into this inner sanctum would be like.

More significant in my calculations, however, was the mischievous thought that my elevation to this obscure but exalted body would annoy the sort of Establishment figures I had been railing against all through my political career, and especially those who desperately aspired to membership themselves.

There had been many of republican tendencies before me who had joined the Privy Council, as was expected of all Cabinet ministers and senior opposition members. These included sceptics such as Tony Benn, Jeremy Corbyn and his shadow chancellor, John McDonnell, who once declared he wanted to see a public execution of papier-mâché models of the royal family.

I did not fool myself as to the origins of the offer. Both the Tories and Lib Dems, as coalition partners in government, had a fixed number of honours and titles to dole out – peerages, knighthoods, Privy Council membership, gongs – and Nick Clegg was simply sharing the Lib Dem allocation around. The baubles were quite numerous. I think by the time the 2010 parliament had drawn to a close, we had more Sirs in the parliamentary party than women, not a happy position for a liberal party to be in.

So, in the end, I said yes and then thought I should do some digging. My first port of call was the Concise Oxford English Dictionary, where I found the following:

Privy

(adj)

    1. sharing in the secret of (a person's plans etc.)

    2. hidden, secret

(noun)

    1. a lavatory, esp. an outside one

It seemed clear that, in etymological terms, the adjectival meaning was the relevant one, not least because of its emphasis on secrecy, a traditional trait of those who rule us, and perhaps also the spatial limitations of the noun alternative, though given the sometimes bizarre origin of British institutions, nothing could be entirely ruled out. The Privy Council, I discovered, dates back to the earliest days of monarchy, when it comprised those individuals whom the monarch had picked to proffer advice. And unlike Parliament, it still meets in private to transact its business.

In due course I was summoned to a meeting of the Council, but as the date indicated was 5 November, the most important day of the year in my home town of Lewes, I declined. We finally agreed on my attendance at the meeting scheduled for 11 February 2015.

More information followed from the Privy Council Office, which is housed in a discreet building about midway between Westminster and Buckingham Palace, at the highly desirable address of 2 Carlton Gardens.

This included the details of the induction ceremony, and specifically the oath that was to be administered to me. This dates back to Tudor times, and is full of arcane phrases such as 'Dignity Royal', 'Heart and Conscience', and 'Foreign Princes, Persons, Prelates, States or Potentates'.

The covering letter reminded me sternly that I should 'keep secret all matters committed and revealed ... in Council' and asked me to destroy the guidance document I had been sent in respect of the swearing-in ceremony. This struck me as rather odd, offensive even. Here was an arm of the state, conducting business as part of the government, and yet in 2015 it was still operating under rules established in Tudor times. Naturally I did not destroy this document. It is reprinted in the Appendix of this volume, along with the oath. Doubtless those who would defend this pseudo-masonic arrangement would call it tradition, and take a dim view of those who seek to change or undermine it.

It is true that traditional ceremonies can be found in many a nook and cranny in our country, whether in government, the church or simply in local communities. Very often these will retain original features, the relevance of which may have changed or been lost over the centuries. In my constituency, for instance, we hold the annual Lewes Bonfire celebrations which include the burning of a Pope and the hanging of 'No Popery' banners across the street. Those who come down to Lewes from London, and maybe are more gentle sorts, are perhaps more used to encountering the problem of no potpourri.

Some from outside Sussex, unfamiliar with the Lewes Bonfire traditions, are aghast, seeing these as a terrible anti-Catholic display. In fact, it is nothing of the sort. Rather, it is an anti-Establishment event, and a topical one, as the creation of four, or was it five, effigies of Donald Trump in November 2016 as an 'Enemy of Bonfire' clearly demonstrated. The Pope in question is a specific one, Pope Paul V, who was Pope at the time of the burning of seventeen Protestant martyrs in Lewes in 1557.

There are many traditions in our constitutional arrangements. Some of them are useful, such as the one where Black Rod, on his way back from the Lords to the Commons following the Queen's Speech at the opening of Parliament, has the door slammed in his face, reminding us all that the elected chamber takes precedence over the unelected one. Others, such as the use of goatskin on which the Queen's Speech is written, are harmless, except, presumably, for the goat. The Privy Council arrangements are neither useful nor harmless.

It might be argued that the historical footprint still to be seen in the Privy Council is akin to that seen in traditional events up and down the country, whether in Lewes on 5 November or otherwise. But the crucial difference, of course, is that the Privy Council has power and passes legislation that affects everyday lives. It is a functioning part of government. Yet its accountability is limited. Its meetings of course are closed, or secret, as the dictionary might put it.

In February 2000, the Labour MP Gordon Prentice challenged the government on the floor of the Commons to 'institute a review of the purpose and effectiveness of the Privy Council'. He went on to complain about the lack of accountability, pointing out his 'astonishment that some Orders in Council are never seen in the Houses of Parliament'. The reply from the junior minister, Paddy Tipping, was that the Council was 'a long-established and effective example of joined-up government which continues to play a useful role in a variety of policy matters'.

How very New Labour to apply the buzz phrase 'joined-up government' to a body largely unchanged over half a millennium. The minister added that this ancient body would shortly have its own website, which he enthusiastically described as 'a real example of new technology and forward thinking'. He also reminded the House that all the Orders in Council, that is the decisions taken, were published and available for public scrutiny. Quite how many were ever scrutinised is debatable.

The year before, a peer, Lord Craigmyle, had asked for clarification on the rules governing the publications of Orders in Council. In reply, the Lord Privy Seal, Margaret Jay, incidentally daughter of former Prime Minister Jim Callaghan, told the House of Lords that unless an Order was also a Statutory Instrument, which only a minority were, it was necessary to request copies of Orders from the Privy Council Office. This of course assumed you knew in the first place that the Order in question actually existed. She added that where the Order related to a chartered body, that body would first be asked for permission to release the Order for scrutiny and, implicitly therefore, that permission could be refused. All a real example of new technology and forward thinking.

I thought I would test the system myself, so in the spring of 2000, I tabled parliamentary questions to both the Prime Minister and the Home Secretary to ask each to list the occasions in the previous three months when the royal prerogative had been exercised under their advice, these being matters that would go through the Privy Council. The Prime Minister, Tony Blair, told me that 'records are not kept of the individual occasions on which such powers are exercised'. Mike O'Brien, a Home Office minister, replied by saying, 'I regret that this information is not held centrally.'

This all seemed to me rather cavalier, so I wrote to the then president of the Privy Council, the Labour minister Margaret Beckett. I asked her to send me copies of all the Orders issued in the previous six months. Paddy Tipping replied. It transpired over 250 had been issued in that period, equivalent to about ten a week, the majority of which had not been made proactively available to MPs, let alone the public. There were so many, Paddy Tipping explained to me, and some were 'very large indeed', that he only sent me a list of titles. He added that they covered a wide range of subject matter, 'some of national or international interest.'

To be fair to Paddy Tipping, his reply did recognise the shortcomings in terms of accountability, and he outlined some limited steps he was taking to improve matters, including depositing Orders in the House of Commons library. The list of 250 or so included some seemingly harmless matters such as amendments to Charters covering bodies such as the University of Wales College of Medicine, or sites where burials were to be discontinued, but others looked rather more significant. There was The European Communities (Designation) (No3) Order 1999, or The Transfer of Functions (Nuclear Installations) Order 1999.

It also transpired that the Council was, like Churchill's description of Russian actions, a riddle wrapped in a mystery inside an enigma. For this obscure body has also spawned even more obscure committees, such as those that concern themselves with the Channel Islands, or with the universities of Oxford and Cambridge.

Again, some of the business transacted here really ought to be given more of a public airing. For example back in 2012, assent was given to the Housing (Control of Occupation) (Sark) Law 2011, despite the fact that a petition opposing this had been submitted by the owners of the Sark dependency, Brecqhou, namely, the reclusive Barclay brothers. The brothers, of course, own the *Daily Telegraph*, but you would have struggled to find a report of this interesting development in their paper. This is indeed a curious oversight, given the zealous way in which the paper rightly delves into similar matters when they involve elected MPs pushing for public action to aid their private interests.

Others in Parliament shared my concern. In 2004, the Public Administration Committee called for comprehensive legislation to require the government to list the prerogative powers exercised by ministers, and to be helpful produced a draft Bill. In 2006, the Lib Dem peer Lord Lester introduced an even more radical Bill, to transfer responsibility for these powers from ministers to Parliament. All this pressure led to the government finally taking action, culminating in a report entitled 'The Governance of Britain – Review of the Executive Royal Prerogative Powers', in October 2009.

It is fair to say that over the past twenty years, some progress has been made to modernise the use of these powers, though important powers do still remain outside the control of Parliament. Most controversial has been the question as to whether these powers should be used to allow the Prime Minister of the day to initiate military action. There seems little doubt that legally they can, though Parliament has increasingly objected to this.

And so it came to the day of my induction into the Privy Council. I duly reported to 2 Carlton Gardens to be transported by a sleek motor car to Buckingham Palace. In a somewhat cavernous space that served as an anteroom, I joined the four Cabinet ministers who were there to represent the government, together with assorted others who, like me, were to be inducted that day, adding to the other 600 or so existing counsellors.

After about a quarter of an hour, the big double doors were opened and we were ushered into a nondescript room where the Queen was sitting on what looked like a less than comfortable chair. It was however more comfortable than the chairs the rest of us had, which were non-existent. We were all expected to stand for the duration of the meeting. This, it seems, was an innovation of Queen Victoria. We all stood in a wide arc which, were the circle described, would have occupied most of the room.

First up was a consent to a royal marriage between two people I had never heard of – Juliet Victoria Katharine Nicolson and Simon Alexander Rood. The bride-to-be was, I discovered later, a great-granddaughter of HRH Princess Patricia of Connaught, which seemed a rather distant connection to require involvement by the Privy Council. Then there followed the swearing in of five new Privy Counsellors, including my Lib Dem colleagues Jenny Willott and Susan Kramer, taken as a job lot. Mine was a solo turn that came subsequently, for, as with the oath taken in the Commons, I did not wish to compound my dubiousness about the oath by involving God as well, so merely affirmed.

For the ceremony, there was a lot of kneeling and moving between footstools, ending with a kiss on the Queen's hand. She looked at me in a hard, quizzical way, doubtless aware of my sporadic trenchant comments on the monarchy and perhaps wondering why I was there, as indeed was I, at that point. I returned to the arc line where congratulations of sorts were mumbled to me. The Chancellor, George Osborne, oozed his sardonic congratulations to me on joining the Establishment.

After that, it was back to the business of the meeting. Nick Clegg, as Lord President of the Council and the most senior minister present, read out various proclamations relating to new currency including a number of special edition coins not for general circulation. It seemed to be a low-level money-making operation for the Treasury, literally.

Then there were new charters, and amendments to existing charters, an Order relating to the Saint Helena Act 1833, an amendment to a naval pension scheme, an Order relating to sanctions on Yemen – the sort of thing that the Commons ought to have had the chance to debate – and an amendment to the Misuse of Drugs Act 1971, which I knew nothing about despite having been the drugs minister for a year until shortly before. There were also burial notices, matters relating to the Channel Islands, and a good deal more besides. To all the Queen assented, as she must, saying 'approved' to each measure as it came forward, unless it related to a petition for a new charter, when she said 'referred'.

Later that week, I was sent a copy of the Order admitting me to the Council. I was a touch surprised to note it was on a relatively cheap and nasty blue A4 piece of paper. At the same time, I was sent a copy of the oath, together with a list of the rights and privileges to which I was now entitled.

The first two paragraphs went into exhaustive detail as to how Privy Counsellors should be addressed: 'Individual Privy Counsellors are entitled to the style "The Right Honourable". This also belongs to all peers below the rank of Marquess. Whether they are Privy Counsellors or not, Dukes have the higher style "The Most Noble" and marquesses that of "The Most Honourable", and so on for a great deal longer.

Besides the form of address, the advice told me that privy counsellors have priority when it comes to taking the oath at the start of a parliament (assuming they are MPs, of course), can sit on the steps of the Sovereign's Throne in the House of Lords during debates, and have the right of personal access to the Sovereign, but only to tender advice on public affairs. I am certainly tempted to book an appointment to offer the Queen my thoughts on various topical matters. I am sure she would appreciate it.

Since my induction, my Privy Council duties have not so much been light as weightless, as is indeed the case with the vast majority of privy counsellors, apart from those who are also Cabinet ministers. It seems, in fact, that there are only two circumstances upon which we will all be called to do anything, both of which entail being summoned to St James's Palace.

The first of these is on the occasion of the announcement of the engagement of a reigning monarch. That seems unlikely to occur in my lifetime. The second is when the accession of a new sovereign is proclaimed. When we are assembled, the Garter King of Arms does the business, accompanied by the King of Arms, the Heralds, and the Pursuivants, whoever they all are.

In 1952, the last occasion when this ceremony occurred, around two hundred privy counsellors attended, most apparently attired in morning dress, though some decided this was not enough and opted for the even more elaborate court dress. It must have been difficult to find a supply for all the cocked hats required, not to mention the odd sword, and will be even more difficult next time round, the size of the Privy Council having tripled since then.

This assemblage, of course, is not there to vote on whether the designated person should become monarch, or anything as vulgarly democratic. Indeed, if the procedure followed in 1952 is repeated, the new monarch's first Privy Council meeting will already have taken place and an accession declaration made behind closed doors.

All this may seem rather quaint and harmless, but there is a hard edge to the activities of the Privy Council. For it is the vehicle by which the royal prerogative is exercised. Once upon a time, this equated to the rights of monarchs to decide upon matters of state themselves, as a one-person law-making, decision-taking machine. The monarch in fact still retains some personal advantages arising from the historic application of the prerogative. For example, the sovereign has personal immunity from being sued in the courts. This derives from the ancient 'prerogative of perfection', or in layman's language, the monarch can do no wrong.

Generally, though, with today's constitutional monarchy, it is the government of the day which has the right to exercise these wide powers. And all without reference to Parliament, with decisions instead being routed through the closed Privy Council. Indeed, it looked at one point that it was the government's intention to shut Parliament for a lengthy spell during the Covid-19 lockdown in the spring of 2020 and rely instead on Orders in Council. Perhaps fortunately for those of us who believe in democracy, a Privy Council meeting requires either the Queen or Prince Charles to be present in person, but both were self-isolating so this route was barred. The fact that the option was considered at all does not suggest the roots of parliamentary democracy run very deep. Like so much in the British system, this is not calibrated in any formal way. If pressed, you will be told it is a feature of our unwritten constitution. Like the absolute monarchs of antiquity, today's governments benefit residually from the 'prerogative of perfection.'

Over the centuries, Parliament has gradually eroded the royal prerogative by passing legislation. The Fixed Term Parliament Act, for example, introduced by the coalition government in 2011, removed the right of a Prime Minister, acting theoretically on behalf of the monarch, to call a general election at their whim. But it has been a long and slow process, so far taking over 800 years since the barons came together in 1215 to demand that the King sign Magna Carta. Perhaps as significant, but oddly downplayed in our schools, was the Battle of Lewes in 1264, which led to the creation of the first English Parliament and forced the King to accede to the demands of the barons, led by Simon de Montfort, to establish a Council of Barons which took precedence over the King's Council, the forerunner to the Privy Council.

Lewes actually has a proud place in the evolution of democracy in our country, and I felt very honoured to represent the constituency in Parliament for eighteen years. Besides the Battle of Lewes, and the staunchly independent Lewes Bonfire celebrations, the town was also home in the eighteenth century to Tom Paine, author of seminal works such as *Rights of Man* and *Common Sense*. He also played an important role both in the aftermath of the 1789 French revolution, and in shaping the constitution of the United States. It is therefore not surprising that he had little sympathy with the concept of monarchy. He wrote: 'Hereditary powers operate to preclude the consent of succeeding generations and the preclusion of consent is despotism.'

And yet, despite all this, hundreds of years on, key royal prerogative powers remain – not least the power to declare war, which has rested with the monarch since 'remote antiquity'. That in turn has led to governments initiating military action without, it would transpire, the support of Parliament or the people. It is debatable whether the folly of Suez in 1956 would have got very far if Parliament had been involved at an earlier stage.

On the other hand, the decision to invade Iraq in 2003 was preceded by a parliamentary debate, but one skewed by dodgy dossiers about non-existent weapons of mass destruction and grotesque distortions of fact by the Prime Minister, Tony Blair, deployed to secure a majority in the House of Commons for invasion. It seems if a government wants to start a war, they will find a way to do so, through the Privy Council alone if possible, but backed by Parliament on a false prospectus if necessary. Unsurprisingly, there have been attempts to wrest control to wage war from the government and hand it to Parliament, but all have failed. In 1999, a Bill to achieve this was introduced in the Commons: the Military Action Against Iraq (Parliamentary Approval) Bill. The Queen, acting under advice (read: *instruction*) from the government, refused even to allow a debate to take place, something most fair-minded people would regard as outrageous.

Back in 1990, British troops had been committed to military action in the first Gulf War and were placed under foreign command, all by means of the royal prerogative without a vote in Parliament. In contrast, both the House of Representatives and the Senate in the United States had debated and voted on a resolution on military action.

When he was Foreign Secretary in the coalition government, William Hague announced he intended to codify in law the convention relating to the need to consult Parliament before military action was taken, a move supported by the Deputy Prime Minister Nick Clegg. That nothing happened can be explained by the reaction of the Ministry of Defence, which firmly told the Foreign Secretary to get back in his box. That notwithstanding, David Cameron decided to follow the precedent set by Tony Blair and sought Parliament's approval for military action in Syria in 2013. He was defeated. When the same issue arose in 2018, Theresa May, leading a minority government, took no such chances and gave the green light for military action without a parliamentary vote, and got away with it.

Nor is it just matters of war which are at issue. In 1984, prerogative power was controversially used without reference to Parliament to ban the employees of the government's intelligence collection and analysis centre GCHQ from being members of a trade union. In the subsequent court case initiated to challenge this decision, the government successfully argued that not only were their powers in this case not open to judicial review, but that the instructions given in exercising them enjoyed the same immunity. And it was also in the 1980s that then Prime Minister Margaret Thatcher told the House of Commons that, 'Where members of the security service do commit illegal acts, there is always the prerogative power not to pursue criminal proceedings.' That gives a whole new meaning to the phrase Royal Pardon.

We rely on our governments to be essentially honest and not abuse the powers they have, but what, in an unwritten constitution with its use of prerogative powers, is to stop an unscrupulous government from using this power not to pursue criminal proceedings for entirely improper, perhaps self-serving purposes? No doubt the public would not tolerate this if they knew, but given the secret nature of prerogative powers, would they ever find out? The truth is that it is all too easy for a government, faced with a difficult Commons vote, or a wish to slip something through, to use prerogative powers if they can.

Nowhere has this been more sharply evident than in the debate about whether Theresa May's government was entitled to use prerogative powers to give effect to the vote in the July 2016 referendum which produced a narrow majority in favour of leaving the European Union. The referendum was legally only advisory, and many baulked at the idea that the government could trigger the now infamous Article 50 without parliamentary approval. In this case the situation was not helped by the fact that it was not clear whether Article 50, when triggered, was irreversible, or whether the UK, should it choose to do so, could withdraw its action. The European Court of Justice subsequently ruled in late 2018 that Britain did indeed have the right to withdraw Article 50 unilaterally if it decided to do so.

Either way, most Europeans would find it astonishing that the government of the day can assign itself the power to enact the momentous decision to leave the European Union without even a hint of legislation to authorise it. The quaint Privy Council looked quaint no more. Subsequently, the Supreme Court decided that parliamentary approval was indeed required, thus usefully establishing case law in this important matter, even if Theresa May's subsequent somewhat churlish assertion that MPs had a duty to pass unamended the Bill that was forced upon her by this court ruling rather spoiled the effect.

The government could, of course, have avoided the problem in the first place by ensuring the law that generated the referendum made the result legally binding in law, or by conceding at an early stage a parliamentary vote, which they would almost certainly have won. Or, equally, David Cameron could have decided that a referendum on such an important issue, when the public had been subjected to a barrage of straight-bananas stories in the press for years, and when people were likely to grab a chance to vote against the government just because they could, was actually a really bad idea, and that he, as Prime Minister, should be putting the interests of the country first, rather than trying to come up with some risky wheeze to try to hold the Conservative Party together.

If the dispute over the use of prerogative powers in this case served to highlight their existence, that can only be a good thing. For the tendency for the government of the day to find ways to use sweeping powers that bypass Parliament is not unusual.

Nor is it unusual for a Prime Minister or a government to be accused, as Theresa May was over Brexit, of behaving like Henry VIII, a peculiarly British line of attack. The notorious monarch actually has a lot to answer for. He behaved in a manner that still has ramifications down to this day. Far too many pieces of legislation have what is called a Henry VIII clause. Even those unfamiliar with what this does may reasonably harbour suspicions that a legislative tool named after one of our less pleasant and more megalomaniac monarchs may not be an entirely good thing, and they would be right.

The clause, inserted into a Bill, gives the government the right to amend or even repeal that piece of legislation through subordinate legislation, often without even having to bring the matter before MPs again. The power is so-named after the 1539 Statute of Proclamations, taken through Parliament by Thomas Cromwell, by which the King gave himself the right to announce whatever he wanted and it would then become law. Move on a few hundred years and for Henry VIII read: the Prime Minister and the government. Concern about the use of such clauses is shared at the top of the judiciary. Lord Judge, the Lord Chief Justice of England and Wales, put it this way in a speech at the Lord Mayor's dinner in 2010:

> Henry VIII was a dangerous tyrant [and] the Statute of Proclamations of 1539 was the ultimate in parliamentary supineness ... Do you remember the Regulatory Reform Bill of 2006 which ... sought to give ministers power to amend, repeal or replace any Act of Parliament simply be making an Order?

That Bill had the objective of cutting red tape, on the face of it an un-controversial purpose, but the method chosen to enact this end was amazingly far-reaching. Fortunately the House of Lords noticed and forced changes. Nor was this an isolated case. Lord Judge went on to quote dangerous all-encompassing provisions in the Banking (Special Provisions) Act 2008 and the Constitutional Reform and Governance Act 2010. This latter Act, dealing with the crucial matter of our con-stitution, gives the government the right to 'amend, repeal or revoke any existing statutory provision'. Even these powers pale into insig-nificance, however, compared to the frighteningly far-reaching Civil Contingencies Act 2004.

Overall, the powers available to government to act without reference to Parliament are very wide-ranging and fundamentally undemocratic. We rely on the government of the day to behave in a reasonable manner and not pull all the levers available to it as far as they will go. But relying on goodwill and self-restraint in a government is inherently a dangerous approach to take. The parliamentary timetable in fact only serves to encourage the use of back doors. There are never enough slots for all the measures a government wants to introduce and in any case the process of drafting legislation and getting it through Parliament is an expensive and time-consuming one. How much easier and quicker for ministers and civil servants to avoid this approach if possible.

When I was a minister, keen to use the opportunity available to me to make a positive difference, my civil servants would helpfully come up with ways to do so that avoided legislation. Often older and unconnected Acts of Parliament would have some provision that allowed me to make progress. And there was always the royal preroga-tive. One rather worrying discovery I made in my time in ministerial office, both at the Department for Transport and then at the Home Office, was the general uninterest in, and ignorance of, Parliament amongst even senior civil servants. As far as they were concerned, their job was to serve the government of the day, and no more, and what happened somewhere down the road was a matter for the politicians, not them.

There was nobody in the tent, minister or civil servant, who saw it as their task to exercise restraint when it came to methods by which Parliament could be, if not bypassed, then kept on the sidelines. So Henry VIII lives on. He may have been discredited by history, but his methods still find a place in the heart of our government in the twenty-first century. And the royal prerogative, also of ancient origin, lives on too, in rude health and getting plenty of exercise.

But then the phrase royal prerogative sounds rather grand, reassuring even, and governments down the ages have realised that the use of comforting language can be a useful way to soften the truth. The old belligerent Ministry of War is now the friendlier sounding Ministry of Defence, for example, but it has not stopped us initiating military action on a regular basis. And you can be sure that any country that feels the need to insert the adjective 'democratic' into its name, such as North Korea or the old East Germany, is anything but democratic.

So here is the language problem with the royal prerogative. Our society encourages respect for and, still, deference to the royal family, so attaching the adjective royal to anything gives it a gloss of respectability and inhibits criticism. After all, most institutions and concepts that bear the adjective royal are ones which command respect, whether it is the Royal Society, the Royal Opera House, or the Royal Society for the Protection of Birds.

So let us rename it for what it is. Perhaps if the power were called the Prime Minister's Prerogative, Parliament would by now have done rather more to curtail it, as it most certainly needs to.

Unequal Before the Law

The law prosecutes the man or woman
Who steals the goose from the common
But lets the greater villain loose
Who steals the common from the goose

This sardonic little verse from centuries ago popped into my head as I was preparing this chapter.

Of course it is far from unusual for those in power, in any country at any time, to seek to fashion the law to suit themselves and their like. Nowadays, in Britain at least, such bias often comes fiscally, rather than through the naked appropriation of land or the institutionalisation of injustice in the courts implied in the old verse. So we might see a right-wing government cutting taxes for the rich or a left-wing government improving workers' rights. Governments, of whatever flavour, are in power because they have been given a mandate of sorts through the ballot box. There are, however, two unelected individuals who, behind the scenes, have acquired the unique right to be consulted on, shape, and even block legislation that affects their private interests in a way they do not like. Those individuals are the Queen and the Prince of Wales.

The precise mechanism is one called 'Queen's or Prince's Consent' and it was sought 146 times between 1970 and 2013. It remains very much alive today and, indeed, updated guidance on how it should operate was issued by the Office of the Parliamentary Counsel as recently as July 2015. It is the Counsel's role to decide if such royal consent is needed for a Bill. If the conclusion is that it is needed, then Queen's Consent has to be obtained *before* a Bill can start its journey through the democratically elected Parliament. It is therefore completely different from royal assent, which is the required rubber-stamping by the monarch *after* a Bill has completed all its parliamentary stages. Assent is uncontroversial. Consent is not.

Royal assent was last withheld by Queen Anne in 1708, and it would now cause a constitutional crisis if a monarch ever exercised his or her nominal right to withhold it. There is nevertheless perhaps one theoretical circumstance in which it might be withheld. That is if Parliament forced through legislation against the wishes of a minority government, and the monarch's ministers, whose advice would be bound to be taken, required that assent be refused. That, of course, would create a constitutional crisis of a different sort.

In general, consent is deemed to be required for matters falling into two categories: those which engage the royal prerogative, and those which engage the personal property or personal interests of the Crown. This process raises two disturbing issues: for prerogative matters, that the government of the day will use this process as a smokescreen to block the passing of, or even debate on, a Bill it does not like; for personal matters, that the monarch or Prince of Wales can influence legislation in a way that helps them personally.

In terms of prerogative matters, there is likely to be no personal gain or loss to the Queen from granting or withholding consent, and indeed she will always act on the advice of ministers. So for instance, the Fixed

Term Parliament Act 2011 required Queen's Consent because it abolished the royal prerogative to decide on the date on which an election should be called, a decision which of course had always in recent times been a matter in any case for the Prime Minister rather than the monarch. The requirement for consent in such prerogative cases is both cumbersome and unnecessary, and throws up the same problems as the use of the royal prerogative does in general, and so strengthens the case for its reform.

Most legislation, naturally, is government-inspired, so the granting of consent by the monarch is merely a formality. Some legislation, however, originates from outside the government, from individual MPs, and may well generate opposition from the government of the day. Advising the Queen to withhold consent is a very effective way of ministers stopping unwelcome bills in their tracks.

How many times this has occurred is not recorded, itself an unsatisfactory aspect of the system, but here are three examples involving Bills introduced by backbenchers. In 1964, the Titles (Abolition) Bill was brought to a juddering halt when the then Tory Home Secretary declined to recommend Queen's Consent, on the basis that it was unlikely the Bill would be debated. It certainly was not after that intervention. In 1969, the Rhodesia Independence Bill was blocked by refusing Queen's Consent. The potential for government embarrassment, it seems, outranked the wish of MPs to debate this issue. And in 1999, MPs were prohibited by the Speaker even from voting on the Military Action Against Iraq (Parliamentary Approval) Bill on the basis that the government had advised that Queen's Consent be withheld.

Here then is the royal prerogative with a vengeance, not simply as we have seen in a previous chapter bypassing Parliament in terms of decision-taking, but now preventing MPs from even debating or voting on a prerogative matter when the government finds it inconvenient for them to do so.

For ministers to then state that a Bill was stopped because Queen's Consent is not forthcoming is to imply that the decision to block even debate on a Bill was one taken by the Queen, and thus to draw her into political controversy quite unfairly and indeed unwisely. *The Guardian*, for example, ran a report in January 2013 which stated, in respect of the 1999 Iraq Bill referred to above, that the Queen had 'completely vetoed' this Bill, which 'sought to transfer the power to authorise military strikes against Iraq from the monarch to parliament'.

Leaving aside the pointlessness of the adverb 'completely', the implication of the piece was that the Queen had unilaterally acted to stop debate on a Bill she did not like, and had decided to veto the Bill in order to keep the power to initiate military action to herself. In reality these motivations were entirely ones of the government, whose wish it was to block the Bill and retain for themselves control over when military action should be taken. The Queen was merely acting as a cipher, and as someone to hide behind.

There is no certainty of course that any of these three Bills would have made it onto the statute book, and indeed faced with government hostility were unlikely to do so, but that is not a good reason for muzzling MPs. Moreover, with the benefit of hindsight, a longer opportunity in 1999 to consider the question of British military action in Iraq might well have been a good thing.

The Political and Constitutional Reform Committee of the House of Commons, which looked into the whole business of royal consent in 2013, recommended that the government should, without exception, secure consent for any Private Members' Bill that was deemed to require it, whether it agreed with the contents of the Bill or not. It also recommended that any letter to the royal household from the government concerning consent or otherwise for a Private Members' Bill be copied to the member whose Bill it was, as a matter of course, to aid transparency.

In Parliament, it was not just this committee that had concerns. In the Lords in November of that year, the Labour peer Lord Berkeley introduced a Bill relating to the rights of the sovereign and the Duchy of Cornwall that, amongst other things, would, if passed, have abolished the notion of consent. Naturally, that Bill itself had to secure consent from both the Queen and the Prince of Wales to get off the starting blocks. It was given, but the government made sure the Bill ran into the sand. The use of Queen's Consent in these cases flows from the general application of the royal prerogative, and is consistent within its own rather idiosyncratic rules.

Yet there is no good reason why such consent should need to be obtained at all prior to a Bill being introduced. Even if the prerogative is to remain unchanged, notwithstanding there is a strong case to reform and curtail it, consent could be implicit in the formal granting of royal assent at the end of a Bill's progression through Parliament.

More concerning, and certainly more opaque, are the occasions when the personal and private interests of the Queen or Prince Charles are engaged. These personal interests include the assets of the Duchy of Lancaster, under arrangements put in place in 1485. This is no abstract theoretical matter. The Duchy comprises well over 40,000 acres, including hugely valuable swathes of land such as the Savoy Estate off the Strand in London, ten castles and land in counties across England. Money derived from the Duchy goes straight to the reigning monarch, as it has done for well over 500 years. The Queen's Consent is required for any proposed law that would affect the Duchy.

Similarly, the Prince of Wales has to give consent for anything affecting the Duchy of Cornwall. So Prince Charles had to agree, for example, to the Pilotage Bill in 1987 as this impacted on the Isles Of Scilly, where he acts as the harbour authority, and also to what became the House of Lords Act 1999, which removed hereditary peerages including in Wales.

As set out elsewhere in this book, there is an argument that the Duchy of Lancaster's income stream is public, not least given that some of the income is used for purposes generated by monarchical requirements, and that its different treatment from those lands that comprise the Crown Estate is both illogical and unsatisfactory. Nevertheless, if the monarch is acting in a capacity as custodian of a public asset, there is certainly a case for engaging her views, though the process by which this is done and the views expressed should be open to public scrutiny, just as when a local council comments on prospective government legislation.

No such argument, however, can be made for those landholdings of the Queen which are defined by legislation as private property, specifically under Section 1 of the Crown Private Estates Act 1862. This includes, for example, Sandringham and Balmoral. Queen's Consent is nevertheless still required for anything affecting these private assets.

There is a clear distinction between an activity carried out by the Queen or other members of the royal family as a public duty, or using public assets, and one where only private activity is engaged.

Our politicians, who, like the Queen, have a public role and are supported by public funds in that role, are required to draw a clear line between that which is a public duty and that which is a private activity. We require transparency for the first and offer privacy for the second. All too often it suits the royal family to blur the line between what is public and what is private, depending on what is most advantageous to them to argue in a particular circumstance. The monarchy, of course, exercising as it does a public function on behalf of the country and doing so with public funds, is a public body. Axiomatically, it should therefore be covered by the seven principles of public life that apply to all such bodies, whether central government, local councils, or the NHS.

They were established in 1995 by Lord Nolan and come under the Committee on Standards in Public Life. The principles are now well established and respected, with sanctions for contraventions – except, it seems, in the case of the royal family. The application of Queen's Consent to matters concerning her private property drives a royal coach and horses through these principles. While personal advantage can be gained in this way on an ad hoc basis, other highly questionable advantages roll on through the decades, indefensible yet unchanged.

When a company is dissolved, its property transfers to the Crown. In other words, the relevant section of the Treasury. If, however, the business was located in either the Duchy of Lancaster or Duchy of Cornwall, the remaining assets would go straight to the Queen or Prince Charles, giving a windfall income. Under the terms of the Companies Act 2006, a company struck off, and so dissolved, can be reinstated and the value of property lost reinstated. Queen's Consent is required because of the possibility of such assets having to be returned. Similarly, consent was required for the Charities Act 2006 as changes might have reduced the windfalls from which the Duchies benefited.

Consent was also required for the Child Maintenance and Other Payments Act 2008, in respect of the provisions relating to deduction from earnings orders. This was because of a possible increase in the numbers of cases where the Queen had to make payments under such orders relating to staff of the Royal Household. Consent was even required for the Animal Welfare Act 2006 because of the powers of inspectors to go onto land to check for welfare offences. The outcome was that a unique exemption was granted for the Queen's private estates, where it is thus theoretically easier to escape prosecution for mistreating animals.

So when the Animal Welfare Act gives the royals a special exemption in respect of their private assets, the legitimate questions are these: why did the royals seek special treatment, why did the government roll over and grant it, and most fundamentally, how can such a request be appropriate in the first place? The Palace will argue that the Queen in these cases, as when the prerogative is invoked, simply follows minis-terial direction and the whole thing is a mere formality. But unlike the straightforward rubber-stamping that is royal assent, the process for consent is considerably more expansive, suggesting otherwise.

The royal household is contacted by the relevant government depart-ment at an early stage to flag up pending legislation, and this clearly gives an opportunity for a response from the Palace to be taken into account before the die is cast. It is very common for the initial contact to be by telephone, through the office of the Queen's private secretary, he being the bridge between the Palace and the government. Naturally, there is no formal written record made of any discussion by phone, but it allows the government to amend its proposals in the light of comments received, so that when the formal letter is finally sent by the relevant government minister to the Palace, a deal has already been hammered out.

Professor Rodney Brazier of Manchester University, who gave evi-dence to the Political and Constitutional Reform Committee as part of their inquiry, told the MPs: 'Royal consent, and the process through which the Royal Households are engaged before it is obtained ... fuel speculation that influence is being brought to bear on the content of legislation of an unknown kind.' This speculation is perhaps hardly surprising when the process involves letters allegedly being sent to the Queen's legal advisors, Farrer & Co., to the Clerk to the Council of the Duchy of Lancaster and to the Secretary to the Duchy of Cornwall, setting out the nature of the legislation and its potential impact.

There is also a minimum window of time given for the Queen or Prince of Wales to respond of not less than fourteen days. As Professor Brazier outlines:

> This procedure indicates that royal consent requires more than the Sovereign being merely asked for formal approval. It raises the

question of why such minimum notice, full explanation, advice from Sovereign's solicitors, and continuing information, are required. By contrast, a request for royal assent to legislation is entirely formal, which is as it should be.

Dr Adam Tucker, then Lecturer in Law at the University of York and now at Liverpool, also gave evidence to the committee. He put it this way: 'This process is wholly inconsistent with any characterisation of the procedure as symbolic. It is designed to facilitate genuine reflection and to elicit informed consent.' He also chipped in, for good measure, with a different but undoubtedly germane point, to assert that 'any involvement of the Prince of Wales in the legislative process is constitutionally unacceptable', the occupier of that position at any given time by definition not being the monarch. In other words, the Prince of Wales being asked for consent is a constitutional impropriety.

Seeking consent from the Prince of Wales is a convention that arose without explanation in 1848, long after the first use of King's Consent, which was from George II in respect of The Suppression of Piracy Bill. The fact that King's Consent existed for so long without a parallel arrangement for the Duchy of Cornwall suggests Prince's Consent has even less constitutional basis. The Information Commissioner was asked to intervene in a 2010 case brought by the indefatigable academic, John Kirkhope, who in 2013 authored the first in-depth analysis of the status of the Duchy since 1837 and who had been refused information from DEFRA about the Duchy's representations on the 2009 Marine and Coastal Access Bill. The Commissioner ruled:

> Making legislation is perhaps the most important function of
> government ... the public interest lies in knowing more about how
> the Prince of Wales in his capacity as Duke of Cornwall may influence

government policy and the process by which his consent is obtained when Parliamentary bills may affect the interests of the Duchy of Cornwall. The Monarchy has a central role in the British constitution and in the Commissioner's view the public is entitled to know how the various mechanisms of the constitution work in practice.

And then he threw in a hand grenade with the pin removed: 'There is no actual legal obligation to give consent…' Ultimately, consent is a matter of parliamentary procedure. If the two Houses of Parliament were minded to abolish consent, they could do so by means of addresses to the Crown, followed by a resolution of each House. Legislation would not be needed.

Consent is but one of the dubious mechanisms used to good effect by the Duchy to advance its own interests. The central mechanism relates to the interpretation of its intrinsic status, and the advantages derived from the opacity of this.

The Duchy, created by Edward III, was the first English dukedom, and the 1337 Royal Grant Charter that gave effect to this created a unique legal arrangement. The eldest son of the monarch, the heir apparent, would be Duke of Cornwall. If this situation did not exist, for example where the heir was female, there was no male offspring or the eldest son was a minor, the dukedom would revert to the Crown with the monarch acting as a sort of legal caretaker until a male appeared who did qualify. The Duchy is never extinguished even when there is no duke, a highly novel concept. By way of illustration, there was no duke between 1936, when Edward VIII came to the throne (he having no male heir, a situation continued upon the accession of her father George VI when a female, Elizabeth, became next in line to the throne) and 1969 when Prince Charles hit twenty-one.

Because the Duke has to be both the heir apparent and the eldest son, that means if Prince Charles had died before fathering a son, Prince Andrew would have become the Duke, but if Charles were to die now ahead of the Queen, then the Duchy would revert to the Crown because the new next in line, Prince William, is not the eldest son of the monarch but rather a grandson. In fact there were only eight years between 1376 and 1714 when there was a duke of full age. The Duchy has in effect been in the hands of the Crown for around two-thirds of the time since it was created.

The recent changes to the law governing succession to the throne to eliminate the male bias have nevertheless left the Duchy arrangements untouched. The pace of constitutional change in Britain tends to be glacial. It is in fact a matter of debate whether the Duchy as a whole has truly existed in unbroken form since 1337. The historian Mary Coate, in her book *Cornwall in the Great Civil War and Interregnum 1642–1660*, writes: 'In one respect Cornwall was singular. The downfall of the monarchs entailed the abolition of the Duchy of Cornwall as an administrative unit, and the sale of its numerous royal manors, thus ending at a stroke a system which had survived intact from the fourteenth century.'

The Duchy was duly abolished in 1650. After the restoration of the monarchy, inducements were offered to the new landowners to facilitate the recreation of the Duchy estate, and the royals acted as if the abolition had never happened because it had not had royal assent. Nevertheless, the claim made today that there is a direct and unbroken lineage to the Duchy going back to 1337 is not correct. Something else that is not quite accurate, and rather more germane to today's situation, is the classification of the Duchy as 'a private estate', a description baldly stated at the top of the Duchy's home page on its website.

John Kirkhope refers to the Duchy as occupying 'a convenient limbo', which claims the benefits of a private landholding when it suits their argument, and claims public status when that is more advantageous. So is the Duchy public or private?

What is a little odd is that the Duchy, and its companion piece, the Duchy of Lancaster, were not surrendered as part of the 1760 deal entered into between George III and Parliament. Under this deal, the King handed over the Crown Estate lands and in return received for the first time a civil list that was meant to be sufficient to meet his requirements. Indeed, it was not until 1800 and the passing of the Crown Private Estate Act that the King was actually allowed to own private property.

The omission of the two Duchies from the 1760 agreement strongly implies that Parliament already considered these to be public lands and certainly as hereditary revenues in which Parliament had an interest, or axiomatically they would have been mentioned for the purpose of exclusion in the 1760 arrangements. The Duchy income had in fact already been surrendered by the Crown in 1697 as part of an earlier deal with William III. Certainly the functions the Duchy enjoyed from 1337 onwards transcended those available to other Duchies and bore all the hallmarks of Crown privileges. They included the right to wreck, the right to Royal Fish, including whales, porpoise, grampuses and sturgeon, wine from every ship that landed and the seizure and confiscation of enemy ships in times of war.

Some of these ancient rights have very modern advantages. Under the right to create mines, for example, the Duchy registered in 2012 mining rights for tungsten and iridium. The right to foreshore gives a nice steady income from tourists parking on some Cornish beaches, or from surf schools that have been established.

Some perhaps seem rather more bizarre in this day and age. As late as 1973 Prince Charles received his feudal dues of a hundred silver shillings and a pound of peppercorn from the Mayor of Launceston. From Stoke Climsland the Duke received a daily bounty of a salmon spear and a bundle of firewood while he was in residence locally, a bow made of alder from Truro, a pair of white gloves from Trevalga and a pair of greyhounds from the manor of Elerky in Veryan. A cottager near Constantine baked a lamprey pie with raisins in lieu of rent.

The original 1337 Charter is now deemed to have been an early Act of Parliament, and how can you create a private estate by parliamentary Act? We know that a select committee in 1800 classified the records of the Duchy of Cornwall as public ones, and that in 1837, at the start of Victoria's reign, the Duchy was classified as an Office of State, again with public records. The passing into law of the Duchies of Lancaster and Cornwall (Accounts) Act 1838 required the two Duchies to present their accounts annually to Parliament, something no ordinary private estate would be required to do.

Fast-forward to 1894 and we find the Duchy describing itself as a 'Department of State' in correspondence, a description repeated in 1921, although it was also being called a private estate by then, which is still the Duchy's preferred description of itself today. Commenting on the issue, Clement Attlee told the Commons: 'The Duchies are historic survivals … they cannot be considered in any way to be private estate.' Mind you, that was in 1936 before he became Prime Minister. Politicians tend to suppress their original views on the monarchy when they obtain power.

This so-called private estate is very happy to behave like a government department or like the Crown when it suits it to do so. In the case of the Tamar Bridge Act 1998, there is a section relating to the Duchy, its rights, powers and privileges. Why is this here? According to Cornwall County Council, the section was included in the Act 'as required by the Duchy of Cornwall'. In other legislation, the law is deemed to apply to the Duchy, but, unlike every other person or body, it cannot be prosecuted for any contravention of the law. It is, for example, exempt under Section 14 of the Nuclear Explosions (Prohibition and Inspections) Act 1998. The main purpose of the Act is given in Clause 1: 'Any person who knowingly causes a nuclear weapon test explosion or any other nuclear explosion is guilty of an offence and liable on conviction on indictment to imprisonment for life.'

So Prince Charles will be able to get out his chemistry set safe in the comforting knowledge that he cannot be prosecuted for causing a mushroom cloud to appear over Tintagel. Similar exemptions are written into Acts as varied as the Transport Act 2000 and the Licensing Act 2003. More insidiously, they are written into the Planning Act 2008, which gives the Duchy a green light to ignore planning restrictions that apply to everyone else.

Perhaps most egregious are the hugely beneficial tax arrangements the Duchy enjoys. These are covered in depth in a separate chapter. In a speech to the Commonwealth Law Conference on 18 April 2013, the Lord Chief Justice, the aptly named Lord Judge, gave a lecture entitled 'Equality Before the Law'. He told his audience:

> If we are looking for a critical ingredient in the rule of law it is that we must live in a society in which every citizen is treated equally before the law ... Neither money nor wisdom nor strength nor social position nor political or financial power should ever attract special privileges or special treatment from the law.

It is not known if Prince Charles or indeed any government minister or parliamentary draughtsman was in the audience. Certainly none seems to have taken on board the learned judge's points when it comes to the matter of leasehold reform. The Crown was given exemption from the 1967 Leasehold Reform Act which was then also claimed by the 'private estate' that is the Duchy of Cornwall. That means that tenants of the Duchy cannot, unlike just about everybody else, buy their property or secure a lease extension. Church and National Trust properties are also excluded, exemptions which are more tightly drawn and most people would regard as not unreasonable.

This matter was taken up by Tony Berkeley, a Labour peer in the House of Lords, on behalf of local residents. The reply dated 12 November 2018 which he received from Sir George (now Lord) Young in the government whips' office was presumably intended to be reassuring, in which objective it notably failed. 'Crown authorities have voluntarily committed, most recently in 2001, to abide by the same terms as private landlords in most circumstances … There are exceptions where the Duchy will not abide by the terms of the law…' The right of a leaseholder to purchase the freehold of the property they lease has been enshrined in law since the 1960s. One Duchy resident, Jane Giddins, who once volunteered for the Prince's Trust, called the Duchy exemption 'outdated feudalism'.

Lord Berkeley complains that leases that are issued are often for only very short periods such as twenty-one years or less. He cites one example where the Duchy allowed someone to fund and build a house on an off-island but then required the leaseholder to sign up to a short lease on which the property transferred free of charge to the Duchy on the death of the leaseholder and his wife. Some people might call that daylight robbery. The Labour peer points out that both the Duchy of Lancaster and the Crown Estates have been much more circumspect in seeking to apply exemptions.

The dice are heavily weighted against the ordinary tenant in other ways. Rents for properties on the Isles of Scilly have been rising inexorably to what the market will bear, which is fine for wealthy incomers but not so good for the families that have long lived there. The *Mail on Sunday* reported that local people had to tender for a bungalow on a two-year shorthold basis, yet the same property was advertised in *Country Life* with a ten-year lease. The increase in rents means that money from housing benefits has been flowing into the Duchy as landlord. In 2014, it was estimated that this source generated an income stream from councils to the Duchy of at least £163,000.

While the 'private estate' receives free legal advice from the Treasury Solicitor and makes full use of it, tenants who want a new lease have to pay not only their own legal costs but also those of the expensive solicitors the Duchy will employ, Farrers, who Tony Berkeley says can be notoriously slow in these matters. The Prince, in common with Buckingham Palace, regularly uses Harbottle & Lewis for legal work, a firm who boast that they 'provide innovative, pro-active legal advice to dynamic and creative clients'.

In 2017 Lord Berkeley introduced in the Lords proposed legislation in the form of the Duchy of Cornwall Bill. This, if enacted, would have removed the unique tax exemptions enjoyed by the Duchy, ended its special status under the Leasehold Reform Act 1967 and ended the link between the Duchy and the Treasury Solicitor. It was met with zero enthusiasm from the government.

Perhaps the principle of special treatment under the law applies in other smaller ways too. Visitors to the Chelsea Flower Show in 2019 may have been surprised to see William and Kate's three children there – George (five), Charlotte (four) and Louis (one). There is a blanket ban on under-fives attending the show, a rule rigorously enforced for everyone else.

Because the royal family so often writes its own rules, and the state both bends to accommodate what is wanted and keeps it secret that rules have been bent, suspicions can be raised where perhaps normal procedures have actually been followed. Philip's driving is a case in point. This has been a topic of interest for the newspapers, dating back even before his marriage to the then Princess Elizabeth, when they reported an incident just after his engagement where the Prince, driving at excess speed, skidded and ran into a hedge. In the last iteration, in January 2019, it seems quite clear that the 97-year-old was at fault when he pulled out from a side road into the path of another car on the main A149. He maintained he was blinded by the sun, in which case the answer obviously was not to pull out rather than to do so and hope for the best.

The accident near Sandringham fortunately left the Duke unharmed, amazing considering both his age and that his sturdy vehicle rolled, which gives some indication of the force of the collision. The occupants of the other vehicle were not so fortunate, however, with one sustaining a broken wrist, and another cuts to her knees. Mercifully, a nine-month-old baby on board was unhurt.

The Crown Prosecution Service operates a two-stage test in deciding whether to take matters forward. The first is to establish the likelihood of any prosecution being successful. In this case, that test will have easily been met. The second, rather more subjective test, is to consider whether a prosecution would be in the public interest. Before any decision was announced, the Duke decided to voluntarily surrender his licence, following which the CPS said it would not prosecute.

There is undoubtedly an argument for saying that the surrender of a licence prevents any recurrence, and given this, there is little point in pursuing a case against a 97-year-old to the courts. Such a view could reasonably be taken whoever the 97-year-old is.

Yet because the royal family has a track record of securing favourable treatment from the law, the suspicion will fester that the failure to prosecute represented preferential treatment. The fact that Philip surrendered his licence sometime after the crash and not long before the CPS decision was announced raises the possibility that Philip was offered a deal – surrender your licence and we will not prosecute, a deal unlikely to be available to others who find themselves in this situation. There is also the fact that Philip was spotted just forty-eight hours after the accident driving on public roads without wearing a seat belt. It seems this matter, which should automatically generate a fine and points on the licence, was quietly buried. The ostensible reason, according to unofficial Palace briefing, was that the Duke had a sore shoulder from his accident and wearing a seat belt was uncomfortable. On the face of it, that suggests his mobility was impaired to a degree, and raises the question whether he should have been driving at all. Crucially, though, it is not as though he had to drive. After all, the royal family is surrounded by flunkeys, any one of whom could have taken the wheel.

Furthermore, the Queen, who was with him in the car, was also not wearing a seat belt, without even the excuse of a bruised shoulder. Naturally, that offence is not being pursued either. Nor can it be, in fact, given that all legal action is taken in her name. You cannot have Regina *v* Regina.

It seems, in fact, that this particular episode was far from an exception. In January 2020, the Queen was caught on camera driving her Range Rover on a public road near Sandringham, again without wearing a seat belt. Moreover, she had the previous May agreed to give up driving entirely on the advice of her security team. The Queen has never taken a driving test and is the only person in the country allowed to drive without a licence.

The Queen of course is a law-abiding individual, her lack of seat-belt wearing apart, but just suppose she had been at the wheel rather than the Duke when that accident occurred, and just suppose a fatality had occurred as a consequence of a driving error made by the Queen. No prosecution would have been possible, no matter how careless or reckless the Queen might theoretically have been. That cannot be right.

For a telling comparison we need only look across the Channel to Belgium, where in 2019 the former King Albert II (they abdicate over there when they get too old) was threatened with a daily fine of €5,000 until he submitted to a DNA test to establish if he is the biological father of a love child, Delphine Boël. He finally succumbed, and the DNA test confirmed that he is indeed the father. Ms Boël is now officially a princess who will share in her father's estate when he dies. It would be interesting to know what results would have been thrown up if members of the British royal family had been required to undergo DNA tests where paternity has been in doubt.

The Queen is patron of the Royal Society for the Prevention of Accidents, whose website offers the firm advice: 'Always wear your seat belt when travelling in the front or rear of a vehicle.' The Duke of Edinburgh is a patron of the Order of the Road, which claims it is 'the only organisation devoted solely to the encouragement of safe and courteous driving.'

Prince Andrew is not the patron of any road safety-related charity as far as I am aware, which is just as well in view of the incident in March 2016 where he found the gates in Windsor Great Park would not open as the sensors had failed. An alternative nearby route was available for Andrew, involving a short diversion, but instead he decided in a fit of juvenile pique to ram the gates open with his Range Rover. His yobbish behaviour caused thousands of pounds of damage to the gates, with the bill for repairs ultimately falling to the taxpayers. The gates are the property of the publicly owned Crown Estates, who picked up the bill for the damage. A park worker who witnessed the event told *The Sun*: 'It was a crazy thing to do. [Andrew] has a bit of a reputation for roaring around like Toad of Toad Hall and he seems to think he can do what he likes.'

The police said they could do nothing until a complaint was lodged. One duly arrived the next day from Graham Smith, chief executive of the pressure group Republic, whereupon the police again decided they could do nothing despite the clear evidence of deliberate criminal damage. Nor did the Crown Estates seek to recover the cost of repairs as they doubtless would have done from anyone other than a royal. Applying the now standard suffix that denotes a scandal, Graham Smith dubbed the incident Gategate.

Yobbish behaviour is nothing new for Andrew, of course. In 2005, he tried to put himself above the law again when in Australia. At Melbourne airport, he refused to go through the normal security procedures to board his Qantas flight to New Zealand. Unlike in this country where the authorities might have buckled to a royal with a tantrum, the Aussies stood firm and barred him from the plane until he agreed to be searched with a hand detector. A security guard who was present told the Australian press: 'Who does he think he is? What a pompous prat. Everyone has to go through security screening. He should be happy to do so and set an example.'

So what can we conclude? It is clear that the royal family gains from a basket of unique financial and legislative advantages that should have no place in a modern democracy, and where the law does apply and they break it, a blind eye is turned to this. Parliament should act. Until it does, the royal family will remain too often above and certainly beneficially unequal before the law.

Where There's a Will

The royal family is inextricably linked with a number of ancient customs, practices and artefacts, the sort that overseas visitors regard as quaint.

These ancient appendices in some instances go as far back as, well, the twentieth century. Or even 2014, the year the 'historic' diamond jubilee coach entered service on ceremonial occasions to provide an impression of centuries-old continuity, a bit like a mock-Tudor house. A harmless deception, you might think. Others are less so. Take, for example, the question of royal wills. The Palace would have you believe that it is an ancient tradition that royal wills, unlike those of anybody else in the country, can be sealed and therefore not available for public scrutiny.

Wills in this country have always been open for inspection, centuries before anyone had ever heard of the modern concept of freedom of information. It is, after all, an essential legal safeguard to prevent theft and malpractice. This concept of openness equally applied to royal wills, until 1911 that is, when the dubious principle was established that if the contents of a will would be embarrassing to the royal family, then it could be sealed. The official reason was to uphold the dignity of the

135

Crown, but surely dignity is upheld by the avoidance of undignified behaviour, rather than by the ability to cover it up.

The catalyst on this occasion was the death in late 1910 of Prince Francis, brother-in-law of George V. Francis was almost a pantomime villain, with his waxed moustaches and his well-earned reputation for gambling and womanising. In his will, he scandalously left prized family jewels to a mistress, one Ellen Constance, the Countess of Kilmorey, with whom he was rumoured to have had an illegitimate child.

Faced with this, the royal family did what they always did, and still do: they decided to hush it up. So Francis's sister, Queen Mary, persuaded a judge to ban public access to the will. In the meantime, Ellen was paid the princely sum of £10,000, equivalent to around £700,000 today, to return them. They were subsequently seen shortly afterwards round the neck of Mary as her husband was crowned George V. They have also been worn more recently by Princess Diana and by the Queen herself. How do we know all this? Not thanks to the royal family of course, for whom inconvenient facts are matters to be kept secret from the public at large, but thanks to the BBC, whose diligent journalism unearthed a copy of the will in the Belfast records office. So an 'ancient' precedent was set and is carried through to this day and used whenever there is something to hide. Royal wills are now locked up in a metal safe behind an iron cage on the first floor of Somerset House.

And so it was in 2002 that a highly questionable arrangement sealed the will of Princess Margaret. Even the sealing of the will was kept secret, and only became known some five years later as a result of a somewhat bizarre legal action initiated by a man called Robert Brown. Mr Brown maintained that he was the illegitimate son of Princess Margaret, though why and how he has reached this conclusion is unclear. At first he looked into whether he was related to Edward VIII and then considered whether Prince Philip might be his father, before settling on the Princess Margaret connection.

He was born in Kenya in 1955 on 5 January, but it took four weeks for the birth to be registered, which he regards as significant, as, he believes, is the fact that a Privy Council meeting was held on the same day. It seems that his mother, Cynthia, had been working as a model for Hardy Amies, a favourite designer of the Princess, but that appears to be as strong as the connection gets. It is also the case that later in that year, 1955, Princess Margaret called off her wedding to Group Captain Peter Townsend. If you have a particularly febrile imagination, you might play this fact into Robert Brown's story.

At the time, it was assumed that the hurdle had been the fact that the former Battle of Britain fighter pilot was divorced, still a stigma in 1950s Britain. In fact the Prime Minister, Anthony Eden, himself divorced, had raised no objections to the marriage and even arranged it that she could keep her HRH title. It subsequently turned out, from a letter discovered in the National Archives at Kew quite recently, that she was simply 'uncertain' as to whether or not she wanted to marry him.

Be all that as it may, Robert Brown has spent years and a great deal of money trying to force the courts to open the will of Princess Margaret, which he believes may throw light on the circumstances of his birth and perhaps even make provision for him in some way. He went to the High Court in 2006, and again the year after, to press his case. He was unsuccessful, with Sir Mark Potter, president of the family division, calling it 'an imaginary and baseless claim'. But Mr Brown resolved to plough on, and then turned to the Freedom of Information Act to help.

This channel proved no more useful for him, with his application being refused, until in 2013 he won permission to seek a judicial review into the refusal.

In ruling in his favour, Mr Justice Phillips said that the case gave rise to 'important points of principle and practice' with regard to open justice and the public interest.

Indeed it did. For while Mr Brown's central belief is hard to take seriously, his persistence has performed a public service in revealing the secrecy surrounding royal wills. It turns out that the wills of Princess Margaret and the Queen Mother, who had died just seven weeks after Margaret, were sealed in 2002 at a secret hearing presided over by the High Court judge Elizabeth Butler-Sloss. The only other people present were legal representatives of the Queen, and the then Attorney-General, Lord Goldsmith.

A parliamentary answer I received in 2010 from the Solicitor-General confirmed the attendance of the Attorney-General at this hearing, and also confirmed that 'the only member of the Royal Family whom the Attorney-General … is on occasion called upon to advise is the Queen'. We must assume therefore that both the sealing of the wills and the secrecy of the hearing were supported, perhaps even driven by, the Queen herself. Lord Goldsmith, nominally at the hearing to represent the public interest, was the Attorney-General who was to change his legal advice on the legality of the Iraq War to come down in favour of what Tony Blair wanted to do, and who was seen to interfere with a police corruption investigation into the arms company BAE. The judge granted a 'practice direction' which sealed both Princess Margaret's will and that of the Queen Mother, and established the principle in law, as opposed to haphazard custom over the previous ninety years, that royal wills should remain sealed.

This hearing was so secret that it was itself kept from Parliament and from the public, and when Sir Mark Potter came to look into the matter as part of his consideration of Robert Brown's claim, he was concerned to discover the written record of this hearing was confidential and one which he, as head of the family division, had not even known had existed. He said at the time that he had never heard of a practice direction that is not in the public domain. Well he wouldn't have, would he? And nor would the rest of us.

It seems clear that the episode in 1911 has established the principle that where the royal family wants something to do with a will hushed up, the legal system will bend to accommodate them. Mr Brown was right to tell *The Guardian* that what had happened threw up an issue of constitutional significance: 'It is constitutionally wholly inappropriate for the Palace and private lawyers with the assistance of the attorney general to enter into utterly secret formal arrangements, to reflect Her Majesty's wishes, with senior judges.'

For the public at large if not for Mr Brown, the question of his birth is secondary to the serious questions raised by the way this matter has been officially handled. Why, and under what legal provision, was there a hearing in private to discuss the sealing of these wills? Why was seemingly no formal record of this hearing made public? Most of all, what does it say about our democratic and legal safeguards if a judge can subvert the law relating to the openness of wills by issuing a 'practice direction' to help the royal family, and then keep it secret that this has occurred? Once again, the classic BBC comedy series *Yes Minister* becomes less comedy and more documentary, as Sir Humphrey, quoting Sir Francis Bacon, tells his minister, Jim Hacker: 'He that would keep a secret must keep it secret that he hath a secret to keep.'

In May 2002, I asked the Prime Minister Tony Blair to publish the Queen Mother's will. He replied that

> in line with a long standing convention for dealing with wills of senior members of the Royal Family, an Order has been made by the High Court for the sealing up of the will of the late Queen Mother,

which means that it cannot be inspected or published. Therefore
I do not intend to take any steps to ensure publication of the will.

What was in the wills of Princess Margaret and the Queen Mother is ultimately less important than the points of principle: why should a member of the royal family, unlike anyone else in the country, be able to keep their will secret anyway; and what justification can there be for bending the law to the royal will in this way?

Mr Brown's lawyer at the time, Geoffrey Robertson QC, bluntly stated that the decisions to seal the royal wills 'were made without juris- diction, according to a practice direction that does not exist as far as the law is concerned'. The constitutional historian Professor Michael Nash told the *Daily Mail*: 'It seems they are making it up as they go along. They are using privileges and prerogatives that should have died out in the Middle Ages.'

It is common knowledge that court cases are pursued by the state in the name of the monarch of the day, hence Regina *v* whomever it is. That means of course total Crown Immunity for the monarch, who can hardly prosecute him or herself. Perhaps this legal immunity has gone to the head of successive monarchs. By seeking to subvert the law to benefit themselves in this case, it looks very much like R *v* The Public Interest.

Besides the points of principle, we might also wonder: why go to such lengths to seal these two wills? It may be of course simply that the royal family is pathologically wedded to secrecy, and certainly their general attitude to the Freedom of Information Act suggests that may be a plausible explanation. Or were there other reasons, perhaps financial ones? After all, if it became publicly known how much was bequeathed, the public might begin to question afresh the level of taxpayers' sup- port the royal family benefits from, or indeed begin asking how it was possible to accumulate such wealth in their lifetimes without seemingly having any external means to do so.

Princess Margaret was revealed to have left an estate of some £7.6 million, and that was after she had apparently previously disposed of some £12 million of assets to her family, including her house on the Caribbean island of Mustique, to minimise death duties. Where did Princess Margaret get £20 million from? Even the generous largesse provided by taxpayers through the civil list cannot explain that.

Some small sum will have been saved by the abrupt way in which her staff were disposed of immediately following her death. Ten long-serving staff were told they no longer had a job and to vacate their royal lodgings without delay. The Princess's personal chef, Kevin Martin, employed for twelve years, was reduced to applying to the local council for help for somewhere to live. It mattered not what dutiful and loyal service they had given. They were now surplus to requirements, like the Princess's personal possessions that needed to be cleared out of Kensington Palace.

But if Margaret's £20 million raises eyebrows, the Queen Mother's reputed legacy raises serious questions. She is rumoured to have left an estate worth a cool £70 million, with whatever was left to the Queen being passed on free of inheritance tax – just one of many tax dodges uniquely available to the royals – representing a multimillion-pound loss to the taxpayer. Amongst the tax-free gifts to her daughter were a priceless Fabergé egg collection, her string of racehorses and a valuable collection of paintings.

Where did this £70 million come from? Doubtless there was some inherited wealth but surely nothing of that order? She is unlikely to have won it at the races. Indeed, she is rumoured to have left a multi-million-pound bookmakers' debt. Nor did she hold back from spending freely during her life. She ran a huge personal staff of sixty, with butlers, footmen, pages, equerries, ladies-in-waiting, housekeepers, gardeners and chauffeurs all falling over each other. At her frequent extravagant luncheons and dinner parties, there was a liveried foot-man posted behind each chair. Nor was any expense spared when it came to the food and drink, with bottles of champagne costing £300 apiece disappearing as fast as water in the Sahara. And run-ning five properties as she did would hardly have helped keep the bills down.

Though her staff were meanly paid, they were so plentiful in number that the wages bill still came to around £1.5 million a year, well in excess of the already generous no-strings-attached, no-questions-asked £643,000 a year the taxpayer was handing to her by the mid-1990s. Even in the last year of her life as a centenarian, she managed to spend £4 million more than her state benefit.

It seems clear she had to be regularly bailed out by the Queen as the overspending mounted, and indeed she also left debts of £7 million when she died, including significant gambling debts and a massive overdraft at Coutts of several million. Doubtless the bank took the view that this was risk-free for them.

Her staff were to face the same abrupt fate that those of Princess Margaret had just a month earlier. Billy Tallon, who had worked for the royals for over half a century, rising to become the leading servant in the Queen Mother's retinue and allegedly her personal favourite, learnt of her death from a tabloid newspaper. Buckingham Palace the next day confirmed to the press that when a member of the family died, their staff died with them, as far as the rest of the family was concerned. Would the now unwanted staff get a pension? 'That would depend on their job and on their contract,' said the Palace. But surely those dispensed with overnight would get a pay-off? 'Um, not necessarily,' replied the Palace. It is to be hoped that the Palace spokesman sent out to parry these journalists' questions prudently checked his or her own arrangements afterwards.

The Queen Mother throughout her life exhibited an extravagance when it came to her own enjoyment, especially if the taxpayer was footing the bill, and a meanness when it came to parting with any of her own money. She protested bitterly to the Treasury that the tips given to Royal Marine bandsmen and to other staff on the royal yacht *Britannia* on the occasion of her visit to Tunisia in 1961 should be met from public funds, and not from her enormous civil list grant. The tips came to 2/6d (12.5p) per day for the bandsmen, 3s (15p) for stewards, and 5s (25p) for some other staff. In total, this came to just over £78 for the entire trip, which was hardly going to break the royal bank.

Her meanness was not unique in the royal family. Queen Victoria decreed that newspaper should be cut into squares to be used as toilet paper by her staff, who also had to tolerate permanent sugar rationing. Queen Victoria's daughter Louise left £239,261 when she died in 1939, equivalent to around £16 million today. It transpired she had been chased for, and failed to pay a bill of 15 shillings, or 75p, to a local tobacconist.

Edward VIII, the Queen Mother's brother-in-law, was known as the millionaire miser. Like the Queen Mother, he was happy to splash out outrageously on his priorities while being tight as a drum with his staff, and always keen to extract money from the state. Nor did it matter which one. The costs of his controversial trip to Germany in 1937 were met entirely by the Nazi regime. In 1940, as Britain was fighting for its very survival, he complained to Churchill about his absence from the civil list. This despite the fact that he was easily a millionaire, having accumulated a great deal of taxpayers' money ever since he had stepped on to the first rung of the civil list ladder with £100,000 a year as Prince of Wales back in 1911.

The British government paid for the rent of his Paris house, and in 1945, despite the fact that information he had allowed to be passed to the Germans had played a major part in allowing the Nazi conquest of the country, the French government granted him tax-free status for life. His top priority, of course, was Wallis Simpson. In the years 1934 and 1935 alone, he presented her with £7 million of jewels, and thereafter an annual allowance of £370,000 (both figures at today's prices). Meanwhile, he sacked royal retainers as a cost-saving measure.

The distasteful dichotomy between the approach taken by royals to expenditure on themselves compared with that on their staff has continued to the present day. In 2010, the Queen decided to cancel the biennial Christmas party for staff, and the Palace presented this as a response to 'the difficult economic circumstances facing the country'. Yet as the party is always paid for by the Queen herself, the only result of this magnificent sacrifice was to personally save her £50,000.

The enormous amount left by the Queen Mother cannot however be explained by her meanness to those who served her. Perhaps part of the answer to the mystery can be found in the windfall from which she herself benefited in 1942 when she was left a large hoard of jewels by a McEwan's brewing heiress, a collection known as the Greville inheritance. Were these given to her personally or as the Queen consort to George VI? In other words, do they really belong to the state? If jewels were the reason for the 1911 cover-up, perhaps jewels played a part too in the 2002 sequel. What is certain is that the sealing of royal wills does not allow the proper checks to be made to ensure that what properly belongs to the state has not slipped across into private property.

It could be of course that there is nothing untoward in these wills, but in which case why seal them? I took up the issue again as an MP back in 2009, without any success, it has to be confessed. I told the papers:

It is a matter of equity and transparency that people are able to see
wills and it is quite wrong that the royal family is treated differently.
They pass on gigantic sums of money without paying death duties.
If we had the wills made public there might be fresh questions
about whether they need quite so much money from the Civil List.

One royal will that was made public was that of Princess Diana, whose
death in 1997 stunned the world. But maybe it was decided her will
could be made public as in a way she was by then regarded by the
royal family as no longer one of them. What happened in her case was
truly shocking. She made clear her intentions in a 'letter of wishes'
attached to the will that a quarter of her tangible possessions be given
to her godchildren. Yet her executors – her mother, her elder sister
and the Bishop of London – simply swept this aside and applied to the
courts to overturn the letter of wishes.

In a secret hearing – yes, another one of those – a variation proposed
by the executors was agreed. This had the effect of disinheriting the
godchildren who instead received mere sentimental trinkets, like a gift
Diana had once received from Argos. Naturally, none of this became
public at the time, for the will that was published was the amended
one, not the original. The truth only came out with the trial for theft
of Diana's butler, Paul Burrell. Incidentally, he scooped £50,000 from
the will as a result of the variations made by the executors, a bequest
that had been totally absent from the original will.

It seems Paul Burrell had powerful friends. On 24 April 2001, the
ex-butler was charged with stealing 342 items belonging to Diana,
Charles and Prince William. The trial, which was conveniently delayed
to avoid clashing with the Queen's golden jubilee celebrations, finally
began on 14 October the following year. It collapsed two weeks later
when the Queen, who had had a three-hour private meeting with

Mr Burrell some time before, came forward at the last minute with information that undermined the prosecution case, just hours before Mr Burrell was about to take the witness stand. He was then cleared of all charges. The taxpayers' bill for the aborted trial was around £3 million. 'What she has done for me, to intervene like this, is absolutely unprecedented,' he told the *Daily Mail*. Indeed it was.

The police raid on Paul Burrell's house that preceded the court action had also uncovered an inlaid mahogany box containing a signet ring from James Hewitt and around twenty secret confessional videos made by Princess Diana, recorded by a former BBC cameraman. As well as Diana discussing her divorce and life thereafter, the videos allegedly contained a series of character assassinations of each member of the royal family by the Princess. They were also said to include a recording of a former aide to Prince Charles, one George Smith, in which he alleged both that he had been raped by another royal employee, and that he had witnessed that same employee giving oral sex to a senior member of the royal family.

One of the police who raided Mr Burrell's house was Detective Chief Inspector Maxine de Brunner. She has said that at a meeting with Charles's lawyer, Fiona Shackleton, on 17 May 2001, she was asked to make the video 'go away'. 'It was one of the lowest points in my professional career,' she told *The Observer* in December 2003. The videos did indeed go away at the time. This of course would have been an enormous relief to the royal family. It seems likely that this disappearance took place before the Queen helpfully intervened to ensure the criminal case against Paul Burrell ran into the sand. Meanwhile, the senior courtier who was very close to Prince Charles was given a £50,000 pay-off, also to go away, though only after he had signed a confidentiality agreement. Material from the tapes was finally given an airing by Channel 4 in the autumn of 2017.

With the shocking treatment of her will, it seems Diana was to be trashed by the royal family in death as she was in life. But as with Robert Brown, the real concerns transcend the individual circumstances. What kind of executors take it upon themselves to totally ignore the wishes of a deceased? And what kind of court agrees to such a request, and further agrees that it should all be done in secret, with the connivance of the Palace?

The sad and worrying conclusion from all these episodes is that the royal family regard themselves as above the law and free to write their own rules, and that the courts and government will, it seems, help them do so.

The remedies are clear: the law must apply to everyone equally, including members of the royal family, and all royal wills should be openly published, just as they are for any other person in this country, from the Prime Minister down.

The Royal Mint

'You can tell a lot about a country which refers to
the Royal *Mint and the* National *Debt'*

– WILLIAM COBBETT

April Fool's Day 2012 was certainly a day for the British royal family to celebrate. The country may have been under the cosh as public services were slashed and wages frozen or cut in an attempt to get the economy back on an even keel following the crash of 2008, but for the royals the pound signs had suddenly got a lot bigger.

It was the day when the Sovereign Grant Act 2011 came into force, providing a new method to fund the royals which replaced the long-established civil list mechanism. Ronnie Biggs would have been envious. No violence, no risk, just an elegant clean cash coup, and not just for one year but for every year thereafter. Here was the Great Gravy Train Robbery.

The figures speak for themselves. For 2001–11, the civil list was set at £7.9 million for each year. This became £13.7 million in 2011. The first year of the Sovereign Grant saw support rise to £31 million in 2012. The then Chancellor, George Osborne, maintained that this figure was overall equivalent to the previous year's as it amalgamated funding streams related to transport and the upkeep of royal palaces.

Then the cash bonanza really took off:

> 2012–13: £31 million
> 2013–14: £36.1 million (up 16.5 per cent)
> 2014–15: £37.9 million (up 5 per cent)
> 2015–16: £40.1 million (up 5.5 per cent)
> 2016–17: £42.8 million (up 7 per cent)
> 2017–18: £76.1 million (up 77.8 per cent)
> 2018–19: £82.2 million (up 8 per cent)

The new method of funding the royals overturned more than 250 years of a settled scheme. Back in 1760, upon coming to the throne, George III did a deal with the government. He would surrender to the nation the lands that would be known as the Crown Estates in return for money from the government to support him and his lifestyle through an enhanced civil list, set at £800,000 a year. The government would henceforth take over from the King responsibility for funding the armed forces, the secret service, the judiciary, and other public functions.

The link between the income from Crown Estates land and income for the monarchy therefore ended in 1760 as it became a public asset, and although the name was kept, this was a misnomer. Over the years, and particularly from the second half of the twentieth century onwards, some royals, especially Prince Charles, have looked with envy at the performance of the Crown Estates, seen how it has prospered, and begun to regret the arrangement entered into by George III. If only the clock could be turned back, the royals could benefit personally from the successful Crown Estates. In other words, they wanted to advantage themselves at the expense of the taxpayer who would consequently lose out.

Successive governments of all colours resisted this self-serving suggestion. When the idea was floated back in 1972, Roy Jenkins, the former Labour Home Secretary, demolished it thrice over: first, it was simply wrong to imply the Crown Estates in any way belonged to the Queen; second, funding the royals in this way would mean less parliamentary scrutiny over royal finances than had existed for over 200 years; and third that nobody, not even the Queen, should be automatically protected against the consequences of inflation.

Successive governments respected the status quo and ignored self-serving pleas for change from the royals, that is, until George Osborne became Chancellor. Despite reservations from his Lib Dem deputy Danny Alexander, he swiftly agreed to the proposal that the civil list be replaced by a scheme whereby a percentage of the profits of the Crown Estate each year went to the royals. This was initially set at 15 per cent but has subsequently been upped to 25 per cent to cover a bells and whistles upgrade to Buckingham Palace.

For the icing on the cake, a hugely beneficial condition was inserted for the benefit of the royals. If in the unlikely event the Crown Estates' income fell one year, the royals would not lose out. They would however gain from above-inflation performances. Heads they win, tails the taxpayer loses. Despite the huge constitutional and financial significance, the change from civil list to Sovereign Grant was not discussed widely in government before it was announced. It was hustled through a small committee in Parliament with only the Scottish National Party objecting.

The draft legislation was, however, supplied by George Osborne to Prince Charles in advance for his clearance. A letter sent to his office on 16 June 2011 read: 'I should be grateful if you could lay this letter, with my humble duty, before the Prince of Wales and seek His consent...' Unsurprisingly, Charles was more than happy to give his consent to what was a massive hike in royal fortunes and the groundless re-establishment of a link between the income of the Crown Estates and payments to the royals.

In the short parliamentary debate that was allowed in July 2011, a number of MPs, including shadow Labour ministers, suggested that the benchmark for annual changes should be based on GDP rather than the performance of a well-endowed and well-placed property company, which is what the Crown Estates is. This would indeed seem to have been more appropriate, and tie the fortunes of the royal family more closely to the ups and downs of the population at large. The Crown Estates regularly produces a rate of return in excess of inflation, which in turn means above-inflation increases every year for the royals, a situation only likely to become more marked in future. In July 2019, for example, the Crown Estates, who hold the right to the sea-beds around Britain, announced an auction for the biggest offshore wind power development in the world. This will provide a bumper windfall of hundreds of millions for the Queen from her 25 per cent share of the Crown Estates profits, a vast sum that before George Osborne's disastrous intervention would have gone back to the Treasury.

But there was another reason for not overtly re-establishing the link with the Crown Estates. Although the 1760 agreement handed to the state the income from this estate, there has still been a technical requirement at the beginning of each reign for the monarch to formally sign over the income to the government. Prince Charles, who has been arguing over decades for the financial link between the Crown Estates income and financial support for the royals to be re-established, has made it known that his personal view is that all the income from the Crown Estates should go to the royals. The total value of the estate was put at £14.1 billion in 2017. In terms of the performance in 2018/19, that suggestion, if enacted, would have handed another £250 million or so, that is around a quarter of a billion pounds, to the royals for that one year alone, at the expense of the public purse.

Of course if Charles really wants to re-create the position before 1760, that would require the monarch once again to personally fund not only the expenses of the royal family, but also the salaries and pensions of ministers, judges and those in the civil service, and the costs of the armed forces and secret services too. It was to lose that heavy burden that George III agreed to a new arrangement. But Charles would appear to be interested only in the beneficial side of the equation that would hugely enrich the royal family, not the side that would entail royal liabilities.

Nor is Charles alone. In evidence to the Public Accounts Committee in October 2013, Sir Alan Reid, the Queen's Treasurer, was also keen to play up one side of the equation while ignoring the other: 'Crown Estate income is the monarch's until they surrender it at the beginning of each reign. If you look at the last five years, the Government, after allocating money to the monarchy, has had a surplus of £1.2 billion.' Actually, if the position before 1760 were re-established, the greedy royals would find themselves billions out of pocket every year. The deal, which they now seem to regret, was one that was very good for them.

In that parliamentary debate of July 2011, the arch-traditionalist Conservative MP Jacob Rees-Mogg raised this issue with the Chancellor, asking him 'to confirm that in the theoretical circumstances that a new monarch decided to keep the Crown Estates revenues, it would be open to such a monarch to do so'. The Chancellor replied by suggesting that that was 'pretty unlikely' and 'pretty theoretical', but did not deny the constitutional possibility. We can expect Charles to pursue this point in private if he feels there is any chance of getting away with it. He would, it appears, have the strong support of at least one MP.

This all raises the question, also asked in the debate but not answered, as to who actually owns the Crown Estate lands. The overwhelming view from constitutional experts is that the government does on behalf of the country. Perhaps the simplest way of looking at this is to ask what would happen to the estates if Britain ever became a republic. It is inconceivable that a deposed monarch could walk away with the Crown Estates.

The one positive element in the Chancellor's announcement was that for the first time, royal finances would be open for regular scrutiny by the National Audit Office and by the Public Accounts Committee. This did lead to an inquiry by the committee in 2013 under the feisty Labour chair Margaret Hodge, but the royal gentlemen sent into bat for the Palace effortlessly blocked the difficult questions, even if they did not trouble the scorers very much. With Margaret Hodge no longer the chair, no subsequent examination by the committee has taken place. Given the massive increases in the Sovereign Grant that have occurred since, it is practically a dereliction of duty that the committee has not returned to the subject.

In setting out the changes to Parliament in 2011, the Chancellor offered this reassurance:

'The Bill ... is a mechanism for helping to continue the current level of spending ... The amount of money going from the public purse will be roughly the same.' The new arrangement, he said, 'delivers value for money for the taxpayer'.

That has now been seen to be wildly wrong, one might even say a travesty of the truth. Aside from the huge rise in the Sovereign Grant, it means that less money is now required to be used for public purposes from the profits of the Duchy of Lancaster, thereby increasing the profits the Queen takes as personal income from this source. The Duchies are considered in detail elsewhere in this book.

We should not be surprised that these changes have turned out rather well for the royals. It is instructive that whenever changes to royal finances have been announced by governments over the last fifty years, we are always told they are prudent and represent good value for money. Yet they nearly always end up increasing significantly the income for the royals.

In 1990, the government chose a time just before the summer recess for a statement on a previous review of the civil list. MPs were given two hours' notice of the debate, allowed twenty minutes for questions, and had to wait for the next day's Hansard to appear to learn, for example, that Prince Edward's annual handout had been upped from £20,000 to £100,000.

The Prime Minister, Margaret Thatcher, proposed a massive increase in the annual sum given to the Queen, up from £5.09 million to £7.9 million. An inflation figure of a whopping 7.5 per cent for each year of the ten-year period covered was assumed for the calculations. At the same time, the opportunity for an annual parliamentary debate on the civil list was removed. It was all wrapped up in silken talk of 'efficiency savings', 'improvements in management', and 'best financial practice'.

Spinelessly, the opposition leader Neil Kinnock, who unlike other MPs had been notified prior to the debate of the changes, fully endorsed this royal windfall, asserting the changes would have 'widespread support' and would 'commend themselves to the House'. The journalist and author Robert Harris suggested that Neil Kinnock had opted to 'roll over on his back and wave his arms and legs in the air'. It was left to assorted Labour backbenchers to rain on the party. Tony Benn suggested that 'many people believe that the sums paid to the royal family far exceed the services rendered'. Dennis

Skinner, less elegantly, wanted to know why the taxpayer should 'hand out large sums of money to the Queen and all the hangers-on at the Palace'.

He was presumably referring to the other members of the royal family who received a regular and generous income from the civil list. It is worth noting that the practice of paying sums to the monarch's relatives, other than the King's wife, only started when the present Queen came to the throne in 1952.

A left-field intervention came from the Tory backbencher Anthony Beaumont-Dark, who asked Mrs Thatcher to agree that it would be better 'if the private wealth and income of however high a person, even the sovereign, were taxed, as is the case for everyone else'. The Prime Minister did not agree. We can imagine that Mr Beaumont-Dark instead got the gamma ray treatment. The absurdly generous nature of the settlement became clear to MPs ten years later in 2000, at the time of the next review. It transpired that the civil list had built up a huge surplus of £35 million, and as with the Sovereign Grant that followed it, there was no mechanism to reduce the annual amount. Money for the royals can only ever go up, never down.

A report at the time in *The Independent* quoted Treasury officials as saying that the Chancellor, Gordon Brown, was 'considering negotiating with Buckingham Palace the historic convention that the civil list ... is never reduced'. Yet Treasury files now available from 1972 show that the parliamentary counsel who drafted the Civil List Act 1972 recommended a power for MPs to cut the payment if required. This idea was neither pursued by the then Conservative government, nor very far by Gordon Brown, as it turns out.

But within the constraints of this royal ratchet, Tony Blair and Gordon Brown did take a robust line in 2000. The £7.9 million figure would be frozen for another ten years. Furthermore, some expenditure hitherto met by departments would be transferred to the Palace, which in effect did constitute a cut in the civil list.

Even so, there were again hostile comments from backbench Labour MPs. Tony Wright called the inability to cut the budget 'extraordinary'. Dennis Skinner, ploughing the same furrow as ten years earlier, suggested the Prime Minister 'kill two birds with one stone by shipping them [the royal family] off to the millennium dome, where they can have a zone apiece'. The dome was at the time Labour's great white elephant in Greenwich, although it would in time transform itself to become the successful O2.

Jeremy Corbyn asked Tony Blair 'to comment on the possibility of relocating the royal family to some smaller and more modest accommodation in the future'. He was in fact echoing comments of the much respected minister Mo Mowlam, who had called for the royal palaces to be vacated, a remark Tony Blair forced her to retract. Mr Corbyn studiously avoided revisiting the matter during his time as Labour leader although he did cause some controversy at the beginning of his term by refusing to sing the national anthem. So now the Sovereign Grant heads for £100 million a year. Meanwhile the royal household report for the year 2017/18 stated that a surplus of £28.7 million had been generated for that one year alone.

It is worth noting that this is far from the only cost to the public purse attributable to the royals. To this we need to add the security, provided in some cases as nothing more than status symbols even for minor royals that most people have barely heard of, the Ministry of Defence spend on ceremonial duties, and the whole sprawling Lord Lieutenant network. Totted up, the true cost to the public purse stretches well beyond £300 million a year.

On top of that are the substantial incomes from the Duchies of Lancaster and Cornwall, which are pocketed by the Queen and Prince Charles but which seem only to have escaped the 1760 deal on the

Crown Estates because at the time they were insignificant. This is covered in a separate chapter in this book. And of top of that is the cost of the uniquely favourable tax treatment which the royal family enjoys and which thus represents an unnecessary and unjustified loss to the Treasury. Even an improper one.

One huge wheeze available only to the monarch is the exemption from inheritance tax for bequests from monarch to monarch. The Treasury is estimated to have lost out to the tune of between £20 to £25 million, and the Queen personally benefited accordingly, upon the death of the Queen Mother. The calculation is based on the estimate of the value of her estate, which is perhaps as high as £70 million, though we cannot know for certain as uniquely royal wills are not published and Gordon Brown, Chancellor at the time, refused my request for the information. If anything, bearing in mind her fabulous collection of jewels and art, this is likely to be an underestimate.

In this case, even more may have been lost to the taxpayer. After the Queen Mother's death, the Inland Revenue was told that valuable items had been given to her grandchildren back in 1993, so more than seven years before her death and thus ruling out the application of death duties which would otherwise have been payable. Yet these items of jewellery were all found in one of her cupboards after her death. The Inland Revenue decided to let it go.

Naturally, what is held in trust by whomever is monarch but which belongs to the nation is rightly automatically exempt from death duties. This would include buildings such as Buckingham Palace and treasures such as the crown jewels and the Royal Collection. But wrongly exempt is everything else when passed from monarch to heir. The argument advanced is that inheritance tax should not be applied to private assets so as to enable each monarch to live in the appropriate manner fit for a king or queen.

But why should inheritance tax not be applied to a monarch's personal property, just as it is for every other person in the country? And if it were applied it would in any case barely make a dent in the enormous private wealth of the Queen. But even if it did, the provision of numerous state-owned palaces and a generous Sovereign Grant hardly suggests that the monarch would not be able to live 'in an appropriate manner'.

A fair comparison might be with the Prime Minister of the day. Nobody is suggesting that the holder of this office needs a minimum level of private wealth to be able to do their job properly. They could in fact be quite poor, for the state rightly provides relevant support: a reasonable but not excessive salary and expenses allowance; an official residence in Downing Street; and a country house to be able to entertain, Chequers, held by the state and available to each new Prime Minister.

There is also the small matter of the law. The Crown Private Estates Act 1862 made it very clear that tax was to be applied, as it was to everyone else, in respect of land. The Solicitor-General in 1910, Sir Rufus Isaacs, was certain that this meant inheritance tax, or 'estate duty' as it was then known, should be applied to private royal possessions such as Balmoral and Sandringham. It never has been.

It is worth considering the varied approaches taken by monarchs to the question of income tax. Queen Victoria paid this when it was reintroduced in 1842. Her son, Edward VII, when he ascended the throne in 1901, argued, behind closed doors of course, that he should be exempt, but this was resisted by the then government, as it was when he tried again in 1904. Significantly, they rejected the notion that Edward was legally entitled to claim Crown Immunity from taxation. This was, they ruled, not a prerogative right. Yet the Palace has continued to insist through to the present day that the Sovereign is not legally liable to pay income tax, capital gains tax or inheritance tax.

The original exemption of the monarch had been a simple practical one. When the monarch in the distant past had been personally responsible for taxation matters, there was little point in a king taxing himself, any more than it would make sense for the government today to tax itself. The Edward VII ruling did not put the matter to bed, however, and royal income tax was ended as part of a somewhat grubby deal between the next King, George V, and Prime Minister Lloyd George to win royal support for the creation of a large number of Liberal peers to force the radical People's Budget through Parliament.

As part of that deal, George V would henceforth pick up the bill for royal travel abroad. The consequence of this is that he only ventured abroad three times in his 26-year reign: to the Indian durbar in 1911, to Paris in 1914, and to Belgium and Italy in 1922. At about the same time as the deal was agreed, the Solicitor-General concluded that the King was liable for estate duty on Balmoral and Sandringham, but nothing was done to enforce this.

In the First World War, George V offered to reinstate the monarch's payment of income tax, but this was not taken forward by the government. The King did however hand back £100,000 from wartime civil list savings.

After that, it was downhill for quite some time. In 1921, the Prince of Wales, the somewhat grasping future Edward VIII, won a specially reduced tax liability. As a result he had managed to stash away around a million pounds by the time he became king in 1936.

At the time of the great depression in the early 1930s, George V ceased paying tax on the money he received from the Duchy of Lancaster. Overall in the inter-war period, royal taxes dropped while those for everyone else rose. This dichotomy became even more pronounced during the Second World War. As the country fought for its very survival, and tax levels for the population increased sharply, the entire tax levy on George VI was removed under a 1937 deal with the government. Ask not what you can do for your country, ask what your country can do for you.

When Elizabeth II came to the throne in 1952, the Prime Minister Winston Churchill was determined that the reign should not begin with an argument about money. He and his Chancellor Rab Butler therefore produced a package that looked prudent, but was actually rather generous. Most importantly, and not made public at the time, they decided that the Queen should pay no tax on her income from investments. Monarchs had always paid this up to the accession to the throne of her father, George VI, who wangled out of it, and without any parliamentary discussion, by simply reclaiming tax deducted at source.

In 2001, investment statisticians from Barclays Capital calculated that a £2 million stock market investment made by the Queen in 1952 would, fifty years on, be worth £1.4 billion. If tax had been paid, the residual figure would have been less than £300 million, meaning a gain to the Queen, and a consequential loss to the taxpayer, of over a billion pounds.

The *Sunday Times* Rich List at the time estimated the Queen's worth to be around £250 million, taking into account all the art, jewels and racehorses she personally owned, but excluding those items held in trust for the nation by the Crown. If these investment statisticians were even just a quarter right, that suggests a serious underestimate on the part of the *Sunday Times*.

Others have gone further. The *Mail on Sunday* in 2001 calculated that the Queen was worth £1.15 billion, with her investment portfolio valued at £500 million. Her stamp collection alone was put at £100 million. Phillip Hall, in his definitive book *Royal Fortune*, describes her as 'without doubt the wealthiest person in Britain'. The American magazine *Fortune* concluded in 1988 that the Queen was the fourth richest person in the world.

Whatever the 2001 figure was, it is a safe bet to assume it has increased substantially since then and there can be little doubt that the Queen is a billionaire. No wonder the royal family is so keen to keep its wills secret. If the true figure emerged, people might begin to question the level of public funding that goes into the monarchy.

In fact, secrecy over the royal family's real wealth has been a constant feature down the years. When the 1972 civil list arrangements were being negotiated, papers in the National Archives show the matter was broached by Treasury officials. They were told that there were matters that were 'sensitive', 'embarrassing' and 'not for disclosure', especially not to ministers and MPs. 'There would be an advantage', officials were told, 'in keeping the paperwork provided for other ministers as brief as possible.' An advantage for whom? Not Parliament nor the taxpayer.

When the Chancellor asked for details of how the royals financed their private spending, the Lord Chamberlain Lord Cobbold said he would only tell him on privy counsellor terms, and nothing could be put in writing. It is clear the 1972 discussions were fraught, and there was even a suggestion of turning the monarchy into a government department, a radical but entirely sensible idea. The Queen's response was to threaten to leave Buckingham Palace if this went ahead.

While the 1952 headline figure given to the Queen was kept down for public consumption, other steps were taken to boost her income besides the exemption from taxation for her investments. For example responsibility for the wages of all workers employed on the upkeep of the royal palaces was transferred from the Palace to the Ministry of Works.

The Queen's position was further boosted by changes to taxation policy in 1963 to concentrate on the landowner rather than on the land, which was interpreted as meaning the only tax liability now for Sandringham and Balmoral was local rates. In 1971 the abolition of

Selective Employment Tax removed another tax liability from the Queen. In 1990, the then Chancellor John Major removed Stamp Duty on stocks and share transactions, one of the Queen's few remaining taxes. This was also the year when the civil list rose sharply.

Then in 1992 came the Queen's horrible year, or 'annus horribilis' as she rather oddly described it. The public was not impressed by a series of private revelations about the family, namely of Charles's shabby treatment of his very popular wife Diana, by a run of royal separations and divorces and by intimate photographs of the Duchess of York having her toes sucked by a man who was not her husband.

In 1992 we also saw the fire at Windsor Castle, and not only was the Queen forced to meet the repair bill without recourse to public funds, but such was the public mood that she and Charles were forced to announce that, from 1993, they would start paying taxes like anyone else (though inheritance tax was still excluded for bequests to the next in line). However the new arrangement was to be a voluntary one, an arrangement I am sure many of us would like. For the first time, tax would be paid on investment income, though forty years of a tax-free holiday will have been immensely rewarding for the Queen.

The 1993 Memorandum of Understanding that encapsulated the changes has a clause within it that allows the monarch to give notice to withdraw from the agreement from the following 6 April. An official briefing from the Palace that year stated that 'The Prince of Wales wholeheartedly supports the Queen's decision to pay tax on a voluntary basis … and intends to continue to do so when he is Sovereign.' This was officially reconfirmed in 2013.

In 2002 I initiated the only debate on royal finances that has taken place since the 1993 memorandum was announced, though there have also been occasional ministerial statements when it has been deemed necessary to increase funding.

The Treasury minister who replied, Dawn Primarolo, confirmed that at that point, the taxes to which the royal family had committed in 1993, which of course did not include inheritance tax, had indeed been paid, and at the rate that would apply to everyone else. 'Income tax is paid on all private sources of income,' she said. It is good news that the 1993 agreement is being respected. It would be better, however, and would remove any worries about a possible future backsliding, if the taxes paid were mandatory rather than voluntary. There is really no good reason why this cannot be achieved. In the past it has regrettably been the case that what seemed to be clear requirements to pay tax have not been applied.

The Crown Private Estate Act 1800 allowed the monarch for the first time to own private property and make a will, and in return William Pitt's government exacted the concession that the monarch was liable for tax on private land held. The next iteration, the Crown Private Estates Act 1862, was even more explicit: 'The private estates of Her Majesty, her heirs or successors, shall be subject to all such rates, duties, assessments, and other impositions, parliamentary and parochial, as the same would have been subject to if the same had been the property of any subject of the realm.'

But while local rates, and subsequently council tax, were from 1952 applied to property held privately by the Queen, other land taxes were not, in contravention of the 1862 Act. So there was no tax on farming profits, for example, until 1993. This matter was pursued vigorously by the senior Labour MP Joel Barnett in a 1971 parliamentary committee examining royal finances. Pushed into a corner, the Queen's representatives lamely tried to argue that farming profit was a trade matter, not an estate one.

Joel Barnett would argue in government that the 1862 Act, which had not been repealed or superseded, required the application of capital gains tax, development land tax and capital transfer tax, as well as stamp duty. One would have thought that someone at the Inland Revenue might have wanted to test the royal interpretation, one which was highly beneficial to the monarch and disadvantageous to the public purse, but no. Easier to let the royals be unequal before the law.

There is in fact an argument that much of the Queen's so-called private estate should be returned to the nation anyway. Sandringham, Balmoral and the Osborne estate on the Isle of Wight were purchased by Queen Victoria from monies given to her by Parliament through the civil list. As a result of Albert's pleadings of poverty they were given more than they needed to enable Victoria to carry out her consti-tutional duties, but then hung onto the cash which had been obtained under false pretences, and invested it in property. In addition, in 1889 a parliamentary select committee established that Victoria had diverted a further £824,000 in her retirement from civil list money provided to enable her to carry out her public functions. Likewise, George V diverted civil list money to extend the estate at Sandringham.

Earlier this century the public was rightly horrified when the grisly details of the abuse of expenses by MPs were uncovered. Here were people in high office taking public money designed to support them in their job as elected representatives, and instead using it to provide duck houses, clear ivy off buildings, clean moats, buy luxurious furniture and the rest. For the royals to use civil list money to buy and help amass a private property portfolio is no different: it is fiddling their expenses.

In *Royal Fortune* Phillip Hall estimated that over five reigns, from Victoria to George VI, the monarchs had between them saved over £67 million from the civil list (speaking in 1991 prices, equivalent to around £140 million today), which was then diverted to them personally.

Albert's pleading of poverty was not unique. It is in fact a regular royal tactic. Nicholas Haslam, the interior designer, described by Kitty Kelley in her book as a 'close friend of the royal family', said: 'The royals love to play at being poor ... They turn each other on with their stinginess.' Sometimes it is the royal employees who suffer. Certainly from 2010 onwards, the general dogsbodies had to endure a wage freeze for several years while the income for the Queen increased inexorably.

In other ways, the stinginess becomes unedifying. At Christmas, some staff at Buckingham Palace are rewarded for their loyalty with gifts like jam from the Palace shop. Recipients are advised to check the sell-by dates. The Queen gets a discount on items that are not selling well, or are close to the end of their shelf life. On the occasion of the fire at Windsor Castle, the staff who battled hard for hours to save valuable artworks and artefacts were offered by way of thanks a free tour. Most declined this generous offer. The meanness and poverty pleading is nothing new. In 1919, for example, Sir Fritz Ponsonby, the King's Treasurer, suggested the King was so strapped for funds that he would have to take a taxicab to go to open Parliament.

The multimillionaire Duke of Windsor was like many royals adept at getting others to pay for activities. In a letter to his brother George VI in February 1937, he wrote: 'Thank you for telephoning me last evening ... I think you'll find you don't have to pay for your telephone calls whereas the long distance is terribly expensive from here [France].' In fact, Edward complained about his financial position at every turn. In another letter just after his abdication to his brother dated April 1937, he wrote:

> I did tell you I was badly off which indeed I am considering the position I shall have to maintain and what I have given up. You now ask me to tell you what my private means are but I prefer not to do so ... secondly I am certain it would be a grave mistake, if

the private means of any member of the royal family were to be disclosed to the Select Committee…

In 1962, Princess Alexandra forced the chartered aircraft she was using for overseas royal duties to divert to Vancouver so she could privately visit friends, and then demanded that the taxpayer meet the costs not simply of the aircraft, but also of the warm clothing she decided she needed to have for the visit. In her view this was two complete outfits. The cost of the detour was around £200,000 in today's prices, and the outfits similarly around £100,000. The government coughed up.

In 1969 it was the turn of Prince Philip to plead poverty, publicly complaining in an interview on American television that the royal family would shortly be 'in the red' and he would have to sell a polo pony or two and perhaps move to a smaller house to make ends meet. Even allowing for Philip's quirky sense of humour, this was breathtaking in its sheer nerve. He also volunteered the view that Britain should worry more about 'the deserving rich' rather than 'the hopeless poor'.

But Prince Philip's ridiculous outburst had the desired effect amongst the sycophantic elements in the Conservative Party, so when shortly afterwards they came to power, it was hardly surprising that an early priority was to divert yet more public money to the royals. As Willie Hamilton argued in his book *My Queen And I*, the Tories had decided that the Queen must have whatever she asked for.

Not everyone was convinced. The *Daily Mirror* front page from 16 December 1971 asked: 'Is it right that you should get the extra [money] and keep secret the size of your private fortune. And be free of all tax?' Nobody would deny that if we are to have a royal family, the monarch must have sufficient funds to enable him or her to perform their duties properly, but the trouble arises when any attempt is made to assess exactly what is needed. The committee set up to examine the civil list allocations in 1972 did not try very hard to find out. They accepted at face value the story of cash shortages without even asking to see a full set of accounts.

The royals were at it again in 2002, just one year after Parliament had been told a £35 million surplus had built up in the civil list. 'Revealed: The Queen is facing a cash crisis' was the front-page headline in *The Independent* on 30 May that year. Underneath, the secondary headline stated: 'Royal family may be forced to ask Parliament for more money'. Inside, there was a full page telling us that the Queen was 'strapped for cash'. It referred to the fact that she had inherited from her mother a £4 million overdraft at Coutts. The paper did not think that the huge tax-free inheritance the Queen received would help. It certainly did not help the taxpayer, who is estimated to have lost between £20 million and £25 million as a result of this unique exemption.

Nor did the paper refer to the huge surplus in the civil list that had built up in previous years and which, as it turned out, was not all spent even by the time of the next review in 2011. And finally, the paper which told us the Queen was 'strapped for cash' did not refer to her very high ranking in the *Sunday Times* rich list, as one of the richest people in the country. It is to be hoped that the journalists responsible for this appalling piece received some recognition from the Palace, for I doubt they would have received very much from other journalists. But it does show the spinning power, and the sheer brass neck, of the royals.

So much concerning the royal family was little short of random. The Queen Mother, for example, had been allocated an annual sum of £70,000 in 1952, rising to £643,000 by the turn of the century. How were these figures arrived at? Nobody knows, and they have all the hallmarks of a finger in the air. Prince Philip, who retired in 2017, now at the age of ninety-nine still receives £359,000 a year direct from the Treasury to enable him to carry out his duties, although such duties have now ceased. We are even asked to believe that this is not enough, with a Palace flunkey briefing the media that as the sum had not changed since 1992, it was now insufficient and the Queen had to make up the balance. If this was meant to evoke sympathy, it merely managed to generate incredulity.

Philip was born on a Corfu kitchen table and slept in an orange box. When he married the future Queen, he was earning £11 a week as a Lieutenant in the Navy, and had no family wealth to inherit. Yet by the turn of the century he was estimated to be personally worth £28 million, thanks to the generosity of the taxpayer, or at least the generosity of successive governments on behalf of the taxpayer.

And it is not just Philip who has benefited in this way. A *Mail on Sunday* analysis in 2001 put the individual wealth of every single senior member of the royal family – the Queen, Philip, Charles, Anne, the Queen Mother and even then William and Harry – at more than £20 million. Andrew and Edward were not far behind.

Regular attempts to nail down the private wealth of the Queen and her family have been consistently rebuffed, on the basis that these are private matters. But if that wealth has in part been created by unique tax breaks to the disadvantage of the public purse or from simple exploitation of public money, then the private position becomes a public matter. If the royals want to insist on privacy for their private funds then they should be prepared to end their unique tax status and pay tax in exactly the same way as everybody else – and be accountable for public money in exactly the same way as anyone else who receives it is.

Back in 2008, an opinion poll suggested 57.4 per cent of people believed taxpayers should spend less on the royals, a view implicitly echoed in 2015 polling, where there was majority support from the public to fund only the Queen, Charles, William and Harry. The total cost in 2008 was thought to be around £50 million a year. It is now many times that.

Duchies All Too Original

The Duchy of Lancaster was established as a crown asset when Henry IV ascended the throne in 1399. It comprises 45,601 acres of prime agricultural land, most of the Lancashire coast, a golf course in South Wales, some property in my town of Lewes apparently, and, most profitably of all, the Savoy estate in central London. It is a 'private' estate which passes from monarch to monarch, with the profits providing the Queen with a large income stream, as well as helping to pay for some royal functions.

Logically, it should have transferred to Parliament in 1760 along with the Crown Estates land. The fact that the Crown Lands Act 1702 specifically prevented Duchy of Lancaster land from being sold clearly underlined its public status. It appears to have been overlooked in 1760 either because it was administered separately or simply because at that point it was worth a pittance in royal terms. The Duchy produced only £16 18s 4d in that year, or £16.92 in decimal equivalent. It escaped again in 1830 when further residual income streams were firmly taken over by the government, after strong protests from William IV. With the great Reform Bill on the stocks, the government did not want to alienate the King unnecessarily.

Since then, however, the Duchy's value has ballooned and its holdings are now worth £533.8 million. Profits have soared in recent years, from £12.9 million in 2012 to the 2018 outcome, which produced a profit for the Queen of just over £20 million. Members of her family, who used to receive money direct from the civil list, now receive their handouts from the Duchy's income, thereby avoiding some of the spotlight that used to fall on them. The Queen claims these payments as a deductible expense, though as the rest of her family play no role in the Duchy this is questionable in the extreme. In any case, the result is to reduce significantly the tax she has to pay on her Duchy income.

Although it is termed a 'private estate', the Duchy escapes paying any corporation tax. Here is another example of the royals alternating between private and public status according to what benefits them more in any given circumstance.

Since there appears to have been an oversight in 1760 when the nation secured the Crown Estates, and the Duchy is unable to dispose of assets without Treasury authority, and not only is some money from the Duchy used to fund official duties, but the Duchy also even has its own government minister, it seems clear that it is a public asset, and the profits it generates should go not to the monarch but straight into the public purse. For the monarch to keep them is royal robbery.

If, on the other hand, it is argued that it is indeed genuinely private, then it should be subject to the same rules as any other private estate, notably in terms of taxation. The royal family cannot have it both ways, but the problem is it seems they can and do.

Much of the Queen's so-called private income from the Duchy has gone on investments, tax free from 1952 to 1993. An investigation by a number of news outlets including *The Guardian* in 2017 revealed that the Duchy was investing significant sums in offshore tax havens, including the Cayman Islands. Amongst the companies invested in was BrightHouse, a retailer accused of exploiting thousands of poor and vulnerable individuals, including using hard-sell tactics on people with mental health issues.

Setting an example? Should the Queen really be investing in offshore tax havens? Just another of the questionable ways in which the hugely wealthy royal family minimises its tax payments. © *Daily Mirror*

The Duchy's complex offshore arrangements, laid bare by the publication of the Paradise Papers, have been curiously absent from its published annual statements. No doubt an unfortunate oversight. The Duchy says it gained no tax advantage from its Cayman Island investments. How odd then that the investment managers seem to have gone to so much trouble to create a complex financial web for no extra return when they could have just deposited the whole lot at the nearest branch of Coutts. The Paradise Papers in fact give a rare insight into the Queen's investment decisions. The fog surrounding these is in fact more like one of the famous London pea-soupers of the 1950s, thanks to a special mechanism she has deployed to prevent public scrutiny. She uses a company called the Bank Of England Nominees, which provides anonymity in trading shares. When it publishes its share register, it is an amalgam of all those it represents so it is not possible to ascertain who the true shareholder is for any specific holding.

A 1973 Act of Parliament forced shareholders to identify themselves when holding shares in the name of a nominee. The Queen, who would have been asked to grant Queen's Consent to the Bill, was exempted. Elected politicians such as MPs and councillors, and indeed even unelected ones in the House of Lords, have to declare their financial holdings so the public can have confidence that they are not acting out of self-interest. No such safeguards exist with the monarchy. Indeed, as politicians have become more open and accountable, the royals have become more secretive and unaccountable.

How can we know that the monarch is not using their position to advance their own interests, that information gained from government papers in red boxes is not being used as privileged information to inform investment decisions? While we can perhaps have a good deal of confidence that the present Queen would never act in this way, we cannot assume that this will invariably be the case with every occupant of the throne. As a key figure occupying a public role, the monarch should register their financial interests for public scrutiny, just as MPs have to.

The royals' subtle manoeuvring between what is public and what is private has its most pronounced manifestation with Prince Charles and the Duchy of Cornwall, who have the game down to a fine art. Not least are the advantages secured by this second royal 'private estate' relating to the tax status of the Duchy. Yet if the case for special treatment for the Duchy of Lancaster is dubious, for the Duchy of Cornwall it is threadbare.

The Duchy, which dates from 1337, has landholdings which are extensive and not simply to be found in Cornwall. Indeed, only 2 per cent of Cornwall is owned by the Duchy, and only 13 per cent of its landholdings are in the county. In fact, it owns four times as much land in Devon, including about a third of the Dartmoor National Park. Elsewhere, there is about 160 miles of coastline, lots of rivers and riverbeds, and residential and commercial properties galore. This includes highly valuable London sites such as the Oval cricket ground in Kennington. Extra cover for the Prince, perhaps.

It also claims the Scilly Isles, though this claim is not without controversy. The Duchy's website asserts that the islands have been part of the Duchy since the fourteenth century, but they were not expressly referred to in the 1337 Charter and there are no records showing it was annexed to the Duchy, which has never been able to answer the questions as to how and when the Isles became the property of the Duchy. It seems clear that the failure to incorporate the Duchy's lands in the package of Crown Estates land that was transferred to Parliament in 1760 was for the same reasons that the Duchy of Lancaster land was not included. It was not as a result of a judgement that it was different and so merited being exempted.

From 1842 onwards, the Duchy of Cornwall paid taxes including property tax, land tax and 'other taxes'. Queen Victoria, who generally took a rather more public-spirited and less selfish view than some of her successors when it came to tax, had already agreed that her civil list income should be taxed, and so it was until her death in 1901. Edward VII did not share his mother's approach and by 1903 had managed to wangle out of paying any tax on the civil list, but his son George, by then Duke of Cornwall and Prince of Wales, remained liable to income and supertax in full on income from the Duchy of Cornwall.

In 1913, the Inland Revenue approached the Duchy about submitting valuations and paying a new landlord's tax on income from mineral royalties under the Finance Act 1910. The Duchy objected, maintaining that the Prince of Wales (not, interestingly, the Duke of Cornwall) enjoys the same prerogatives as the King. The particular relevant point being deployed here is to suggest that the Prince of Wales, like the King, was not bound by legislation unless it specifically referred to him. In other words, he benefited from Crown Immunity.

The academic John Kirkhope has diligently produced a detailed study of the Duchy of Cornwall in his thesis *The Duchy of Cornwall – A Feudal Remnant?* in which he points out:

> The solicitor to the Board of the Inland Revenue maintained the Prince of Wales is a subject of the Crown albeit the 'first of His Majesty's subjects' and the estate is a 'private estate'. In those circumstances the King could not choose to suspend an Act of Parliament as it applied to that 'private estate'.

In other words, there is only one King and therefore only one person who can benefit from Crown Immunity. He goes on to quote the 1688 Bill of Rights: 'That the pretended Power of Suspending of Laws or the Execution of Laws by Regal Authority without consent of Parliament is illegal.' Despite the fact the Inland Revenue had gone into the matter of the Duchy's status quite exhaustively and concluded there was no case for its exemption from taxes, the government's law officers, in a very short ruling, and one without any explanatory arguments, disagreed, and that was that. Their view was reconfirmed in 1921.

When Parliament looked at the matter some fifty years later, MPs were not impressed. A select committee examining the civil list stated:

The income from the Duchy of Cornwall is exempt from all taxes. The exemption is based on an opinion given by the Law Officers of the Crown in 1913 and again in 1921. The tax exemption apparently arose from 'the peculiar title of the Prince of Wales to the Duchy of Cornwall'. The judgement was very short and a little inscrutable. It did not say what was peculiar or special. Nevertheless, the Inland Revenue accepted it without question. There has been no further explanation or elucidation.

One might ask how it is that this 'private estate', like the Duchy of Lancaster, manages to be exempt from corporation tax. What is less opaque is the fact that this exemption represents a huge tax break for the commercial enterprise that is the Duchy, and therefore for the royal family. The Duchy argues that it is 'not subject to Corporation Tax as it is not a separate legal entity for tax purposes'. This is something of a self-fulfilling assertion lacking in any explanation. It merely says corporation tax is not paid because it is not payable. The escape clause comes in the last three words of the quote, which accurately capture the illogical and indefensible position that presently applies in tax terms. For, in other regards, the Duchy most certainly is a separate legal entity.

First and foremost it continues to exist when there is no Duke of Cornwall, which clearly proves that the Duchy has a legal entity separate to that of the Duke. During such times, the Duchy reverts to the Crown, which is obviously a public entity. The separation between Duchy and duke is reinforced by the fact that Charles himself as duke has individual trading arrangements with the Duchy.

For instance, there is the one that covers his property at Highgrove. In a delightfully circular way, Charles pays the full rent to the Duchy, which sounds impressive until you realise that it comes straight back to him personally as Duchy profit without any deductions for tax. Charles has also used Duchy land to grow trees, nurtured and maintained by Duchy employees, the timber from which he then sold to the Duchy for £2.3 million, paid to Charles, again without any tax being deducted.

We have seen the Health and Safety Executive issue an Improvement Notice on the Duchy under the 1974 Health and Safety At Work Act. They were only able to do so because the Duchy is a legal entity. The Notice was not disputed. Similarly, the Environment Agency regularly issues environmental permits to the Duchy, permits that can only be served on a legal entity. The Information Commissioner has ruled that the Duchy is by definition a public body as it carries out public functions, such as its role as harbour authority for the Isles of Scilly. Furthermore, the Information Rights Tribunal in 2010 unequivocally ruled that the Duchy is a separate entity. It concluded:

> Taking into account all the above evidence and other statutory provisions, the practices of the Duchy and the way it has presented itself to the world including Parliament, the differentiation of the Duchy and Duke in commercial and tax matters as well as under legislation and the contractual behaviour of the Duchy, we are led to the conclusion that the Duchy is a body of other person.

Charles will, however, have taken some satisfaction from the decision of the Upper Tribunal's Administrative Appeals Chamber, which in 2016 overturned the decision of a lower court and ruled that the Duchy was not obliged to disclose environmental data, in this case about an oyster farm it controls in Port Navas in Cornwall. It is indisputable, therefore, that the Duchy is a separate entity from Charles himself, and so even if the case is made – and it is certainly a ropey one – that Charles himself has Crown Immunity, the Duchy clearly does not, and yet this is how it is treated, at vast financial advantage to

Charles. Perhaps some determined person at Her Majesty's Revenue and Customs would like to take this up.

In his defence, it is argued that Charles pays income tax so it would be unfair for him to be taxed twice. This looks seductive at first sight, but not upon closer examination. For a start, Charles only pays income tax 'voluntarily', and could therefore stop doing so at any time, an option many of us would like but which is not available to the public at large. The double-taxation argument is flawed in a more fundamental way too. It is standard practice for a company to be taxed on its profits, and then for individual shareholders to be taxed on dividend income. On top of that, the Duchy is exempt from capital gains tax and inheritance tax. The Duchy's own figures show that in 2012, Charles handed over £4,496,000 to the Treasury in tax. He says he pays at the 40 per cent rate, yet the profit that year was £18.3 million. That suggests he has managed to identify expenses of more than £7 million to deduct, thereby leaving the Treasury £2.8 million short. By 2018, profit was up to £21.7 million.

A further tax wheeze for the royal family comes from the interaction between the Crown Estates, whose income falls to the Treasury in the first instance, and the Duchy of Cornwall, where it heads straight to Charles, tax free. It is therefore beneficial for the royal family, and for Charles in particular, for the benefit of doubt in any particular case to be given to the Duchy. Because many of these matters go back to medieval times, it is not always clear when an asset belongs to one or to the other. John Kirkhope lists many of these in his treatise. Disputes have included the claims of the Duchy to parts of Dartmoor forest, the right to gold and silver mines within Cornwall, and the extent to which the Duchy can claim the right to the foreshore within Cornwall.

We should not be surprised that it has been regarded as unseemly to have a public dispute, involving public money, between the Crown and the Duchy, so these matters have invariably been sorted behind closed doors, without parliamentary or judicial oversight, and decided mostly in favour of the Duchy.

One interesting dispute occurred in the short reign of William IV and saw the Crown challenge the entitlements of the Duchy to the Scilly Isles. As there was no Duke of Cornwall at the time and the Duchy had therefore reverted to the Crown, the Crown was technically in dispute with itself. Leaving aside the merits of the argument, this could be seen as a power grab by the Crown in the absence of a Duke of Cornwall.

The Duchy is big business, and becoming much more professional, some might say ruthless, in driving up its profits. These were under £10 million as recently as 2003, yet had more than doubled to £21.7 million by 2018. Under Charles, the Duchy has transformed itself from a somewhat sleepy property company with a mixture of agricultural land and prime London sites to something much more commercially aggressive. As part of this, in 1992 Charles created the 'Duchy Originals' label. The first product was an organic biscuit made from cereals grown on Duchy land. The Prince has a genuine commitment to the environment and to sustainable agriculture, so here was a good way to promote those beliefs and also to add value to the Duchy.

So far, so good. But the biscuits and the other product lines that were developed were marketed with the Duchy's coat or arms, or the Prince of Wales's royal feathers. Here was the use of official marques for a commercial purpose. By way of comparison, the portcullis used for official parliamentary business is carefully protected and any MP or Lord who uses this for their own personal gain risks being censured by the House authorities. Prince Charles's confusion of the official and the commercial was therefore unwise, but may have been just about acceptable when the policy was to transfer all profits to charity. However, by 2008, interest in the Duchy brand was falling off, and the previous year's operating profit of £57,000 turned into a loss of

£3.3 million. As a result, the Duchy brand was in effect rescued by Waitrose, who bought a majority share in September 2009.

Part of the deal, it seems, was the continuing endorsement by Charles, and continuing use of official marques. These are thus now being used to generate profit for a private sector entity, namely the John Lewis Partnership which owns Waitrose. As value is being added to the products by use of official marques, logically Waitrose ought to pay a sum in recognition of that value back to the public purse. Indeed, the Duchy brand is little or nothing except a brand. The vast majority of products do not originate from the Duchy but have merely been endorsed. Naturally the supermarket chain is pleased to able to market the Duchy products with an endorsement from the Prince, but should official symbols be used in this way? Jon Temple, in his book *Living off the State*, certainly thinks not:

> It is highly questionable whether the Duchy … or the Prince really ought to have the right to assign its coat of arms in this way for commercial purposes to a limited company … One could argue that the right to assign use of these logos rests firmly with the Crown and thus Parliament's approval needs to be sought.

The Public Accounts Committee in the House of Commons conducted an inquiry into the Duchy's finances and practices in 2005. This was the first such inquiry for over 600 years, so a review was somewhat overdue. The committee's conclusions called for the direct involvement of Charles in the Duchy management to be ended, saying this created a conflict of interest. It pointed out that there was indeed such a separation in the case of the Duchy of Lancaster and the Queen.

It also drew attention to some dodgy accounting practices, and revealed that amongst the tax-deductible expenses were the costs of employing twenty-eight personal staff – butlers, valets, gardeners and the like. Also included were 'some personal costs of Mrs Parker Bowles', long before they were married. These costs covered staff at her Wiltshire home, her travel, her bodyguards, jewellery, clothes, and stabling for her horses – all again tax deductible. How was expenditure on his Mistress of the Bedchamber in any way a legitimate Duchy expense?

Charles even tried in 2003 to get his polo bills listed as a business expense. It has been a consistent and consistently unedifying feature of his tenure as Prince of Wales that this fabulously wealthy multimillionaire will always try to get someone else to pay for what he wants, whether a rich starry-eyed royalist, an ambitious social climber or the poor benighted taxpayer. The committee called on the Treasury to justify the tax treatment of the Duchy, in particular the exemptions from corporation tax and capital gains tax. It pointedly asked the Treasury whether the arrangements created in 1337 were appropriate in the twenty-first century.

These medieval arrangements included a handy provision whereby the Duchy scooped up the legacy of every person resident in the Duchy who died intestate with no relatives to speak of. A similar arrangement has applied to the benefit of the King or Queen in the Duchy of Lancaster. The monarch used to be able to claim the estate of anyone in the country who had died intestate without any traceable family, but this was otherwise abolished in 1830.

In June 1936 Edward VIII took advantage of this provision to give himself a windfall equivalent to several million in today's terms by transferring virtually the entire contents of the No Kin Investment Fund to his personal account. The Fund had been kept healthy in case any successful hitherto unidentified claimant should come forward.

Edward left just £1,000 in the fund. George VI personally benefited even more, distastefully pocketing the money from service personnel based in the Duchy of Lancaster who died intestate as a result of active service during the Second World War.

The provision, known officially as Bona Vacantia, continues to this day, and covers not just those who have died intestate, but also treasure trove and funds from dissolved companies. Since the 1970s, however, the derived funds are handed over to charity, though 'voluntarily'.

The Duchy of Cornwall received £552,000 from this source in 2012, of which it kept £86,000 or about 15 per cent to cover 'costs'. By contrast, the Duchy of Lancaster received £705,000 in 2005 with just 3 per cent being deducted to cover costs.

The ancient and obscure nature of the Duchy has meant that public accountability is limited and further shrouded in secrecy by the fact that the Duchy audits its own accounts and there is no right of access for the National Audit Office. Indeed, a Duchy memo written in 1936 during a select committee inquiry into the civil list stated: 'What is essential is to keep out audit by the Comptroller and Auditor General [the National Audit Office].'

Edward Leigh, the then chair of the Public Accounts Committee, said at the time his committee's report into the Duchies was published in 2005:

> I cannot understand why these accounts are not subject to the same disclosure requirements as other accounts presented to Parliament. More information and explanation need to be given to readers of the accounts, not the least of which is Parliament. And the best way for Parliament to get that information and explanation is for the Comptroller and Auditor General to be given the power to audit the Duchies' accounts.

Sir John Bourn, then head of the National Audit Office, told the committee that he would like to look at the books, as part of his duty to Parliament. The recommendations landed on the table with a thud which echoed away to be followed by a deafening silence from the government. Charles called the report 'a travesty' and 'fundamentally wrong'. The bottom line is this. If the Duchy lands are public, as I conclude they are, then they should be absorbed into the portfolio of land held by the Crown Estates with the income then going to the Treasury. Charles could then be supported from public funds via the Queen as are other royals. That in fact is in line with a confidential internal government document prepared in 1897, but never followed through.

If, however, the Duchy is regarded as private, then all the unique benefits it enjoys, including tax exemptions and Crown Immunity generally, should cease to apply and the estate should be treated like any other. So we have two 'private estates' which arguably belong to the state but each instead providing millions of pounds of income every year to two of the very richest people in the country, and even exempt from the taxes every other estate has to pay.

Charles has been quoted as saying: 'I think it of absolute importance that the monarch should have a degree of financial independence from the state ... I am not prepared to take on the position of sovereign of this country on any other basis.'

What does this mean? Such independence could be achieved, I suppose, if all public support for the royals ended, but I very much doubt this is what he had in mind. It seems more likely that he is arguing for the opposite – for the state to provide him with copious amounts of public money, free from taxation or other irritations like accountability. We as citizens should worry that our future king has subscribed to a view familiar to autocrats down the ages, more in line with the practices of Henry VIII or Idi Amin.

Costing the Earth

One theme that Charles has returned to again and again is the need to protect the environment, a matter he embraced rather earlier than most and which he seems genuinely to care about, whether it is the damage being wrought by climate change or the serious threat to endangered species.

But just as he apparently sees no conflict between his concern for some animals and his unbridled enthusiasm to hunt or shoot others, so he seems oblivious to the environmental damage he himself is responsible for while he cajoles the rest of us to minimise our green footprint.

How to explain this behaviour? Some would classify it as simple hypocrisy on his part, some as a sort of Orwellian doublethink where he can hold in his mind two inherently contradictory positions at the same time. Perhaps it arrives as a consequence of royal arrogance, where he feels it appropriate to lecture the world at large from on high while believing he has the right to exempt himself from the strictures he seeks to impose on others, just because he is of royal blood, and important royal blood at that.

He has regularly intervened in architectural matters, to defend the countryside or to champion traditional design. He famously derailed the proposed extension to the National Gallery back in 1984, calling the design a 'monstrous carbuncle on the face of a much-loved and elegant friend'. In 2002 he threatened to withdraw his patronage from the National Trust if it proceeded with a design for its new Swindon headquarters which he did not like. And Charles pushed to have the French architect Jean Nouvel elbowed off a £500 million project next to St Paul's Cathedral.

In 2009, he was accused by leading architect Richard Rogers of subverting the planning system when he called in a royal favour to scupper plans for the redevelopment of Chelsea Barracks, by persuading the Emir of Qatar, whose family was behind the development, to abandon their plans. He had also personally lobbied London's deputy mayor, Sir Simon Milton, who had responsibility for planning in the capital.

Yet not all inappropriate development exercised him. In 2011 he infuriated locals in the Truro area by proposing to build ninety-eight mock-Georgian houses and a supermarket equipped with 1,200 parking spaces on farmland next to the town. Then there was his plan a couple of years earlier to build two thousand new homes on Duchy land just west of Bath. This greenbelt land was being used for organically farmed wheat and rapeseed and was home to kestrels and buzzards, hares and deer. Of course, changing farmland into housing land massively increases its value. It really is appalling, as Charles himself might have said.

And let us not forget the Duchy proposal to wipe out a wildlife sanctuary on the edge of Newquay to build a so-called eco-village made up of 200 homes, only a minority of which were planned to be officially 'affordable'. The Cornwall Wildlife Trust took the not unreasonable view that the best way to secure a good eco-result was to leave the land just as it was.

Unsurprisingly, some might say cynically, the Duchy is rather keener to use glossy and comforting pictures of its agreeable buildings, such as its Welsh slate-roofed holiday lets or refurbished farm buildings, for its public image, rather than the industrial sheds and other ugly commercial properties that have featured recently in Duchy developments and which are far more lucrative for Charles.

The Prince also had locals up in arms with the plan he supported for a hugely damaging new harbour development in Penzance. This was opposed by English Heritage, the then local MP Andrew George, and the local town council. When the scheme was put out to consultation, there were 672 objections and just eight responses in favour. It would of course have benefited St Mary's on the Scilly Isles where the Duchy is the harbour authority. The entire project was estimated to cost £62 million, with Cornwall County Council on behalf of the Route Partnership asking for £35 million of government money to enable it to proceed. As it happens, the decision on that fell to me in 2011 as Transport minister. I was horrified by how the scheme had been inflated in scale quite unnecessarily, and by the cavalier damage proposed to Penzance. I refused to make any contribution from the taxpayer until the Route Partnership had come up with a smaller and much more sympathetic scheme, the sort of scheme one might have expected Prince Charles to support. A big sulk from the scheme's advocates followed.

Charles also decided back in 2006 to allow the cultivation of alien Pacific oysters to begin in the Lower Fal Estuary and Helford River in Cornwall, thus providing another handy income stream for the Duchy. The Duchy owns 85 per cent of the stretches of water in question, and the entire riverbed. The problem is that these oysters are highly destructive to the marine environment, a sort of water-based equivalent of Japanese knotweed. They damage the riverbed, kill mussels and provide the sort of threat to indigenous oysters that grey squirrels on land pose to red squirrels.

The stretches of water in question fell within a Site of Special Scientific Interest, an Area of Outstanding Natural Beauty and a special conservation area. In 2008, Natural England warned the businessman given a licence for this operation by the Duchy about the marine damage being caused. It transpired that the Duchy had failed to carry out an Environmental Impact Assessment, as required by law, before issuing the licence. The Duchy tried to palm responsibility off on to DEFRA or some other government body, but Natural England was adamant that as the Duchy was a public body established by an Act of Parliament (the 1337 Charter), it was solely responsible.

Naturally, no prosecution followed and with the passage of time, the fears about the damage these invasive non-native species can do has proved to be sadly accurate. Meanwhile the alien oysters turn up in expensive London restaurants, described as 'sustainable'.

But it is in matters to do with travel where the greatest disconnect comes between what Charles says and what Charles does. The Prince clearly understands the threat from climate change and has publicly articulated well both the extent of the problem and the necessity for urgent and far-reaching action. To be fair, he has taken a number of worthy steps to green activities within his control, but has drawn the line at anything that would affect the choices he personally wants to make.

The 2007 Annual Review, for instance, reported that the Duchy had managed to reduce carbon emissions by 9 per cent. With the exception of his Aston Martin, which was now only covering 100 miles a year, all the Duchy vehicles were running on bio-diesel. By 2008, even the Aston Martin had been converted to run on bio-ethanol produced from surplus wine. Charles was very keen on cleaner alternatives to diesel. On one occasion, when we shared a platform at a Prince's Trust event, he proudly told me, apropos of nothing, that the royal train was now running on used cooking oil. I congratulated him, and meant it, even if the royal train is hugely expensive in terms of cost per mile covered.

Moreover, the Prince in 2007 was by this point urging all his staff to cycle to work, although he had no such plans to do so himself. He also that year committed to using public transport 'where appropriate', though it subsequently appears to have been appropriate on very few occasions.

When it came to energy, the installation of four hydro-powered turbines at Windsor Castle will have helped reduce royal carbon emissions, though, as is par for the course, no royal money was spent on these. Rather they were completely funded by the electricity generating company. It is certainly easier to go green when someone else is paying.

Yet sadly all these small but worthwhile moves pale into insignificance in carbon terms when his flying proclivities are factored in. Aviation is an enormous generator of greenhouse gases, dwarfing any other activity an individual would typically engage in.

For instance, when I flew to Tasmania one year on a commercial flight to help the local campaign against vandalistic forestry, I asked my office to work out how many trees I should plant to offset the carbon emitted by me as just one passenger on the flight. The answer was nineteen, a figure that logically would need to be multiplied by however many hundred were on my plane. In carbon terms, that one flight equated to around half my total carbon emissions for the year.

So it was in 2007, the same year that Charles was taking genuine steps to reduce the Duchy's carbon footprint, that he was awarded the Harvard Club's Global Environmental Citizen Award. What should have been a good-news accolade turned into a bad-news own goal. He decided to fly, at public expense, to Philadelphia to pick it up accompanied by an entourage of twenty others, commandeering the entire first-class cabin. Such bloated arrangements are par for the course. In April 2018, Charles took thirteen Clarence House staff with him to the Commonwealth Games in Queensland, which racked up a bill for the taxpayer of £155,000 in transport costs alone. Perhaps prudence of a sort is kicking in, as on the previous visit to Australia in 2012, his support team numbered eighteen.

On the latest trip, the entourage included a doctor, a dresser, a valet and a travelling yeoman. The responsibilities this particular post entails seem rather eclectic. On this tour, the yeoman was involved in choosing Charles's clothes, which makes you wonder what the valet was doing. Michael Cooney, national director of the Australian Republican Movement, said he thought that the Travelling Yeomen were a Tom Petty tribute band. A previous yeoman in 1999 was captured feeding gin and whisky to the Queen's corgis at Buckingham Palace.

On another occasion, Charles set off round Europe to give a series of speeches on climate change. But rather than use commercial flights or indeed even the train, he commandeered a private jet, adding vastly to the problem he was earnestly lecturing about. The tour included such difficult-to-reach places as Rome, Berlin and Venice. The carbon footprint of the private jet was estimated to be 52.95 tonnes, or five times that of the average person in a whole year. Travelling by commercial airlines would have reduced the emissions by around 93 per cent.

Much of this has earned Charles richly deserved criticism and charges of hypocrisy from the press, and has undoubtedly blunted the environmental message he is aiming to convey. Yet still he turns the tinniest of ears to the world. In January 2020, he met the teenage climate activist Greta Thunberg in Davos. The Prince, we were told, had arrived in the Swiss resort in an electric Jaguar. What we were not told, but which emerged shortly afterwards, was that he had clocked up 16,000 miles in three private jets in the fortnight before, as well as a gratuitous helicopter ride. The jet travel is estimated to have resulted in 162 tonnes of carbon emissions and cost the taxpayer £280,000.

The following month he flew 125 miles by helicopter to Cambridge to make a speech about lowering aircraft emissions. The round trip generated a further 2.4 tonnes of carbon and cost the taxpayer around £12,000. Taking the train or car would have cost less than £100 and emitted less than 0.2 tonnes of carbon. In his speech, Charles urged his audience to 'act quickly to rescue this poor old planet'.

Nor is Charles's aviation footprint limited to the carriage of royal personages. On arriving on Victoria Island on a tour of Canada, the Prince was furious to discover that his favourite shoehorn had been left at the previous stop in Winnipeg by his valet. A Canadian air force jet was the answer. It covered the thousand or so miles gaily burning kerosene, no passengers on board, and was met at the airport by a police convoy, all to reunite Charles with the misplaced item. We can imagine that the valet was given a severe dressing down for his heinous error.

Now any pretence that the Prince should use a means of transport that minimises his carbon footprint has drifted away like so much hot air. Private jets are now the default option, with Charles's predilection reinforced by Camilla. Charles himself vowed not to use British Airways again, declaring their first-class seats deeply uncomfortable. He should try economy! The *Sunday Times* reported that his BA flight in April 2000 to Klosters for a skiing holiday was only the second time ever he had flown abroad using a commercial air service.

In July 2017 Charles ran up a travel bill of £30,414 for a one-day trip on a charter plane to Belgium. Presumably it was not 'appropriate' to take the excellent Eurostar service direct from London to Brussels. That October, Prince Edward and his wife Sophie managed a five-day trip to Brunei for two-thirds the cost, around £21,000, while Charles and Camilla, using the RAF Voyager, burnt their way through £362,149 on the travel for their trip the same month to Brunei, India, Malaysia and Singapore. Overall for the year 2017/18, Charles spent well over £700,000 on those individual journeys costing over £15,000, which are publicly reported. The bill is even higher when those no longer separately identified and which individually cost less than £15,000 are factored in.

Charles also tops the list for travel extravagance again in the latest accounts, managing to burn through £1.3 million in this one year. This is an increase of around a third on the previous year, when £416,576 went on the tour of the Caribbean in March 2019 by Charles and Camilla. Even a trip to nearby France and Greece cost £159,820, but then the RAF Voyager, unlike commercial flights, does not come cheap. But why worry? After all, they are not paying. We are.

The 2018/19 figures show that it is business as usual for the pampered royals: private jets and helicopters instead of commercial flights and timetabled rail services. Grimly, this all led to a doubling of carbon emissions from royal travel in the year, up from 1,687 to 3,344 tonnes.

The Palace argues that trips are undertaken at the request of the government, and indeed they often are, but nobody in government requires the use of private jets and helicopters that massively and quite unnecessarily increase carbon emissions. And certainly nobody has required them to waste £200,000 on private jets in this one year to ferry them between London and their private residences in Scotland.

Prince Charles deserves full marks for spending half an hour of his meeting with President Trump on the occasion of the American's state visit, trying to convince him of the reality of climate change and the need to take action. We can, however, perhaps be grateful that the American President's knowledge of, and interest in, climate change is so sketchy that he is unlikely to have pointed out the hypocrisy of Charles's position.

Charles is also the heaviest user of the royal train, with the Queen really the only other member of the royal family to deploy it. It is an expensive luxury, costing well over half a million a year just to maintain before it even moves. In 2010, he accounted for eleven of the nineteen journeys the train made, the Queen the other eight. The royals took normal trains fifty-two times that same year. The royal train is surprisingly basic and lacking in modern creature comforts. An attempt by the new Labour government in 1997 to find other users for the train when it was not on royal duties soon hit the buffers.

If it was unattractive to potential other users twenty years ago, it is even more so now. In truth, it is operating well past its natural lifespan and there has been talk of retiring it for some years. It has been kept going really for the Queen's benefit. The key decision time will come when Charles succeeds to the throne. Economic logic strongly points to the train being withdrawn at that point and not replaced. However, given Charles's attachment to the train and his cavalier disregard for the impact of his activities on the public purse, we can expect him to argue for a replacement, dressed up as an environmental move.

Inside this country, virtually all the members of the royal family now regularly reach for the helicopter to cover even quite short distances and often where a direct rail service is available. I queried this while Transport minister and was told by officials that 'short single journeys in the helicopter are discouraged by the Royal Household'. You could have fooled me.

In March 2019, Prince Harry, echoing his father, took a helicopter (at a cost of around £6,000 to the taxpayer, compared to £34 for an advance first-class rail ticket) to travel from London to Birmingham (a journey that by rail takes around ninety minutes on a twenty-minute frequency), before two days later telling a packed Wembley Arena to 'wake up' and act 'on the damaging impact our ways of living are having on the world'. He was accompanied on stage by his wife Meghan, who a month earlier had taken a carbon-heavy private jet to indulge in a 'baby shower' event in New York. There are over thirty scheduled daily flights each way each day between London and New York.

Yet Harry and Meghan seemed oblivious to the charge of green hypocrisy. In August 2019, it was revealed that they had taken four private jets in eleven days, just weeks after Harry had both flown to a Google summit in Italy to warn of the terrifying dangers of climate change, and used the columns of *Vogue* to call for urgent action to save the planet.

Unsurprisingly, Harry and Meghan ran into a good deal of adverse comment for what was widely viewed as hypocrisy. The Prince lamely replied to this by saying that he only 'rarely' used private jets, which is an interesting recalibration of that adverb, given their recent itinerary.

We then had Sir Elton John, who had paid for two of the flights, weighing in to defend them. The private jets were necessary to limit press intrusion, he claimed, as reported on the front page of a number of papers. The singer famously tweaked his song 'Candle in the Wind', originally written about Marilyn Monroe, to refer to Harry's mother, Princess Diana, at her memorial service in Westminster Abbey. Perhaps he could now do the same for her son, dropping 'Bennie' and instead giving us 'Harry and the Jets'.

Shortly afterwards, in a bit of sibling rivalry, William and Kate and their children were captured alighting from a £73 budget FlyBe flight from Norwich to Aberdeen.

Officially, we are asked to believe that the royal household carefully weighs up the options for each journey, balancing matters such as safety, value for money, and the length of the journey. A minority of the royal family, including the Queen and Princess Anne, do seem to do this, but most clearly do not.

The indisputable fact is that most members of the royal family have no compunction about using very expensive forms of transport when much cheaper alternatives are available, and no compunction about leaving a huge carbon footprint while lecturing others on the need to tackle climate change. It is an attitude that combines arrogance and hypocrisy in equal measure. Nor do the royals mind charging the taxpayer for journeys most people would regard as private, for example, to travel to their private holiday homes each year.

Challenging Charles for the dubious honour of the royal who, per mile, costs the taxpayer most and who emits the most carbon is Prince Andrew. In 2005, the National Audit Office, normally sober and careful with its public comments, produced an official report that was a blistering attack on his travel predilections. It revealed that in just twelve months, the Duke of York ran up an expense sheet totalling £325,000 on helicopters and planes. His defence was that the train was 'too unreliable', hence for example a £3,000 bill to take a helicopter from London to Oxford that year.

The Palace response when such excesses are queried? 'The Duke has also used public transport in the past.' Is that the best line they can come up with? Perhaps it is. Andrew's attitude to the public purse is typified by a trip he made to India in 2012. Instead of taking up the offer of staying at the British High Commissioner's luxury Delhi residence, as Charles had done on a previous visit, Andrew insisted on checking in to the Maharaja Suite at the Leela Palace, just about the most expensive hotel accommodation in the city. The Foreign Office should have shown some backbone and refused to pay. Meanwhile, Sarah, by then his ex-wife, was tweeting in support about his 'gruellingly busy trip'. Yes, I really do not see how he coped.

Andrew even brazenly calls on public money to enable him to pursue his golfing interests. In June 2006 the government finally gave me the information I had been pushing for regarding Andrew's use on two occasions in 2004 of Ministry of Defence 32 Squadron aircraft.

The first 'official duty' involved his attendance at a meeting of the Royal and Ancient Golf Club in St Andrews, which cost the taxpayer £4,686. Sir John Bourn, the then head of the NAO, noted that a return air flight to London was available for £254, but taking that would have meant Andrew could not have completed the eighteen rounds of the course. He noted acidly that the Duke's next royal engagement was four days later.

The second occasion was his attendance at a meeting of the Royal Portrush Golf Club in Northern Ireland. On each occasion he also attended an event nearby, which, it was uncharitably suggested, was a device to enable the whole cost to be charged to the government. In fact, a contribution of £636 was made towards each flight to defray costs, though naturally not by Andrew, but rather by the Royal and Ancient.

On the second occasion, in a display of shocking discourtesy, he arrived at the royal garden party where he was the key royal several hours after the event had begun, having first played a round of golf. Over the years, there has for Andrew been a curious overlap between royal tasks to be undertaken and the proximity of golf courses. Just months after the blistering NAO report, he used the Royal Flight to visit Orkney where once again he managed to take in a round of golf. Par for the course.

In 2009, he racked up a bill of some £2,000 for a helicopter to take him 113 miles from Windsor to a golf course in Kent where a party was taking place. He also visited the Royal Cinque Ports Golf Club in

Deal, where he spoke exclusively about golf before leaving around an hour later. A spokesman claimed it was 'an entirely justifiable expense'.

As with golf, so with tennis. In 2018 Prince Edward took a private jet at an estimated cost of £10,000 to travel from Tamworth to Bournemouth. He then nipped along to Poole to visit a luxury yacht company, Sunseeker International. A first-class turn-up-and-go rail ticket from Tamworth to Poole would have cost £254. The next day he visited the Hyde Real Tennis Club, before making the 67-mile journey home by royal helicopter. The M3 and M27 would have got him back in under an hour and a half, as was equally the case when he ostentatiously flew into Eastbourne for a lunch in 2009. The town is served by a half-hourly train service to London with the journey taking around eighty-five minutes.

The royals have form going back some distance. When Prince Philip sailed off for months aboard the royal yacht *Britannia* in 1956 on what was rumoured to be largely a 'wenching expedition', he racked up a bill of at least £2 million. The cost was increased by his demand for a 'commando raft' to unload his Rolls-Royce at places where there were no car-docking facilities. He also travelled with his own sports car. The royal yacht ate up another million pounds of public money the following year when Princess Margaret commandeered it for forty-four days for her honeymoon. As she lounged on deck sipping her cocktails and taking in the sun, it would be nice to think she spared a thought for those poorly paid British servicemen who had suffered a deduction in wages in order to club together for a wedding present for her.

So the abuse of public money is not new, but it has got markedly worse. Over the last twenty years, we have seen a steady stream of stories in the newspapers, revealing incident after incident where private jets and helicopters have been gratuitously used. As Kevin Maguire the *Daily Mirror* journalist put it to me: 'The royal family wants to travel on magic carpets.' Air Miles Andy is a well-established moniker, joined now by Air Miles Eddie. Heavily critical pieces in the press have been followed by outrage from public and politicians alike. Yet it has all simply washed over the royals, who blithely carry on as before.

There is no doubt if a politician splashed out public money on themselves in this way, they would face opprobrium, and rightly so. We can recall the dent in the credibility of the then Deputy Prime Minister John Prescott when the label 'Two Jags' was attached to him. He too was busy lecturing people on climate change. Yet the cost to the taxpayer and to the planet of running a Jaguar is a tiny fraction of the cost of a helicopter or private jet. If John Prescott, or indeed any minister, had used a helicopter at public expense to make a short trip to be able to play a round of golf as Prince Andrew has, they would have been run out of office. Of course, Prince Andrew cannot be run out of office because he has not been democratically elected. He is a hereditary fixture and we are stuck with him.

The only real response from the royal family to the torrent of negative travel stories has been to attempt to bury bad news by choking them off. Twenty years ago, the annual list that was published itemised all journeys costing more than £500. By 2010, the threshold had been raised to £10,000. The figure was upped again in 2016 to £15,000, conveniently hiding all those gratuitous helicopter journeys, 202 of them in fact that year, or around four a week, as well as forty-three charter flights that now slip in just under the bar. As most journeys by royal train cost just over £15,000, can we expect the reporting threshold to be raised to £20,000 soon?

They have also adopted the technique perfected by the Blair government of choosing the time and method to release information to try to minimise coverage. So, in 2017, the royal accounts were issued on the day of the funeral of Countess Mountbatten, attended by the Queen and Prince Philip. In 2018 they topped this by choosing a day that coincided with the high point of Prince William's Middle East tour, when all the royal correspondents were out of the country. That same day the Queen cancelled an engagement due to illness. There is only so much space for even royal stories in our papers, and as a result, a lot of embarrassing information did not make it into the press. In 2019, however, the tactic did not work. The royals may have thought that the myriad antics of Boris Johnson would give enough cover for the release of their annual report, but even Boris and his domestic disputes could not keep the multimillion-pound bailout for Prince Harry's new residence at Frogmore Cottage off the front pages.

This example shows very clearly that royal extravagance is not simply limited to travel. It applies to any area of life, in fact, where the bill can be offloaded on to the public, and none more so than when it comes to the royal estate. The portfolio held in trust for the nation comprises, as well as Buckingham, St James's and Kensington Palaces, Windsor Castle, the Royal Mews and Paddocks at Hampton Court, Holyroodhouse in Edinburgh, and a staggering 296 'grace-and-favour' properties, most let out rent-free to distant relatives or Palace employees. This list does not include the many private properties held by the royals. The cost to the public purse of maintaining this vast swathe of properties is naturally very considerable, particularly when substantial upgrades are identified.

Until the end of George VI's reign, the monarch was required to fund the upkeep of Buckingham Palace entirely from the civil list. Yet by 2016, the government was agreeing on behalf of the nation that public money should be used to foot the entire bill for a no-expense-spared £359 million revamp of Buckingham Palace. The Queen was reported to be 'fully supportive' of the project. I imagine she was. It was waved through the Commons by a small group of MPs who took just thirteen minutes to approve the plan. Only the SNP representatives objected, and then only to the method of funding, but not to the principle of all this public money being used.

It is interesting to contrast this with the last time there was major expenditure on a royal palace, namely that which was required to restore Windsor Castle after the serious fire there in 1992. Sir Peter Brooke, speaking on behalf of the government on that occasion, blithely said they would be more than happy to pay for the restoration from public funds, but he did not reckon on the popular outrage that this idea generated.

Janet Daly, writing in *The Times*, summed up the public mood succinctly: 'When the castle stands it is theirs, when it burns down it is ours.' A hasty way forward was landed upon. Buckingham Palace would open its doors to tourists for a few weeks every year, and the money raised from some pretty steep entrance fees would be used to pay for the restoration. It was a neat solution that avoided further public money being committed, and also allowed a peek inside the Palace for those who wanted to pay for the privilege. And it was successful. In the five years from 1993, £25.9 million was raised.

But hang on, over twenty years later, in 2019, the doors are still open and money is still flowing in. The restoration of Windsor was paid for long ago so what is happening to the money now? It transpires that it was diverted to pay for the restoration of art works in the Royal Collection, which may be a worthwhile cause, but the public at large might have expected this money instead to be used to keep down royal calls upon the public purse. Naturally there was no debate about the options before this one was undemocratically selected. The Public Accounts Committee in 2001 asked who had decided that income from visitors to Buckingham Palace should go towards the Royal Collection. They were told that no approval had been sought for this decision 'because

The taxpayer is facing a bill for £359 million for an upgrade of Buckingham Palace while the Queen, one of the richest people in the country, contributes nothing. Meanwhile she pockets the millions in admission fees from visitors. It makes the £2.4 million of taxpayers' money being spent for Harry and Meghan on Frogmore Cottage look like small change. © *Daily Mirror*

the income belonged to the Queen'. As the Palace performs a public function and its upkeep is paid for by the taxpayer, it would seem clear that in fact the money belongs not to the Queen but to the Treasury.

One might have thought that years of income at this level from ticket sales would mean that the Royal Collection was now fully restored, but Sir Alan Reid told the Public Accounts Committee in 2013 that that was still where all the money was going. Cynics might suggest that this looks rather more like a slush fund. It is perhaps also worth recording that the Royal Collection is a public asset, held in trust by the monarch, though Prince Philip disputed this in a television interview in 2000 when he asserted that the Queen was 'technically at liberty to sell' masterpieces from the collection. Perhaps we should rename it the National Collection before any action is taken to advance this royal annexation.

In any case, the Palace has continued to pocket the money from entrance fees to see the collection, as well as the profits from the mugs and other artefacts visitors can buy. The collection is extensive and despite much fanfare about the opening in Buckingham Palace of the £20 million Queen's Gallery to display works, only 0.1 per cent of the collection is ever on display to the public. Its value is difficult to determine, but could easily be as much as £20 billion. The six hundred Leonardo da Vinci drawings it holds are alone probably worth about £5 billion.

It is alarming that the need to catalogue the collection properly seems to have been a relatively recent idea. The then Chancellor, Gordon Brown, told me in 2000 that there was 'a computerised inventory of the Royal Collection that identifies assets held by the Queen as Sovereign and as a private individual'. Yet two years later, the Treasury minister Dawn Primarolo told me in a letter that an inventory of the collection had only been 'substantially completed'.

One might ask why the income from ticket sales to enter Buckingham Palace, or to visit the Queen's Gallery, is not being used to offset the cost of the extensive and expensive refurbishment that has been agreed for the building, rather than resorting to the further diversion from the public purse of income from the Crown Estates. One might also query why the refurbishment cost itself has rocketed since the idea was first mooted.

In 2007, Sir Alan Reid warned that tiles and bits of stonework were falling off the building, and said an extra £1 million was needed to fix the problem. By 2008, the Palace estimated that the backlog of repairs to the occupied, that is to say the publicly maintained, palaces would require between £32 and £55 million to be spent by 2015. This, note, was for all the palaces – not just Buckingham Palace – which, in 2010, was identified as needing £10 million. In his evidence in 2013, Sir Alan suggested that the new Sovereign Grant should allow, if the diversion of 15 per cent of the Crown Estates profit remained constant, 'major inroads' to be made into both the maintenance backlog and the interior furnishings.

In 2016, the then Prime Minister David Cameron and the Chancellor George Osborne were of the view that an extra allocation of £50 million would be enough to deal with the problem, but then they were replaced by Theresa May and Philip Hammond, who got taken for £359 million by the Palace who could not believe their luck. Now money is being spent on the building as if there is no tomorrow, with little concern about value for money. It will not be surprising if they come back for even more in due course.

So while the taxpayer signs off £359 million, the Palace continues to pocket all the lucrative stream of entrance fees to the building, to other royal palaces and to the Royal Collection. Admissions to Buckingham Palace alone brought in £10.35 million in 2017. Total admission income for the various buildings reached £181 million over the five years to 2017. To paraphrase Janet Daly, it is theirs when it is an income stream, it is ours when it needs to be repaired.

The refit of Buckingham Palace is an extreme example, but it is by no means a unique one. Indeed it seems that almost every time there is a change of royal in one of the public homes they occupy, there is an obligatory refurbishment. When Prince Charles moved into Clarence House after the death of the Queen Mother, over £3 million of taxpayers' money was used to bring the interior up to a standard he deemed appropriate. His contribution towards the decoration costs was

£78,000 including VAT. Despite receiving £643,000 a year from the state, the Queen Mother had paid no rent on the building.

A highly favourable rent arrangement was also in place for Prince Michael of Kent. The Michaels moved into an apartment in Kensington Palace in 1978 on a rent-free basis courtesy of the Queen, having pleaded poverty. 'We live at home on yoghurt and cornflakes,' Princess Michael said at the time. The following year, they bought an eight-bedroom country house in Gloucestershire for £300,000, valued at £5 million by 2000. That year, the House of Commons was assured that the Michaels, who were not undertaking any royal duties, were contributing £3,500 a year towards maintenance. Letting agents at the time estimated the commercial rental value could be as high as £500,000 a year.

By 2002 the rent paid had crept up to £69 per week. Under intense public pressure, not least from MPs who described his occupancy as 'the grandest housing benefit scheme in the country', Prince Michael conceded he would have to move towards, but not reach, a market rent.

In 2005 we discovered that Prince Andrew had been able to lease the thirty-room Royal Lodge at Windsor, along with seven cottages and a hundred acres of land, at a huge discount. He paid just £1 million for a 75-year lease. At the same time brother Edward had agreed a rent for the 57-room Mansion House at Bagshot Park in Surrey, sitting within fifty acres of land, for well below the market price. This was fixed at £90,000 a year, compared to the £720,000 it was estimated it would reach on the open market. In addition, the Ministry of Defence paid half the costs of a £3 million refurbishment, although it had been vacated by the MoD back in 1996.

In 2000, a building firm employed by Edward to handle repairs to the house went into receivership, blaming Edward's 'dithering' for their demise. Eighty-five people lost their jobs. Edward had set up a separate company to oversee the renovation project, Eclipse Nominees. The only obvious reason for such a move would have been to enable him to liquidate the company and so avoid paying any bills due.

The National Audit Office examined these cases and concluded that the Crown Estates had behaved appropriately. One crucial consideration, it seems, was that the Queen could simply have designated the properties as grace and favour, and the Crown Estates might have received nothing at all. The Crown Estates also came to a deal with Princess Alexandra, the Queen's cousin, where she was to pay an annual sum of £10,500 for the Thatched House Lodge in Richmond Park, a grand dwelling which came with a gardener's cottage, stables and summerhouse. The market rental is estimated at the time to have been £85,000. Both properties are in the portfolio of the Crown Estates, a body charged with maximising the return for the taxpayer from its holdings.

Scroll forward to 2017 and we find £24 million being allocated for a three-storey building in the grounds of Kensington Palace, one storey above ground and two below. This, incidentally, was to rub shoulders with the 323-year-old Grade I listed Queen Anne's Orangery designed by Sir Christopher Wren. This is just the sort of scheme we might have expected Prince Charles to become exercised about and describe as 'appalling', but he has been strangely silent. The building also contravenes the planning policy of the local council, which rules out two-storey basements. Permission to build was granted in September that year.

Subsequently, Harry and Meghan decided that they wanted to live elsewhere, and £3 million was allocated to refurbish Frogmore Cottage for them, a ten-bedroom property on the Windsor estate. The papers and the public were outraged. For once, deference was replaced by some hard and entirely appropriate questions.

Why should the public pay for the move of Harry and Meghan from the secure and entirely adequate quarters they enjoyed at Kensington Palace to Frogmore Cottage just because they were, as alleged in the tabloids, falling out with William and Kate? And if they did have to move, given that Harry has amassed at least £20 million in terms of personal wealth, why could he not pay for this relocation? And why should the public purse pay for the huge extra security costs that this move would generate, and that would have continued for as long as they were there?

Richard Kay in the *Daily Mail* also pointed out that over the previous eighteen months, Meghan had amassed new jewellery worth an estimated £600,000. She now boasts a 91-piece collection including seven necklaces, twenty-three bracelets, twenty-six rings, and thirty-five pairs of earrings. The pair did not seem short of cash.

Meanwhile, even those properties regarded as private have benefited from public largesse. The government has picked up the bill for the heating at Balmoral, for example, on the basis that while there, the Queen is still working, going through her red boxes. The same argument presumably explains why the public pays for the mass movement of staff north from Buckingham Palace to serve the monarch on holiday in her private capacity at Balmoral.

The royals have also literally been costing the earth in another way, too. Like any large landowner, they have benefited hugely from the operation of the Common Agricultural Policy whose rules reward the mere possession of land. An analysis by Greenpeace in 2016 revealed that the Queen was one of the top recipients of EU money, with her Sandringham farmland alone coining in £557,707 that year, with a similar sum every year. On top of that the royals have been keen to look for other public money sources they can tap into, including applying to the Forestry Commission for a grant of £300,000 for fencing work.

There is even a scheme to offload most of the costs of the Maundy Money the Queen hands out every year. This ceremony, held on the day before Good Friday, derived from the washing of the feet of the poor by Jesus. But by the eighteenth century, British monarchs had decided that handing out specially minted coins was preferable to washing feet. The Royal Household pays face value for the coins that the Queen distributes, which, given that these are pennies and the number of recipients is linked to the age of the monarch, is hardly going to break the bank, even with the Queen at ninety-four. The taxpayer, however, pays for the cost of the minting. It is not difficult to assess which is the more expensive. In 2002 I asked the Treasury for the cost of manufacturing the coins, but was unconvincingly told that this was commercially sensitive.

One huge cost to the public purse comes from the security allocated to protect the monarchy. No figures for this are ever published, as it is argued that to do so would give useful information to those with malign intent. While it is sensible for this reason not to break down the cost by individual protected, it should be perfectly possible to provide an overall figure. What we do know is that the cost is substantial. Estimates vary, but all suggest the annual bill is in excess of £100 million. Dai Davies, a former head of royal protection and Chief Superintendent of the Metropolitan Police, told me that over 450 personnel are deployed to protect the royals, a huge drain on police resources when numbers of front-line officers have been cut back. On overseas trips, protection officers will fly out to reconnoitre the places to be visited. A second team will then go out to check, and a third team will accompany the royal in question. In all cases, the officers hold the rank of Inspector or above, fly business class and are entitled to claim an allowance for extended hours. The question of providing security for Harry and Meghan in Canada and the United States has proved a particularly charged one.

We live in an uncertain world, and there is no question that it is right to provide protection for key people in society, including of course senior members of the royal family, who might be targets for deranged individuals. Yet we are entitled to ask whether the routine and very expensive protection afforded to minor royals is really necessary. That was certainly the view of Sir John Chilcot who, in 2000, had been asked by the then Home Secretary Jack Straw to conduct a review into the ballooning costs of royal security.

Sir John's recommendations latched in particular onto the costs of protecting Prince Edward's sprawling property, Bagshot Park, which even back then were estimated to be £1 million a year. He suggested civilians could be used rather than police officers, and that Edward should bear some of the cost. Naturally, the Prince opposed this, preferring the taxpayer to meet the entire bill.

Sir John also recommended scaling back on the provision of police escorts. This followed the public outrage when in May 1999, traffic in central London was held up on several occasions so a party of unimportant royals could have their passage to the Chelsea Flower Show eased. The Duke and Duchess of Gloucester, Prince and Princess Michael of Kent, and Princess Alexandra each had a team of police outriders and police back-up. The scene, captured for posterity, was more akin to what might be found in a country ruled by some self-important despot, except here the banana republic was replaced by a banana monarchy.

It seems the less important the royal, the more they want to flaunt their royal status. The Queen has regularly travelled round London without outriders, and for years Prince Philip drove round the capital on his own in a black cab. In 2008, Dai Davies, who had recently retired as head of the Royal Protection Squad, publicly called for a review, pointing out some royals had 24/7 protection, while others had none. The level afforded did not seem to have been based on any rational assessment. Dai Davies told me: 'I don't know of any real threat to any minor royal over twenty-five years.' This has not stopped round-the-clock protection being provided for barely known royals like Princess Alexandra. Allowing for shift work and holidays, that level of protection requires the deployment of twelve full-time officers, which alone pushes costs up to around the half-a-million mark.

The cost of such protection comes out of the Scotland Yard budget, meaning less is available to tackle serious social problems like knife crime, and in 2010 Scotland Yard expressed its concerns at having to provide cover for royals such as Princess Eugenie as they partied the night away. Protection that year was being given to twenty-two royals. One royal bodyguard told the *Daily Mirror*: 'Looking after the Duke of York's daughters when they are out nightclubbing or swanning around the world does stick in the throat of some Royal Protection Officers.' Another added: 'We feel we've been reduced to mere chauffeurs and gofers.'

The protection that was put in place for Eugenie and Beatrice was reported in the *Sunday Times* to be the result of pressure from Andrew. In the absence of any real threat, this looks more like a question of securing a status symbol. Both women are non-working royals, as are their cousins Zara Tindall and Peter Phillips, who have always managed perfectly well without protection. Their mother, Princess Anne, apparently considered it both unnecessary and a waste of public money.

Yet if anyone was going to demand extra security you would think it would be Anne, who was subject to a kidnapping attempt in 1974. Her car was forced to a halt by another vehicle on the Mall, and a man appeared with a gun. It was no light-hearted affair. Both her police protection officer and her chauffeur were shot. The gunman demanded that she get out the car but, showing admirable courage and a cool head, she simply refused. The stand-off lasted a good ten minutes with the gunman eventually being overpowered.

Of course the royal family, now and in the past, is in one way no different to any other. All families have heroes and villains, and over the years there have been royals who have taken their duty to serve the public seriously, including being prudent with public money entrusted to them, and those who have been rather more venal in nature and been much more interested in serving themselves than serving the public.

The difference between the royal family and most other families is the scale of opportunity both for public service or for self-aggrandisement. And there is another crucial factor. The sense of deference in the country towards the royal family, and of course the fact that they cannot – unlike politicians – be removed from office, must make temptation for those of the more venal variety that much greater.

We are entitled to expect Parliament, the government and especially the Treasury to take much firmer action to protect the public interest.

Charity Begins at Home

What do you do if you are Prince of Wales? It is a unique role for which there is no job description. The glib answer is that you prepare yourself to take over as king, an event that could happen at a moment's notice and on any day.

Or, if you are Prince Charles, you can begin your preparation while you are still a child, and find yourself still waiting after you have long since passed normal retirement age. For almost everyone else, their working life has come and gone. For you, it is seventy and still counting.

A traditional royal response has been to associate yourself with worthy organisations, ideally uncontroversial ones, and to 'do good works'. In this vein, Prince Charles established the Prince's Trust back in 1976, using the £7,000 severance pay he received from the Royal Navy. It is arguably the most useful thing he has ever done. The Trust's aim is to help disadvantaged young people, and in its forty-plus years, it has helped nearly 900,000 of them, aged eleven upwards, with education and training, and generally preparing them for life.

The official website is really rather heartening, and Prince Charles can take genuine satisfaction from the fact that his initiative, which incidentally was originally opposed by the government of the day, has made a real and beneficial difference to so many young people's lives, even if the percentage raised spent on overheads has been uncomfortably high.

It is fair to say, however, that despite good intentions, not all his charity endeavours have been as successful. Charles seemed to want to measure his success, and depth of charitable involvement, by the number of charities he could establish, even though frequently this meant overlapping or duplicating the work of other charities, including his own. At one stage, he had twenty-four, each with its own chair and overheads. Very sensibly, if well overdue, Prince Charles recently brought all his charities under a single umbrella, named the Prince's Foundation. Unfortunately, there has been a more concerning side to his charity work. In an effort to maximise the income stream, questionable practices have been adopted and questionable individuals engaged.

Even the Prince's Trust has not been immune from this. With the prospect of unlocking big bucks a realistic one, Charles developed close links with Enron, the American energy company. On the face of it, here was a great success story, a business that in just fifteen years had gone from nowhere to become America's seventh largest company, employing 21,000 staff in more than forty countries. A company awash with profits to devote to good causes.

In the case of the Prince's Trust, this came in the form of donations amounting to a million pounds between 1991 and 1999. Executives from Enron became regular visitors to Charles's residence at St James's Palace, and in return Charles travelled to Houston to be guest of honour at a lunch at the home of Enron founder Kenneth Lay. But Enron's success proved to be as solid as candyfloss. It turned out that the company had lied about its profits and engaged in a range of shady dealings, including concealing debts so they would not show up in the company's accounts. Bankruptcy followed.

It must be tempting to accommodate people who are in a position to make substantial donations to your charities, but that does not mean it is always wise to do so. Indeed, it is not fanciful to suggest that some people may be seeking to donate, not out of benevolence or generosity to a good cause, but to secure the implied connection with someone prestigious who can improve or cement their reputation.

In his book *Rebel Prince*, Tom Bower revealed how in 2000, Cem Uzan, described by the *Daily Mail* as 'a shady Turkish billionaire', paid £200,000 for his wife to sit next to Prince Charles at a dinner to celebrate the setting up of a charity to further the Prince's interest in architecture and urban design. The dubious arrangement was negotiated not by Prince Charles of course, but by his loyal servant Michael Fawcett.

The day after the dinner, photographs of the Uzans with Prince Charles appeared on media sites across the world. The trick was repeated the next year with another dinner, this time at Buckingham Palace, and another £200,000. It was followed the next day with dinner at Highgrove, where the entertainment was provided by Shirley Bassey. It is unknown whether she performed her big hit 'Goldfinger' about 'The man with the Midas touch'.

And on it went. Another dinner at Buckingham Palace, a polo match at Cirencester, drinks with Princess Margaret's son Lord Linley, a day's racing at Ascot, and meanwhile the money rolled in… Unfortunately, this all came to an end when, in 2003, Cem Uzan, who had been under investigation in the United States for racketeering, was sentenced to jail for fraud-related offences.

Charles's cash for access approach has since been adopted by Prince William. At a private reception and dinner in New York in 2014, for example, the price for sitting down with William and Kate was $50,000 a seat. The event, held at the Manhattan residence of British entrepreneur Sir Martin Sorrell, was used by William to raise money for his favourite wildlife charities. This is undoubtedly a laudable aim, even if Prince William's predilection for shooting birds and going on wild boar hunts does weaken his moral case somewhat, just as his grandfather's presidency of the World Wildlife Fund was compromised by his predilection for shooting tigers, or indeed virtually anything that moved. But William seems to be falling into the same trap that ensnared his father, namely to seek to maximise the amount raised for good causes while skating over the appropriateness of entertaining those who are coughing up.

In this case, some controversy flowed from the presence at the dinner of John Studzinski, managing director of the Blackstone Group, owners of the SeaWorld marine parks. A documentary had accused the parks of cruelty towards killer whales and dolphins in the parks, and indeed some would say that the keeping of such large and intelligent creatures in confined spaces axiomatically must be cruel. SeaWorld rejected the claims, but whatever one's views on such marine parks, it does suggest it might have been more prudent if Mr Studzinski had not been present at the Prince's dinner.

Another episode that looked like cash for access this time involved Harry and Meghan. George and Amal Clooney laid on a private $43 million Gulfstream G450 jet to fly Meghan back to the UK after her ostentatious New York baby shower. Weeks later the Clooneys were guests at a slap-up dinner at Buckingham Palace hosted by Charles to celebrate the Prince's Trust.

One recurring concern with Prince Charles's charities was the amount spent on overheads. As well as the duplication of chairs and boards referred to above, there was the employment of Robert M. Higdon, who had been named managing director of the Washington-based Prince of Wales Foundation in 1997, and in which capacity he raised huge sums for Charles's pet interests, including architecture and the environment. The usual tactic was the cash for access route: arranging a personal meeting with Prince Charles in return for a large cheque.

But Charles's charities were not the only beneficiaries of this technique. Another was Mr Higdon himself, who received an extensive salary and generous expense reimbursements for his troubles. In 2011, the last year before his contract ended, $600,000 of the money he had raised was reportedly paid in salary and expenses to him personally, almost the same as the total amount disbursed by the foundation. But at least there was some money left to distribute, unlike from A. G. Carrick, the obscurely named entity set up by Charles to distribute to charity the proceeds from the sale of his watercolours and other art works, and which now handles the products available in his Highgrove shop. Rather inconveniently for the Prince, the *Daily Telegraph* reported in 2011 that not only had no money been distributed to charity for two years from the turnover of £4.35 million, but A. G. Carrick had actually received £40,000 from his charitable foundations, diverted from good causes.

Initially a spokesperson for the Prince maintained over £25,000 had been distributed, itself of course merely a tiny fraction of the turnover. When the paper queried even this paltry allocation, the story changed. Now the story was that the £25,000 was in fact used to cover a loss from the previous year 'as is standard procedure'. The loss, it seems, was a 'once-off due to reorganisation'. The paper reported that, according to the accounts, A. G. Carrick had liabilities in excess of £1 million. There was, however, no question of not paying the annual employee bill of £500,000, or around £75,000 in 'emoluments' to the firm's directors, including Michael Fawcett, whose company also raked in £18,600 for 'services' that year.

The Highgrove shop website reads: 'All profits from the sale of

Highgrove products, garden tours and events are donated to The Prince of Wales's Charitable Foundation.' With a 'limited edition Highgrove Harry Bear' at £125, and a 'Highgrove Prince of Wales Check Throw' at £150, there ought to be a healthy profit, and those paying through the nose for such items should at least be able to take some satisfaction from the knowledge that their spending is helping those less fortunate than themselves.

Another questionable use of monies raised for charity came in 2010 when the Charity Commission announced it was considering an investigation into the purchase made by Charles's Foundation of Dumfries House in Ayrshire. Three years earlier, on a whim over a generous dinner at Windsor Castle, an excitable Prince Charles learnt of the sword hanging over the remote and little-known property. Here was a house with all its original furniture and paintings still retained, but about to go under the hammer. He decided there and then, without ever having seen the house, that it must be saved. At that point, lorries laden with the house's contents in packing cases were literally on their way to Christie's in London. They were stopped and turned round at one in the morning in Cumbria.

Only £12 million at that point had been raised towards the estimated sale value of £43 million, and while Charles's subsequent tin rattling succeeded in reducing the deficit, a yawning gap of £20 million was left. 'I'll make up the difference myself,' he defiantly declared. Of course, he did not mean by putting his hand in his own bulging pocket. That is not something one does if one is Prince of Wales. No, he meant diverting hard accumulated and much needed funds from his charitable foundation. In the end, a £20 million loan was taken out so Charles could buy the property at the price asked by the vendor, the immensely wealthy Marquess of Bute, with no attempt to negotiate the price down. The arrangement was surprisingly signed off by the normally careful Sir Michael Peat, his private secretary. The security for the loan was the waterlogged farmland that surrounded the house, farmland Charles intended to use to build a model community, a sort of Scottish Poundbury. It was to be called Knockroon, which sounds like something out of *The Goon Show*.

The local council had previously rejected an application for building on the seventy-acre site, but Charles, with well-placed royal arrogance, simply assumed the council, which under planning law is supposed to be applicant-neutral, would cave in to a prince of the realm. Indeed they did, but even the paper windfall given by the timid council to Charles still left his investment well adrift. The financial gap in the foundation's account was partly plugged between 2009 and 2011 by donations totalling $200,000 via a now-defunct investment bank. The payments came from a shell company called Quantus Division Ltd based in the British Virgin Islands, part of a network of more than seventy offshore companies handling billions of dollars moved out of Russia. The network was managed at that point by a Moscow bank, Troika Dialog. The chief executive of the bank was one Ruben Vardanyan, although he denied to the BBC having any involvement in the day-to-day operations of the bank and strongly denied any involvement in any criminal activity.

In any case, the donations, which Mr Vardanyan said were to 'preserve architectural heritage in England' (though Dumfries House is in Scotland) helped establish a relationship between him and Prince Charles. In 2013, the two met when Charles visited Armenia where Mr Vardanyan was establishing a college. A tree-lined avenue of sycamores at the college would be named Prince Charles Alley. A partnership between the college and Dumfries House was agreed to allow Armenian students to study at the Scottish location. In 2014, a delegation led by Mr Vardanyan came to Dumfries House where

Charles was able to thank donors. The banker had managed to raise a further £1.5 million from assorted Russian businessmen, who were duly rewarded by Charles with a black-tie dinner in 2014.

Ministers in the British government have made clear they want to see better due diligence by British institutions before they accept money from offshore companies. Charles's foundation says it carried out such diligence, and that that exercise raised 'no red flags'. It does not seem to have been very thorough if that is the case.

Building at Knockroon started in April 2011, but more than five years later *The Scotsman* reported that of the planned 770 houses, just thirty-one had been completed. The target had been for 330 to be ready by 2017. Moreover, of the thirty-one, fewer than half were owned by members of the public. Rather, the majority had been sold to a multimillionaire benefactor of Charles's charitable trust. The selling prices, typically £190,000 for a three-bedroom house, will not have helped. In nearby Cumnock, the same could be picked up for as little as £40,000. The project's main housebuilder withdrew from the venture in 2015.

Charles also ran into trouble with his suggested street names, with just three of his seventeen being accepted by the Knockroon Community Liaison Group. Greenmantle, named after John Buchan's 1916 Richard Hannay thriller, was rejected as having sectarian overtones. Others that bit the dust included Wandering Willie's Wynd, Blind Harry's Wynd, Shanter, Balwhidder Brae and Tillietudlum, another Goons-sounding name.

Meanwhile, *Scotland On Sunday* discovered that the foundation had waived a loan of £1.71 million to Dumfries Farming and Land Ltd, a real-estate subsidiary tasked with making the Prince's vision a reality. This is a sizeable proportion of the £3.82 million raised that year for the foundation from donations. The Charity Commission duly contacted the foundation to clarify what was going on. Its guidelines state that a charity should not invest in a subsidiary 'if it is reasonably foreseeable that the subsidiary may not be able to service the loan or repay it when the time expires'.

A 2016 analysis by the subsidiary calculated that the Knockroon site was worth just £2 million, as opposed to the £14.85 million figure assumed when planning permission was secured. And rather than providing profits for Charles's foundation, the subsidiary clocked up an accumulated loss of £430,000 between 2007 and 2014. 'The present value of the land is not relevant,' a Clarence House spokesman haughtily declared.

The Dumfries House project is currently being overseen by Charles's very loyal servant Michael Fawcett, for which his company, Premier Mode, was paid £276,000 from charitable funds in the most recent year for which figures are available. Despite antipathy from William and Harry, the former toothpaste-squeezer, as *Private Eye* calls him, has now been appointed chief executive of the Prince's charitable foundation. Achilles and Patroclus reunited.

Part of the problem has been Charles's unwillingness ever to listen to advice which displeases him and, just like the medieval courts of old, those who proffer it tend to find themselves on the way out. Those who remain will tend to tell him what he wants to hear.

Yet Charles's judgement can be far from perfect, so the inevitable consequence of a failure to listen to those around him who have his best interests at heart can land him in hot water.

Many in his circle tried to dissuade him from filming an interviewed rebuttal to the Princess Diana *Panorama* programme that had gripped the nation, the one where she had talked of there being three people in her marriage, but Charles would not listen and went ahead with the interview with Jonathan Dimbleby. When his exercise in self-pity turned out to be a public relations disaster, it was the unfortunate

Richard Aylard who got the blame. He was Charles's fourth private secretary in seven years.

Charles was also cautioned about getting too close to Cem Uzan but to no avail. Even Prince Philip described him as a 'rent-a-royal' for the way he raised funds for his charities. If he was warned about his close friendship with the disgraced TV star Jimmy Savile, he paid no attention. There were mutterings about Savile's disgusting activities as far back as the 1980s, when he was quietly dropped by British Rail. He had headed up a long-running series of successful television adverts for the state-owned railway operator ('this is the age of the train'), but then BR heard rumours that Savile was engaged in necrophiliac practices at the morgue at Stoke Mandeville hospital, and he was axed. Savile himself even referred publicly to these accusations in the 1990s in order to deny them.

Meanwhile, the garish BBC star, who was knighted by the Queen in 1990, enjoyed almost unparalleled access to Clarence House and to Prince Charles. According to Sarah Goodall, then Lady Clerk to the Prince, incredibly, he acted as a sort of marriage guidance counsellor to Charles and Diana, though on this occasion Jim was a long way from fixing it. Charles, who agreed to be patron of one of Savile's charities, the Stoke Mandeville Appeal, would even sometimes ask Savile to read over his draft speeches and offer comments, according to the journalist Catherine Mayer in her book *Charles: The Heart of a King*.

There were undoubtedly concerns in the Prince's household. Dickie Arbiter, who handled media relations for Charles and Diana between 1988 and 2000, found Savile's behaviour odd and disturbing. 'He would walk into the office and do the rounds of the young ladies, taking their hands and rubbing his lips all the way up their arms if they were wearing short sleeves. His bottom lip would curl out.' Sir Roger Jones, the former chairman of the BBC's charity Children in Need, said of

Savile: 'We all recognised he was a pretty creepy sort of character.' He was kept well away from Children in Need.

The same year, 1999, Charles accepted an invitation to a private meal at Savile's Glencoe home, the house which after his death was daubed with the phrase 'Jimmy the beast'. Charles did receive letters from the public making accusations about Savile, but he dismissed them all as mad, or showing jealousy. On Savile's eightieth birthday, Charles sent him a box of cigars and a pair of gold cufflinks, with a note that read: 'Nobody will ever know what you have done for this country Jimmy.' Well, they know now.

When Savile died four years later, having escaped justice for his terrible crimes, Charles and Camilla led the public tributes. How's about that then? Even more embarrassing for Charles were his links with the disgraced Bishop of Lewes, Peter Ball. Here was another character who, like Savile, had easy access to Prince Charles and who, like Savile, formed a close relationship with Charles. And it was Savile who first opened royal doors for him.

It was in 1993 that the bishop admitted gross indecency. He had persuaded a seventeen-year-old, Neil Todd, to pray naked with him and had whipped him so he would 'bear the marks' of his faith. The penalty was a light one, which the Crown Prosecution Service now admits was wrong: he was given a police caution. No doubt the reams of supportive letters from the great and the good, including my predecessor as MP for Lewes Tim Rathbone, played a part in this.

The Establishment had rallied round and showed no signs of deserting him, even after he had admitted his guilt. Prince Charles was particularly supportive. 'I wish I could do more,' he wrote to him in 1995. 'I feel so desperately strongly about the monstrous wrongs that have been done to you and the way you have been treated.' Charles was not alone. The Queen herself offered her support to him after he had received his caution, holding out her hand to him at a public event in Truro, saying: 'My love and encouragement, Bishop.'

Peter Ball continued to be on close terms with the Queen Mother and with Princess Margaret, and was invited to preach at Sandringham. He also gave communion at Highgrove. Here was a man who had admitted a charge of gross indecency, of whipping a seventeen-year-old, yet royal sympathies were with the perpetrator. The victim, insofar as he came into the picture at all, was trashed. 'The young man who accused me keeps on harassing,' Peter Ball wrote to the Prince. 'The last was a few weeks back with a fax, threatening to say more.' On 23 March 1997 Charles wrote to the bishop:

> I can't bear it that the frightful terrifying man is on the loose again … I was visiting the vicar … and we were enthusing about you and your brother and he then told me that he had heard that this ghastly man was up to his dastardly tricks again. I'll see off this horrid man if he tries anything again.

The 'ghastly man' would in due course commit suicide.

All this tumbled out in July 2018 in evidence at the independent public inquiry into child abuse. The inquiry was to conclude that Charles had been 'misguided'. What also tumbled out was that the sex abuse bishop had offered marital advice to Charles and Camilla, just as Jimmy Savile had done for Charles and Diana previously.

Peter Ball was to attend their wedding in Windsor in 2005. He also delivered the address at the funeral for Camilla's father the following year. Charles had also arranged for Peter Ball to be able to live in a Duchy property, Manor Lodge in the Somerset village of Aller. He lived there from 1997 until 2011. The inquiry heard that Charles also gave him 'small gifts of money'.

So why on earth was Prince Charles so seemingly unaffected by the bishop's admission of gross indecency in 1993? His excuse was that he had been told by the bishop that he had been 'involved in some form of indiscretion' that prompted his resignation. We are asked to believe that he never asked what form this indiscretion took. The Prince says he believed that Ball had been falsely accused, but admits that he knew that Ball had been given a police caution. How to square this? Incredibly he states that he was 'not aware until recently that a caution in fact carries an acceptance of guilt'. Yet the meaning of a caution has been crystal clear since official guidance on the matter was issued in 1931. In order to be allowed to accept a caution, according to the latest official Home Office guidance, 'you have to admit an offence'.

William Chapman, who represented survivors at the inquiry, called it 'frankly astonishing' that the Prince did not understand what a caution meant. 'The prince had access to the best advice that money can buy.' Presumably the Archbishop of Canterbury at the time, George Carey, also did not understand what a caution was, for he allowed Peter Ball once again to conduct church services, this time as a retired priest.

So just when did the Prince discover that a caution was an acceptance of guilt, and when did he find out what the indiscretion was that he had so mysteriously failed to identify back in 1993? He told the inquiry: 'I ceased contact with Mr Ball once the judicial process had concluded and he was found guilty of serious offences against young people.'

In other words, he either did not show any interest in understanding what a caution meant or what the 1993 'indiscretion' had been until after Peter Ball's conviction in 2015, or he had found this out but did not see this as a reason to discontinue contact until that year's guilty verdict was delivered. In 2015, Ball was convicted of sexual offences against eighteen young men and handed down a 32-month prison sentence.

Prince Charles said: 'My heart goes out to victims of abuse and I applaud their courage as they rebuild their lives.' Sadly it was too late for Neil Todd.

The Grand Old Duke of Sleaze

An heir and a spare. The essential royal approach through the years to ensure a natural line of succession. So the Queen produced four children, Charles two, and now William three. That does, however, leave a problem – what to do with the children who were once needed as an insurance policy, but have subsequently been eclipsed by later developments? Andrew, for example, was once second in line to the throne after Charles but has now slipped down the royal charts to number seven. Edward was third and is now tenth.

Some, such as Princess Anne, accept their lot and get on with it. She continues to quietly undertake many royal duties, and seems satisfied with her niche. She is now probably the most respected of the royals after the Queen herself and for the three years from 2015 undertook more official engagements than any other member of the family. The same cannot be said for Andrew and Edward – the brothers grim.

Andrew in particular appears not to have become reconciled to his diminished status. One way this manifests itself is in his strident demands that his daughters be treated in the same manner as Charles's sons. So he and their mother Sarah Ferguson insisted that Princess

Eugenie's wedding in Windsor should include an open-top ride through the town, so as not to be outdone by the recent nuptials of Harry and Meghan. The fact that this generated a security headache and an estimated bill of £2 million for the taxpayer was of course of no concern to Andrew and Sarah.

Much to their chagrin, the BBC decided it was not worth covering the wedding, so it appeared instead on downmarket daytime ITV. A week after her daughter's wedding came the announcement that Meghan and Harry were expecting a child. Within an hour, Sarah had taken to Twitter, not to congratulate the two but to say she was 'so proud of Eugenie and Jack'. She followed this up with a tweet thanking Eugenie's dress designer and then posted another photo of the wedding. These attempts to divert attention were seen as being in very bad taste and looked opportunistic. The comparison that springs to mind is a music industry one: when in the early 1970s David Bowie had become perhaps the pre-eminent cult figure with his *Ziggy Stardust* album, his old record label Decca cashed in by re-releasing a track he had recorded many years before and which he wished he had not, the quite terrible 'Laughing Gnome'.

Andrew also stamped his feet to ensure 24-hour security cover for his daughters, to keep up with Charles. But while cover is certainly justified for William, third in line, and probably Harry too before he renounced royal duties, it is frankly difficult to make a case for lesser royals. It is notable that neither Anne nor Edward has requested nor required security for their children. Another sharp difference exists in the comparison with Anne's children. The Princess Royal sensibly did not want them to have royal titles so they could live as normal a life as possible. Harry and Meghan are following the same path with Archie. Andrew and Sarah, on the other hand, insisted their daughters be dubbed HRH Princess. Andrew was even rumoured to have pushed hard for titles to be bestowed upon their husbands, though he denied having made any interventions. Whatever the truth of the matter, in April 2019, it was confirmed that Eugenie and husband Jack would be known as Mr and Mrs Brooksbank.

This approach is not without precedent. In 1919, Princess Patricia of Connaught, a granddaughter of Queen Victoria, gave up her title upon marriage. So obsessed was Andrew, however, about status for his daughters' husbands that he unwisely issued a petulant personal statement on Twitter about this back in December 2016 in response to a single paragraph in the gossip column of the *Daily Mail*. Unwise for several reasons: firstly, because it elevated the story that would otherwise have passed unremarked; secondly, because it was in the first person and issued on his personal Twitter account rather than handled professionally by the Palace communications team; and, thirdly, because its grammar and spelling left something to be desired.

Andrew was pushing for his daughters to be given taxpayer-funded roles, and to be moved to more extravagant accommodation in Kensington Palace. In his tweet, he described the Princesses as 'modern working young women', which is pushing it a bit. The previous year, Beatrice managed to squeeze in eighteen foreign holidays, including a break in Ibiza on Roman Abramovich's £1.5 billion super-yacht.

In fact, his daughters appeared more reconciled to their status than he was. Eugenie secured a post with an art dealer, while Beatrice found work with an investment firm in New York. He has also complained when his daughters have been absent from the rather dry Court Circular that is issued daily and which lists royal engagements. On one occasion in 2016, he went ballistic when the Duke of Kent and Princess Alexandra were name-checked but his daughters were included as 'other Members of the Royal Family'. Following heated exchanges with

Palace officials, he appears to be winning on this front, and the largely inconsequential and intermittent activities of his daughters can now be followed. Any activity they do undertake, such as when Eugenie was present at the Queen's Maundy Money ceremony in 2019, is hyped up on her father's Twitter feed.

The main flashpoint has been between Charles and Andrew. The Prince of Wales has made it clear that he wants to see, at least publicly, a slimmed-down monarchy, with the royal also-rans quietly retired. He was rumoured to want to restrict royal duties to himself, William and Kate, and Harry and Meghan, though subsequent events will have shortened that list even further. As the Queen hands over more responsibility to Charles, the squeeze to a slimmed-down royal family is one he is exerting now. It was perhaps the publication of a photo in the papers from Buckingham Palace the day before Andrew's petulant tweet that spurred the latter on. There stood the Queen and Prince Philip, Charles and Camilla, William and Kate. Here was the core team, dressed to the nines for an event for members of the world's diplomatic corps, and Andrew was not part of it.

While many would applaud the retirement of minor royals from the payroll and from the public eye, if Charles's leaner approach is to work then his offspring and their wives, not to mention Camilla, are going to have to undertake rather more royal duties than they do at present. In 2018, Charles clocked up 507 engagements, compared to just 220 by William and 193 by Harry. Camilla's total was just 219. The then 92-year-old Queen undertook an impressive 283.

In the past, a royal second son would have been sent abroad to become governor-general in one of the colonies, but with empire now a distant and receding memory, that particular avenue has long since been closed off. Andrew did complete twenty-two years in the armed forces and served with courage and distinction in the Falklands War of 1982. The trouble is that after his retirement from active duty, he found himself at a loose end, and the rest of us found ourselves with a loose cannon.

The Duke of York fancies himself on the international stage, especially in the more exotic parts of the world. So in 2001 he took on the role of Special Representative for Trade and Investment.

Unfortunately, the way he undertook this diplomatic role was far from diplomatic. One former royal aide described his approach as 'the worst combination of arrogance and stupidity' – hardly the ideal combination. Increasingly he became something of an embarrassment and a liability to Britain. In Rome, when he was introduced to the head of a major fashion house, he breezily replied, 'Never heard of you.'

Hidden in the thousands of WikiLeaks files is one from Tatiana Gfoeller, the United States ambassador to Kyrgyzstan in 2008. The cable recounted a lunch in the capital Bishkek addressed by Andrew in which he slagged off France as corrupt and, in the presence of the US representative, asserted that Americans 'don't understand geography. Never have. In the UK we have the best geography teachers in the world.'

Warming to his saloon bar theme, he used his overseas platform to attack those back home in the Serious Fraud Office who had been investigating bribery allegations related to the al-Yamamah arms deal between BAE and Saudi Arabia, describing their actions as 'idiocy'. He also denounced reporters from *The Guardian* who had been investigating the bribery allegations as 'those fucking journalists … who poke their noses everywhere'.

One might have thought that for the Prince to openly slam a respected British organisation while abroad, to implicitly accept corrupt practices as a legitimate way of doing business, and to criticise the free press while in a country where it was not free would be grounds for ending his role, but he was allowed to carry on.

Before he had left Britain for this visit, he had demanded a special briefing from the Serious Fraud Office on the progress of their corruption investigation. The head of the SFO, Richard Alderman, duly met Andrew in Buckingham Palace on 13 May 2008. Senior officials in the SFO described the request for a briefing as 'well out of order', and said they felt 'very uncomfortable'. The SFO was at pains to stress that the information they supplied to Andrew was only that already in the public domain, which may account for his undisciplined rant against them in Bishkek.

After he returned home, Andrew was given a tour of the SFO's head office in London and again pushed for privileged information about the sale of arms by BAE. Again, he was politely rebuffed. Was the Serious Fraud Office merely following good practice in deploying a 'need-to-know' approach, as would be only sensible for a sensitive and complex fraud investigation, or did they perhaps worry that information they provided to Andrew might somehow find its way back to the Saudi royal family? In 2011, when this all emerged, Vince Cable, the then Lib Dem Business Secretary, said in restrained terms that it was 'not helpful' for Andrew to comment on government policy, and reiterated that 'we regard bribery overseas as illegal and unacceptable. That is not a matter for Prince Andrew, that's a matter for the government.' Prime Minister David Cameron, however, who is distantly related to the Queen, reiterated that the Prince had his full support.

That support appeared to be absent from Britain's career diplomats. Simon Wilson, who served as deputy head of mission in Bahrain between 2001 and 2005, reported that Andrew was 'more commonly known amongst the British diplomatic community in the Gulf as HBH – His Buffoon Highness'. For good measure, he was withering about the vast entourage that Andrew took everywhere and the cost to the taxpayer.

> The style in which I observed him carrying it [the role] out beggared belief. He travelled with a team of six … There was also a 6ft-long ironing board that he insisted went everywhere he went. It was hilarious to witness the valet struggling off the plane with it and placing the precious object carefully into the minibus.

It was not just Andrew's undiplomatic language that was a worry. Simon Wilson was most concerned that Andrew would frequently articulate a view at variance with official government policy, and officials were too afraid to challenge this. An even more basic concern was where he was going and whom he was meeting – matters which, to a large degree, he seemed to decide for himself.

For example, between November 2001 and May 2008, he officially visited the United Arab Emirates on nine occasions, Qatar five times and Kuwait, Bahrain and Egypt four times each, as well as undertaking visits to Oman, Dubai, Jordan and Saudi Arabia. In 2006, I asked the government in a parliamentary question to itemise the contracts won in the previous year as a result of visits by the Duke of York. The Trade Minister, Ian Pearson, told me that 'it is not possible to directly attribute contracts won to any individual contribution'. In other words, they could not point to one.

Just what was the value to Britain in these repeated visits to Middle East countries by Andrew, visits paid for, at considerable cost, by the British taxpayer? When the Queen or Prince Charles go abroad to represent Britain, they generally operate to a tight timetable, with relatively little down time. Andrew's schedule frequently allows for 'private' meetings, and indeed private visits to the same countries he was on other occasions visiting officially.

In 2011, for instance, the Prince's office offered no explanation as to why he did not arrive officially in Qatar until 27 November, when he had left Britain four days earlier. Had his private jet (courtesy of the taxpayer) developed a fault en route? The explanation was to be found in the *Daily Mail*, which reported that Andrew had stopped off in Azerbaijan, widely recognised as one of the world's most corrupt countries. It turns out he had also been to that country eight times in the previous six years, with two of those visits described in the WikiLeaks cables as 'very private'.

On at least one occasion, in 2009, he flew there and back using a private jet, leaving the taxpayer to pick up the £60,000 bill. There are daily commercial flights between London and the capital, Baku.

Azerbaijan's President, Ilham Aliyev, was widely believed to engage in the torturing of political opponents and the rigging of elections. This did not seem in any way to deter Andrew. Indeed, he is said on one occasion to have visited a luxury spa owned by the President, where a blind Russian masseur with reportedly 'the best hands in the world' is employed. But it is perhaps his strong connections with another former Soviet state, Kazakhstan, that have raised the most questions, and the most eyebrows. Here again a smattering of official visits have been supplemented by private ones.

Kazakhstan is home to some of the richest gas and mineral reserves anywhere in the world and has economically performed very strongly over the past twenty years. However, it has also had a reputation for corruption, though steps are slowly being taken to improve matters, as I saw when I visited the country on behalf of the Westminster Foundation for Democracy in 2019.

Just as I arrived, President Nursultan Nazarbayev surprised everyone by suddenly standing down. He had led the country without a break from the dissolution of the Soviet Union through to 2019. He did, however, retain control of a number of important levers behind the scenes. Nazarbayev and the Duke of York are patrons of the British-Kazakh Society. They have known each other for some considerable time and have even gone goose hunting together.

Other Britons who have been keen to cultivate relationships with the country include Tony Blair, who was richly rewarded for consultancy services with a contract worth £8 million. By 2012, *Private Eye* estimated that his take had reached £16 million. And after Blair took the golden road to Kazakhstan, Peter Mandelson was not far behind, a guest of Samruk-Kazyna, the country's sovereign wealth fund. Prince Andrew has been keen to arrange meetings between British investors and companies in Kazakhstan. Throughout his period in office, an absolutely central figure was the President's billionaire son-in-law, Timur Kulibayev. He was befriended by Andrew, who also formed a bond with Goga Ashkenazi, a leading businesswoman and mother to a son by Kulibayev. Andrew was photographed with her at Ascot in 2007, where she was invited into the royal box. In 2008, he felt he was on close enough terms for him to join her for dinner just days after she had given birth to the boy. And in 2010 he attended her thirtieth birthday party at a country house in Buckinghamshire.

In 2007, Andrew sold Sunninghill Park, the house that was a wedding present to him and Sarah from the Queen. The sprawling house would not have won any architectural awards from his brother Charles, looking as it did like an off-the-shelf branch of Tesco, missing only the toytown clock that adorns so many of their leaden outlets. Nor was the interior much of an improvement, with its musical toilet roll holders that played 'God Save the Queen'. The house sat empty after 2004, when Andrew vacated it, and there had been precious little interest in the property since it was first decided to market it in 2002, or in its asking price of £12 million. After all, if you had such a sum to spend on a house, why would you buy that uninspiring one?

For some time, Andrew had been hawking the house round,

including on official trips abroad, such as one to Saudi Arabia and Bahrain in 2004. He was still pushing the case on another visit to the Middle East in 2005. It transpires that he was controversially cleared by the Foreign Office to raise the matter. But then something rather odd happened. The house was sold for £15 million, and not by anyone approaching the estate agent, Savills, with whom the property had been placed.

According to the Land Registry, the buyer was identified as an outfit based in the tax haven that is the British Virgin Islands, the Unity Assets Corporation. It was only in 2010 that some diligent journalism from the *Sunday Times*, stripping away the layers of front companies, proved that the ultimate buyer was Timur Kulibayev, though he had denied his ownership to the paper just two days before publication. In 2011, Andrew reportedly lobbied Rory Tapner, chief executive at the Queen's bank, Coutts, to take on Mr Kulibayev as a client, even asking senior figures at the bank if they would travel to Kazakhstan to meet him. The meeting never took place, with one bank official observing that 'Kazakh oligarchs are the sort of people we generally don't touch with a bargepole'.

It was rumoured that the go-between for the Sunninghill deal was Ms Ashkenazi. In fact it was Kenges Rakishev, a Kazakh tycoon whose financial interests cover much of the country's natural resources and who at the time was engaged in the construction of a £2.5 billion petrochemical plant in Kazakhstan. Andrew had several private meetings with him in London, which sometimes lasted hours. It is not known what was discussed. Commenting on the meetings, Artur Krivov, a senior employee of Mr Rakishev's, offered this cryptic observation: 'I know that usually Mr Rakishev does not meet with anyone more than once if he does not need anything.' The property for which the billionaire Kazakh had paid £3 million in excess of the asking price, when it had sat empty for years and for which there were no other bidders, was then left to rot and never occupied again. Demolition began in 2016.

At the same time as he bought Prince Andrew's house, Mr Kulibayev bought four adjoining houses in Upper Grosvenor Street in London for a cool £44.4 million, again using front companies for the purchase. They too were left unoccupied and by 2010 were partly boarded up. The obvious question, to which no satisfactory answer has ever been forthcoming, is why would Mr Kulibayev pay Prince Andrew £3 million over the asking price for a property he apparently never intended to occupy? A second question might be: why did he take such elaborate steps to cover up his ownership of the property?

In 2016, President Nursultan Nazarbayev visited London and Prince Andrew arranged for him to have lunch with the Queen and Prince Philip at Buckingham Palace, which, given the Queen's age, is a rare honour these days for a visiting head of state. The same year, it was reported that Andrew had been in line for a commission payment of £3.85 million, that sum being 1 per cent of a Kazakhstan infrastructure deal he had helped broker by sending a handful of emails.

The Prince's spokesman initially denied that Andrew, who was then still the UK's special representative, had played any part in this deal. When presented with a copy of an email sent by Andrew which unquestionably proved the opposite, he tried to suggest it was a forgery. When that did not work, the law firm Harbottle & Lewis was instructed to try to block publication of what was now accepted as a genuine email, on the basis that it breached Andrew's privacy. Fortunately, the *Daily Mail* was not intimidated, rightly recognising the public interest in the story. In the event, the deal collapsed after Kazakh police opened fire on a group of striking oil workers, killing fourteen, and investors took fright. The episode did, however, lead some to question whether the Prince was using his role more to help himself rather than to help Britain.

Andrew's colourful connections with powerful individuals abroad also included being hosted in Jeddah by the Saudi Binladin Group, a multinational construction conglomerate founded by the father of Osama Bin Laden. Then there was 29-year-old Sakher El Materi. The Prince hosted a lunch for him at Buckingham Palace, but only just in time, for shortly afterwards his father-in-law, the autocrat Ben Ali, was deposed as Tunisian President in a democratic uprising.

Stephen Day, a former British ambassador to Tunisia, abandoned the diplomatic niceties, describing Materi as a 'crook ... the worst of all of them'. He told the BBC, 'I advised my clients to go nowhere near him.' He said he could not imagine how Materi had ended up in Buckingham Palace: 'The embassy in Tunis was very clear that this was a man who carried an awful lot of baggage.' It transpired he had written to William Hague, then Foreign Secretary, about Andrew to say that 'an entirely new role should be found for him as soon as possible'.

And let us not forget Tarek Kaituni, a convicted Libyan gunrunner, with whom Andrew shared a holiday in Tunisia before the two went on to Libya. Andrew accepted a 'private' gift from him of an £18,000 diamond necklace for his daughter Beatrice. The Palace, when asked about this, haughtily replied that they do not comment on private gifts to members of the royal family. In the abstract, what this means, of course, is that they do comment on official gifts given, which axiomatically then belong to the state, but if, in theory, a gift were given to a member of the royal family in questionable circumstances, it need only be labelled 'private' for it to vanish into the ether as far as the Palace is concerned.

Meanwhile, Bahrain continued to loom large in Andrew's activities. The country injects a good deal of money into the Royal Windsor Horse Show, so it was perhaps unsurprising that the King turned up at the

Queen's tent for a photo in 2011. But if that was embarrassing, given that a popular democratic uprising in the country had just been rather violently put down, what was worse was that he brought his son Sheikh Nasser bin Hamad with him. It transpired that the arrival of both at the Queen's tent had been engineered by Andrew, who tried to get them invited back to Windsor Castle for tea, a suggestion the Queen firmly refused. Nasser, a friend of Andrew's, had been accused of engaging in torture during the uprising. The accusations were disputed and, in the end, no charge was pursued.

Andrew also met Colonel Gaddafi, the former Libyan dictator, more than once and, separately, his son Saif Al-Islam Gaddafi several times. It was public knowledge that Andrew made a five-day trip to the country in November 2007. When questioned by the *Mail on Sunday*, Buckingham Palace implied that this was his only trip to the country and that he had not met Gaddafi while there. Eventually, they conceded that the Prince had indeed met the Libyan dictator on a visit in 2008 and had also undertaken two other private visits. Part of the reluctance to come clean may be that on one occasion, ministers wanted Andrew to raise with the Colonel the ongoing issue of the Lockerbie bombing, and in particular to try to avoid a major diplomatic incident should the convicted bomber have died in a Scottish prison. His close relationship with the dictator may have been seen as a plus on this occasion.

So, had the Palace deliberately sought to mislead the paper with their original response, or did they have to go back to check with Andrew and only then discovered the facts? Either explanation is rather worrying: either the Palace deliberately told the media something they knew to be untrue or they were in the dark about where Andrew had been travelling to.

The Palace added, 'We do not comment on private visits of the members of the royal family.' How convenient, and how wrong. Nobody would suggest a member of the royal family should make public a genuinely private visit, say, to an old friend, but there is a world of difference between that and what Andrew was doing. We know he was undertaking private visits to places he was also visiting officially, but there may well be even more visits we do not know about, and for all of them, known and unknown, we have no official record of who paid for what, why the visit took place and what was discussed with whom. We do know that in many cases, his flights and hospitality were paid for by others, putting Andrew at least morally in their debt.

A register of interests rightly exists for MPs and peers to record gifts and hospitality, and overseas visits are listed. That way people can take a view on whether any particular speech or action by an MP or peer might have been influenced by a gift or hospitality received. No such assessment is possible in the case of members of the royal family if even the Palace is in the dark.

Back in 2001, around fifty MPs signed a Commons motion tabled by the Labour MP Gordon Prentice calling for the creation of a register of business interests held by members of the royal family. The spur for this was the furore over the perceived exploitation by Sophie Wessex of her royal connections to boost her public relations company. But the move ran into the sand. Tony Blair, the Prime Minister, neatly sidestepping the specific issue as he so often did, said he was '100 per cent behind the monarchy', and that was that.

A register would also have required Andrew to come clean about his involvement with shady offshore companies. In December 2019, the *Mail on Sunday*, in an excellent piece of investigative journalism, revealed that the Duke had a 40 per cent share in an outfit called Inverness Asset Management that ended only the previous March. The business, jointly owned with the former Conservative Party treasurer David Rowland, was based in the tax haven that is the British Virgin Islands. The aim of the company was to target royal families, heads of state and the like and to persuade them to put their money into an investment fund based in another tax haven, the Cayman Islands. The carrot was a tax-free income.

A fortnight later, it emerged that Andrew had also set up a company with the sports tycoon Johan Eliasch, a former Conservative Party deputy treasurer. This outfit, Naples Gold Ltd, dates from 2002, and the fact that Andrew's participation took seventeen years to come to light might be explained by the fact that he called himself 'Andrew Inverness' – his favourite Scottish city, it seems, when it comes to creative financial dealings. The Duke was created the Earl of Inverness by his mother when he married Sarah Ferguson in 1986. In 2009, 'Andrew Inverness' was also a creditor of a luxury ski company, Descent International, that collapsed owing £27,000. Perhaps this was an apposite vehicle, as the Duke has demonstrated an impressive ability to go downhill fast.

In the registration documentation for Naples Gold, 'Andrew Inverness' described himself as a 'professional consultant' and misleadingly gave his address as a grand building in South Audley Street, Mayfair. According to the *Daily Mail*, this was actually the offices of Mr Eliasch, with the building controlled through another offshore company based in the British Virgin Islands.

The *Daily Telegraph* discovered that the Duke was also the owner of a company called Urramoor Ltd, incorporated in February 2013, with three subsidiary companies. It was described as 'The Private Investment Office of HRH Duke of York'.

It is worth remembering that for the years from 2001 to 2011, until he was bundled out of the position following the revelation of his links with convicted sex offender Jeffrey Epstein, Andrew was acting as Britain's trade envoy, and was supposed to be drumming up business for Britain, not himself. He continued to make numerous trips abroad at public expense even after his role had officially ended. There is a clear conflict of interest between what Andrew's role required and what he was doing. No minister, MP or Lord could possibly have got away with this, and to be fair, I doubt any would have tried, so blatant and heinous is the conflict.

Andrew's engagement with David Rowland and his son Jonathan certainly demonstrated a blatant and heinous disregard for proper behaviour on the Prince's part. In November 2019, the *Mail on Sunday* reported that the Duke had allowed Jonathan to join him on an official trade visit to China and accompany him to meetings. On 11 March 2010, ahead of the visit, he sent Jonathan an email stating, 'This is my outline programme for China. Which events do you need to be at?'

It was alleged that Mr Rowland then used this access to generate business for the family's bank in Luxembourg. A meeting with Louis Cheng, then president of the world's largest insurance company, was shoehorned into the schedule at Mr Rowland's request – but perhaps attendance at meetings was not essential, as the Rowlands were afterwards passed a copy of a Foreign Office diplomatic cable detailing the conversations Andrew had had with leading Chinese politicians. On another occasion Andrew asked for an official briefing note from the Treasury about the Icelandic financial crisis, which was then live, and duly forwarded this on to the Rowlands. Not since Edward VIII passed on information from his red boxes had we seen such a highly improper use by a royal of privileged government information.

The Duke's engagement with David Rowland goes back a long way. He even unveiled a bronze statue of the financier on the sprawling estate the latter owns in Guernsey.

The *Mail on Sunday* discovered that on at least one of Prince Andrew's secret trips to meet Gaddafi, he was accompanied by Mr Rowland, who also flew with Andrew to the World Economic Forum in Egypt in May 2008, an occasion when the Prince had dinner with Nursultan Nazarbayev. In 2009, David Rowland secured control of the failed Kaupthing Luxembourg bank, which then came back to life as Banque Havilland with Prince Andrew as guest of honour at the reopening, where Andrew was effusive in his praise for Mr Rowland.

In what some saw as an unfortunate coincidence of timing, Mr Rowland shortly afterwards made a gift of £40,000 to Sarah Ferguson's aide Kate Waddington to help clear Fergie's debts, which then stood at around £5 million. The root problem was that Sarah wanted to carry on a particularly expensive lifestyle, and seemed to make no adjustments to take account of what she could actually afford. Rather than cut back, she flailed around looking for money from a variety of sources. So, in a multimillion-dollar deal, she became the face of Weight Watchers in the United States. The Palace was suitably aghast. Other business ventures have followed, including one where she appeared on a US shopping channel to promote a juicer. The House of Orange?

One of her most profitable ways to bring in money came through her writing, and specifically her *Budgie the Little Helicopter* book. When I first came across this, it seemed oddly familiar. I scoured my bookshelves and found what I was after – a brightly coloured hardback book my father had given me when I was about five. It was called *Tommy the Tugboat*, by a writer called Dora Thatcher, and first appeared in 1956.

As I fondly skimmed *Tommy* for the first time in decades, I marvelled at the similarity in storyline between *Tommy* and *Budgie*, and then it turned out that there was even more overlap with a book called *Hector the Helicopter* by the English author Arthur Baldwin. Naturally, Sarah has denied that she is guilty of plagiarism.

Critics slammed Sarah's book as 'utter rubbish' and 'ghastly', but she had a royal name and was not afraid to use it. The book sold in copious numbers and TV rights in the United States followed. Whether the book would ever have sold, or even been commissioned, if the author had not been a royal must be doubtful. However, Andrew at least, with his deep attachment to helicopter travel, will have liked it.

Since *Budgie* first appeared in 1989, Sarah has put her name to twenty-five books, and in February 2020 it was announced that she had signed a deal with an Australian publisher for seven more.

It is interesting to compare Sarah's literary activities, solely designed to enrich herself, with Meghan Markle's involvement with the publication of a cookbook authored by the Hubb Community Kitchen, the proceeds from which went to help the victims of the terrible fire at Grenfell Tower. Meghan had written a foreword for the book, and by March 2019 it had sold 130,000 copies and raised £557,638 for the Hubb Community Kitchen.

Also in February 2020, it was revealed that Sarah was intending to go into the film business. Her plans included a trilogy of films under the banner *The Royals*, with each focusing on a member of the family from over a hundred years ago. To help this endeavour, the Queen has given her special access to the Royal Archives in Windsor, which looks like the privileged exploitation of a national asset for personal wealth creation. Given Sarah's track record in business, there is of course no guarantee that this enterprise will be any more successful than others she has been involved in. She would certainly be wise not to tap into Prince Edward for advice. His foray into royal films, Ardent, was a calamitous failure.

Other ventures by Sarah were less successful than *Budgie*. In 2006, she started a lifestyle company called Hartmoor, but it collapsed just three years later with debts of more than $1 million. Of course, none of this was apparently Sarah's fault, with a source close to the Duchess saying, 'She had business partners who were supposed to manage the business and they didn't do that. She was the talent. She was not the CEO. There were far too many people being paid far too much in swanky offices.' In 2011, Sarah sold her story to Oprah Winfrey for a six-part reality series in which she was joined by her daughters. The general impression created was that they were all victims. In the meantime, the colander that was Fergie's economic model meant that as soon as money came in, it disappeared out the other end. As well as that welcome contribution from David Rowland, it is clear that Andrew was having to bail her out regularly. *Vanity Fair* in 2011 suggested that he had paid down a lot of the debts at a rate of 25p in the pound, and that that money may have come from the Queen.

Other sources of money proved far from trouble-free. Sarah was an executive director of Gate Ventures between July 2017 and December 2019, during which time she borrowed at least £287,000 from the company. Her main role, according to Gate's former chairman, the Hong Kong businessman Johnny Hon, was to 'introduce a few people to me in Hong Kong'. She also received a £72,000 retainer from another company, Global Group, controlled by Hon. A further £232,000 was loaned from Gate to Ginger and Moss, a tea company she had set up but listed at Companies House as a dormant company from 2016 to 2018. Her friend Manuel Fernandez's tech start-up was also loaned £36,000. By February 2020, none of these sums had been paid back. Gate Ventures, established in 2015 to invest in films and start-up businesses, attracted more than £24 million from around 3,500 mostly Chinese investors, who received no return, and by early 2020 the matter had reached the courts. One investor, Zheng Youngxiong, claimed he was owed £2.5 million. That March, Judge Sebastian Prentis appointed two insolvency practitioners, one of whose tasks was to investigate whether 'misapplication of monies' by directors had occurred. Sarah is supposed to have stood down from Gate Ventures in December 2019, but a cursory glance at the company's website shows that she was still prominently listed as executive director in July 2020.

Mr Hon is an ambitious sort. According to his website, 'Johnny is often consulted by Presidents, Prime Ministers and other state leaders from many countries who value his advice and insights.' He is undoubtedly well connected and has engineered several meetings with senior British royals – and then billed Gate for the meetings. The judge called his expenses, which also included shopping sprees and the use of private jets, 'simply extraordinary'.

Hon's contacts with the royal family reach beyond Sarah Ferguson. His largesse has also extended to Zara Tindall, daughter of Princess Anne. In exchange for £100,000 a year, she was appointed a non-executive director of Global Group and required to attend two board meetings by telephone and four company functions, and to advise on horse racing. Her lawyer initially declared it 'wholly untrue' that she had held this position until presented with documentary evidence of the contract between Mr Hon and Ms Tindall by the *Daily Mail*. In the summer of 2019, Hon also signed up Peter Phillips in a deal that provided a salary for him in exchange for a figurehead role at a new horse racing members' club, a far from onerous task that should leave him enough time to sell Jersey milk to the Chinese.

But it was an episode in 2010 that was most embarrassing for Sarah Ferguson. Painfully, in May that year she was caught red-handed on film promising to secure access to Andrew, and therefore privileged influence, in return for a modest £500,000. But she had been reeled in on a line cast by the 'fake sheikh', *News of the World* reporter Mazher Mahmood, who was posing as an Indian businessman.

Mr Mahmood had already back in 2001 trapped Sophie Wessex, Prince Edward's wife, into making some unwise comments about politicians. Sophie attacked 'President Blair' and his 'horrid, horrid' wife, Cherie, who 'hates the countryside', slammed Gordon Brown's 'frightening' tax rises, and for good measure lampooned the then Tory leader, William Hague.

In 2005, it was the turn of Princess Michael of Kent to fall into Mahmood's trap, making unguarded remarks about other members of the royal family. Apparently, Charles had merely married 'a womb', and Diana had been a 'bitter' and 'nasty' woman – epithets that might, in light of such comments, be applied more accurately to Princess Michael herself. The Princess also defended Harry, who had been pictured wearing Third Reich insignia at a fancy-dress party – unlike her father, who, as a Nazi SS officer, wore it for real.

Sarah's sting was arranged after a royal associate let it be known that she had allegedly been taking money in exchange for arranging meetings between businessmen and Andrew. The exchange between Sarah and Mahmood was captured on film for posterity. 'I could bring you great business,' she gushed. 'For example if I introduced you to…'

'Andrew, for example?'

She continued:

> Andrew, for example … and he opened doors for you which you would never possibly do. Then, depending if it was a very big deal … then each deal you and I discuss the percentage of it … Andrew said to me, 'Tell him £500,000 … Look after me and he'll look after you … you'll get it back tenfold.'

The two agreed the £500,000 arrangement, including a $40,000 down payment, which, it appears, had been negotiated by aides at an earlier initial meeting with Mahmood in a New York hotel. The $40,000 was produced in notes from the safe. Sarah then encouraged him to hand over the dosh by opening and closing her fists and beckoning with her fingers.

In 2013, Sarah was asked about this episode on the Australian Channel 9 programme *60 Minutes*. Despite some gentle questioning, she lost her cool, at one point instructing someone off camera to 'delete that bit' and then, shortly after, walking off set for a break in the middle of the filming.

In one sense, what Sarah Ferguson does is a private matter. She has no formal role and is no longer a member of the royal family. But incidents like this become public if she can promise that Prince Andrew, as a public figure representing the nation, can be accessed in exchange for cash. That too might be regarded as simply very embarrassing if she was baselessly hyping up her influence, but it is worrying when she suggests that Andrew and she discussed the matter beforehand and that the figure of £500,000 came from him.

If there was prior collusion between Sarah and Andrew about this – and Andrew has categorically denied that – then that would amount to malfeasance in public office, except of course that the royals are not obliged to play by the rules that exist to keep elected representatives and public officials on the straight and narrow. Subsequently it was reported that Sarah was demanding compensation of £45 million from Rupert Murdoch on the basis that the sting interview wrecked some business opportunities she was working up.

But if that episode was the most cringeworthy for Sarah, it was another offer to help pay off her debts that has hung like a stone round Andrew's neck. In December 2010, Andrew was photographed walking through Central Park in New York with financier Jeffrey Epstein, who had been released the previous year after serving thirteen months of an eighteen-month sentence for a sex offence involving a minor. It emerged that Andrew and Mr Epstein had known each other since the 1990s. In

July 1999, the financier had enjoyed a weekend at Craigowan Lodge, a seven-bedroom property in the grounds of Balmoral that is the royal family's favourite hideaway.

Three months earlier, Andrew had attended a party held in his honour by Mr Epstein. The party took place at Donald Trump's Mar-a-Lago private Palm Beach club in Florida, where Mr Epstein was a member. Mr Trump was amongst the guests. The financier owned a luxury sugar-pink beach property nearby and was close friends with the future President. Independently, Andrew was described in British newspapers at the time as being a friend of Trump. He appears still to be, with the papers reporting in 2018 that Trump wanted to play golf with Andrew when he came to Britain. It is not known whether Trump was aware of Andrew's comment in 2016 that a Trump presidential win would 'tear things apart'. Maybe he approved.

In 2002, Donald Trump said of Jeffrey Epstein, 'I've known Jeff for fifteen years,' and called him a 'terrific guy'. He went on: 'He's a lot of fun to be with. It is even said that he likes beautiful women as much as I do, and many of them are on the younger side.' Later he would change his tune and maintain he barely knew him, even though the New York media had regularly chronicled his frequent appearances at Epstein's luxury Upper East Side residence and the two had frequently been seen together in Florida. In 2019, an old film clip from NBC resurfaced, showing Trump enjoying himself with Epstein while surrounded by attractive women. This suggests the President must have an extraordinarily bad memory.

When Epstein's 'black book' of contacts emerged, it was found to contain fourteen separate telephone numbers for Trump, including one for his wife Melania. Police evidence demonstrated that Trump had called Epstein on the phone, flown on Epstein's plane and eaten in Epstein's Florida home. 'Mr Trump's only connection with Mr Epstein was that Mr Epstein was one of thousands of people who has visited Mar-a-Lago,' was the story given to Buzzfeed by the Trump attorney in 2015. Trump's memory loss now extends to his meetings with Andrew as well. By December 2019, he was telling an audience at the US ambassador's residence in London, 'I don't know Prince Andrew,' despite the existence of plenty of photographs showing the Prince and the future President together. He seems also to have forgotten that in 2000 he made his private jet available to Andrew to fly him to Mar-a-Lago.

In the notorious 2005 recording which captured Trump talking about women, he said, 'When you're a star, they let you do it. You can do anything. Grab 'em by the pussy. You can do anything.'

The Palm Beach police first became interested in Epstein in 2005 following an allegation that he had molested a fourteen-year-old girl. When Epstein's mansion was searched by police, they found receipts for explicit books, such as *Slave Craft: Roadmap for Erotic Servitude Principles*. They collected around forty statements from women alleging molestation by Epstein, accounts which tended to corroborate each other. Despite all this, the US government, in the form of Alexander Acosta, the attorney in Miami, reached a secret agreement with Epstein which allowed him to plead guilty to just one count of soliciting prostitution from a minor. He was sentenced to eighteen months in prison, much of it to be spent on work release. He also agreed not to contest around forty civil claims brought by the women. Had these been prosecuted, it is thought he might have received a life sentence. The Palm Beach police chief, Michael Reiter, termed the way the authorities had reached a deal with Epstein 'very unusual'. The *Miami Herald* called it 'the deal of a lifetime'. Acosta was appointed Labor Secretary by Donald Trump in 2017. The US Justice Department notified Congress in early 2019 that it had opened an investigation into the federal handling of the Epstein case.

At the same time as the 1999 Mar-a-Lago party in question was held, with Andrew, Epstein and Trump in attendance, the club was employing a sixteen-year-old called Virginia Roberts, who was earning $9 an hour as a locker room attendant. In 2015, she filed an explosive court submission to allege that she had been recruited the year before Andrew's party, in 1998, as a sex slave for Jeffrey Epstein, that she was used to satisfy the sexual needs of important people with whom Mr Epstein wanted to strengthen his relationship, and that Prince Andrew was one of those people. Her affidavit recorded that she had three times had sex with Andrew when she was legally a minor, as far as the state of Florida was concerned. Of the episodes she alleges took place, one was in London, one in New York and one at an orgy on Mr Epstein's private island, part of the US Virgin Islands chain.

She claimed that Epstein told her 'to give the Prince whatever he required' and to report back on the details of what occurred. She said Epstein's aim was to ingratiate himself with powerful people, in order to gain influence, 'as well as to obtain potential blackmail information'. Others have reported that Epstein had installed hidden cameras in rooms across his property. Prince Andrew and the Palace have always strenuously denied that any such encounter between Andrew and Ms Roberts ever took place, and indeed originally even claimed the Prince had no record or recollection of having met her. But then a 2001 photograph emerged of a happy-looking Andrew with his arm around Ms Roberts's midriff.

Although the denials from the Palace have been strong and unequivocal in respect of the allegations that sex took place, they have never explained why Andrew was in the company of a seventeen-year-old with his arm round her. Nor has the Palace provided a narrative to counter the claim that flight logs appear to place Andrew and Ms Roberts together at the times and in the locations she alleges the sex sessions took place.

The Palace has also refused to answer questions about Andrew's friendship with Epstein, or to address the fact that the flight logs for Epstein's private plane place Andrew with Epstein on a regular basis. Nor have they ever given any explanation for the 2010 walk-in-the-park between Andrew and Epstein, who was by then a registered sex offender. However, three senior officials in the Palace were reportedly sufficiently worried to take the exceptional step of writing to the Queen to draw attention to the damage Andrew was doing to the monarchy. They even dared to raise the question of whether Andrew should be suspended from undertaking royal duties.

But the Queen was having none of it. Andrew could do no wrong in her eyes. Her only response to finding Andrew in the mire was very publicly to invest him with a special honour at a private ceremony at Windsor Castle. He was awarded the insignia of a Knight Grand Cross of the Royal Victorian Order, for 'personal services' to the Queen. This Order is one of the few where the Queen alone, rather than the government, determines the recipients.

Worryingly, Andrew featured even more prominently than Trump in Epstein's black book. The financier listed sixteen numbers for the Prince, including a Palace number marked ex-directory, one for Balmoral and one for Sandringham, as well as a personal mobile number. Other well-known figures also to be found included Peter Mandelson, for whom ten numbers are listed, and Tony Blair. But it was Sarah Ferguson who topped the list. He had recorded eighteen separate numbers for her.

Epstein was to be another one of those people leant upon to help clear Sarah's mountain of debts. She received £15,000 from the convicted sex offender as a contribution, days after Andrew had been photographed with him in Central Park in December 2010. In the storm that followed this saga being uncovered, Sarah publicly called Epstein a 'paedophile' and said he had been 'rightly jailed' in 2008. That had not, of course, stopped her from accepting his money. She subsequently admitted to a 'gigantic error' and vowed to repay the money. When asked in 2015 if she had done so, her spokesman replied, 'No comment.' It is a reasonable assumption that the word 'comment' was superfluous.

Perhaps she was taking a leaf out of Andrew's book. Back in 1993, the Prince launched Kelly Associates to collect payments for the use of his photographs. Andrew, as one of the directors (described as 'retired naval officer'), pledged that whatever came in would be given to charity. When *Private Eye* reported on the endeavour in 2004, no money had been given to charity, at least for the previous two years. Kelly Associates was dissolved in 2008.

It was a similar story with Key to Freedom, a charity set up by Andrew in 2012 to help young women trafficked for sex in India – or set up to improve the Duke's image, depending on your interpretation. Andrew termed this a success story, but the truth was rather different. The charity was supposed to offer a 'route to market' for products produced by the girls, particularly hand-printed silk scarves. A deal was reached with Topshop, but within a year, sales had withered away to almost nothing. By late 2019, no scarves had been available to buy in the shops for at least eighteen months, but that did not stop the Duke that year from letting it be known that he was 'particularly dismayed' that his efforts to help victims of sex trafficking had been ignored.

More charity-related embarrassment followed when in the summer of 2020 it emerged that Andrew's charitable trust had broken the law by diverting £355,297 from the charity to the Prince's household to make up for time one of his employees, Amanda Thirsk, had spent on other activities. The money was repaid and the trust notified the Charity Commission of its intention to wind up its activities and distribute the funds left to other charities with similar objectives.

Epstein's black book contained the contact details for a great many women, listed under 'massage'. One of those was Virginia Roberts. It was reported that Epstein eventually reached an out-of-court settlement with her.

Virginia Roberts's story was first uncovered in 2011 by the diligent *Mail on Sunday* journalist Sharon Churcher, but it was with the publication of the Central Park photo that the British press really took an interest. And it was shortly after that when we learnt that Epstein had donated £15,000 to the Help The Fergie Fund. These developments forced Andrew to relinquish his role as special representative for the British government, though he had to be crowbarred out of it. However, it was not as painful for him as it might have been, as he simply carried on as before but without the handle.

He also had to deal with the association with Epstein that had been captured that day in Central Park. Prince Andrew had not only been walking with Epstein but had been a guest at his luxurious residence, the largest private dwelling in Manhattan. His spokesman told the media, 'There is recognition that the December visit [to Epstein] was a mistake, and I think you'll find that there will be no repetition of that visit,' an assurance that stopped short of a promise to cut all ties.

The story would not go away, and the embers that had been ominously smouldering away burst into life again when in July 2019 Epstein was re-arrested and charged with sex trafficking crimes between 2002 and 2005. One of the statements read out in court came from Ms Roberts. Another, in a deposition from a Johanna Sjoberg, then twenty-one, accused Prince Andrew of putting his hand on her breast. But then on 10 August 2019, Epstein was found dead in his cell. It appeared he had committed suicide. This is despite the fact that he had been found semi-conscious with injuries to his neck on 25 July and subsequently placed on suicide watch. A CCTV recording that should have been available was apparently erased due to 'technical errors'. There will have been many rich and powerful people who would have been waiting anxiously to discover what Epstein might have said from the witness box and for whom his death and the absence of his highly publicised criminal trial were welcome developments. But Epstein's death did not relieve the pressure on Andrew, which continued to grow. Footage emerged of him inside Epstein's New York apartment, while the Palace issued ever shriller denials of any wrongdoing. *The Times* labelled him 'the duke of hazard'.

Andrew was captured peering cagily round the solid oak door that was the entrance from the street, and then waving goodbye to a pretty brunette. He then appeared to check whether his presence had been noticed. Epstein left in the company of a young blonde wearing a thick fur-lined coat and little else soon afterwards.

Then an email exchange between the author Evgeny Morozov and the literary agent John Brockman was published in full by the magazine *New Republic*. In one email Brockman wrote that he walked into Epstein's Manhattan house in December 2010 to find a 'British guy in a suit getting foot massages from two young well-dressed women', and then identified him as Andrew.

That Prince Andrew is fond of the company of attractive young women is hardly a revelation. He was snapped on holiday on a yacht surrounded by topless women in Phuket, Thailand, in 2001. He was with his friend Jeffrey Epstein, who is thought to have hosted Andrew's holiday. Epstein's former butler, Juan Alessi, in a 2011 sworn deposition, said that Andrew attended pool parties with naked women at the mansion, where the Prince allegedly enjoyed massages from adolescent girls.

At least three of the girls were questioned under oath as to whether

Andrew had any sexual contact with them or other masseuses. They exercised their right to remain silent under the 5th Amendment to the US constitution. Andrew has denied being present at any pool parties. He was captured in attendance at a Hallowe'en sadomasochistic 'Hookers and Pimps' themed party in Manhattan in 2000. He was accompanied by Ghislaine Maxwell, the woman who allegedly procured girls for Epstein, including Virginia Roberts.

A couple of days after the footage of Andrew's presence at Epstein's Manhattan house was released, a phalanx of more than twenty women assembled to testify before a judge in New York. One was Virginia Roberts, now known by her married name of Giuffre, who told the waiting reporters: 'He knows the truth and I know the truth ... I hope he comes clean about it.'

But Andrew seems to have been studiously determined not to answer any legal questions, and keen to keep as far as possible away from the FBI – indeed, from the US legal system in general. Geoffrey Berman, the top federal prosecutor in Manhattan, finally made his exasperation public in January 2020. Andrew, he told reporters, had said he was 'willing to help any law enforcement agency with their investigations if required', but had so far given 'zero co-operation'. Lisa Bloom, representing the women who say they were abused by Epstein, called Andrew's refusal to answer questions 'a slap in the face' for the women.

Meanwhile, any pretence of public respect for Andrew was disappearing fast. At a press conference in London with the Foreign Secretary Dominic Raab and the US Secretary of State Mike Pompeo, the refusal of the US authorities to extradite Anne Sacoolas was raised. She was the American who had been charged by the Crown Prosecution Service with causing the death by dangerous driving of nineteen-year-old Harry Dunn, by driving on the wrong side of the road. Very shortly after the tragedy, she scuttled out of the country and back to the US, claiming diplomatic immunity. To laughter from the audience, one journalist said, 'We want Anne Sacoolas, you want Prince Andrew. Is there a deal to be done?'

At one point back in 2015, it looked as if the Duke of York might be subpoenaed to give evidence, but the judge ruled that the allegation of Virginia Roberts being forced to have sex with him was 'immaterial and impertinent' to the wider case being heard. Ms Roberts's legal team had twice tried to serve legal papers on Andrew, once via the British Embassy in Washington and once by recorded delivery to Buckingham Palace. Receipt of the papers was refused on both occasions.

Andrew's strategy in the autumn of 2019 was to avoid any legal entanglement and instead use the media to try to dampen the story. Of course, the Duke was busy taking his own legal advice, though both he and the Palace refused to identify who was being consulted. In September, however, Andrew was photographed on the golf course – where else? – with Paul Tweed, a leading celebrity media lawyer. Sources said the two were old friends and that this was not a professional meeting. Then in March 2020 we learnt that Andrew had hired Clare Montgomery QC, the talented barrister who had represented the vile Chilean dictator General Augusto Pinochet in his efforts to avoid extradition. The press gleefully linked the Prince and the General. Andrew seemed to be continually walking into bad headlines. The engagement of this top barrister with extradition experience did, however, suggest that the Duke was genuinely concerned that there might be an attempt to extradite him to the United States, where pressure to get him to testify had been unrelenting.

Andrew's attempt to use the British media to dampen the story was to backfire spectacularly. It began in earnest with an exclusive report in the *Evening Standard* on 28 August 2019 when he complained that he was the subject of a 'witch-hunt'. He even suggested that the incriminating photo of him with his arm round Ms Roberts's midriff could be a fake. Few were convinced, especially not Ms Roberts, who took to the airwaves via NBC News to label the Prince 'an abuser'.

But the real damage was done in an extended BBC interview with the forensic Emily Maitlis on 16 November. Incredulity piled upon incredulity, and the interview contrasted sharply with a BBC *Panorama* programme about a fortnight later, when Ms Roberts was interviewed and was generally accepted to have presented herself as credible. In the Maitlis interview, Andrew admitted he had been a guest of Epstein on many occasions, both in Manhattan and in Palm Beach, and had been to his private island and on his private plane, but maintained he had never witnessed or suspected anything untoward. He also admitted that Epstein was invited to Windsor Castle in July 2006 for Beatrice's eighteenth birthday bash, and said he was unaware that an arrest warrant had been issued for Epstein two months earlier for sexual assault of a minor.

'He never said anything about it,' the Prince lamely told Ms Maitlis.

One of the free trips Andrew took aboard Epstein's private jet he shared with a former Miss Russia, Anna Malova, travelling from the US Virgin Islands to Palm Beach in Florida. Ms Malova was later jailed by the US authorities for failing to comply with a court order unconnected with Epstein or Andrew. Press reports have suggested that MI6 is concerned that the Russians may have evidence to link Andrew to the Epstein saga.

In the BBC interview, we were then asked to believe that the reason for the visit to Epstein in New York in 2010 was in order to break off the friendship between the pair. Most people wanting to end a friendship would simply let it wither, or perhaps make a phone call, or send a text or email. It is somewhat peculiar to travel all the way to the United States to achieve such an end, even more so when you then spend four days living in the property of the person whose friendship you intend to terminate, a convicted sex offender, and allow yourself to be guest of honour at a small dinner party in the house.

'I went there with the sole purpose of saying to him that because he had been convicted, it was inappropriate for us to be seen together,' Andrew told Ms Maitlis – which of course they were when they strolled through Central Park. He had rehearsed this argument earlier in the year, as reported in a *Sunday Times* piece on 6 October, and clearly the sceptical public response to this explanation had not deterred him from repeating it.

If the purpose of the visit was indeed to discontinue the friendship, then it was very generous and understanding of Mr Epstein shortly afterwards to make a sum available to help clear Sarah Ferguson's debts, a point that Emily Maitlis unfortunately did not pursue in her otherwise excellent interview.

'Witnesses say they saw many young girls coming and going at the time,' Ms Maitlis put to Andrew. 'There is video footage of Epstein accompanied by young girls and you were there staying in his house.'

'I never saw them,' replied Andrew.

He then said he had no recollection of ever meeting the then Virginia Roberts, despite the frequently reproduced photograph of him with an arm round her bare midriff. It seems his memory, like President Trump's, is failing him. He also suggested that the photo was taken upstairs in Ghislaine Maxwell's house but then said he had not been upstairs there, which invites the question: in that case how was he able to place the location of the photo?

Yet the Prince's memory seems razor-sharp in other respects. Questioned by Ms Maitlis, Andrew was able to state with certainty that he had not been at Tramp nightclub on the specific evening he was allegedly there dancing with Ms Roberts in 2001, but was actually with his daughter Beatrice at the Pizza Express outlet in Woking. Clearly this must have been a joyous occasion to leave such a deep and lasting impression and etch the date firmly in the Prince's mind almost twenty years on.

Others have a different memory of the evening in question. The *Mail on Sunday* reported that two new witnesses had been found to corroborate Ms Roberts's accusation that she was with the Prince that night at Tramp. The paper also reported a statement from 'a highly respected former Royal protection officer' who told the paper that Andrew may have returned to Buckingham Palace late that night, rather than being at home as he maintained. Meanwhile, a second victim of Jeffrey Epstein alleged that Andrew had also had sex with her. And model Johanna Sjoberg claimed that when she was twenty-one, the Prince groped her breasts, while Ghislaine Maxwell used a *Spitting Image* puppet of Andrew to fondle Ms Roberts's breasts.

The fallout from the car-crash interview included renewed pressure on Scotland Yard to explain why it had not pursued complaints about Prince Andrew's alleged engagement with Ms Roberts and specifically the allegation that she had been trafficked to Britain to have sex with Andrew at the home of Ghislaine Maxwell. The police first received a complaint in 2015 following the matter bursting into the open in the United States, when Assistant Commissioner Dean Haydon decided not to progress the complaint to a full investigation, even though the police policy at the time was that 'victims must be believed'. Lawyers acting for Ms Roberts independently contacted the Metropolitan Police in 2016 without effect.

The fallout also forced Andrew to move his office out of Buckingham Palace and to stand down from all 230 of his patronages, a decision he presented as a temporary move. He had little choice. He had already been dropped as chancellor of the University of Huddersfield, and other organisations were lining up to review his position, including the Foundation for Liver Research, the Sea Cadets, the Whitgift School in Croydon and, perhaps most hurtfully for Andrew, the Royal Portrush Golf Club. The Grenadier Guards, one of the Army's most distinguished regiments, made it known that they had not wanted him as their figurehead in the first place when he was appointed in 2017 and had asked for a different royal but were told firmly by the Palace that they were getting the Duke of York.

The point of no return was perhaps reached during one of the leaders' debates in the 2019 general election campaign when Sue from Leeds asked, 'Is the monarchy fit for purpose?' Jeremy Corbyn was applauded when he replied that it 'needed a bit of improvement'. A couple of days later, Andrew issued a statement announcing that his role as a publicly funded royal was over 'for the foreseeable future'. It is not hard to imagine that the thrust of this statement will have been in effect dictated to him by senior members of the royal family, alarmed by the damage he was doing to the institution.

Andrew's withdrawal from the front line meant he faced losing his royal security, a status symbol he had always valued. A Scotland Yard source told the *Evening Standard*, 'Those in charge of security cannot write a blank cheque for anyone who does not have a public role for the foreseeable future.'

There had, however, been a blank cheque to cover the security costs racked up by Andrew for his pet project, Pitch@Palace. For this aspect alone the taxpayer was presented with a bill for a quarter of a million pounds. But Pitch was another casualty of the BBC interview, ignominiously holed below the water line.

Pitch@Palace was a vehicle the Prince established to bring entrepreneurs and rich investors together. Andrew likes to style himself as an entrepreneur, although, as he never puts any money in himself, it has been suggested that his first investment should be in a dictionary.

Private Eye likened his performance at these events to being in the presence of Kim Jong-un, with attendees expected to take copious notes of the pearls of wisdom flowing from his mouth, or visibly hold up their electronic devices to record them. These exaggerated mannerisms were not functional but rather served to massage Andrew's ego, just as a person taking their driving test will often greatly exaggerate looking in the rear-view mirror to ensure the examiner knows they are doing so.

Pitch@Palace began in 2014 with two events. By 2018, he had clocked up forty-five events that year outside Britain. On the day I checked the website, in early April 2019, it turned out that the most recent event had been a seminar at Buckingham Palace for, yes, Bahrain. Days later, Andrew turned up in Bahrain on an official visit, paid for by the taxpayer. His ex-wife and his daughter Beatrice then joined him, guests of the Crown Prince, at the Bahrain Grand Prix, with Sarah happily posting a selfie taken with the jockey Frankie Dettori. Andrew was due to visit Bahrain yet again when the sky fell in after his disastrous BBC interview. For once, the visit was pulled.

Meanwhile, Pitch was hit by a succession of major funders making known their intention to end funding. One by one, they pulled the plug: Standard Chartered, Barclays, KPMG, Inmarsat. Initially, Andrew indicated his intention to continue leading the venture, but his case, already very shaky, was demolished by the revelation in the *Daily Telegraph* that the company Pitch@Palace Global Ltd, a commercial enterprise, had written into the small print of its terms and conditions an entitlement to take 2 per cent of any investment in the first three years. Andrew had therefore opened up the possibility of benefiting personally from the use of public buildings where Pitch events were held, namely Buckingham Palace and St James's Palace.

Rich Wilson, who co-founded a technology hedge fund and had attended a Pitch event, was scathing in his reaction to this revelation. 'What on earth is a member of the royal family [doing] using his status to take equity from early-stage tech founders for essentially nothing?' What indeed. Very shortly after the *Telegraph* piece, the clause relating to the 2 per cent cut was quietly removed from official documentation.

Again, *force majeure* took over and the next day Andrew very reluctantly conceded that he would step back from Pitch, which would henceforth be headed by Amanda Thirsk, the Duke's private secretary, who had been running the initiative on a day-to-day basis and would now become chief executive. At about the same time it emerged that Ms Thirsk was leaving the royal household after fifteen years. Within the Palace, she was held largely responsible for the decision to proceed with the disastrous BBC interview. The Duke's advisor Jason Stein had counselled strongly against the idea but was overruled. He left Andrew's employ shortly before the broadcast, after only a month in office. Ms Thirsk, when she left, did so with a five-figure ex gratia payment, according to Sky.

The new arrangements at Pitch did not hold for long, and in April we learnt that Ms Thirsk was leaving to take up a private sector posting. Pitch@Palace was to be relaunched as Pitch Connect, though who was going to handle the damaged goods, and how, was far from clear.

Come the New Year, and the Palace let it be known that Andrew's sixtieth birthday celebrations on 19 February would be a muted affair, with the planned glitz abandoned. Instead, there would be a small dinner party at his Windsor home. According to media reports, several invited guests hurriedly developed subsequent engagements and Sarah was left to cast around to make up the numbers.

The hitherto unremarked practice of flying the Union Jack on public buildings to mark the Duke's birthday now generated a good deal of public hostility after councils were reminded to fly the flag on his birthday. *The Sun* ran a front page with the headline 'Union Joke'. A number of councils said they had no intention of complying and the government was left with little option but to say that flying the flag was optional. More *force majeure*. And to ward off more unwelcome headlines, Andrew quietly made it public that he had 'declined' a promotion to the rank of Admiral that had been due to come up with the rations on his sixtieth birthday. This putative promotion, like the vast majority of honours handed out by the Queen to her family, naturally bore no relation to the achievement of anything that would remotely justify it. Andrew, who collects medals as some collect stamps, will have to put up with being a mere Vice-Admiral for a bit longer.

Andrew is the Queen's favourite son and the turn of events will have distressed her deeply. She allowed herself to be photographed with Andrew out riding, and then attending church, to show her support for her wayward offspring. In January 2020, the Palace let it be known that Andrew had been 'a tower of strength' as she dealt with the unfolding saga involving Harry and Meghan. The Queen was also keen to have Andrew present in his military role for the annual Trooping the Colour ceremony in June, as a step towards his rehabilitation, but perhaps fortunately in this regard, it was cancelled due to the coronavirus.

Despite Andrew's toxic association with Epstein, it is possible his position would have been treated with more sympathy had his arrogance and rudeness not alienated so many people over the years. Over the years, Paul Page, an armed police officer from the royal protection squad, revealed details of Andrew's behaviour at Buckingham Palace where the officer was stationed. The information came out in a court case in which Mr Page was being charged with running a fraudulent pyramid scheme within the squad. He told the court of one incident in which Andrew had rung through to instruct the police, contrary to their security procedures, to allow through a car containing two guests. The guests, when they arrived, turned out to be two young women, both provocatively dressed, and each swigging from a can of Coke. The car was waved through without even the names of the young women being recorded. The women left about an hour later.

Andrew seemed quite keen to waive the strict security he had demanded be provided for his daughters. In another incident, when Mr Page and other protection officers discovered through electronic means that somebody was wandering along the corridor near the Queen's bedroom, they went to investigate and found it was Andrew. They were met with a stream of abuse. 'This is my fucking home, I can go where I want, now fuck off.'

On another occasion – which the officer concerned believes may have been the time Andrew said he was at home all evening after visiting Pizza Express in Woking – a royal security officer alleges that Andrew arrived back at the Palace in the early hours and began blaring his horn and flashing his lights. The Prince was, it seems, furious that the gates had been closed, as quite properly they would have been, and used his bodyguard's radio to shout abuse at the guards on the gate, including a yelled demand to 'open these bloody gates, you buffoons'. One royal aide told the *Daily Telegraph*, 'I've seen him treat his staff in a shocking, appalling way. He's been incredibly rude to his personal protection officers, literally throwing things on the ground and demanding that they "fucking pick them up". No social graces at all.'

He has also been accused of using racist language. Rohan Silva, a Sri Lankan who was a key aide to the then Prime Minister David Cameron, said he had been left 'reeling' when Andrew used the phrase 'n****r in the woodpile' in an official meeting. Andrew denied he had said this. But then former Home Secretary Jacqui Smith announced that Andrew had made 'unbelievable' racist jokes at a state dinner for the Saudi royal family. One particularly egregious 'joke' that left the MPs present 'slack-jawed' involved camels. Once again, the Palace was forced to issue a denial.

Andrew has become a royal pariah and a return to public life any time soon is unthinkable. Yet his association with Epstein, and the allegations of his involvement which have ultimately destroyed his position, are far from the only aspect of his behaviour that is of major concern and needs to be properly investigated.

So we should start by detailing exactly where he has been jetting off to at public expense, and what he has been doing in parallel privately, and determining what he has actually achieved – and, for that matter, the damage that he has done.

To date, no proper assessment has been made of the value for money for the country of his multiple overseas trips. Back in 2009, it emerged that Andrew himself had commissioned a report into his activities from PricewaterhouseCoopers. The government refused my request to publish the report, maintaining that it was 'private'. It is rumoured that the report identified Andrew's travelling practices as excessive. In the ten years to 2011, his special representative role cost the taxpayer £4 million, with another £10 million to be added on for his police protection.

Despite being forced to resign his role in 2011, Andrew simply carried on much as before, with the Palace explaining that he was undertaking royal visits abroad just as other members of the family do. 'Why is Air Miles Andy still funded by taxes?' asked the *Daily Mail* in 2012. Andrew in fact undertook trade missions to seven countries in the six months after he allegedly stood down from the role.

One of the visits was to Bahrain, which has continued to feature prominently in his schedule. In 2014, he again met the King, this time at the economic summit in Davos. Andrew seems unperturbed by the country's poor human rights record. Indeed, in general he seems drawn to tyrants and torturers in his choice of contacts and countries.

It seems that despite the acute embarrassments, the shady company he keeps and the pointed questions about his activities, Andrew would not modifiy his behaviour one iota. Each year the Prince has received a handout from his mother, a tax-free sum of £249,000 to fund his private office, to which he can add a small naval pension of £20,000. Yet his spending habits have suggested an income way beyond that, and we are entitled to know where that has come from and what Andrew has delivered in return.

Most strikingly, in late 2014, Andrew and Sarah, who as a couple never quite seem either married or divorced, bought a £13 million ski chalet in the upmarket Swiss resort of Verbier. Of course, this is no ordinary chalet. It has seven bedrooms, a massive indoor swimming pool, a sauna, sun terrace and bar. Until they purchased it, Chalet Helora was being rented out at £22,000 a week. In May 2020, we learnt that the Yorks were facing legal action, having failed to meet a deadline the previous December to pay the remainder of the sum due for the purchase of Chalet Helora. The pair apparently let the seller know that they intended to dispose of the chalet to clear the debt, but that cut no ice. It seems he preferred hard cash to vague promises. In the past, there have always been individuals willing to stump up cash to help the Yorks out of yet another self-dug hole, whether it was Jeffrey Epstein, David Rowland or some dodgy contact from one of the -stans, but Andrew was now perceived as so toxic, and perhaps more significantly lacking in influence, that false friends were now hard to find.

At the same time, Andrew was spending £7.5 million to refurbish Royal Lodge, his home in Windsor Great Park. Nor was he scrimping on personal possessions. In early 2015, he was snapped wearing the latest eighteen-carat gold Apple Watch, which would have set him back around £12,000. Unless of course that was another 'private' gift.

So how can someone with the declared income he has possibly afford a £13 million Swiss chalet, and to support an opulent lifestyle that clearly requires far more? Unless he has come up trumps in the National Lottery and told nobody, he is clearly gathering in significant sums that we do not know about. Yet people do not generally hand over large sums to other people out of the goodness of their heart. They generally want something in return.

The media have often been more interested in his sex life than his finances. Yet ultimately who Andrew has sex with, and what form that sex takes, is a private matter, assuming no law has been broken, security has not been compromised and undue influence has not resulted. He is entitled to privacy on that front.

But we are entitled to be told where all Andrew's hidden wealth has come from, and what steps now need to be taken in terms of royal rules and accountability to ensure that the financial abuse Andrew has been allowed to get away with can never happen again.

The Royal Free

B ack in 2006, Prince William took Kate Middleton on a romantic
holiday to the island of Mustique. This select Caribbean location
has long been a regular haunt of the rich and famous, including members
of the royal family such as Princess Anne's daughter, Zara.

The royal connection began in 1960 when Princess Margaret was
given a piece of land by the island's then owner, Colin Christopher
Paget Tennant, later the third Lord Glenconner, as a wedding present,
which is certainly a few steps up from the set of saucepans most people
could expect to receive.

Mustique is renowned for its pristine white sandy beaches, turquoise
sea and, of course, for the ever-present sun that bathes the island. On
that occasion, William and Kate stayed in a five-bedroom hillside villa
overlooking the sea, equipped with a twin gazebo and an infinity pool.
The normal rent for this splendid spread at the time was £8,000 a week.
Fortunately, William did not have to pay. He let it be known he would
like to holiday on the island, but complained that he was only a poor
student and could not afford to go.

Obviously this was tragic, if untrue, but fortunately a white knight
stepped in. No, not his father or grandmother, nor any other member

of the royal family, any number of whom could, if they had wished, have paid for this holiday for William and Kate from their small change. Instead, it was a millionaire clothing tycoon, John Robinson, who took pity on the bereft Prince and made his Villa Hibiscus available. While this was undoubtedly very generous of the founder of the Jigsaw fashion chain, it would be interesting to know on how many occasions he has made his villa available to people who genuinely cannot afford it.

William's rather crude plea could perhaps be forgiven from someone still maturing into adulthood, especially as he was following an example set by his father. Back in 1999, Charles flew William and Harry to Greece to soak up a free cruise on the *Alexander*, one of the largest yachts in the world, courtesy of the Greek shipping billionaire Yiannis Latsis, one of the twenty richest people in the world. Prince Charles does not appear to have delved too closely into Mr Latsis's background or the rumours circulating about him before accepting his generous hospitality. After all, a free cruise is a free cruise. Charles had in fact first borrowed Mr Latsis's yacht in 1991 for a second honeymoon with Diana, and then again in 2002 for an intimate holiday with Camilla. It must be good to be able to conduct your romances in such opulent and glamorous surroundings, knowing that someone else is picking up the bill.

Having tasted the sweet fruit, William has been keen to keep eating. The Cambridges were subsequently only too willing to accept an offer for the use of another Mustique property, the Villa Aurora, owned by Mark Cecil, a hedge fund millionaire.

Then in 2015, for a change of scenery, they descended on the Villa Rocina along with the extended Middleton family, courtesy of Violeta Alvarez, the Venezuelan millionaire. In 2018, visitors to Mustique might have seen not just William and Kate but again the extended Middleton family, too, soaking up the sun and knocking back cocktails in the five-star Cotton House resort. The *Daily Mail*, which has reported on the royal couple's trips to Mustique, quoted an island source in one of its pieces: 'The Cambridges never have to pay for anything when they are in Mustique. They are always looked after. They have drivers, private chefs and a team at their disposal.'

It is perhaps no wonder that the paper labelled the couple the 'King and Queen of the freebie holiday'. Is this really the example we want our future King to set? It seems the visits to Mustique occur with regularity, as the Cambridges work their way round the island's villas. But one they are unlikely to be staying at is Les Jolies Eaux, previously owned by Princess Margaret.

In 1996, with her health failing, she transferred the property to her son, Viscount Linley, to try to avoid death duties. Somewhat callously, he decided shortly afterwards to sell it and deprive his mother of her Caribbean retreat. As a sop, he negotiated that she was to be allowed to spend three weeks a year in the villa, courtesy of the new owner, a fabulously wealthy American called James Murray, the son of a cattle farmer. But Mr Murray decided on a drastic conversion of the quaint villa to make it rather more vibrant and American, which took away the memories and magic for Margaret.

Lord Glenconner subsequently told his friend Sharon Churcher, then chief American correspondent for the *Mail on Sunday*, that Linley's sale of her villa plunged Margaret into a deep depression. The day in early 1999 when the estate agent showed potential buyers round the property, with Margaret in situ, was, according to friends, one of the most traumatic days of her life. This all added to her physical woes, and when she attended Prince Edward's wedding that year, she was in a wheelchair. She had lost her sanctuary that meant so much to her, and lost her health too. She felt adrift and alone back in Kensington Palace.

Lord Glenconner, in whom Margaret confided, claimed the Queen brusquely pooh-poohed the notion that her sister needed any sort of treatment for her mental anguish or even, it seems, her physical symptoms, simply telling her to 'buck up'. She believed Margaret was not as ill as she made out, and perhaps might even have been malingering. The Queen, who no doubt thought she was acting in her sister's best interests, told her to stop feeling sorry for herself and is even alleged to have banned wheelchairs at Sandringham and Balmoral, believing shock therapy was the way to get Margaret back on her feet, literally.

For Margaret, the cool response from her family only exacerbated matters. She was to die shortly afterwards, in 2002. We can only speculate whether Margaret might have overcome this depression and lived to a royal ripe old age, as so many women in her family have done, if her condition had been received rather more sympathetically.

So it has been trips galore to Mustique for the Cambridges, but it would be naive to assume that their freebie holidays are limited to this idyllic island. William has an open invitation to use any of the luxury lodges in the Kenyan game reserve run by the family of his former girlfriend Jecca Craig, which he has eagerly accepted. Indeed, it was on a visit there in 2010 that he proposed to Kate. Perhaps they are all good friends, for in 2014 Ms Craig joined William for a boar hunt on a 32,000-acre estate in Spain owned by the Duke of Westminster.

Then there are the trips to France. In 2012, they availed themselves of a hunting lodge, the Château d'Autet, owned by the then Viscount Linley, now Earl of Snowdon. In the spring of 2016, William and Kate were able to enjoy a four-day skiing holiday at Courchevel in the French Alps, courtesy of the Duke of Westminster, who flew them out. According to the *Daily Mail*, Kate's mother asked around to see if someone could provide a chalet for them. Heaven forbid they might have to pay for one themselves. It is not as though William could not afford to pay for such holidays. His estimated wealth is already in excess of £20 million.

And they were hardly back in Britain when, in July that year, the ever-generous Duke of Westminster made available a private jet to convey them to a delightful sixteenth-century chateau in the south of France, owned by Michael Green, the communications guru.

The freeloading by our future monarch and his wife is not unique to them, it has to be said. On the contrary, it is all too normal behaviour for the Windsors. There seems no limit to what members of the royal family will seek to avoid paying for. William's father got in on the act early. Aged twenty-one, Prince Charles managed to land it that Major Ferguson, whose daughter would much later marry Prince Andrew, took responsibility for the time-consuming task of arranging his polo games – an unpaid role, of course. The major pulled in sponsors like Rolex and Cartier, so Charles ended up having to pay nothing to partake in this highly exclusive and expensive sport.

In 1988, the tabloids gleefully ran a story about Major Ferguson's sorties into massage parlours. Much fun was had by all. *Private Eye* even ran a Ronald Ferguson anagram competition, which generated entries such as 'old groaner's fun' and 'organ flounders', the latter presumably mere supposition. In any case, Prince Charles, with his usual absence of loyalty and lack of gratitude for services rendered, abruptly sacked him. The dismissal came in a letter from a private secretary. The major had served Charles for twenty-one years. He told the *Daily Telegraph*, 'I was appalled by the way it was handled. The Prince of Wales did not have the guts to send for me and tell me straight to my face.' Of course, what Major Ferguson did or did not do in massage parlours had no impact one way or the other on his ability to organise Charles's polo matches, but Charles decided to adopt a holier-than-thou response to the tabloid stories, thus adding the exercise of double standards to his brutal actions. After all, this was the time when Charles saw no problem in maintaining a relationship with Camilla while still married to Diana.

Charles and Camilla have also been very happy to accept free holidays, and not just those courtesy of Yiannis Latsis. At the turn of the century, the loss of the royal yacht *Britannia* was a great saving to the Treasury but a bitter loss to the royal family. Still, there was consolation in the free holidays that could be garnered: the pair were able to enjoy the delights of the Mediterranean, for example, relaxing on a luxury yacht owned by the Iraqi-born banker Nemir Kirdar.

Princess Michael of Kent, known unaffectionately as 'Princess Pushy', requested ten colour TV sets for her servants' quarters from Thorn EMI as a price for her to attend a cocktail party. A nice gesture, perhaps, but then nice gestures come cheap when someone else is paying. Oh, and she demanded an appearance fee as well for herself. One particularly extraordinary incident involving Princess Michael occurred when she saw an ivory bear in the window of a London jeweller's and on impulse walked in and unashamedly asked for it to be given to her.

There is no record of the exact exchange that took place, but one imagines it might have gone something like this: 'Good afternoon. I'm a member of the royal family. That rather nice ivory figure in your window – I would like you to give it to me for nothing.' That, in any case, was what it amounted to.

The shop duly complied and in return got a thank-you letter to frame and display. It might have been more satisfying for the shop owner, and certainly more appropriate, simply to have told her, to use Princess Anne's famous phrase, to naff off. Perhaps Princess Michael was keen to emulate the example of Queen Mary, wife of George V. She was a great collector of rare and expensive items, especially those belonging to other people – tiaras, Fabergé eggs, figurines – and did not mind where she collected them from. Her normal technique would be to visit friends, browse through their collections and then show enormous interest in anything she found that caught her fancy.

Some of this was blatant, such as informing her intimidated host that she had a matching piece in the Palace, and would it not be marvellous to reunite the pair. And who could say no to a queen? If a host seemed resistant to making an unconditional gift, a piece could always be 'borrowed' and then simply not returned. Anyone who had any sense would hide their prize possessions away prior to her arrival and bring out the junk instead.

And it is not as though Mary was short of jewels. She had snapped up at fire-sale prices many of the famous Imperial pieces smuggled out of Russia during the revolution. Sadly, the Tsar and his family were not in a position to reclaim them subsequently as they were executed, Mary's husband George V having refused them the lifeline of asylum in Britain. Still, every cloud has a silver lining.

Then there is the generosity of Manuel Colonques, the Spanish tile manufacturer. You can see his quality tiling in Prince Charles's kitchen and bathroom at Birkhall, or indeed in many other royal homes, though of course you may have to pay to get in. On one occasion Prince Charles subsequently flew to open a new wing of Mr Colonques's factory in Spain and attend a dinner there. The following year, the Spaniard's company installed an Islamic garden at the Prince's home at Highgrove – free of charge, of course. No doubt he and his wife will have been delighted to have subsequently received an invitation to William and Kate's wedding. They in turn received tiles for their bathrooms, too.

The enthusiastic receipt of gifts even extends to the clothes they wear. While protocol suggests that the royals should not accept clothes as gifts, that does not stop them borrowing fabulous designer outfits which would cost thousands to buy, and then returning them afterwards. In Kate's case, the negotiations are handled by her stylist, Natasha Archer, who picks the outfits for the Duchess to wear. To be fair, Kate has been spotted shopping alone – for instance at Jigsaw, where she used to work before marrying William, and whose creator is John Robinson, the very same one with the Mustique villa. And she does actually buy clothes herself – in fact, around £50,000 worth in 2012 alone. The *Daily Mail* in 2017 estimated that over one year the figure had risen to around a quarter of a million pounds.

The deeply unattractive culture of brazenly soliciting something for nothing is of course made easier by those who are prepared to go along with it. They might be overawed, they might want the kudos, or they might want a commercial advantage. But whatever the reason, they nearly always say yes.

Sarah Ferguson came unstuck, however, when she tried to blag outfits from the designer Zandra Rhodes in return for securing media coverage for her creations. 'Darling, I don't need the publicity,' was the cool response.

That the royals exude a sense of entitlement, expecting ordinary people to provide goods and services free, rewarded only by the satisfaction that they have served their betters is perhaps unsurprising when so many appear willing to reinforce it by their own actions. Wimbledon in 2018 made a jaw-dropping seventy-four royal box seats available every day of the tournament. Hospitality packages included lunch, tea and end-of-day drinks.

The royal mindset is not far removed from the droit de seigneur mentality of medieval times. In fact, those familiar with the long lineage of royal traditions may see a parallel in the customs of Queen Elizabeth I. Every summer she would set off, hundreds of carts and hundreds of servants in tow, and descend on some unfortunate local worthy who was expected to house and feed this hungry horde, naturally without any payment being made, and for as long as the Queen decided to stay, even if this effectively bankrupted her host. The towns through which this cart train passed were also expected to hand over some token of esteem like a silver plate, and perhaps some gold too. They were royally robbed, but it was ever so elegantly done, with the supplicants conniving in their own loss. And as it was in the reign of Elizabeth I, so it is in the reign of Elizabeth II.

In *Rebel Prince*, Tom Bower sets out numerous occasions when Prince Charles has exhibited this haughty attitude of entitlement. He tells how the art historian and landscape designer Sir Roy Strong was summoned to advise on the cultivation of hedges at Highgrove. After many days' work, he submitted an invoice for £1,000 to cover the costs of the gardener he had brought with him, whereupon the temperature dropped to below zero. Sir Roy was frozen out, never asked to return, and was not even thanked for his efforts. A personally inscribed copy of his book on gardening which he had brought for Prince Charles was left to languish in a waiting room, barred from the library.

Charles, it seems, was offended by the sight of an invoice. But why on earth should somebody in this situation providing a service subsidise one of the richest people in the country? Most normal people would instead be offended by the rude and ungrateful way in which he dealt with people who were helping him out.

Camilla soon learnt the ways of the royal family. Upon discovering that a billionaire banker to whom she had been introduced owned a luxury yacht and a huge estate in the south of France, she made it known that she would like an invitation. One duly appeared. It is difficult to decide if such behaviour should be classified as shameful or shameless. Perhaps both.

Princess Margaret was another royal who made it very clear that she wanted the free use of a yacht here and a villa there from her star-struck rich friends. If it was not a free holiday, then money would do. Never mind the good causes, Margaret expected to be paid to attend overseas charity events and would travel first class, and expect a first-class hotel and a personal appearance fee. The going rate for an event in New York was $30,000. Naturally, this will all have come out of the money raised for the charity.

While she valued the big-ticket items, she did not neglect the lesser-value opportunities either. Like most royals, Princess Margaret was the recipient of unsolicited gifts from supplicant well-wishers, many of whom will doubtless have spent money they could ill afford to enable them to make their humble offering. One such gift was an enormous basket of bubble baths, perfumes and oils, so enormous that it took two people to carry it – specifically, to carry it to the Crabtree & Evelyn shop in Kensington, where Margaret demanded a cash refund. Store policy was only to issue a credit note in respect of returned goods, but, being a royal, she got the cash she wanted. It would be interesting to know what the donor of this gift would have thought of this shabby behaviour.

The unsolicited gifts come in all shapes and sizes on an endless conveyor belt, like an upmarket version of the one that used to feature in the BBC programme *The Generation Game*, except that with the royal version, there is no need to memorise the gifts, as they get them all anyway.

The 2016 visit of the Cambridges to Canada is not untypical. The indigenous peoples who hosted them gifted them 150 separate items, from a pair of gloves to a miniature totem pole. Their political hosts also showered them with gifts, including woollen wraps, bow ties, a guitar and a ukulele, books, a hockey jersey and an elaborate candlestick holder. Then there are the offerings from the public at large. With thoughts of the children clearly in people's minds, there came a deluge of soft toys, socks, crayons and books. Perhaps the oddest gifts were four lace snowflakes and a package of bread mix, though presumably William and Kate need little help when it comes to making bread.

The official gifts received by the Queen from other heads of state can be equally varied and idiosyncratic. In 1997, for instance, these included a bronze sculpture of giraffes, a book of antiquarian maps, two water colours of orchids, and a carved wooden elephant.

As so often with the royals, there is a blurred line between what is private and what is public – and, in this case, what is a personal gift and what is an official gift. Andrew Morton, in his book *Theirs Is the Kingdom*, refers to an incident in which Charles and Diana, while on an official visit to Bahrain, were publicly presented with mere tokens by the Emir. A year later, it transpired that Charles had been given a 'private' gift of a brand-new Aston Martin, and Diana a 'private' gift of a fabulous set comprising a sapphire and diamond necklace, bracelet and earrings. That these gifts were made on an official visit to individuals representing Britain makes it clear that these should have been regarded as official gifts to the nation. The fact that they were made in secret strongly suggests that the objective of this subterfuge was to allow the royal couple to divert the gifts from the British nation to themselves. Naturally, any official gifts from the Queen or members of her family are paid for by the taxpayer. In 2002, the then Chancellor Gordon Brown told me that the cost for the year before had been £47,854.

The nexus between private and public gifts came to the fore back in 2002 with the inquiry into Charles's household affairs conducted by Sir Michael Peat. That followed the collapse of the trial of Paul Burrell, formerly butler to Diana, Princess of Wales. He was alleged to have systematically plundered her estate. The court proceedings were progressing well from the point of view of the prosecution until the Queen suddenly announced, halfway through the trial, that she had known all along that he was holding on to Diana's possessions for safekeeping.

Mr Burrell was hugely loyal to the Princess and seems to have been genuinely concerned that her possessions might have been wrongfully removed after her death. It was her relatives who alerted police to their suspicions that Mr Burrell was improperly taking Diana's possessions.

One day he was invited to take tea with the Queen at Buckingham Palace. The etiquette for these occasions normally requires the guest to sit in a chair at right angles to the Queen for an event that typically lasts about twenty minutes. On this occasion, the Queen patted the settee on which she sat for Paul Burrell to join her on it. The two had known each other for a long time. Mr Burrell started life in the Palace as a page boy to the Queen. Tea lasted an hour and a half. It was on that occasion, it seems, long before Paul Burrell's trial began, that he apparently told the Queen that he was storing Diana's possessions for safekeeping.

It is extraordinary that it was only in the middle of the trial that the Queen revealed details of this conversation. After all, it was on 19 November 2000 that it became known that the police wanted to question him about the alleged theft. It was on 16 August 2001 that he was charged with stealing 342 items belonging to Diana, Charles and William. It was on 14 October 2002 that Mr Burrell's trial began. But it was only on 1 November 2002 that the Queen revealed the conversation she had had with Mr Burrell which immediately caused the trial to collapse.

Why did this take so long? Did the Queen really not understand what was happening? Had the penny dropped that this conversation would emerge as part of the defence case, putting the Queen in an embarrassing position? Were members of the royal family worried, notwithstanding his fierce loyalty, about what else Mr Burrell would say when questioned? Certainly the defence were in no doubt that Mr Burrell would be acquitted if the trial continued to its conclusion.

One interesting aspect is that criminal cases in this country are undertaken in the name of the sovereign, hence this one would have been Regina *v* Mr Paul Burrell. It is therefore perhaps the first time the monarch has intervened to destroy what is technically her prosecution.

The police did not emerge with much glory from this episode. They told Charles and William that Mr Burrell had sold some of Diana's artefacts in the United States. This turned out to be a case of mistaken identity. They told the royal pair that Mr Burrell had acquired three properties. This was misleading, if not incompetent. One was his residence which he was selling, one was held on a bridging loan prior to his move and the third was a flower shop that was, to all intents and purposes, connected to one of the other two. In any case, such was the furore about the facts and allegations that did surface, including about his household, that Prince Charles was obliged to set up an inquiry. This was not, however, to be an independent inquiry, let alone a police investigation. Rather, it was an internal one, trusted to Sir Michael Peat.

Sir Michael was the consummate insider. He had by this point served the monarchy for twelve years, including as Keeper of the Privy Purse. He is credited both with advising the Queen in 1993 to start paying tax, and for putting the royal finances in better shape generally. He moved across to work for Prince Charles in 2002 as private secretary.

Sir Michael is widely regarded as both competent and a man of integrity, but surely even he would have found it challenging had he found that some of the more sensational allegations, particularly one alleging an incident of male rape within the Prince's household, had any validity. And, unsurprisingly, he concluded in careful wording, 'The suggestion that the disclosure [by the Queen] was made for an improper motive and in the expectation of preventing the trial continuing finds no support in the available evidence.' As it was, he did actually produce what was, overall, a critical report, one which buffeted the boat, but not so much that there was any chance of it sinking.

Out of his report tumbled an unsavoury picture of the way Prince Charles's household affairs were being run. It found that staff, including Charles's trusted right-hand man Michael Fawcett, had accepted gifts and hospitality from outsiders, even though the rules forbade this. The gifts Mr Fawcett received included a watch worth £2,500 and a club membership worth even more. Nor were these officially declared, although he had made no secret of them, suggesting such behaviour was standard practice. The report, however, found that Fawcett was not guilty of actual financial impropriety.

Perhaps it was, as Paul Burrell said, simply a staff perk 'as old as the monarchy'. For staff were also given unwanted gifts by Prince Charles himself, particularly items such as pens and bottles of champagne. Others were variously sold off for charity by Michael Fawcett, given to charity or simply destroyed if they could not be passed on. These included drawings or home-made tapes specially and lovingly made for the Prince.

Sir Michael's report revealed that between 1999 and 2001, Charles was the lucky recipient of an astonishing 2,394 presents. These included 249 CDs, videos and tapes, fifteen items of arms and armour, twelve toiletry items, five animals, and most likely a partridge in a pear tree.

As mentioned, there was again confusion over what was an official gift and what was personal. In the end, Sir Michael traced only 180 that could be called official, which is of course a tiny proportion of the gifts received. Within even that small number, nineteen had disappeared without trace. Crucially, he concluded that there was no evidence of staff selling or disposing of gifts without authorisation, which implicitly pointed the finger at Prince Charles himself.

The 111-page report made uncomfortable reading for the Prince, painting as it did a picture of sloppiness and incompetence. Someone had to be seen to be carrying the can. Obviously Prince Charles decided it would not be himself, so step forward Michael Fawcett, who duly fell on his sword. Charles was nevertheless unhappy at the outcome. 'I can manage without just about anyone, except for Michael,' he confessed.

The sword Mr Fawcett fell on, however, turned out to be one of those trick stage ones where the blade disappears into the hilt and the victim emerges unscathed. He was given a pay-off believed to be in the region of £500,000 and set up his own event management company, with Prince Charles as a principal client.

In 2017, the former footman was made a director of Charles's private company, A. G. Carrick Ltd, which handles the mementoes that can be bought at his Highgrove shop, just the place to go if you want an overpriced stuffed corgi. The business reported a two-year turnover of more than £4 million.

Over the years, many have resented the influence Mr Fawcett has appeared to exert over Charles, not least Diana, but it is far from unique for a senior royal to have a very close relationship with a servant. Queen Victoria, for instance, had John Brown. Following the embarrassing fiasco of 2002, the rules on royal gifts were tightened and a new code introduced. This stated:

> The fundamental principle governing the acceptance of gifts by Members of The Royal Family is that no gifts, including hospitality or services, should be accepted which would, or might appear to, place the Member of The Royal Family under any obligation to the donor. In this regard, before accepting any gift, careful consideration should always be given, wherever practicable, to the donor, the reason for and occasion of the gift and the nature of the gift itself.

This is all sensible, and usefully includes hospitality and services in the definition of gifts. Sometimes, however, a member of the royal family, when on official business, will receive a gift which is more akin to a hand grenade with the pin taken out.

Back in 2012, Prince Edward and his wife found themselves on a visit to Bahrain. As with all official overseas visits, the decision to send a member of the royal family was taken by the Foreign and Commonwealth Office. On the trip, the Countess of Wessex was presented with two sumptuous sets of gems worth a fortune. She was subsequently criticised for accepting them, given the appalling human rights record of the Bahrain regime, but that is perhaps unfair. She could hardly refuse a gift from a head of state where she was an official guest. The gifts were subsequently properly recorded, and published in the annual list of official gifts received.

The former Foreign Office minister Denis MacShane called for the jewels to be sent back, or sold, with the proceeds being used to help those who had suffered at the hands of the regime. Had that advice been followed, it would have negated any value Britain derived from the visit. Rightly or wrongly, it was the Foreign Office view that it was better to engage with Bahrain and to try to influence its policies, and that using the royals in the Middle East where monarchs abound is a good strategy. So, if there is a fault, it is with the FCO, who decided on the visit in the first place, not with the Wessexes.

The code also seeks to tackle the most egregious practices that Sir Michael Peat had uncovered, for example making it clear that 'under no circumstances' should an official gift be sold or exchanged. It also required a much more rigorous approach to record-keeping to be adopted. The robustness of the code is, however, weakened by the question that occupied Sir Michael Peat: what is an official gift, and what is a personal one? The code itself concedes that 'there may be occasions when the classification of gifts is not obvious'. As we have seen from Sir Michael's analysis, the vast majority fell into the applied definition of personal.

Personal gifts are those which are 'given by people whom the Member of The Royal Family knows privately and not during or in connection with an official engagement or duty'. There is no requirement, it seems, to keep a record of such gifts, let alone publish any list, so it is not possible to assess whether gifts have been correctly classified as personal. Nor do the royals seem to apply the 'fundamental principle' referred to above when it comes to personal gifts. If they did, it would, for instance, be difficult to explain how Prince Andrew accepting money from a paedophile to help clear Fergie's debts would qualify. And if, in theory, a member of the royal family were to receive a questionable payment, all they would have to do is treat it as a personal gift from a known recipient, and the requirements of declaration would have been met. This is deeply unsatisfactory.

In terms of unsolicited personal gifts from private individuals not personally known to the royal recipient, the code says that if worth in excess of £150, they should be returned to the donor. It would be interesting to know how many such gifts, of the thousands of unsolicited gifts received since this code came into force, have actually been returned. And what about the clothes they borrow to wear on official engagements? The value will be over £150, but, as they are returned, it is unlikely they are listed.

Then there are the cars. William and Kate are amongst several royals who have benefited from cut-price leasing deals for top-notch Audis. Others include the Queen, Prince Charles and Prince Harry. These special terms, worth rather more than £150 a shot, were not, of course, available to the general public at the same time.

It must have been very pleasant for William and Kate to have been ferried round California's Santa Barbara Polo & Racquet Club in a top-of-the-range Audi 8 when they attended a charity event there in 2011. Audi in fact paid £350,000 just to be associated with the royal event. Like any hard-headed business, they will have calculated that the economic return for them from this sponsorship was greater than the cost of the sponsorship itself.

No doubt the company's public relations executive, Jon Zammett, will have been delighted subsequently to have been invited to William and Kate's wedding breakfast.

The point is not that it is wrong for members of the royal family to use Audis. But their choice of vehicle should not be based on who gets through the door and offers a discount on lease terms, particularly if that advantage falls to them personally rather than the poor put-upon taxpayer. Politicians, especially ministers, have generally been thoughtful about the car they choose to use. Is it British made? Is it environmentally friendly? Does it have safety features to protect pedestrians and cyclists? Not all of them will weigh these questions heavily, but all will be aware of them and conscious that in a democracy they may at some point be called upon to defend their choice, as Two Jags Prescott can definitely attest.

It is standard practice these days for businesses to line up celebrities to use and therefore endorse their products. Someone like the ever-popular David Beckham will have made far more money from sponsorship than from football. When Mr Beckham lends his name to something, there is a simple transaction taking place. He is transferring some of his good reputation onto a product and so associating it with him in the eyes of the public. In return, he receives a sum of money for his troubles, and good luck to him.

But Mr Beckham is a private individual whose decisions as to what he wants to be associated with affect him and his family alone. Members of the royal family are not purely private individuals, however much they might like to try to argue they are. Rather, they are people who hold public positions, just as MPs and members of the House of Lords do, and need to be held to the same rules. A royal family endorsement should not be for sale to the highest bidder.

If the royals exploit their position to accept, even elicit, freebies, some have gone even further by seeking to gain financial advantage by trading on the family name. Prince Edward, for instance, had desperately wanted to make a success of television and film production. His first attempt was in 1987 when he organised an excruciatingly bad royal version of *It's A Knockout*. There were four teams, captained respectively by Edward, Andrew, Anne and Sarah.

The programme, filmed at Alton Towers, involved contestants having to perform somewhat ridiculous tasks. In one round, they had to dress as giant vegetables and throw fake hams at each other. *It's A Knockout* was already past its sell-by date by 1987, but Prince Edward's foray made sure the item was soon after pulled off the shelf altogether. He was at that time to the royal family what Gavin Williamson is to the Conservative Party today – the house nerd.

He set up Ardent Productions, his own film company, but it was never profitable except for one year when Edward did not draw a salary. Almost everything produced sought to cash in on his royal connections in an increasingly desperate attempt to keep his failing company afloat. He even went to the lengths of trying to film Prince William at his university when all the media had been warned off filming Charles's sons until they came through their education (and, amazingly, by and large they had respected that wish). Charles, who knew nothing of Edward's film plan until it was under way, was less than pleased.

Ardent finally gave up the ghost in 2009 with assets of just £40. It would undoubtedly have failed very much earlier had it not been for Edward cashing in on the family name – that, and an 'investment' of £200,000 by the Sultan of Brunei and a mysterious further £350,000 in 2005.

Malcolm Cockren, the chairman of Ardent at the time, gave an astonishing interview to *The Observer* about this donation from an outfit called Intercap Ventures Incorporated, based in an offshore tax haven. He told the paper that neither he nor Edward knew who was behind this company, and agreed it could be anyone, even the Mafia. He also described the day of the interview as a good one, saying, 'We got a cheque for $10.'

Prince Michael of Kent was blatant when it came to cashing in on his royal position. In a stunt worthy of Fergie, he appeared on television to promote something he called the House of Windsor Collection, a rather grand name for a rather tacky mail order business selling cheap royal trinkets. Mercifully, the scheme was a financial flop and before long was washed away into the royal gutter.

He will have been comforted, however, by the receipt of around fifty payments over more than ten years, totalling £320,000, and channelled through offshore companies. They all came from the Russian oligarch Boris Berezovsky, who claimed through his lawyer that he 'never sought or obtained any benefit or service' from the Prince.

Peter Phillips, son of Princess Anne, will have been delighted to have won the contract to organise the £150 per head lunch in the Mall to mark the Queen's ninetieth birthday. With around 10,000 people buying a ticket, his company, Sports and Entertainment Ltd, made a profit of £750,000 from the event.

For sheer neck, it is difficult to top the antics of Simon Rhodes. Surely you have heard of him? He is the third child of the daughter of the Queen Mother's sister. As reported in *Private Eye*, Mr Rhodes was the man to go to for exclusive and very expensive 'Privileged Royal Tours', which were 'guided by a member of the royal family', that is to say Mr Rhodes. Yet he undoubtedly had strings he was able to pull. The fact that his wife is a lady-in-waiting may not have been entirely irrelevant. His tours of Buckingham Palace fell outside the normal hours, and he seemed to have access to parts of the royal estate not normally open to the public. Maybe he would like to donate the profits from his enterprise to offset the costs of the major refurbishment of Buckingham Palace.

The Committee on Standards in Public Life has set out seven tests for those holding a public position. The tests are widely applied, amongst others to those in the civil service, local government, the police, the courts and probation services, and the health, education, social and care services. MPs rightly have a tighter code of conduct, and ministers a yet more onerous one. The royal family, it seems, has exempted itself.

Here are the first two of the seven tests:

1. **Selflessness**
   Holders of public office should act solely in terms of the public interest.

2. **Integrity**
   Holders of public office must avoid placing themselves under any obligation to people or organisations that might try inappropriately to influence them in their work. They should not act or take decisions in order to gain financial or other material benefits for themselves, their family, or their friends. They must declare and resolve any interests and relationships.

The pervasive culture within the royal family of accepting freebies and exploiting the royal name for personal gain clearly violates these two tests. Instead of acting with financial integrity, there are too many in the royal family who see their status as a way of enriching themselves. Individuals in other areas of the public sector who behaved in this way would find themselves subject to disciplinary hearings, sacked or even prosecuted.

Royal supporters will argue that they receive this largesse in a private capacity. Leaving aside the observation that the royals cite private status when they want to sidestep the rules that apply to public status, and claim public status when it suits them to do so – especially when they want to call upon public funds – individuals employed in public roles elsewhere are required to declare private activities where this might affect their public roles.

Councillors, for instance, have to withdraw from discussions on planning matters if the application being considered may affect their private position, whether beneficially or adversely. Members of Parliament are required to register any income from whatever source above a low threshold, whether or not it has any obvious connection with their parliamentary activities. These safeguards are there to keep elected politicians on the straight and narrow, and to give the public confidence that their actions are not being driven by personal benefit.

And the system, while not perfect, does work without fear or favour. Back in 2006, I discovered that David Cameron, then Leader of the Opposition, was using his publicly funded office in the House of Commons to hold fundraising events for the Conservatives. I lodged a formal complaint, the system kicked in, he was ruled to have transgressed and he had to discontinue the practice and make an apology to the House.

No such constraints or safeguards apply to the royal family. They can accept any free holiday, free use of a castle, the use of a private jet, a luxury car or designer clothes, all without any requirement even to record these gifts. It is only thanks to the media that occasionally, and despite the best efforts of the Palace, some grubby arrangement has a spotlight thrown on it.

As a basic step, each member of the royal family should be required to register anything worth in excess of the £150 referred to in the 2003 code which hitherto has been classed as personal, unless it is genuinely from close friends or family. They should also be required to register gifts in kind with a value greater than the £150 limit, where there is a public aspect to this, such as clothes worn on official engagements. We have a right to know who is buying favour with those who comprise one leg of our constitutional structure, namely the monarchy, and they should have a duty to make that information public, just as others in public office have to.

Killer Wales

On one day in 1913, George V and his party shot and killed 3,937 birds. The King himself accounted for 1,000 pheasants in just six hours, or almost three a minute. The numbers might imply a machine gun had been deployed, but the King and his companions achieved this feat with simple shotguns. Enough birds to feed a medium-sized town for a day. But of course the birds were not shot for the pot, and certainly not to feed any locals. No, they were shot for fun, for the King enjoyed killing them. The overwhelming majority of carcasses would have been buried or simply left to rot.

The lust for blood sports has always been an integral part of royalty in this country, and the present incumbents are just as keen as their forebears in centuries past. But then old habits die hard. The odd calamity, such as King William II being killed by an arrow in 1100 while out shooting deer, or Prince Charles falling off his horse and fracturing his shoulder in 2001 while out hunting, does not seem to be a deterrent. The image of a King from a few hundred years ago out hunting may seem very natural, part of our idea of merry old England. And truth be told, if you were a royal in those long-gone days, there were a limited number of activities to pursue beyond fighting, fornicating and forcing vast quantities of food into yourself.

Of course by Victorian times, the country had moved on. The industrial revolution had occurred, and the advent of the railway was binding the country together as surely as a pair of bootlaces being tightened. So what should we make of the activities of the future Edward VII, who in 1868 chased a deer all the way from Harrow to the goods yard at Paddington station where he shot it dead, to the amazement of the railway staff present. Was this, even in 1868, normal civilised behaviour?

Edward loved killing animals, and the larger the better as far as he was concerned. In Nepal in 1876, he shot dead twenty-three tigers in two weeks, topped off by an elephant.

His son, George V, is portrayed as a somewhat dull and worthy sort, patiently sticking his stamps into his collection, but he enjoyed the kill just as much as his father and spent the best part of seventeen years before he became king shooting grouse at Sandringham. Not that his passion left him after he acceded to the throne. Indeed, so keen was he on grouse shooting that he kept the clocks at Sandringham an hour forward so as to give more time for shooting.

Nor was his killing limited to grouse. In 1911, he killed twenty-one tigers, eight rhinos and a bear during a ten-day hunting trip in India. His passion was in turn shared by his sons. Edward VIII was also an avid hunter, killing anything and everything from a tiger to a bull elephant, a crocodile to a kudu.

Next up on the throne was George VI who, like his father, was frustrated that becoming king meant he would have to cut back drastically on the grouse shooting. His exchange of letters with his brother, by then Duke of Windsor, were frequently fraught with issues to do with Edward's plight, or talked about world affairs, but almost always included at the end references to 'sport', that is to say shooting and hunting. A typical letter from George to Edward in October 1948 observed that 'after a wet summer the partridges have done badly', then moved on to discuss the United Nations ('no better than its predecessor') and the situation in France, before observing that 'we did quite well with the grouse and stalking'.

Nor was this sport just a male pursuit. The future Queen Mother, out on safari in Africa, had written enthusiastically to her father-in-law George V:

> I took to shooting with a rifle ... I enjoyed it so much, and became very bloodthirsty. First of all I shot birds as big as capercailzie [wood grouse] for the pot, and then I shot buck, and by great flukes managed to kill and not wound, and then I shot a rhinoceros.

She and her husband, George VI, as he would become, blasted their way across the continent, also killing oryx, giant gazelles, antelopes and even a bull elephant. By January 1952, the King was dying, but he still managed to rouse himself from his bed for one last time to lead a party that bagged ninety pheasants, seventeen rabbits, three mallards and two pigeons.

The macabre remnants of royal slaughter can be seen in the gruesome trophy room at Sandringham. Stuffed animals and mounted heads, sixty-two in number, lend an oppressive air, a museum of violent death. There are the stuffed lions, the rare rhinos, a leopard, an Indian tiger, and the ivory tusks of an elephant.

The defence from the Palace is that this is a historical display, with nothing included that dates after 1941. That may be so, but is it really very tasteful to keep a room dedicated to the killing of animals, particularly as many of those exhibited are now endangered species, not least as a result of recklessly excessive hunting? Yet in one way the room is entirely appropriate, because the enthusiasm of the royals for killing animals did not end in 1941. It is very much alive today, unlike the tens of thousands of animals they have enthusiastically despatched.

Prince Philip can make the dubious claim of having killed more living creatures than any other royal alive. One estimate in 1996 reckoned that in the previous thirty years he had shot at least 30,000 pheasants. On top of that, he was known to have shot at least one tiger and two crocodiles, not to mention wild boar, stags, rabbits, and ducks too numerous to count. With breezy chutzpah, he has brushed off suggestions that there was some sort of conflict between his taste for killing vast numbers of animals and his role as President of the World Wide Fund for Nature, a post he held for fifteen years. He remains President Emeritus.

The Prince was a founder member of the World Wildlife Fund, as it was then called, in 1961. That same year, he caused a furore by shooting a tiger while he was a guest of the Maharaja of Jaipur. The Queen kept him company on that hunt, riding on the back of an elephant, any discomfort mitigated by a bearer shading her from the sun with a parasol. It was nice to know that despite India's independence some years earlier and the collapse of the British Empire, the old hallmarks of the Raj were still there to enjoy.

Two hundred beaters drove the poor tiger into a clearing. The Duke, standing on a wooden tower, then delivered the fatal bullet to the head. The body was taken to the maharaja's palace and laid out on the ground as a prop for a photograph for Prince Philip, the Queen and other hangers-on to crowd round. Afterwards, the maharaja had the corpse of the tiger skinned and stuffed and shipped to the Prince at Windsor Castle.

On that trip, Philip also killed a crocodile and six urials, a type of mountain sheep, all of which led to loud and widespread condemnation in both India and Britain. One would have thought that the World

Wildlife Fund might have quietly sought to distance itself from Philip and his killing spree, an enthusiastic indulgence that suggested he had instead signed up for World Wildlife Fun, but no, it instead offered him the position of president, a post held from 1981 to 1996.

The spineless charity has argued that what the Duke does in his private capacity 'is beyond the sphere of our relationship with him'. How very convenient. The average member of the public might naively have assumed that the charity would want as its president someone who respected animal life rather than someone who enjoyed killing it. It seems the World Wide Fund for Nature, as it now is, will tolerate any activity from a royal, however inconsistent with its aims. In Britain, Prince Charles, a keen hunter and shooter, became the head of the organisation's UK arm. Yet before this appointment, in 1978, his participation in a boar hunting expedition in Liechtenstein led the RSPCA, that is R for Royal, to describe him as 'Hooligan of the Year'.

And then there was King Juan Carlos I, who was head of the Spanish arm. The King included in his 'conquests' a wolf, nine brown bears (one pregnant and one allegedly forced to consume vodka), and an endangered European bison. An elephant hunt in Botswana proved to be the final straw and he was forced to relinquish his WWF position in 2012 after 94 per cent of the ordinary membership voted he be stripped of the role. But the Spanish King can take comfort that his hunting excesses have not caused any sort of breach with Britain's royal guns. He thoughtfully sends Seville oranges across so that the shooting party can add its trademark royal homemade orange vodka to the royal hampers.

In 1960, the year before Philip's Indian tiger kill, the British press reported unfavourably on the fact that he seemed keener on stalking the grouse moors at Sandringham than supporting his wife at the birth of their son, Andrew. The *Sunday Express* offered this sarcastic comment: 'We are edified that he was able at last to leave his bird shooting at Sandringham and re-join his wife at this exciting moment of her life.'

The Duke of Edinburgh has always glibly maintained that his shooting activities were about culling rather than killing. Philip made sure he introduced Prince Charles to shooting when he was just eight years old, keen to instil macho activities in the thoughtful boy. Charles seemed to take to it like a duck to water, though in his case, a protected one.

Although not close, father and son did bond when it came to shooting. At nine, Charles shot his first grouse. The year after, the pair went to Hickling on the Norfolk Broads to shoot ducks. When eleven, he wrote to Lord Mountbatten: 'I have been having great fun shooting lately,' he said. 'Yesterday I got twenty-three pheasants and today I got ten and a partridge, a moorhen and a hare.' At thirteen, he downed his first stag. On a visit to some of Philip's German relatives, the pair are reported to have killed no fewer than fifty wild boar. On another occasion, in 1967 and also in Germany, the pair notched up twenty-seven hares and four foxes.

Prince Charles was also an enthusiastic fox hunter, so much so that he very improperly overstepped the constitutional line to defend his personal activity against the threat of abolition by the Labour government in power as the twenty-first century began. According to the *Daily Mail*, he unwisely vented his feelings at a well-attended meeting: 'If the Labour government ever gets around to banning fox hunting, I might as well leave this country and spend the rest of my life skiing,' he told his audience.

The Labour MP for Nottingham South, Alan Simpson, called that 'a very generous offer'. Prince Charles followed up his broadside with a letter to the Prime Minister. He had no compunction about using privileged access to protect private and personal pastimes. The letter reiterated the views of a Cumbrian farmer who had told him: 'If we, as

a group, were black or gay, we would not be victimised or picked upon.'
Alan Simpson was scornful: 'His comparison with ethnic minorities
is bizarre. The issue about their treatment is not remotely comparable
to the treatment of people in the countryside.'

Prior to her marriage, Diana had been dragged up to the Scottish
Highlands in pursuit of animals as part of some peculiar royal courtship
by Charles. She even ended up shooting and wounding a deer at
Balmoral 'because they wanted me to. What is it with this family that
they love killing things?' What indeed. Diana found no support from
the female members of the royal family. The Queen herself enjoys
grouse shooting and in years gone by, she would follow the shoot and
wring the necks of injured birds.

In a repulsive rite of passage that has come down the ages, Diana was
'blooded' by gillies: her forehead smeared with the blood of her first
kill by the hunt's attendants. Her enthusiasm for hunting and shooting, such as ever existed, soon wore off, and according to her police
protection officer Ken Wharfe, she came to regard the royal obsession
with pheasant shoots in particular as 'repugnant, requiring little or no
skill, a pre-planned carnage of wildlife bred specifically for slaughter'.

Meanwhile, as the enthusiasm of her husband and her boys for the
activity seemed only to increase, she sardonically dubbed them the
'killer Wales'. If any animal lover hoped that a new generation of royals
would eschew the kill, they were to be sadly disappointed. Like their
father before them, William and Harry were introduced to shooting at
an early age and it has been central to their lives ever since. William
shot his first stag at fourteen, and seemed unmoved by the barrage
of criticism from the public and from MPs that followed. One, Tony
Banks, called it 'disgusting', and 'a throwback to the nineteenth century'.

Even his admission to St Andrews University was marked by Charles
with the not very academic gift of a handmade sporting rifle.

In 2007 Harry was questioned by police after a member of staff from Natural England and two other members of the public witnessed two very rare and protected hen harriers being illegally shot from the sky near Sandringham. The penalty for this offence is a £5,000 fine or up to six months in prison. Hen harriers are very scarce – at the time there were only about twenty breeding pairs in the whole of England. But they are disliked by those who maintain grouse moors as they feed on game birds, though given that thousands of these birds can be shot each year at Sandringham alone, it is difficult to think two hen harriers could have made much impression on the overall grouse population.

Harry was out shooting with a friend from the van Cutsem family, who own the nearby Hillsborough estate, the only people known to be out shooting in the area at the time. When questioned by the police, they denied any knowledge of the incident and the matter was dropped. It was regrettably not possible for the police to compare the bullets used to kill the protected birds with those used by Harry and his friend.

In 2014, as Crime Prevention minister, I part-chaired a ground-breaking international event in London pulled together to coordinate and improve the protection of endangered species. It is an issue I have long felt strongly about. Staggeringly, 26 per cent of all mammal species now face extinction, and there are now more tigers in American zoos than in the wild. Prince William, who had for some time expressed his concern about the threat to endangered species, was brought in to add weight to proceedings. The conference was a success and led to the London Declaration, signed by forty-one countries.

Unfortunately, the gloss was taken off when it emerged that William, with brother Harry, had flown to Spain to take part in a wild boar hunt at Finca La Garganta just a day before he made a plea to end the illegal wildlife trade. Those defending the hunting of wild boar point out that they are not a protected species and are held responsible for damage to commercial crops. But is this not the same argument used in the past to justify the mass killing of tigers and elephants?

A royal spokesman, defending William, told the media: 'His track record in this area speaks for itself.' Indeed it does. And then a picture emerged of Harry, rifle in hand, posing by the body of a one-ton water buffalo which he had shot dead while on a big-game hunt in Argentina. The firm that organised it, C. H. Hunting, offers the chance to kill red stag, deer, puma, antelope, boar and birds aplenty. In 2017, Harry told the US magazine *Town and Country*: 'This is God's test. If we can't save some animals in a wilderness area, what else can't we do?'

There is no reason to doubt that Prince William is sincere in his wish to help save signature species like the elephant and the rhinoceros. The organisation he leads, United for Wildlife, is doing good work. But William's ongoing obsession with killing living creatures – an obsession shared across his family – seriously damages his credibility in this important matter.

Moreover, what exactly is his objective? Is it only to protect a species when its numbers drop to critical level and to regard everything else as fair game? If that is the objective then it is one attained to a degree at least by the world's zoos. Would he in fact, like so many in his family before him, be out there shooting tigers if their numbers were rather greater and the population stable? If William and Harry are serious about protecting endangered species, then they need to develop a respect for *all* animal life as a concept, which they clearly do not have at the moment.

By and large, the British public has turned against the hunting and killing of animals for pleasure. But rather than respond to this clear public mood, the reaction from the royals has been to try to keep their hunting and shooting out of the press as much as possible while carrying on as they always have. The photo of Harry and his dead water buffalo has now mysteriously become unavailable. And when Prince Charles was snapped carrying a gun during a shoot at Sandringham, he called the police. They told him the photographer was on a public footpath and was doing nothing wrong. Charles then got his flunkeys to contact the papers to try to stop the story appearing. Fortunately the press were not intimidated and indeed even reported the royal attempt to muzzle them.

If the royals are so convinced that shooting large numbers of grouse is morally justified, or necessary for land management, why do they not come clean and make that case? The answer, almost certainly, is that they know they would lose the moral argument, so instead they try to choke off information about their questionable activities.

William said at the time of the 2014 international conference: 'This year I have become even more devoted to protecting the resources of the Earth for not only my son, but also other children of his generation to enjoy.' A laudable aim but one woefully distant from his own behaviour. The same year, William announced that he wanted to destroy all the ivory held by the royal family. This is no small matter. Some 1,200 items containing ivory can be found in the Royal Collection, including even an ivory Indian throne.

The view was that this action would encourage other countries and heads of state to follow suit, and return the world's spotlight to the plight of the elephant. The animals that provided the ivory are of course long gone, but such a gesture would nevertheless be useful. In 2019, I contacted William's office to ask what progress had been made. Eventually, after some prompting, the answer turned out to be that none had been destroyed. A spokesman told me: 'The Duke has ensured there is no ivory from the collection at Kensington Palace. He does not have control over the full Royal Collection Trust. Nor does his father at the moment.'

The implication is that both William and Charles want to take action on the ivory held by the Palace but to date have been blocked. We do not know if the blockage is Prince Philip or the Queen, but it is not difficult to imagine Philip telling William not to be 'so bloody stupid'.

Of course the explanation may be different. The Royal Collection Trust holds artworks for the nation and it is not strictly within the remit of the royals to dispose of its contents. At the same time, however, it is a tiresome and distasteful habit of the royals to lecture other people on what they should do, whether on animal protection, the environment or anything else, while breezily failing to put their own house in order.

Sadly, that prospect seems a million miles away. Entry into the royal circle seems still to depend upon the willingness to pick up a gun and repeatedly kill animals. Kate Middleton was certainly very clear that this was a prerequisite if she was to land William. After her first appearance with gun in hand in 2007, a spokesperson for the campaign group the People for Ethical Treatment of Animals accurately observed: 'Kate is obviously trying to endear herself to the Royal Family.' She was photographed practising with a formidable bolt-action hunting rifle under the guidance of Prince Charles and two gillies.

The *Daily Mail* quoted friends of Kate revealing that she had never been a particularly enthusiastic supporter of blood sports. Her presence was described as part of a 'concerted campaign' to prove to William that she 'has what it takes' to be his wife. 'She is a solidly middle-class girl but has suddenly developed a remarkable interest in the hunting, shooting and fishing lifestyle,' friends told the paper. Kate has now embraced the shooting lifestyle lock, stock and barrel.

By contrast, Meghan Markle has, as in so many ways, not been prepared to buckle. In 2018, she joined the royals for their regular Boxing Day shooting fest at Sandringham, but if anything that seems to have hardened her views. That she dislikes cruelty to animals is clear, and although she is painted by some as extreme in her views, that is only really true by comparison to the rifle-blasting royals. Meghan's views are actually quite mainstream with the British public: she does not like cruelty to animals or people deriving pleasure from killing them. She is not even a vegetarian (though she is said to be a flexitarian). As her influence over Harry grows, we are likely to see the semi-detached Prince abandon hunting altogether. That in turn would make any future reconciliation with his brother and the rest of the Windsors even more challenging.

Meanwhile, it seems another generation of royal children is being inculcated in the pleasures of shooting living creatures. Prince Andrew took his daughter Beatrice on a shoot when she was six. Edward did likewise with his son James, as witnessed by the publication by the *Mail on Sunday* of a photograph showing Edward recklessly pointing his raised gun in the direction of his then eight-year-old son, reminiscent in fact of the image of William Tell having to shoot an apple off his son's head. Unsurprisingly this led to his mother Sophie banning her son from future shoots, according to the paper.

Sadly, William is now following the long royal tradition of introducing his children at a very early age to shooting animals. In the summer of 2018, Prince George, aged just five, was taken along to his first grouse shoot. William had been four when he was first introduced to the activity. George was seen clutching a toy rabbit on the way to the shoot. By the time he returned, that lovely childhood innocence will have been corrupted. He will learn that for his father and the rest of the royal family, rabbits are not to cuddle but to kill.

If the younger royals are genuinely serious about protecting wildlife, we now need action rather than words. As well as keeping his outstanding ivory promise, let us see William arrange for the trophy room at Sandringham to be dismantled and replaced instead by contents related to efforts to protect endangered species. But most of all, if he and Harry are serious, there is one very simple and effective step they can take. They can lay down their guns and promise never to pick them up again to kill any animal. Such a statement would do more than anything else to move public opinion, both here in Britain and abroad. It would save the lives of thousands of animals, and not just those that would otherwise fall to royal guns.

We Are Not Amused

The Duke of Edinburgh was at it again. Referring to a messy fuse box, he quipped that it looked 'as though it was put in by an Indian.' 'Surely he means a cowboy?' was the witty response from a letter-writer to one of my local papers, the Brighton *Evening Argus*.

Why is it, I wonder, that the Duke equated messy fuse boxes with Indians? Had he perhaps surveyed a good number in his life that had definitely been installed by Indians and were indeed messy? Or was he merely gratuitously uttering an offensive and racist slur without any evidence? The Duke, as we know, has a long track record in making 'jokes' based on race.

In 1986 while in China, he warned British students that if they stayed there too long they would come back with 'slitty eyes'. Meeting an Aboriginal man in Australia in 2002, he asked: 'Do you chaps still throw spears at each other?'

'You managed not to get eaten then,' was his offering to a British trekker he came across in Papua New Guinea. At a reception for influential Indians, he said to one: 'There's a lot of your family in tonight.' And in Cairo, unhappy with the traffic chaos, the father of four barked out: 'The trouble with you Egyptians is that you breed too much.'

For a variation from racist comments, how about these sexist remarks? To a female solicitor: 'I thought it was against the law for a woman to solicit.' To a female sea cadet: 'Do you work in a strip club?' And to a female fashion writer: 'You're not wearing mink knickers, are you?'

These sorts of comments, while generating disapproving noises in some circles, were generally laughed off. To be fair, some of his inoffensive rudeness was sometimes funny. Undertaking an official opening in Canada, he offered the unconventional: 'I declare this thing open, whatever it is.' Less amusing was when in Peru he was handed a history of the town of Lima, which he immediately handed to an aide with the observation: 'Here, take this, I'll never read it.'

At home, his suggestion in the wake of the shooting in Dunblane of sixteen schoolchildren that guns were no more dangerous than cricket bats managed to be crass, deeply offensive to those who had lost their children, and to cross over into political comment when the government was taking forward measures to tighten gun control. On this occasion, an apology from the Palace followed.

There is nevertheless a certain freshness, a certain honesty about how Philip approached his public duties. So the general response has been to see him as a bit of a harmless loose cannon. Yet I wonder if the same casual attitude would have been taken had the remarks come from a television celebrity, or a footballer, or a politician.

But if the Duke's undoubtedly racist comments were tempered by the intended humour with which he encased them, the same cannot be said for other royals. Edward VIII surrounded himself with Nazi sympathisers and regularly espoused a forceful anti-Jewish stance.

The Spanish foreign minister, Colonel Juan Beigbeder, outlined his perceptions of Edward's attitude to the war in a 1940 missive to his government: 'He throws all the blame on the Jews and the Reds and

Eden with his people in the Foreign Office and other politicians all of whom he would have liked to put up against a wall.'

And then there was the Queen's sister, Princess Margaret, whose utterances make Prince Philip look positively benign. According to author Kitty Kelley, she walked out of the film *Schindler's List*, stating to her companions that she did not 'want to hear another word about Jews or the Holocaust'. It was, she said afterwards, 'a tedious film about Jews'. Ms Kelley further suggests that when the Princess was introduced to the columnist Ann Landers, she asked: 'Are you a Jew?' then moved on when she received an answer in the affirmative. Of the President of Guyana, Dr Cheddi Jagan, she opined: 'He's everything I despise. He's black; he's married to a Jew; and furthermore she's American.'

Then there was the Queen Mother. Art historian Sir Roy Strong revealed in 2017 that some of her comments to him were so awful that he had to self-censor himself at the time. On one occasion when he was sitting next to her at lunch, she leant over and cautioned him: 'Beware the blackamoors.' The dictionary defines the term as denoting black people originally from North Africa who worked as servants and slaves in wealthy European households.

Quite why she should suddenly think it appropriate to utter this caution, or why he should beware of them, was not clear, but perhaps the clue lies in a quote from her, as reported in *The Guardian* by one of her ladies-in-waiting: 'The Africans just don't know how to govern themselves ... What a pity we're not still looking after them.'

'Beware the blackamoor brooch' might have been a more useful warning. Insensitively, Princess Michael of Kent, whose father was a Nazi SS officer, wore one to a Christmas lunch at Buckingham Palace attended by Meghan Markle, who of course is of mixed race. At least she had the good grace to apologise afterwards, though it is worth noting she has form in this area. In 2004, she told some black diners in a New York restaurant, whose noise was irritating her, to 'go back to the colonies', wherever they might have been. She denied she had said this, insisting what she had actually said was 'you should remember the colonies', which, to be honest, is not a great improvement.

Other views of the Queen Mother were equally reactionary. She was against democratic elections in India and in favour of white supremacist rule in Rhodesia. According to her official biography penned by William Shawcross, upon arriving at a reception for a Japanese prince, she issued this cringeworthy opening gambit: 'Nip on! Nip on!' On another occasion, the Queen Mother, who had of course been captured on film enthusiastically giving a Nazi salute back in 1933, volunteered the view that she had 'some reservations about Jews'.

Naturally, this reactionary racist picture of the Queen Mother was not the one the public were given. Instead she was lauded as 'the nation's favourite grandmother', and a hero of the Second World War (notwithstanding her strong support for appeasement before it began and indeed after it had started).

To be fair, social norms were different even fifty years ago, and what was acceptable then would not be so today. Nevertheless, with racist remarks attributable to the Queen's husband, mother and sister and others in the royal family, we are indeed fortunate that the Queen herself has not been identified with such comments, either because she genuinely does not think in this way or because she has kept her thoughts to herself.

Nor are all the younger royals entirely innocent. In the early 1990s, Sarah Ferguson came in for sharp criticism for attending a dinner party at the Everglades Club in Palm Beach in Florida, a club that banned blacks and Jews, and doing so on the same day as she had posed for pictures with black children suffering from AIDS.

Old prejudices die hard. It would be quite some time into the reign of the present Queen before anyone Jewish could be found employed at Buckingham Palace in anything other than a menial role. And notwithstanding her strong support for the Commonwealth, by the 1990s only ten of her nine hundred employees were black, and like the Queen's Jewish employees before them, were confined to menial positions.

It is perhaps fortunate that the terms of both the Race Relations Act and the Sex Discrimination Act mean the Queen cannot be prosecuted for any offence. Phillip Hall noted that for the first thirty-nine years of her reign, the Queen had 'not made a significant black or Asian appointment' to her 400-strong household. This is odd indeed for a monarch who has so championed the Commonwealth. It took until 2017, sixty-four years into her reign, for a black person to be appointed to a senior role (apart from one Nigerian equerry who worked for a few weeks in 1956). This time, Major Nana Kofi Twumasi-Ankrah has been appointed, also as an equerry. The major previously fought in the war in Afghanistan. Moreover, until recently you will have struggled in vain to find a woman who has occupied any of the Palace's key roles, from Private Secretary to Keeper of the Privy Purse, Chief Press Secretary to Royal Librarian.

On the occasion of the Queen Mother's hundredth birthday, Parliament, led by the media-savvy Tony Blair, queued up to pay glowing tributes and send a Humble Address to her. She was 'a source of inspiration', gushed the Prime Minister. Every occasion was 'enhanced by her presence'. The leader of the Opposition, William Hague, was even more effervescent. The Queen Mother 'radiates warmth, charm and dignity'.

There was much reference to her wartime activities, and it was indeed commendable that the King and Queen stayed in London through the war and did provide a point round which to rally. One Christmas a photo of the future Queen Mother was put on a card and sent to every soldier. It proved immensely popular. Naturally, the positives were played up at the time to help the war effort, and the negatives swept under the carpet. For instance, it was put about that as well as staying in London, the King and Queen were voluntarily sharing the same deprivations as the rest of the population.

That was not exactly true. The rules on rationing in effect ended at the gates of Buckingham Palace as the royals were able to freely use food sourced from their farms. So inside, life carried on as normal. Roast beef and champagne abounded. The King had six rashers of bacon and two eggs for breakfast every morning and grouse every evening. The Queen gorged on her favourite oatcakes, gaining almost a stone in weight in a year. The seams on her gowns had to be let out. Illness in the Palace was attributed to a surfeit of grouse.

Listening to the speeches in the Commons, it was difficult to escape the conclusion that MPs were using this royal event, as they had used many others such as the untimely death of Diana five years earlier, for their own benefit. This was even more so two years later, when Parliament would be recalled at very considerable cost for an emergency session when the Queen Mother died. MPs were flown back at vast public expense from wherever they were in the world, and likewise all the House of Commons staff brought back to ensure the bars and restaurants were open. The usual contingent of men in swords was present, and all for a tribute session that lasted just an hour and which heard leading MPs make a series of repetitive speeches.

In an article for *The Independent* the next day, I wrote that while I genuinely had every sympathy for the Queen and other family members who had lost someone close, there was really no good reason why any tributes that MPs wanted to make could not have waited until Parliament was due to sit again less than a week later.

The image had been created, bolstered by one visit to the East End during the war, that the Queen Mother was somehow in touch with ordinary people. In reality, she did little to hide her contempt for them. She was 'rather mocking, not very kind', according to the wife of the British ambassador in Paris. She would make fun of people who rhymed Ma'am with harm, rather than with spam.

The Queen Mother will not have welcomed the tabloid splash in 1987 that catapulted an individual the world had never heard of into the spotlight. 'Queen's Cousin Locked in Madhouse', ran the front page of *The Sun*, accompanied by a photo of a wrinkled and bedraggled old woman. The cousin in question was Katherine Bowes-Lyon, niece of the Queen Mother, cousin to the Queen, and the daughter of the Honourable John Herbert Bowes-Lyon and the woman he married, the Honourable Fenella Hepburn-Stuart-Forbes Trefusis.

Katherine, and her sister Nerissa, were despatched one dark day in 1941 to a home for people with learning disabilities, the Royal Earlswood in Redhill, Surrey, a grim establishment that had opened in 1853 as the National Asylum for Idiots. Three others, second cousins to the then Queen, later the Queen Mother, were also packed off to the same institution that day as an unwanted job lot: Idonea, Rosemary Jean and Ethelreda Fane.

No explanation has ever been forthcoming as to why, and by whom, it was decided to deposit the two sisters, then aged twenty-two and fifteen, into this home, and at this time. What is clear is that, as far as the royal family were concerned, the sisters were to be written out of the story as non-persons. *Burke's Peerage* reported the death of Nerissa in 1940, before she even arrived at the forbidding Surrey establishment, and that of Katherine in 1961. The truth is that Nerissa survived until

1986, and Katherine until 2014. *Burke's Peerage* does not invent entries, but reports information passed to them by reliable sources.

Harold Brooks-Baker, the editor, said: 'Any information given to us by the royal family is accepted, even if we had evidence to the contrary.' According to nurses at the Earlswood, neither of the sisters was ever visited by any member of the royal family, or indeed the Bowes-Lyons. They were never even sent a Christmas or birthday card.

When Nerissa died in 1986, she was given a pauper's funeral (at state expense, naturally). Her grave in the council-run Redhill cemetery was identifiable only by means of plastic tags and a serial number. When Idonea died in 2002, she too was given a pauper's funeral, though this time a basic headstone was provided. Her death was not announced by Buckingham Palace, but by the client assets manager for the relevant local NHS Trust.

Her funeral was naturally in stark contrast to the hugely expensive state affair that marked the funeral of the Queen Mother shortly after-wards, though considerably cheaper for the taxpayer. At the time there were two MPs who asked how much that lavish funeral was costing the public purse – myself and Jeremy Corbyn. Neither of us was given the figure. The Labour MP Gordon Prentice did manage to establish the cost of just one element – the bill to the Commons just for the lying-in-state came to £495,000, so not including the huge costs of recalling Parliament. He also discovered that the cost to the Ministry of Defence, which was only marginally involved, was £301,000.

The 'nation's favourite grandmother' told the *Daily Express* in 1996 that she had only learnt in 1982 that Katherine and Nerissa were shut away in the Royal Earlswood when the hospital's League of Friends wrote to her. Yet she must have known full well about the fate of her nieces when they were packed off in 1941, and may well indeed have been part of the decision-making process. And if indeed she was not involved, did she not notice that they were suddenly not around and ask what had become of them? Presumably even if she had only been alerted to the facts in 1982, would she not have been shocked at their fate and taken action to remedy matters? But she did not. She did nothing.

The Queen Mother, who was a patron of Mencap, the charity dedicated to helping those with learning disabilities, never once visited them, not before or after 1982. Nor, despite her fabulous wealth, her sixty servants and £300 bottles of champagne, did she provide her nieces with even the most basic essentials. Until 2002, the royal family did not even provide Katherine with her own underwear. The fees for her stay at Ketwin House, also in Surrey, to where she had been transferred upon the closure of the Royal Earlswood, were picked up by the ever reliable NHS. Ketwin House was in fact closed while Katherine was resident there after allegations of physical abuse, the washing of female residents by male staff, and question marks over the handling of patient finances.

Nor did the Queen Mother show any interest in her nephew Timothy, a chronic alcoholic, who was likewise a non-person as far as she was concerned. She did not even attend the funeral of his wife who killed herself after the death of her child, the Queen Mother's great-niece.

It seems that the stubborn adherence of the royal family to practices and attitudes long past their sell-by date extended too to the Victorian custom of shutting away or shutting out awkward relatives, and not asking too many questions afterwards. Out of sight, out of mind. Perhaps this approach is one that just came naturally to the family at the time. It was what was done under such circumstances.

But perhaps there was also felt to be a conscious need to present the family as flawless. After all, the basis of the hereditary principle is that it invariably generates a bloodline perfectly formed to assume the highest offices in the land, a dubious intellectual position at the best of times and one unpleasantly redolent of the theory of Aryan purity of the 1930s. Any developments that suggested otherwise needed to be suppressed, or people may conclude that a system that enabled people to choose at any given time the most appropriate leader, in other words, an open democratic election, might generate someone more suitable.

It was impossible to hide the madness of George III, whose reign had to be punctuated by periods of regency, but other aberrations from the norm were easier to disguise. In 1905, George and Mary, who would five years on become king and queen, had a son, John, whose birth was much celebrated within the family and throughout the land. Then poor John had an epileptic fit and his blossoming public presence was brought to a shuddering halt.

His horrified parents ensured he was thereafter excluded from family photographs and kept well away from his father's coronation. He became the one of whom one did not speak. Early in 1917, to avoid any risk the public might discover the truth, John was taken to Wood Farm, a secluded spot on the Sandringham estate where he lived with a nanny and two male attendants whose job was to contain him when fits occurred. Dying two years later, he never saw his parents again.

Within the Bowes-Lyon line, there was also the tale of the 'monster of Glamis', the location referring to the castle owned by the family near Dundee. According to *Debrett's*, there was in 1841 a male heir directly related to the future Queen Mother, Thomas Bowes-Lyon. Officially he died shortly after his birth, but rumour persisted that the sorry individual, deformed and mentally ill, lived for many decades locked up in a hidden room in the castle. It seems to have been a regular technique to announce to *Debrett's* or *Burke's Peerage* the premature deaths of inconvenient relatives still alive.

We know that the child had been baptised at birth, yet had no grave-stone to mark his apparent early demise. This, and the information contained in family records, would appear to lend some credence to the story. It may be that the passage of time will have modernised the approach of the royal family to such circumstances. Yet it is salient that the two royals in recent times who have shown a more modern and compassionate approach – Princess Diana in embracing those with AIDS, and her son Harry's clear and genuine concern for disabled veterans and for those with mental health issues – both ended up on the outside of the unreformed world of the Windsors. It remains the fact that Katherine was left abandoned in an anonymous Surrey home until her recent death in 2014.

If we are to have a modern royal family, what does it matter if the genealogical line throws up someone who is disabled or has a mental health condition, or if a prince wants to marry a divorcee or a Catholic or someone with a different skin colour, or what is patronisingly called a 'commoner'? What does it matter if a member of the royal family is gay? The fact that William has responded with equanimity to the possibility that he and Kate may have a child who is gay is a welcome development.

What is more important than outdated prejudices is that there is honesty and compassion, two qualities that were sadly lacking when it came to those poor women packed off to the darkest corners of Surrey.

There were hopes that Harry's decision to marry Meghan Markle, an American divorcee with an African-American mother, would help drag the royal family towards the present day. Yet the last person who tried to do this was his mother, and that did not end well. Sadly, the royal family in 2020 have proved to be even less tolerant of Harry's wife than they were of his mother a generation earlier.

The Royal Box of Tricks

I t was George III who appointed the first spin doctor, around two hundred years before Tony Blair and Alastair Campbell made the phrase common currency. The King had become irritated by generally accurate newspaper stories about his activities, and decided a counter-balance was required. So a 'Court Newsman' was appointed, and given the task of distributing daily to the press information about royal engagements. It was called the Court Circular, and can still be found tucked away somewhere in *The Times*, and now also on the Palace website.

Come the age of photography, and it did not take the royals long to work out that photographs of themselves were useful in consolidating support. The first family photo appeared in 1857, and five years later one taken of the Prince of Wales and his bride Alexandra sold a staggering two million copies.

Between that year and her death in 1901, Queen Victoria registered 428 official portraits for sale. They appeared everywhere, including on household products like toilet soap. It was the nineteenth-century version of Duchy Originals, where a royal imprimatur is used to sell, with similar lucrative results for the royals. The use of royal images continues unabated to the present day, except nowadays the purveyors are largely newspapers and other media. The Palace, which sternly argues that royal children should be protected from press intrusion, is nevertheless quite content to make available photographs of them on special occasions such as birthdays.

The pictures are invariably used, and prominently in the tabloids in particular, for the simple reason that the editors believe – with good reason – that such pictures sell papers. But it is an uncomfortable deal for the press. It is the Palace that controls the supply of pictures, both in timing and content. Naturally only those which show the image the Palace wants to convey are made available. They are, in effect, securing space in the papers for their message, just like an advertiser, except in this case, the space comes free, and indeed with a supportive editorial line.

The result is a never-ending diet of exaggerated and sycophantic headlines, that being the only real direction in which the headline writers can go.

So we are told by the *Daily Mail* that on a public outing where he was present, the five year-old Prince George 'stole the show'. Had he displayed some extraordinary ability for a boy his age? Had he done something which suggested he was something of an amusing rascal? No, he had simply been there, behaving as any five-year-old would. No more, no less.

The same paper published 'twelve pages of joyous photos' in a 'Charlotte and George magical pull-out'. Other tabloids act in the same way. Local papers, if anything, are even worse. The Brighton *Argus*, normally a rational and factual read, went into hyperdrive for an October 2018 royal visit. 'Harry and Meghan stun the crowds,' shouted the front page. I wondered at first if they had been using Tasers, but it transpired they had just been walking about. The royal couple were certainly well received but fortunately nobody seems to have been stunned. 'See inside for 20 pages of pictures on the royal day plus full website coverage,' the paper helpfully suggested.

Or take the *Metro*. 'Charlotte is such a charmer,' gushed its front page, as the paper published photographs taken by her mother and supplied by the Palace to mark the little girl's fourth birthday in May 2019. Perhaps she is a charmer, but then any child that age could generate that response, given a competent photographer and a supply of flattering pictures. She might be a horror for all we know.

We saw the same routine for Prince Louis's first birthday the week before, except that on that occasion, news of the American President's state visit to Britain leaked out, somewhat trumping the Palace's planned media management of the young prince's birthday.

Still, there will be plenty of other opportunities, and the Palace will make sure the captive media has just the photos it wants them to have at just the right time. We will be invited to celebrate the same repetitive diet of events: births, children's birthdays, engagements, weddings and other milestones. Not really any meaningful achievements, just procreation – the perpetuation and expansion of the royal family.

The press produced an astonishing feat of journalism when Archie was born. The *Daily Mail* and *Daily Telegraph* the next day managed thirty-one pages in royal baby supplements, based on nothing – at that point there were no pictures of the new baby, who did not even have a name.

A similarly over-the-top approach is taken to royal weddings. In May 2019 we were treated to double-page spreads in the papers on the occasion of the wedding of Lady Gabriella Windsor. Who? It turns out she is daughter of Prince Michael of Kent and fifty-second in line to the throne, the royal family's two of clubs, so hardly a court card. Just how far down the line of succession do we have to go before the media decide an event is not newsworthy?

Down the decades, official pictures have been used to reinforce the notion of the royals as a normal, happy family. The truth has been somewhat different. Unlike in most families, royal children – especially the Queen's – have often been left with nannies for months on end while their parents are abroad. Prince Philip managed to miss all of his son Charles's first five birthdays. And when the young Charles was rushed to hospital for an emergency appendectomy at midnight, the Queen stayed tucked up in her bed. When Anne, at a tender age, had her tonsils removed, it was nanny who stayed with her in hospital overnight, while her mother remained in Windsor Castle.

Nor do the seemingly normal family photos which are made public always reflect reality. You would not guess, for example, from the early photographs of Charles with his parents that the rules of the house meant that he always had to bow to his mum before he left the room. No photograph of that has ever been released by the Palace. Nor one subsequently of Prince Charles's servants backing out of his room, just as they might have done in Imperial China.

Of course, on the occasions that the press publishes photographs that the Palace does not want the public to see, they protest in vigorous terms, such as when in 2015 *The Sun* published pre-war pictures of a young Elizabeth and the future Queen Mother giving a Nazi salute, egged on by the future Edward VIII.

What the Palace wants is a succession of pictures and stories of which it approves, and over which it has editorial control, appearing in the papers, while retaining the right to complain, cajole, even take court action in respect of printed pictures and stories it does not like. It is natural that any entity, whether a political party or a business, a rich individual or a so-called celebrity, would welcome the opportunity to be able to use the press as a sort of free publicity machine, and one that has the benefit of appearing independent in the reader's eyes –

and especially if negative coverage can be minimised. But it is not the job of the press to meekly facilitate that.

One early example of spin came in 1936 with the death of George V. At 11 p.m. on 20 January, he was injected with fatal doses of morphine and cocaine. Death would certainly have happened within days at most, probably hours, but it was brought forward in order that this would, according to the notes of the royal physician Lord Dawson, appear 'in the morning papers rather than the less appropriate evening journals'. At 10 p.m., the physician arranged for *The Times* to be tipped off that the King would die that evening, and they held back publication accordingly. George V was not consulted about this medical intervention. Legally speaking, Lord Dawson committed murder, and indeed treason, to secure what he deemed the appropriate newspaper coverage, although it might well be argued that his actions also prevented unnecessary suffering. In a House of Lords debate later that year, he called such interventions a 'mission of mercy'.

In more spin, the King's last words were reported to be: 'How is the Empire?' It was also suggested he had said 'Bugger Bognor', which is pure fiction. Lord Dawson's notes tell us his last words were in fact 'God damn you'.

Yet spin can only take you so far, as the Blair government of the early years of this century discovered. It can, for a while, create a positive image in excess of the objective reality, but when the truth does finally emerge, and the effects of spin are revealed, there is public anger at having been deceived. Ultimately the game is not worth the candle.

Patrick Jephson, who was private secretary to Diana, warned in 2017 that the royal family's addiction to spin was dangerous for them.

We forgive politicians their spin doctors … because we can vote them in or out. But if your purpose constitutionally is to be a unifying force, a symbol of continuity ... then you are on thin ice. What we have now is a determination to control the message, to control the image.

He accused the Palace, as Diana split from Charles, of spreading a 'vile diagnosis that she had a clinical personality disorder, a slur then systematically spread by royal spin doctors and still whispered to this day'. The raw truth about the state of the marriage between Charles and Diana was that much more shocking when it finally emerged precisely because the public had been sold the union as a sort of royal fairy tale.

Yet the Palace will always try to control the public image presented as a way of dealing with difficult issues rather than tackling and remedying the underlying problem in any situation. Whenever they can, they will always paint over rotten wood rather than replace it.

The Palace has even adopted the technique perfected by the Blair government of issuing lumps of bad news together. In June 2018 for example, they issued three potentially difficult financial reports on the same day in the safe knowledge that this would mean one critical story in the press rather than three, and just to be on the safe side, they chose a day when they could bury bad news, the day Prince William was on a Middle East tour and most of the royal correspondents who would normally cover the release of financial reports were out of the country with him. The spinning and controlled release of information is the first trick in the royal box. The second is to take advantage of the deference shown to the royal family.

While the world was agog with stories of Edward VIII and Mrs Simpson, hardly a word appeared in the British papers. They had been asked not to touch the story and duly complied. Those returning to these shores from the United States knew far more than the average person in Britain, until of course the dam broke.

In 1952, when the Queen ascended the throne, deference was still pretty much absolute. A third of the British population believed she had been chosen for the role by God. At the coronation, the six girls carrying her train had to be virgin daughters of earls. Apparently, British troops in attendance were ordered to abstain from sex for forty-eight hours beforehand (though how would anyone have known if the command had been obeyed?).

Afterwards the Archbishop of Canterbury declared that 'This country and Commonwealth last Tuesday were not far from the Kingdom of Heaven.' Another cleric declared the coronation 'a miracle which might save civilisation'. It was even reported that prisoners in a corrective training centre had gained great spiritual benefit from seeing the coronation on television.

Doubtless the perceived magical nature of the event helped mute any public concern about the £2 million cost of the extravaganza. A week after the coronation the Chancellor spoke of the need for financial stringency when considering wages for railwaymen, miners and shop assistants.

Back in 1952, divorced persons were not allowed into the presence of the monarch. Given what happened subsequently to the Queen's own family, it is a good thing that that antiquated rule at least has been abandoned.

A few months on from her coronation, when a journalist, Gwen Robyns, wrote in one report that 'the weary Queen slipped out of her shoes', the newspaper's editor was contacted by a furious Palace and the reporter was told to 'lay off the Queen'.

Another reporter, Maurice Weaver, quoted in Kitty Kelley's book *The Royals*, said: 'We were not allowed to write anything other than what the Queen wore and how she looked. The Palace press secretary would come out and give us a description … and we dutifully took it all down and reported it that way.'

Anne Edwards of the *Daily Mail* put it succinctly: 'No dictator ever muzzled the press quite as tightly as the Queen of England muzzles hers today on every aspect of royalty.'

Mostly the media muzzled themselves when, on their tour of Australia in 1954, the Queen had a public spat with Philip, which involved throwing her shoes and a tennis racket at him. As it happened, the action was captured by a documentary film-maker who promptly handed the footage over. Don't hold the front page.

This self-censorship, for that is what it is, extended to book publishers. *Royal Service* and *Royal Secrets*, two volumes of memoirs by Stephen Barry, a valet to Prince Charles for twelve years until 1981, appeared in the United States, but British publishers refused to handle them in deference to the Palace. This is despite the fact that he had much to tell that would have been of interest and that would have helped sales. For instance, his US agent told me that very close to Charles's wedding to Diana, Mr Barry was sent on a pre-arranged mission to deliver to Camilla a gold bracelet with the letter C embossed twice.

In 1955 the journalist and broadcaster Malcolm Muggeridge publicly suggested that another photo of the royal family was for some people 'more than they could bear'. He came home to find his house covered in graffiti. In 1958 he called the Queen 'a nice homely little woman' and was promptly removed from all BBC outlets for a suitable period. In 1966 the Palace threatened to withdraw Court Circular information from the *Daily Telegraph* because the paper consistently failed to put the word 'the' in front of 'Princess Margaret'. It is difficult to imagine anything more absurd.

This may seem like ancient history, but in 2016 comedian David

Baddiel had his radio show pulled after mocking the Queen's sex life on her ninetieth birthday. Tasteless, yes, and certainly many listeners thought so, but a reason to take him off air? Apparently so. The bigwigs at the BBC dutifully apologised to the Palace.

Even now, the Palace seems to arrogantly think that the media is there to be respectful and act as some sort of agency for the royal family and, when the media carries out their proper constitutional role of reporting the news and holding the royals to account, however inadequately, they seem to regard this as some sort of treasonous behaviour.

Linked with this is the third trick in the royal box: downgrade or remove access for those journalists or media outlets who do not behave as the Palace wants. After the famous BBC *Panorama* episode where Diana sensationally talked of there being three people in her marriage, the Palace responded by giving ITV pole position for the Queen's next Christmas message. They are also increasingly trying to set the terms for any interviews given, and, if necessary, will use an outlet that will play ball with their demands rather than one which will not. In the past, Charles was relaxed enough to take any question an interviewer wanted to pose, even to appear on the odd live chat show. Now strict pre-conditions are imposed.

This does not, of course, mean that the press will not print stories critical of the royal family. One paper in 1959 ran the cheeky headline 'the Duke visits Britain' upon the return of Philip from a long trip overseas, but even that paper drew the line at reporting the gossip that was circulating in Fleet Street about the various female companions Philip had been spending time with while out of the country. Or in the country, for that matter. Outside Britain, you could find stories about Philip's 'bachelor apartment close to Berkeley Square', or his attendance at meetings of the Thursday Club 'in the infamous Soho district', but you would search the British press in vain for these items. There were at best occasional hints that all was not quite as it seemed, such as when the *Evening Standard* reported that Philip had ordered a new bed for his room at Windsor Castle, and that it was a single.

Some areas the press has generally regarded as fair game, particularly where public money is concerned, entirely appropriately given the enormous cost to the nation of the royals. Air Miles Andy is rightly a regular target.

The *Morning Star*, perhaps unsurprisingly, has tended to go further than most. While the rest of the press were falling over themselves to report the wedding of Charles and Diana in breathless terms (and not mentioning the rumours of Diana's unhappiness which even then were circulating round Fleet Street – she had been filmed by the BBC in tears at her wedding rehearsal, footage of which was destroyed), the ultra-left paper ran a whole page headed 'for richer, for richer'. It even somewhat tastelessly, but perhaps not inappropriately as things turned out, referred to the precedent of Princess Margaret and Lord Snowdon, whose wedding had also been gushingly reported in 1960 and which had ended in divorce eighteen years later.

On the occasion of Andrew's wedding to Sarah, the *Socialist Worker*, or *Socialist Striker* as it was sardonically known, ran the headline 'Parasite to Marry Scrounger', though it was not immediately clear which was which in their minds.

While deference is still upheld for the Queen, it is no longer automatically given to others in the royal family. Sometimes that means we see proper questions of accountability being asked, such as over Prince Charles's habit of seeking to influence ministers behind the scenes. On other occasions, the tabloids in particular lapse into outright rudeness, such as unkindly labelling Sarah Ferguson the 'Duchess of Pork'. When the wind lifted her skirt, it generated the headline 'her royal thighness'. It is noticeable that this juvenile reporting is only ever applied to female members of the family. Males rarely have comments made about their appearances. If they were, we would have heard about the Duke of Pork as well.

On other occasions, suffocating sycophancy can take over, even leading to seriously misleading reporting of an important story. For sheer breathtaking idiocy it is difficult to top the *Daily Express* front page of 27 June 2018 which reported on a trip by Prince William to Israel. 'In the never-ending turmoil of the Middle East and the intractable deadlock between the Israelis and Palestinians, could a seemingly impossible breakthrough be achieved by... WILLIAM THE PEACEMAKER.' Spoiler alert – the answer was no.

The distinctly shaky legs on which this whole story rested was the mild request by Israel's President to pass a 'message of hope' to the Palestinian premier whom William was to meet later. 'William The Postman' would have been a more accurate headline for the paper. Could anyone, even at the *Express*, seriously believe that William merely passing on an envelope could end decades of what the paper itself rightly called 'intractable deadlock'? Or perhaps the paper had reverted to a medieval mindset, when the King's touch was thought to be able to cure evil. Really, we all deserve better than this garbage.

The love-hate relationship the media shows the royals all too often manifests itself in their reporting of the trivial, including by invading what should genuinely be the private space of individual members of the royal family. Public figures should expect to be held to account for their public roles, but they are also entitled to a private life away from public gaze. Increasingly, the royals have turned to their expensive solicitors to tackle some of the more egregious intrusions, and here is the fourth trick in the royal box to keep control. We can sympathise entirely with the robust line taken by Prince William when in 2012 the French magazine *Closer* published some surreptitiously taken photos of a topless Kate while the couple were on holiday in France, at a private location well off the beaten track. This gross intrusion must have been particularly sensitive for William given what his mother had to endure. The Prince sued for damages and was awarded £92,000, though the couple had asked for £1.4 million. Crucially, though, the successful action prevented the further dissemination of the pictures.

We can sympathise too with Meghan Markle when the plaintive and highly personal letter she wrote to her wayward father was released by him to the media, who gleefully published its contents. Harry and Meghan were understandably furious when intrusive photographs of their home appeared in *The Times* and elsewhere online. The pictures, taken from a helicopter, even went so far as to show the interior of their bedroom. Harry accepted 'substantial damages' from the news agency that had taken the photos but the damage was done.

We can even sympathise with the very heavy hand that was, in the spring of 2019, applied to the British media to prevent them reporting strong rumours of an affair involving a senior male royal. Even if the rumours are true, so what? Has this impacted on the public duties of the royal in question? Has it cost the taxpayer money? Is there a security issue? If the answer to these three questions is no, as I believe it to be, then the affair, if it exists, is nobody's business apart from the parties involved and affected.

Just because there is interest from the public in a particular matter, this does not make it a matter of public interest. The problem comes when the threat or indeed instigation of legal action is used, not to protect a genuinely private matter, but to prevent the public from learning something which they are entitled to know, but which the royals wish to hush up because it is embarrassing.

A case in point is the Nazi salute picture already referred to, where the Palace wished to take legal action, citing issues of copyright and 'criminality'. But it is an important part of our history to understand that the future Edward VIII and Queen Mother were sympathetic to the fascist movement in Germany. That may well be embarrassing for the royals but is not a good reason to censor the truth. Similarly, Charles wanted to take legal action after comments he had written to a small circle of people appeared subsequently in the press. In these, he referred to the 1997 return of Hong Kong as 'the great Chinese takeaway' and described the Chinese leadership as 'appalling old waxworks', a description in fact that many at the time would have agreed with.

But if he found the publication of his comments embarrassing, then the answer would have been not to commit them to paper in the first place, or to choose his friends more carefully. The *Mail on Sunday* was quite right to publish them. To try to use legal force in such a case is to seek to curtail the freedom of the press without good reason.

The appointment in 2012 of Kristina Kyriacou as his communications secretary worsened matters. She left in 2015 but her style of emails to media outlets demanding corrections and retractions persists, along with more legal warnings from Charles's solicitors, Harbottle & Lewis.

Charles in fact has an unattractive habit of wanting to be free with his views and to wield influence in private, but not be held in any way publicly accountable for this.

The royal family has overall become far more willing to resort to legal action than it was in the past, and does not seem to distinguish between cases which represent a genuine invasion of privacy, and cases where it is simply that they would rather a particular story did not appear.

In 2015, a BBC documentary *Reinventing the Royals* was delayed at the last moment after the corporation received a warning letter from Harbottle & Lewis. Clarence House had originally given the green light, but developed cold feet when it appeared the programme might actually be a proper piece of research rather than the hagiography for Charles they had assumed was on its way. The BBC to its credit did broadcast the two-parter a few weeks later.

Back in 2002, Prince and Princess Michael of Kent complained to the body then adjudicating on stories in the papers, the Press Complaints Commission. The *Daily Mail* had run three stories about the couple's occupation of Kensington Palace. Amongst the allegations it made were that the Kents were paying a mere £70 per week rent for a highly desirable central London property worth £15 million which had seven bedrooms and five reception rooms. The Kents protested that they were paying £115 a week, and that the property only had five bedrooms and four reception rooms. The pampered pair might have been wiser to keep quiet. Their litany of petty complaints was mostly not upheld by the PCC.

But it is the fifth trick in the royal box that is the most powerful, and the most sinister. It is the fog of secrecy with which they have managed to envelop themselves, and inside that fog to behave in ways they simply would not dare if the public knew what they were doing, or to lock away records of the past which they do not wish to see the light of day, even to pervert and destroy our history where it suits them to do so.

Dr Piers Brendon, the eminent Cambridge historian, told me:

> It is well known that the royal family have systematically sanitised the documentary past in their own interest, from the destruction of the Prince Regent's compromising correspondence, via the production of an improved version of Queen Victoria by Princess Beatrice and others, to Princess Margaret's burning masses of her mother's letters.

This royal approach is not new. In the nineteenth century, entire records from three centuries earlier were destroyed because they reflected adversely on the private life of Edward I. Similarly Edward VII left instructions that all his letters were to be burnt, and the same fate befell a painting of George V that its subject did not like.

There seems to be a common theme of locking away – literally – of both relatives of the Queen Mother and their consequential erasure from history, and of embarrassing information, to the extent of falsifying the record in definitive publications.

Perhaps most egregious has been the way in which the clear pro-fascist and pro-appeasement views of the royal family in the 1930s and into the 1940s have been cleaned up or airbrushed out. At the end of the war, many embarrassing documents, revealing the pro-Nazi views of many in the royal family and the wider British Establishment, ended up in the hands of the new civilian German government, or the American forces. Anthony Blunt, later uncloaked as a Russian spy, was repeatedly sent to Germany on the orders of George VI to retrieve all the damaging material he could so that it might be destroyed. Amongst other files, he rounded up sixty-two volumes of correspondence between Victoria and her eldest daughter who married Frederick III of Prussia in 1858 and who mothered the future Kaiser Wilhelm II. He was rewarded for his efforts with a knighthood and a CVO (Commander of Victorian Empire).

Clement Attlee's new Labour government had been only too keen to exploit Nazi files that they now had in their possession, but changed their mind when faced with the problem of incriminating royal material. A batch entitled the 'Windsor File' was regarded as particularly sensitive. This contained comments of the Duke of Windsor while he was on the continent and which found their way at the time into German intelligence. Two copies of the file now held by the civilian

German government had been made, one being handed to London and one to the Americans. Securing the return to Britain of the American copy, or its destruction by them, became a major objective of British foreign policy at this time, and a good deal of scarce political capital was expended on it in Britain's engagement with the Americans, who became irritated with this British obsession.

The State Department's director of European Affairs, John Hickerson, wrote in a top-secret message that he expected the British government to resist strongly the publication of any material relating to the Duke of Windsor. 'There is throughout the United Kingdom an unreasoning devotion to the monarchical principle and an almost fanatical disposition to do everything possible to protect the good name of the institution of the monarchy.'

Anthony Blunt was allowed to continue his cosy role at the Palace as Surveyor of the Queen's Pictures even after the truth about his treachery began to emerge. The Queen asked in 1964 what was to be done about him, but in the meantime he was allowed continued access to the Palace, even giving guided tours to friends. Peter Wright, the MI5 employee of *Spycatcher* fame, was asked in 1967 to undertake a complete investigation into Blunt, but was told to lay off one area – his activities in retrieving royal material from Germany. He was only finally brought to book by Margaret Thatcher in 1979.

The zeal with which the Palace and the British government wanted after the war to rewrite history was not actually the inspiration George Orwell used for Winston Smith's work changing the contents of old newspapers in *Nineteen Eighty-Four*, written in 1948, but it could have been. He who controls the past controls the future. Or to quote a Russian joke circulating during Stalin's time as leader of the Soviet Union, you never know what's going to happen yesterday.

We might expect the Royal Archive to be the place to find the truth about the past, and it is certainly true that there is a vast treasure trove of documentary evidence about the past held there. It is also true that the staff employed are courteous and helpful. However, there is one over-riding problem. The archive is classified as private, the property of the monarch. Yet hidden away in the turrets at Windsor Castle is the history of this country, and specifically the history of how one leg of our constitutional arrangements, the monarchy, has acted up and down the decades. It is our history, not just theirs. So some material is available, but what is released is not governed by the same objective standards that apply in the National Archives at Kew.

Back in 1997 one of my first actions as an MP was to introduce a Bill to reduce the time public records are held before being considered for release. I suggested that the period should be reduced from thirty to twenty years. Although I was unsuccessful then, that policy was subsequently adopted by Gordon Brown's government after a review of public records policy carried out by Paul Dacre of the *Daily Mail*. The National Archives are now progressively releasing more and more of our history, and earlier and earlier.

But some files stay locked up beyond the twenty- or even thirty-year period, and it is no surprise that the biggest bulk of these relate to royal matters. A visit to the excellent National Archives at Kew is an unrewarding experience if royal files are your subject of interest. On the day of my visit, there were 3,629 closed files on the royal family. Here are some of the titles:

- PM's Office: Correspondence – Family name of Royal Family members (1951–1964)
- Relations between the media and members of the Royal Family – possible legal measures (3 January 1984 – 18 January 1984)
- Future career of the Prince of Wales (31 May 1979 – 21 December 1981)

- Prince of Wales article: 'Help for Self-Help' for publication in *The Economist* (11 March 1983 – 18 March 1983)
- Visit of Duke of Edinburgh to countries in Far East and Pacific (1959)
- Discussions on civil list (11 January 1965 – 13 November 1969)
- British nationality for German descendants of British royal family (1957)

On the face of it, there would seem to be no good reason why these files, all of them over thirty years old, and the vast majority of the rest, cannot be released, with names redacted where necessary. Yet many closed files, it has been decided, will stay that way for 100 years.

I pursued with the National Archives the file referred to above relating to Prince Charles's article 'Help for Self-Help'. In return I received a comprehensive reply explaining why I could learn nothing more about this. How can an article written almost forty years ago on what appears to be a benign subject possibly qualify for the same level of protection as a genuine state secret of the most important kind?

At least in Kew we can learn the titles of the closed files. In Windsor, there is not even a list. What we do know is that it is the policy not to release anything that relates to the present reign. That means that the most recent file you can possibly access, if it has not been specifically closed for a longer period or destroyed, will date from 1952 – a 67-year rule, and counting.

Some closed files have even been transferred from Kew to Windsor, which means the chances of seeing them will be adversely affected. One batch relates to correspondence with the Treasury dating from 1993, the year the Queen was effectively forced into paying tax. We will no doubt now have to wait a very long time before that file sees the light of day, if it ever does.

The same highly restrictive approach applies to records held by the

Duchy of Cornwall. When John Kirkhope sought to access these, he was loftily told that access to Duchy records was a 'privilege and not a right'. When they finally granted him the right to see papers, he duly requested access to various documents dated between 1832 and 1913 but was told they were all confidential.

It is time for the National Archives to take over both the Royal Archive and the records of the Duchy of Cornwall, and apply the same rules for disclosure as it does to other categories of information, with the same privacy protections applied where appropriate. That includes producing as a first step a comprehensive list of what is actually held.

As the access to archive material has been kept tightly controlled, so steps have been taken to strangle the release of recent material relating to the royals which is held by public bodies. Before the coming into effect of the Freedom of Information Act 2000, Rosie Winterton, then a minister in the Lord Chancellor's department, told me in a parliamentary answer in 2002 that the Open Government White Paper (1993) states that 'records relating to the royal family will be treated in the same way as all other records'. She also added that 'under the Open Government Code, "potential embarrassment" is not a factor in determining closure or release'.

The 2000 Act, while quite liberating in most respects, opened up a gulf between royal and other material. Its original terms, despite throwing open the doors of the state, made it quite difficult to secure the release of documentation relating to the royals. Access was far from automatic. A public interest test had to be met.

Tightening came in other ways too. Around the same time, Dr Piers Brendon was contacted by the Cabinet Office and Royal Archives, who asked him to return a file that had, it seems, been opened in error. He described the material in the file, which related to matters of patronage, as 'flimsy' and 'insignificant', and pointed out it had already been widely seen by scholars, but the Cabinet Office was adamant. 'I was struck by how much fuss was being made about so much trivia,' he told me.

In 2010 the Labour government introduced a Bill to update the Act. In general this led to some further liberalisation. Yet there was one exception to this direction of travel – the monarchy, where even the small crack in the door provided by the 2000 Act was closed off. The new position in law is that even if the release of information is overwhelmingly in the public interest, it cannot be provided. This new draconian regime applies to the Queen, Prince Charles and, added as an afterthought, Prince William. The public interest test remains valid for other royals.

This tightening represented a major victory for the Palace in its secret and forceful lobbying to achieve changes to legislation for the benefit of the royals. A Palace spokeswoman, questioned on this, told *The Guardian*: 'The royal household was consulted by government on the changes to the freedom of information act but as with all official matters, the royal household relied on the advice of Her Majesty's ministers with regards to the issue.'

This is dissembling at its very worst. It is both accurate and totally misleading, in that it fails to mention the first key element of the process. The Palace lobbied hard for the changes and Jack Straw, the relevant minister at the time and never a great fan of freedom of information, agreed to do what the Palace wanted. Only then, and this is where the Palace quote starts, did the government formally ask for Queen's Consent and were naturally given it.

So why was the Palace so keen to secure these changes? It did so because Charles wanted the ability to influence matters in secret without being in any way held accountable, and because his interventions were beginning to leak out. One such matter that became public was his improper intervention in the proposed redevelopment of Chelsea

Barracks, a scheme he managed to scupper. Another was the long battle being fought by *The Guardian* for the release of letters written by the Prince, lobbying government ministers on a wide range of topics.

It took the paper nine long years to win its Freedom of Information Act case for the 'black spider letters', covering the period 2003 to 2009, to be released. It was a campaign that was fought bitterly all the way, not just by the Palace, but by both the Labour and then the coalition governments, who between them spent £400,000 of public money fighting to keep Charles's letters secret.

Part of the case for suppression put forward by the then Attorney-General Dominic Grieve was that there was, in his view, a risk that the Prince would not be seen to be politically neutral if they were released. But that is because he was not politically neutral. He was adopting political positions on a wide range of topics and lobbying accordingly. Painting over rotten wood again. The answer was not to hush up his lobbying, but to ensure he discontinued it.

You might think that the response of government ministers to the constant lobbying would have been to remind Prince Charles of his non-political constitutional role. Some hope! Andy Burnham, now the Mayor of Greater Manchester but then Labour's Health Secretary, was only too eager, as the democratically elected minister, to sign off his reply to the unelected prince with a cringeworthy flourish: 'I have the honour to remain, Sir, your Royal Highness's most humble and obedient servant.' Keep the red flag flying, Andy.

Eventually forty-four letters were released. They included Charles pressing for a cull of badgers, arguing against government plans to cut funding for homeopathic remedies, and calling for better equipment for British troops in combat zones. Charles had also lobbied on farming issues. The Duchy of Cornwall, the profits from which go to Charles, is as we know a large landholder of agricultural land and the recipient of handouts from the state in that connection, yet he failed to declare an interest, as MPs, peers or councillors would have had to have done, when he advocated policy positions. Now, since the change in the law, he is free to lobby for his own interests without that being officially discoverable.

The Information Commissioner, in considering the question of release, observed that there was 'overwhelming public interest in revealing details because the Prince of Wales's contact with government ministers raises legitimate questions about [his role] in a parliamentary democracy'.

Indeed it does. The Scottish Information Commissioner, Rosemary Agnew, went even further, saying that 'giving the royal family absolute exemption ... would be in direct conflict with the public interest'. Scotland subsequently rejected the changes accepted south of the border. There is now a total prohibition on the release of any further letters for a period twenty years after their creation, or until five years after Charles's death, whichever is later.

It would be surprising if the meddling Prince (his own description) did not see the outcome as a green light to embark on a new round of letters, perhaps even less nuanced than previous ones. We will not know for a long time. The royal family may think they have won an important point but actually they are storing up trouble for themselves in the future.

Freedom of information is important, not just because it empowers the citizen, but also because it is a major driver in keeping people honest and behaving responsibly. If you have the ability to spend public money and influence decisions, you are much more likely to do so wisely if it is likely your activities will be made public in due course.

If there is any doubt about this, we need only look at the whole saga of MPs' expenses. Would anyone really have planned to spend money on duck houses and moat cleaning if they had thought it was all going to end up on the front page of their local paper, or worse? So how can it be justified for freedom of information to be applied to all public bodies except the royal family? Like the Department for Transport, or your local council, or Network Rail, or the Environment Agency or countless other bodies, the royal family performs a public function with public money. They should be properly accountable for that. Why should they alone be unequal before the law? Even if an argument can be made for the Queen, who has a well-established constitutional role to offer advice, no such position exists for Charles, let alone William. We only have one monarch at a time.

Yet we now learn that Charles has been regularly receiving red boxes full of confidential papers since 1992. Apart from anything else, this conflicts with the long-held 'need to know' policy of successive governments. That in turn may partly explain why the Cabinet Office fought for three years to conceal this fact before it finally emerged in 2015. We now learn that William too is receiving boxes of confidential material. It must of course be very frustrating for Prince Charles to have strong views on topics and to have to keep those to yourself, or at least couch them in very careful terms, but that is the lot of the constitutional monarchy. The roll of the dice that has won them a hugely privileged position in society also brings with it a requirement to avoid making political or controversial comments. If he finds the constitutional restrictions too onerous, then he can always absent himself from the line of succession and become a normal citizen.

Prince Charles has very obviously found the requirement to keep out of politics something of a yoke around his neck, and has pushed the constitutional envelope as far as it will go, some would say beyond bursting point. So we know the Prince's views on a wide range of matters, everything from architecture, where he is a traditionalist, to climate change, where he is a strong believer and advocate for action, to China, where his distaste for the ruling Communist leadership and his support for Tibet is not hidden. We even heard him on Radio 4's *Thought for the Day*, in December 2016, arguing for a tolerant approach to refugees, and warning of a return to the dark days of the 1930s. To many, this sounded like a thinly veiled attack on UKIP-type attitudes.

As it happens, I tend to agree with most things he says, but that does not change the fact that he frequently crosses the line into political areas. If the function of the royal family is to unite the nation, adopting sometimes controversial viewpoints that alienate sections of the population is not the way to achieve it.

There is a sentiment often attributed to Voltaire (but actually penned by an English writer, Evelyn Beatrice Hall, succinctly capturing what Voltaire might have said): 'I disapprove of what you say but I will defend to the death your right to say it.' For Prince Charles it might be: 'I approve of what you say but I will defend to the death our right to have you not say it.' Well, perhaps not to the death.

One of the reasons the Queen's time in office has been a success, as it undoubtedly has, is because even after decades on the throne, we do not officially know what she thinks on most issues, although we can probably make a shrewd assessment. Studious, conscientious and boring is what is required and what she has broadly delivered.

Obviously everyone, including the Queen, is entitled to their views, and indeed it would be an odd person who did not have their own views on the major issues affecting the country. Nor would it be surprising, given her background and age, if hers were on the right of the political spectrum, and there is nothing wrong with that. What is wrong, however, is if the systems in place allow the monarch or the Prince of Wales, or indeed any other member of the royal family, to exert influence beyond that which is appropriate for a constitutional monarchy, and secondly, if the public are not able to hold them to account for their actions because the law has been skewed to prevent this from happening.

Prince Charles has chosen a different route from his mother, and therein lies danger for the monarchy. If as king he is seen as simply another politician, support for the monarchy will soon ebb away. As *The Times* acidly put it in an editorial, 'a head of state with an opinion is called a president, not a prince'.

Charles, under pressure, has said that of course he would behave differently as king. But old habits die hard. Is not the most likely scenario that he will continue to advance his views strongly on a wide range of subjects, many political in nature, but will do so in secret, confident that the avenues for discovering his actions have been largely closed off?

Weak at the Knees

'As a believer in Republican principles, I can see no use for a Royal Family.'

Labour's first ever Member of Parliament, Keir Hardie, could not have been clearer when he addressed the House of Commons in 1901.

Although you would have been hard pressed to find many other MPs at the time willing to express such views publicly (although a fair number of Liberals in private had a good deal of sympathy with the sentiment), the statement in itself was far from exceptional. In Britain, there had long been a radical strain that opposed the continuation of a monarchy. Indeed, it might be argued that with the execution of Charles I in 1649 and the assumption of power by Oliver Cromwell, we were the first major power to effect a move to a republic.

In the eighteenth century, the talented and acerbic cartoonist James Gillray mercilessly satirised George III, particularly his miserly nature and his pretensions to be an expert in art. The French revolution of 1789, which saw the execution of Louis XVI four years later, inspired republican movements the world over, to the alarm of monarchies everywhere. In Britain, a republican flag was created. Inspired by the French tricolour, it consisted of three horizontal stripes: red, white and green. It could be seen on occasions such as Peterloo, scene of the infamous massacre in 1819 when troops on horseback charged into the crowd of some 70,000 protesters, and the causes of social justice and republicanism became intertwined.

In France, in Britain and in the United States, those promoting the end of monarchy were enthused by the one-time Lewes resident Thomas Paine, who wrote: 'One of the strongest natural proofs of the folly of hereditary kings is that nature disproves it, otherwise she would not so frequently turn it into ridicule, by giving mankind an ass for a lion.'

It is indeed unarguable that the monarchs thrown up by accident of birth since the time Thomas Paine wrote those words have not comprised the best person available at the time. Amongst the diligent and dutiful, there have been the playboys, the lazy and, in the case of Edward VIII, the dangerously fascistic.

The further upheaval of the old order in 1848, which touched around fifty countries and saw the removal of monarchy in France (again, and for the final time), and the limitation of monarchical power in Denmark and the Netherlands, had only ripples in Britain. Yet there was sufficient alarm for the government to pass into law that year the Treason Felony Act, largely with an eye across the water to Ireland. Section 3 of the Act made it an offence

> If any person whatsoever shall, within the United Kingdom or without, compass, imagine, invent, devise, or intend to deprive or depose our Most Gracious Lady the Queen, from the style, honour, or royal name of the imperial crown of the United Kingdom, or of any other of her Majesty's dominions and countries.

The penalty was transportation to Australia. The law remains on the statute book to this day, though transportation has now been replaced by a maximum sentence of life imprisonment. However it is doubtful that a successful prosecution could be brought, particularly given the personal rights embodied in the 1998 Human Rights Act. With that in mind, *The Guardian* in 2001 mounted a legal challenge to the Act, arguing that it was a basic right to be able to argue for a republic and that the 1848 legislation was therefore unconstitutional. The action failed, the court deciding that the question was hypothetical, as *The Guardian* was not being prosecuted under the Act. Most of the judges nevertheless accepted the paper's point that the part of the Act 'which appears to criminalise the advocacy of republicanism is a relic of a bygone age and does not fit into our modern legal system'. That makes the events of 2013 rather curious. In that year, the Ministry of Justice erroneously announced that Section 3 had been repealed, and later had to contradict itself. But why? Why has this obsolete provision been left on the statute book?

A small number of prosecutions followed its enactment in 1848, but the last was in 1883. In any case the existence of the Act has never deterred those peacefully opposed to the British monarchy. Queen Victoria's retreat into the life of a recluse, following the death of her beloved Albert in 1861, gave oxygen to those who questioned the value of a monarchy and in particular how much it was costing to keep Victoria invisible.

The early 1870s were a high point for republicanism in Britain, and in 1873 the National Republican League was formed. In Parliament, the Liberal MP for Chelsea, Sir Charles Dilke, led the charge, openly argu- ing in 1871 that Britain should become a republic. On 6 November that year, he told a packed public meeting in Newcastle: 'If you can show me a fair chance that a republic here will be free from the political corruption that hangs about the monarchy, I say … let it come.' He also tore into the pointless sinecures and extensive waste of money associated with the monarchy. He demanded a parliamentary inquiry into royal expenses.

Sir Charles was a man well ahead of his time. As well as his advocacy of republicanism, he championed labour rights, the feminist movement, and universal suffrage. His route to the top was only halted by a messy divorce. The febrile republican tide was only turned in 1874 when the Prince of Wales contracted typhoid fever and the resultant newspaper coverage generated a wave of sympathy.

But still republican sentiment persisted amongst politicians. Keir Hardie himself was unambiguous in his views, Speaking in 1894 on the occasion of the birth of the royal child who would become Edward VIII, he said:

> From his childhood onward this boy will be surrounded by sycophants and flatterers by the score and will be taught to believe himself as of a superior creation. A line will be drawn between him and the people whom he is to be called upon someday to reign over. In due course ... he will be sent on a tour round the world, and probably rumours of a morganatic alliance will follow, and the end of it all will be that the country will be called upon to pay the bill.

His analysis of the operation of monarchy was as true then as it is today. The royal family is indeed surrounded by sycophants, and most members of the family do appear to regard themselves as superior to ordinary people. His prescient prediction of a morganatic alliance – a marriage between a person of high rank and one of a lower rank – proved to be spookily accurate. His second prediction, that the poor old taxpayer would have to foot the bill, was even more so.

The Liberals had no love for Edward VII, who improperly connived with the Conservative opposition to try to thwart the radical programme

of the 1906 Liberal government, including the People's Budget –
ultimately unsuccessfully – but it was to the fast-growing Labour Party
that republicans looked for action. They were to be sorely disappointed.

The 1923 Labour Party conference considered two motions relevant
to the monarchy. The first was 'that the Royal Family is no longer a
necessary part of the British constitution', and the second was 'that the
hereditary principle in the British Constitution be abolished'. Respond-
ing from the platform, George Lansbury adopted an approach that
was to become all too familiar in the Labour Party. He too was a
republican, he told the conference, but the issue was a 'distraction' from
more important issues. A republic, but not now. Both motions were
soundly defeated.

It was perhaps a good thing that Keir Hardie died in 1915, before he
had to witness the embarrassing approach adopted by his successor,
Ramsay MacDonald, on the occasion of the formation of the first Labour
government in 1924.

The initial shock of the Establishment at the infiltration of 'socialists'
to government, even if the party was in a considerable minority in the
House of Commons, was soon replaced by a more pragmatic thought:
bring them inside the tent, albeit superficially. The new ministers were
all given, and meekly accepted, a crash course in courtly behaviour by
the Cabinet Secretary, Sir Maurice Hankey. What a relief it must have
been to those fearful of socialism to see Mr MacDonald turn up in full
court dress for his first formal Court reception. Doubtless he cut a fine
figure in his blue and gold braided tailcoat and white knee breeches,
not to mention his sword. Willie Hamilton, the radical Labour MP,
described the scene thus in his book, *My Queen And I*: 'So it was that
Ramsay MacDonald and his motley crew heralded in the revolution,
like circus clowns enjoying the paint, powder and ridiculous garb – all
symbols of a society they had been elected to destroy.'

The one minister who refused to conform, the Minister of Health John Wheatley, widely regarded as the most successful minister of the short-lived 1924 administration, was found no place in the 1929 Labour government. He had committed the unpardonable sin of refusing to buy a silk top hat and court dress. A Labour minister sacked for not wearing a tail-coat and a top hat! What would they have thought in the mining villages of South Wales or the north-east?

But it meant that after the election in 1929 when the Labour ministers attended the Palace to collect their seals of office, to a man they were decked out in morning coats and silk hats, united in obsequious conformity. Perhaps this pathetic behaviour influenced the young socialist writer George Orwell. There are certainly similarities between the actions of the pigs in *Animal Farm* and those of Labour ministers around this time. Normal garb good, morning dress better.

They had thrown in the towel on day one and the Labour Party, whenever in government, has been mechanically repeating the action ever since. Small gestures can make statements. If the first Labour Prime Minister and his Cabinet had insisted on wearing normal clothes, that would have sent a clear signal that theirs was a new world. By adopting the rules of the old, the message they sent was business as usual.

Keir Hardie, when first elected, refused to wear the expected attire of black frock coat, silk top hat and starched collar, instead opting for a plain tweed suit and red tie, topped off with a deerstalker hat. He was viciously attacked for this, but his reputation today is markedly higher than that of Ramsay MacDonald. It is very British for those who rise outside the ranks of the established order, even for those who have opposed it on principle, to leap at the chance to join it when the opportunity presents itself.

It happened with the northern entrepreneurs who made their fortune in the industrial revolution. Being a huge financial success was not enough. They craved access to the top table of old. Richard Cobden, an industrialist who was an exception to the rule, observed that 'manufacturers and merchants seem to desire riches that they may be enabled to prostrate themselves at the feet of feudalism'. He became a radical MP and principal opponent of the Corn Laws.

So it was with the Labour Party of the 1920s. The Labour government may have accepted the Establishment but the gesture was not reciprocated. They had come to power at the start of 1924 but were forced to go to the country in October that year, having lost a motion of no confidence in the House of Commons. Four days before the election, the text of a letter was published in the *Daily Mail*. It purported to come from one Grigory Zinoviev, head of the executive committee of the Communist International, and Arthur MacManus, a British representative on that committee. It was addressed to the Communist Party of Great Britain.

The letter talked about 'close contact between the British and Russian proletariat', and how to 'extend and develop the propaganda of ideas of Leninism in England and the Colonies'. (I wonder if Scotland and Wales were colonies, in the writer's mind?) This was fake news, 1924 style. Ramsay MacDonald called it out as fake straight away, but it was in vain. There were too many, including in the civil service, who believed it was authentic or found it convenient to do so. The letter had actually been received by the Foreign Office two days after the vote of no confidence and there is some evidence (set out in a 1968 publication, *The Zinoviev Letter: A Political Intrigue*, by Lewis Chester, Steven Fay and Hugo Young) that officials colluded with the Conservative opposition to breathe life into it.

Grigory Zinoviev's refutation, two days before the election, was lost in the whirling winds of fear. The consequence of the publication of this letter was to reduce to zero Labour's already vanishingly small chance of forming the next government, though the real price was paid by the Liberals, as what we would today call 'soft Tories' ran to the Conservatives to ward off this apparent Bolshevik threat.

Labour lost forty seats, dropping to 151, but the Liberals went from 158 to just forty, their biggest collapse until 2015. In 1998, I asked Robin Cook, then Foreign Secretary, to release for public scrutiny the files held by MI6 on the Zinoviev letter. It seemed to me it was time for the full facts to come out. In his response, he said he could not release the papers, but to be helpful had commissioned a Foreign Office historian to write a memorandum on the letter.

Fast-forward a year, almost literally to the day, and the report from that historian, Gill Bennett, concluded that it was impossible to know who had written the letter, but her best guess was that it had been commissioned by so-called White Russians, opposed to the Communist regime. It seemed clear, in any case, that it was a fake.

Ramsay MacDonald is widely regarded in Labour circles as a traitor to the movement, notably for his role in heading a coalition from 1931 onwards, rather than for any stance relating to the monarchy. He was not alone, however, in finding it very comfortable to hobnob with the highest stratum of society. A record number of Labour MPs attended the Buckingham Palace garden party that year.

The abandonment of republicanism in the Labour Party was brutally demonstrated some five years later. At the abdication of Edward VIII, easily the biggest crisis of the twentieth century for the royal family at least until the death of Princess Diana over sixty years later, a Labour MP, James Maxton, proposed an amendment to the Abdication Bill which, if passed, would have established a republic in Britain. Just five MPs voted to support the amendment, and it was lost by 403 votes.

Socialists might have been entitled to expect a purer response from Clement Attlee, who, in the five years after 1945, introduced a whole range of genuinely radical policies that changed the direction of Britain for good – in both senses of the phrase. He was unprepossessing by nature. Churchill described him rather cattily as 'a modest man with much to be modest about' and rather rudely quipped on one occasion that 'an empty taxi drew up and Attlee got out'.

But the Labour Prime Minister was effective and Churchill was churlish. Attlee was certainly the nearest the party has ever come to actually having a socialist in No. 10. Yet his radicalism did not stretch to the royal family. In opposition back in 1936 he had called for the revenue from the Duchies to be transferred to the Treasury, but by the time he became Prime Minister, he was asserting that the royal family led 'simple lives' with 'no excess of luxury'. This assertion was so manifestly untrue that you have to conclude he had taken a pragmatic decision not to take on this issue at the same time as he was challenging so many long-established shibboleths. Or, more depressingly, that like so many of his Labour colleagues, he had been transfixed by the glamour and the charm offensive launched on him, and had lost his sense of judgement.

By the time Harold Wilson had become Prime Minister, all vestiges of Keir Hardie's resolute republican position had left the Labour leadership like a will-o'-the-wisp. Harold Wilson was a consummate politician and had probably concluded, rightly, that there would be no votes in being hostile to the monarchy, and indeed votes to be gained by being seen to cosy up. It was gently put about that the Queen and Harold got on well.

The acquisition and maintenance of political power is a powerful disincentive to chance-taking and boat-rocking. Even the application of political pragmatism, however, cannot excuse the suffocating sycophancy shown by Neil Kinnock when he enthusiastically supported a massive pay rise of 7.5 per cent a year for the royals in the 1990 review of the civil list.

Yet there was still some republican fire in the party smouldering in the grate. In 1991, the veteran Labour MP and former minister Tony Benn introduced the Commonwealth of Britain Bill. (Mr Benn preferred his adopted proletarian-sounding name to the alternative which he abandoned in 1973, Sir Anthony Wedgwood Benn, itself a hard-won step-down from Viscount Stansgate). The Bill proposed that, in place of the monarchy, there should be an elected President and, for the first time, a written constitution. It was never even debated.

Then came Tony Blair. In 1994 he had floated the idea of a move to a leaner, more modern monarchy, a sort of bicycling monarchy. His reading of the public mood was sharp, for that was probably where the majority of the public was. Of course, he did nothing about it when he became Prime Minister three years later. For his first visit to Balmoral, he donned a tweed suit. Whatever his private views of the monarchy, he knew a good publicity prop when he saw one. His sure-fire media touch kicked in upon the death of Princess Diana, when he captured the public mood much more skilfully than the Palace. The US ambassador, in a diplomatic despatch to Washington, termed Blair's handling 'another triumph'. The royal family, by contrast, had been 'wrong-footed' and displayed 'styles that lack empathy'.

At least with Tony Blair and his exaggerated emotion over the 'people's princess' Diana, we all knew it was cynical play-acting. We even admired his lump in the throat, his chutzpah. Now, you would be hard-pressed to find many overt republicans in the Parliamentary Labour Party. The veteran Dennis Skinner lost his seat at the 2019 election, and the articulate and principled Paul Flynn sadly died earlier that year.

But what of Jeremy Corbyn and John McDonnell, old socialists the pair? In 1991, Corbyn had backed Tony Benn's radical Bill. In 2000, he asked Tony Blair about 'the possibility of relocating the royal family to some smaller and more modest accommodation in the future'.

However, during his 2015 campaign for the leadership of the Labour Party, Corbyn stated that republicanism was 'not a battle that I am fighting'. He said he would not seek to abolish the monarchy while he remained leader, and he was true to his word. Presumably that means he will again argue for it now he is not in a position to deliver it. Jeremy Corbyn is following the intellectually incoherent Labour tradition set by George Lansbury almost a century earlier. Jam tomorrow and jam yesterday, but never jam today. Nor can republicans expect very much in this direction from the new Labour leader, Sir Keir Starmer, who may have been named after Keir Hardie but as far as republican sentiments are concerned, there the similarity ends.

There are, in fact, many in the party whose opposition to the royal family is significantly greater when they are not in office or when talking in private. A 1993 poll of Labour MPs found a quarter in favour of becoming a republic. Nor is this submerged ambivalence to the royal family limited to Labour politicians. In the Commons one day, I ran into Charles Kennedy in the Lib Dem Whips' Office. He had just become Lib Dem leader. 'I've just come back from the Palace,' he volunteered. 'I can see why people are republican.'

The fake sycophancy shown by left-of-centre politicians is, however, as nothing compared to the real thing shown by Conservatives. Even the Queen herself found it somewhat ridiculous how low Margaret Thatcher would curtsey when they met, like an Establishment limbo dancer.

That, however, was elegance personified compared to the absurd curtseys of Theresa May, at the time our most senior elected politician, to Prince William and any other member of the unelected royal family she met. The jerky and ungainly body movements conjured up nothing so much as Olive Oyl in the Popeye cartoons of old.

By indulging in such demeaning deference, the Prime Minister was conveying the message that those elevated by democracy must nevertheless acknowledge the superiority of an unelected family who individually happen to be where they are merely through accident of birth, and indeed the abdication of Edward VIII in 1936.

Apart from piloting a helicopter and producing children, what has Prince William actually done? Certainly nothing that merits a degrading curtsey from one of our most senior politicians, a woman twice his age. The Palace is at pains to say that it is no longer necessary for those who meet members of the royal family to bow and curtsey. This is not an enlightened view from the Palace but a recognition of a fait accompli: increasing numbers simply refuse to behave in this abject medieval way.

If the Palace were enlightened, then they would simply announce that henceforth they would prefer those who meet royals not to bow or curtsey. But of course the opposite is true. They love it and clearly regard it as appropriate. Those who do not show due deference are greeted politely, but ever so slightly more frostily. The hierarchy is rigorously enforced within the family itself. Meghan Markle was even required to curtsey to the Queen at her own wedding. Princess Diana, after she was brutally stripped of her HRH status, was henceforth required by etiquette to curtsey even to the dreadful Princess Michael of Kent, a greater ignominy it being difficult to imagine. Whether she ever did, of course, is another matter.

Most Conservative politicians are highly deferential. Depressingly typical is the former Home Secretary Douglas Hurd, who in 2015 produced a slim volume entitled *Elizabeth II: The Steadfast*. If the title does not betray the likely drift of the book, the fact that it contains an introduction written by Prince William probably does. You would struggle to find a single word of criticism of any member of the royal family anywhere in the book.

And so Prince Philip is described as having been 'a good-looking young man'. Indeed he was, but that is not the aspect of his personality most would alight on first. References to his colourful language, and his language describing people of colour, are entirely absent from the text.

'The Queen's traditional Christmas broadcast to her people … is a much-loved part of Christmas,' states Douglas Hurd. Well, up to a point, Lord Copper. Elsewhere, the Queen is described as having almost magical powers, like the medieval king's touch that could cure all ills. Her visit to Dresden was 'binding up the wounds as only she could do'. In fact, in Dresden the Queen was booed and had eggs thrown at her car.

This followed the unveiling in London shortly beforehand of a statue of Bomber Harris, the architect of the catastrophic carpet bombing of the medieval city in February 1945 in the death throes of the Second World War. The statue was unveiled by the Queen Mother, an event that was subject to jeering and chants that Bomber Harris was a war criminal. The statue had to be guarded round the clock for months to ward off the continual attacks upon it.

Douglas Hurd then asserts, without any justification, that 'as the years passed, the Queen and Diana would have found a way of working together … Diana had become an ally of the Queen.' This working together seems to have been some way off, judging by the famous 'squidgy' tapes, in which Diana fulminated: 'My life is torture. Bloody hell. And after all I've done for this fucking family.'

As part of the divorce arrangements, the Queen supported removing the ability of Diana to continue to use the title of Her Royal Highness, much to Diana's deep dismay. At the same time, on the Queen's instructions Diana's name was removed from the daily prayers in the House of Commons, and any products containing her image were removed from royal gift shops. The idea that they had become allies is complete nonsense.

Throughout the book Douglas Hurd adopts ultra-royalist positions. The failure to replace the royal yacht *Britannia* in 1997 was 'a blunder'. No, actually it saved a huge amount of money. But it is common knowledge that the Queen was very attached to the boat, so doubtless Douglas Hurd will have done himself no damage in royal circles by making this statement. Some Tory MPs of the Brexit variety, living in their heads in about 1954, buoyed by their success, began clamouring for a new royal yacht. Jake Berry, then minister for the Northern Powerhouse, told *The House* magazine in March 2019 that a new royal yacht would 'unite' the country after Brexit and act as a boon to overseas trade – 'a great symbol of a newly independent Britain'. Also clamouring for a new yacht, irrespective of cost, is prime freeloader Prince Andrew. Of course none of these people has carried out a proper cost–benefit analysis. I suspect the Treasury has, which is why they are so steadfastly against the idea.

These delusional, backward-looking Tory MPs seem to think the world can be bewitched by a new royal yacht. If only such a grand boat can sail into distant ports and a member of the magic royal family can sprinkle some royal fairy dust over the locals, the knees will bend and the trade deals will come tumbling out, in terms very favourable to Britain of course – just like it was in the days of the empire.

So are the governments of Australia, Angola and Argentina, even Andorra, likely to realise they had forgotten the grandeur of Britain, be overawed and sign up to some one-sided trade deal as is only our due? I think not. More likely, they will conclude that Britain is retreating in a sort of infantile way into its past because it does not know where it wants to go in the future. Indifference, or at best gentle pity, rather than admiration is the probable response.

Douglas Hurd even criticises the much cheaper and more down-to-earth monarchies to be found elsewhere in Europe. 'Her subjects

… would not relish the pedestrian and undramatic style of her Scandinavian and Dutch counterparts,' he confidently states. Actually, insofar as public opinion can be gauged, that is exactly what they would welcome – yes to a monarch, but a royal family at a much lower cost to the public purse and with far fewer hangers-on.

Judging by the hostile reaction to the Queen's 2018 Christmas broadcast where she referred to poverty while sitting in front of a gold piano, gold fireguard, gold clock and gold mirror, the royals would be well advised to hide their oozing opulence. Even the supportive *Daily Mail* called it 'tone deaf'. And 'subjects'? 'Her people'? What century is he living in?

I have no reason to believe that Douglas Hurd is anything other than a sincere and honest man, but it is worrying if someone of his intellect and political savviness can assert that everything in the royal garden is rosy, like Dr Pangloss in Voltaire's *Candide* that it is the best of all possible worlds, when there is so much evidence to the contrary. More likely, he will have concluded, and he would not be alone in this, that the royal family must be protected from criticism at all costs, and if that means turning a blind eye to some unsavoury elements, then that is a price worth paying. And if his book gets him a special invitation or two where he can schmooze with the royals, well that is a bonus, is it not?

So the result is a book that even a public relations employee at Buckingham Palace would have been embarrassed to issue. Such books, however, are far from rare. I am sure, for example, that the royal family would have been delighted by the largely uncritical tone of William Shawcross's biography of the Queen Mother.

Boris Johnson, while London mayor, decided to rename Crossrail as the Elizabeth Line. According to the former Transport Secretary Andrew Adonis, he did so after lobbying from the royal family. What was wrong with Crossrail? It does what it says on the tin. It even had its own logo to match the name. London's Underground lines have tended either to refer to geographical direction (Central, Circle, Northern) or to key stops (Piccadilly or Bakerloo, that being a combination of Baker Street and Waterloo).

It is a relatively recent trend for monarchical connections to be deployed. The Victoria line, opened in 1968, fitted into the pattern of referring to key stops, even if this one did also namecheck the nineteenth-century Queen. Next came the proposed Fleet line, which opened finally instead as the Jubilee line, referring to the Queen's silver jubilee in 1977. And now the Elizabeth line, the first time a royal name with no geographical connection has been used.

Andrew Adonis also wanted to ditch Crossrail as a name, and instead call it the Churchill line, in recognition of Britain's wartime leader. But in the end, just as with Theresa May's curtseys, the elected took second place to the unelected. Opinion polls consistently show that between about 15 and 25 per cent of the population favour a move to a republic, compared to up to 80 per cent who want the present system to stay. That latter represents in part respect and admiration for Queen Elizabeth II personally. It may well be that the figure will drop when Charles ascends to the throne, though probably not by that much.

Nevertheless, even 15 per cent suggests – if the population's views are to be proportionately represented – that there should be around a hundred MPs who are of a similar mind. There may well be, but the numbers prepared to declare this openly are in single figures. The oath of allegiance, as discussed elsewhere in this book, presents a challenging hurdle. But more so does the reluctance to put your head above the parapet while others are sheltering. And then there is the calculation that there are no votes to be gained by opening up this issue.

So we find the House of Commons populated by those at one end of the spectrum who are slavishly loyal to the monarchy, and those at the other who rather wished it had vanished but keep quiet about it. For George Lansbury, for Jeremy Corbyn, and for many others, it is always number ninety-four on the list of priorities, and number ninety-four is never reached. Indeed, if it were to come into view, then the priority order would be changed to demote it still further, echoing Evelyn Waugh's pithy sentiment in *Brideshead Revisited*, derived from St Augustine: 'O God, make me good, but not yet.'

And what of the royals themselves? Their constitutional position demands that they be politically neutral and each person who has occupied the throne over the last century would doubtless argue that that requirement has been met.

Yet episode after episode has shown that their instincts are most certainly on the right of the political spectrum. The Nazi sympathies of Edward VIII have been well rehearsed, but less so the fact that all the royals at the time were in favour of appeasing Hitler, seeing his aggressive and brutal regime as less of a threat than Communism. The first was distasteful, the second would threaten their interests.

The Royal Archives reveal that Attlee's post-war government, elected on a majority, did not find favour with the royals. In a note to George VI on 10 November 1946, his brother the Duke of Windsor wrote:

> I can readily sympathise with you over the situations in which you must sometimes find yourself placed, vis-a-vis the socialist government and their crazy and dangerous policies … The Socialist's [sic] concerted attack upon any form of wealth, their determination to nationalise many industries, and their continuation of rationing for rationing's sake is … alarming.

And in another letter to George VI almost five years later to the day, the former King wrote: 'Its [sic] too bad that the Electorate didn't give Winston and his Conservatives a proper mandate to clean up the appalling and dangerous mess in which the Socialists have left the country after six years of crazy experimentation based on class hatred.'

There is plenty of evidence of right-wing bias from the royals in the reign of Elizabeth II as well. One shocking example relates to events in Australia in 1975 which betrayed improper behaviour from the Queen and her representatives to favour the right-wing Liberal Party against the incumbent Labor administration. In short, the Governor-General Sir John Kerr connived with the opposition led by Malcolm Fraser to force a change of government and the reinstatement of the Liberals who had been rejected at the previous two general elections. Sir John simply sacked the Prime Minister Gough Whitlam to prevent him taking forward his plans for a half-election to the Senate to gain support for his economic plans and announced he was sending for the Liberal leader to form a caretaker administration.

As the Queen's representative, the Governor-General's constitutional duty was to take advice from the Queen's Prime Minister. To go behind his back and cook up a plot with the opposition was treacherous. It was subsequently stated that Sir John had acted alone, without consulting the Palace, a line peddled by Sir William Heseltine, then assistant private secretary to the Queen. But private papers belonging to Sir John, and uncovered by the diligent Australian campaigner Jenny Hocking, show that the Governor-General in fact had extensive discussions with the Palace before acting, including conversations with Prince Charles going back to the spring of 1975, the best part of a year before the dismissal of the Prime Minister. And the Queen's private secretary, Sir Martin Charteris, assured Sir John that the Queen had personally read all the letters Sir John had sent.

The Governor-General was playing a dangerous game, for had his intentions been rumbled by Gough Whitlam, the Prime Minister could have advised the Queen to sack him and she would constitutionally be bound to accept that advice. Sir Martin Charteris had an answer to this, though, telling Sir John that in that eventuality, the Queen would 'try to delay things' as long as possible.

So we have clear evidence that both the Queen and Prince Charles were over a period of months aware of a plan to install a right-wing administration in Australia without an election, and not only failed to alert the Prime Minister Gough Whitlam to the plans but actually connived at their implementation. This gives a whole new meaning to the phrase 'palace coup'. Does anyone think Sir John Kerr would have taken such an extraordinary step without a green light from the Palace?

The appointments made by the royals betray the same right-wing bias. The rarefied segment of society from which Lord Lieutenants, Heralds and all the other weird and wonderful positions are drawn from show this only too clearly. The Ladies of the Bedchamber who, in Victoria's time, would alternate between Whigs and Tories depending on the government of the day are now almost totally and consistently Conservative. Aides tend to be drawn from the same narrow segment of society, such as Laura Hutchings, who went to work for Prince Andrew having been director of the Conservative Party's Middle East Council. It was not a pattern Harry and Meghan followed, which only confirmed the view of the Palace establishment that they were unsound.

We know from various statements from different members of the royal family, on everything from Philip on taxation to Charles on fox hunting, that they broadly favour policies embraced by the Conservatives. Sophie Wessex described Gordon Brown's taxation policies when he was Chancellor as 'frightening' and Cherie Blair as 'horrid' for her perceived attitude to countryside activities. We know Charles threatened to abandon his post – and that is how he phrased it – if the Labour government brought in a ban on fox hunting.

And what of the Queen herself? She has sought to be a constitutional monarch, impartial in party terms, in this country if not in Australia. But she cannot help the fact, as none of us can, that we are influenced by our circumstances, our family and our upbringing. Enough is known to conclude that she comes from a deeply conservative mould.

That she takes comfort in the Britain that existed in the early part of her life rather than the one we have now can be deduced by her strong attraction to the Commonwealth, her opposition to Scottish independence, indiscreetly leaked by David Cameron, and most recently and tellingly by her support for withdrawal from the European Union.

Laura Kuenssberg, the BBC's political editor, has quoted a source from a lunch at Windsor that had the Queen saying: 'I don't see why we can't just get out. What's the problem?' The story had earlier appeared in *The Sun*, which had run a 'Queen Backs Brexit' headline during the referendum campaign. The paper stood by its story, for which it had two sources, even after a successful complaint by the Palace to the press regulator IPSO. There is also the fact that her favourite paper is the *Sunday Telegraph*, probably the most right-wing turn-the-clock-back national in Britain. A small pointer, perhaps, but a clear one.

We cannot expect any individual, in the royal family or otherwise, not to have views and partiality like everyone else. What we should do, however, is to ensure that the unelected cannot exercise undue influence on the policies the elected government adopts.

The Fab Four:
Let It Be

18 May 2018 proved to be a bad day for Pornhub, the world's largest pornography website. Traffic to the site from across the world dropped 10 per cent, in Britain 21 per cent, and in France 23 per cent. The explanation was to be found in Windsor, where Prince Harry was due to marry Meghan Markle. The only occasion to have caused a greater dip in traffic to Pornhub that year was the World Cup final. Reports of the nuptials on internet news sites racked up 1.1 million hours of reading time. It was the wedding of the decade. All royal weddings attract a level of interest, but this one was in a class of its own. In the UK, more than eighteen million people watched the event on television, as well as twenty-nine million in the United States and literally hundreds of millions globally.

The public had warmed to Harry. He was seen as a likeable ordinary bloke, the sort you have a laugh with over a pint, and someone who had undoubtedly shown courage and commitment to his fellow soldiers while on active duty, and indeed after. He was in fact the first royal since, well, his mother who was from a different mould than the narrow rarefied one that typifies other members of the royal family. He had even been seen boarding an easyJet flight to return to Britain from a holiday abroad.

And if Harry was different, multiply that many times for Meghan Markle. Here was an independent woman with an independent mind who had by her own efforts become a successful actor worth millions in her own right. Moreover, she was of mixed-race parentage, a welcome contrast to the starchy whiteness of the Windsors.

It seemed the royal family was beginning to reinvent itself for the twenty-first century, and not before time. The Queen, bless her, was already past ninety and clearly could not go on for ever. Charles was widely regarded as petulant, out of touch and a bit weird, and William as dull and boring. Of Charles's siblings, Anne was invisible, Edward the family nerd, and as for Andrew...

Even within the traditions of a royal wedding, innovations were made. The ceremony was held on a Saturday, rather the weekday normally preferred, and allowed to clash with the FA Cup final. The service included an element of African-American culture, while the Archbishop of Canterbury diplomatically quoted Martin Luther King Jr in his address, and in the evening Meghan made a speech at the reception, which may not sound revolutionary to most people but was most certainly a break with established royal practice. Meghan may have become 'Princess Henry of Wales', but there was zero chance of her ever using that title.

The birth of their son gave more evidence that they intended to do things their way, not least in the name they chose for him, Archie Harrison Mountbatten-Windsor. It is a name that might have belonged to one of Ethel's boyfriends in the *Just William* books rather than to the seventh in line to the throne. It has a curious 1920s feel to it. Yet it was somehow refreshing, even if we are unlikely ever to see King Archie I, that Harry and Meghan chose to eschew the narrow and uninspiring band of former kings: George, William, Henry and Edward. And, somewhat inauspiciously, Charles. Thoughtfully and sensibly, Meghan made it known that if people wanted to send baby gifts, she would prefer them to donate to a charity. The couple also turned down a title for the lad, who could apparently have become the Earl of Dumbarton. That would indeed have been a surprise for Dumbarton, just as it was for Sussex when Harry's dukedom was announced. Had the pair even ever been to Sussex? It was also refreshing after the birth to see a photo which included, as well as the child and his happy parents, his dual-heritage family. Both Harry and Meghan in their own ways were bringing new dimensions to the Windsors, and the public generally welcomed this fresh approach.

Yet in less than two years the couple were attracting a slew of unfavourable headlines, had moved to the United States and were in effect no longer members of the royal family. How had this happened? The union of Harry and Meghan may have seemed like a breath of fresh air, an all-round positive development, but, like a Shakespearean tragedy, the seeds of later destruction were there in Act One.

The royal family is an innately conservative, even hidebound, institution which changes only very slowly, or indeed not at all. The idea that Harry and especially a feisty Meghan could, from their speedboat, manage to turn the royal oil tanker was rather fanciful. There was no question of their infection – for that was how some palace insiders saw it – being allowed to spread. The only question was whether their modern style could tolerably if uneasily sit within the existing framework. We now know the answer was no.

The antecedents were not good. The last American divorcee to marry into the royal family was Wallis Simpson. And the last feisty women to marry royals were Diana Spencer and Sarah Ferguson. None of these matches turned out well.

Royal women have generally been expected to accept a role which is secondary to royal men. This has included until very recently the legal priority given to males over females in the line of succession. Even now, only sons can inherit hereditary peerages, which means if Archie had been a girl, Harry's dukedom could not have been passed on. Before the UK left the EU, this discrimination was taken before the European Court of Human Rights by a number of women personally affected in comparable cases.

The Palace, and Charles in particular, tried to confine Diana to a secondary straitjacket. On her first visit to the United States, she was not allowed to say anything, and reporters were told not to ask her any questions. Her role was to look beautiful and be a simpering sidekick to Charles. For the first three years, Diana uttered fewer than five hundred words in public.

But the traditional approach was never going to last long with Diana, who was an independent spirit and had strong views of her own. To Charles's irritation, the public at large soon concluded that Diana was both more interesting and more attractive than he was. Rather petulantly, while on a walkabout, he spat out, 'I'm just a collector of flowers these days ... It really would have been easier to have had two wives. Then they could cover both sides of the street and I could walk down the middle, directing operations.' Of course, in a way, he did have two wives.

While Diana accumulated positive international headlines for making physical contact with an AIDS sufferer, Charles barely got a mention when he became the first royal to give blood, which he did as his way of giving reassurance after the AIDS scare.

Meghan is Diana-plus. With her background, this is hardly

surprising: a star of the American legal drama series *Suits*, a skilled calligrapher, a charity worker and a divorcee whose previous wedding took place on a beach and lasted just two years. At the age of eleven, she took exception to a television advert for washing-up liquid that implied that this was a matter only for women and wrote letters to the great and the good to object. She succeeded in persuading Procter & Gamble, the makers of the product, to change their strapline. No longer was it 'women all over America are fighting greasy pots and pans' but now 'people'.

She wrote a revealing and sometimes poignant piece for *Elle* magazine back in 2015 which flagged up the racism, mild and overt, she had to endure growing up with a white father and black mother. As a child, she wanted a set of Barbie dolls, but the sets only came in white or black. Her father bought one of each and created a mixed set for her. When at school, the girl whom Andrew Morton in a recent book suggested was descended from slaves on her mother's side and Robert the Bruce on her father's had at one point to tick a box to record her ethnicity: white, black, Hispanic or Asian. She did not know what to tick so she left it blank. She told her father, who said that next time it happened, 'draw your own box'. She has been doing that ever since.

In Britain, she sadly if inevitably encountered undercurrents of racism, even if here it is generally a less virulent strain than in the United States. After Archie's birth, Danny Baker seemed to think it was amusing to tweet a picture of a staid couple emerging from what looked like a hospital each holding the hand of an attired chimpanzee. Thankfully, the public reaction of revulsion made him delete this pretty sharpish.

Meghan's whole ethos was a million miles from that of the royal family she was joining. While she agreed to be at Sandringham when the Boxing Day shoot was under way, she was never going to participate. Nor was she going to abandon her alternative lifestyle, her Pilates, her dabbling with veganism and the rest – and why should she? She was never going to be a suitable candidate for simpering sidekick, and indeed has elegantly said, 'It's time to focus less on glass slippers and more on glass ceilings.'

But rather than embrace her personality and use it to help modernise the monarchy, the knee-jerk reaction of the Palace was to try to force her into the mould they expected royal women to fit into. Much quoted was Harry's outburst to Palace staff that 'what Meghan wants, she gets'. There are plenty in the Palace who were determined to ensure that she absolutely did not get. Early on, an aide was assigned to her to make sure she understood the royal rules. These range from the prohibitions, such as signing autographs, eating oysters, or hugging her husband in public, to the archaic customs of the court, such as learning to whom to curtsey (including Kate, much to the latter's grim pleasure), and ending your meal immediately when the Queen does, even if you have not finished.

Then there are the colours, carefully controlled. Nails must be in natural tones – nothing garish or too common, you understand. As for her clothes, she was gently but firmly propelled towards frumpy beige and grey. Her skirts were lined and weighted to avoid any Marilyn Monroe-type moment. This all served to submerge her natural vibrant personality, but then that was the point. In the run-up to her wedding, we were told by the Palace that Meghan would have 'six months of listening' and would 'proceed with humility'. In other words, you will be taught to keep your modern American views to yourself and learn your place, madam. Simper, smile and shut up.

Just to make the point, it was discreetly put about that she had become known in the royal corridors as Duchess Difficult, including bombarding her aides with texts at five in the morning after her regular 4.30 a.m. yoga sessions. There certainly seems to have been a clash of cultures, with a number of staff falling by the wayside. This includes Melissa Touabti, her personal assistant, who left after only six months, having previously managed a rather longer time with Robbie Williams, himself not the most placid member of the human race. The off-the-record briefings said Meghan reduced her to tears. True, or just more spiteful Palace spin? Then there was Samantha Cohen, personal secretary to the Sussexes, who handed in her notice after seventeen years with the royal family but only a short time with them. In January 2019, we learnt that the protection officer assigned to Harry and Meghan some six months earlier was leaving the force. She was described by colleagues as 'brilliant' and was highly regarded. Then little more than a month later, Amy Pickerill, Meghan's assistant private secretary, announced she was off, again after only a short sojourn. By August 2019, the couple were onto their third nanny for Archie. And Edward Lane Fox, Harry's right-hand man, quit after fifteen years of service. Now, it may well be that this is all just a coincidence. After all, people do leave jobs as a matter of course. Ms Pickering, for example, was said to be moving abroad. Yet the accumulation of departing aides did not look good.

Meghan's independent spirit contrasted sharply with the approach taken by the conforming and conventional Kate, another element latent in Act One that was to play out virulently. It is a staple of the tabloid press to present an undercurrent of 'bitchiness' that is supposed to exist between apparently competing female royal women. We had Diana and Fergie scrabbling around for position, except that they seem to have got on rather well, and now it was Kate and Meghan, with the media looking for the smallest cigarette paper between them. Was that a deliberate slight when Kate looked the other way outside the church as Meghan seemed to be talking to her?

It is certainly true that Kate and Meghan are out of very different moulds, a difference that has been exaggerated by their response to inclusion in the royal family. Kate has sought seamlessly to adopt the royal customs and habits, adhering religiously to guidance (well, instruction really) on what she can and cannot say and wear. Learning, and enforcing, the somewhat absurd hierarchical practices within the royal court is meat and drink to her. She sits neatly, hands clasped on lap and legs crossed at the ankle. She has even taken up shooting, indeed did so as a way of proving her suitability as a wife for William. She had previously shown little interest in the activity. Kate is intelligent, in fact is destined to be the first wife of a monarch to have a university degree, but she has opted for the traditional slot of dull but worthy wife, so that even the most minor deviation generates a media response. It was news apparently when she dropped a water bottle while getting out of a car. And she picked it up! Hold the front page.

The two women are not natural soulmates, therefore, and in some respects could not be more different, so it was predictable that the media would hype up the alleged rivalry between them. Like any soap, there need to be running storylines, and ones the public will recognise, to keep them tuning in for the next episode. But this is not *EastEnders*, and indeed the storyline has had a darker side. It generated an avalanche of offensive and hate-filled messages on the social media platforms operated for the royals. Staff had to spend hours each week deleting those, and help had to be sought from the social media companies themselves.

Much of this vitriol derived directly from stories in the media, with those posting frequently taking the side of one wife against the other. Some posts threatened violence, while some directed at Meghan were overtly racist. Social media has many positive attributes, but it does seem to have unleashed the worst of human nature as well, particularly where women targets are concerned, and as female MPs will readily testify.

Michael Cole, the former BBC royal correspondent, told me, 'I witnessed the grief when Diana and Fergie, who started as friends, were driven apart by newspapers. If one was in, the other was out. It was a nasty game that ended badly. No decent person would want a repeat performance.'

Unfortunately, that is exactly what we have had, and to a large degree because the tension between the two women is not a tabloid invention, even if they have stoked it, but all too real. This in turn has caused friction between Harry and William. The two brothers had for some time been following increasingly divergent paths, and not just because William almost certainly has kingship before him and Harry almost certainly does not. Just as their appearances are strikingly different, so too are their futures. The rumours of a rift between the brothers followed informed gossip that William, who was best man at his brother's wedding, gave advice to Harry about Meghan, advice that was not well received. That, along with a weekend the four spent together which misfired and a row between the wives about Meghan shouting at Kate's servants, seems to have played a part in the decision of the Sussexes to move from Nottingham Cottage in the grounds of Kensington Palace not into Apartment 1 there, as had been planned, but instead to the isolation of Frogmore Cottage in the royal estate of Windsor Great Park. Apartment 1 was literally next door to that occupied by William and Kate – there was even an adjoining door – which was clearly too close for comfort.

So the papers, which were reporting in October 2018 that the year-long renovation of Apartment 1 to meet Harry and Meghan's needs was very nearly complete, were the following month reporting that they would now not be moving in. The fact that at least £1.4 million had been spent on the property in the meantime to meet the couple's specific needs seemed to bother none of the royals, but then why would it when the taxpayer was picking up the bill as usual? It certainly did not bother William and Kate, who had been very relaxed to see a seven-figure sum spent on their own apartment in the recent past, again courtesy of the taxpayer.

Naturally, with the move to Frogmore Cottage, another bill for conversion beckoned for the taxpayer, this one for at least £2.4 million. It seems every time a royal moves somewhere, a multimillion-pound bill for 'renovation' lands on the taxpayer's doormat.

Part of the explanation is that Frogmore is not a cottage in any sense of the word that you or I would understand. It is an 1801 Grade II listed building with ten bedrooms. According to the magazine *Marie Claire*, the changes have included the transformation of the building from split apartments into a single house, and the installation of a *Gone with the Wind* double staircase. I am sure that these radical alterations will have been considered most carefully by Windsor & Maidenhead Council as part of their legal duty to protect listed buildings, as will the retrospective application for alterations to the grounds.

In a repeat performance, Harry and Meghan decided, after the money had been largely spent, that they did not actually want to live there after all and intended to move to Canada, though they did intend to retain Frogmore Cottage as their British base. This time there was a public outcry and in May 2020 it was announced that the couple would repay the costs of the renovations in instalments over the course of more than a decade, though there seems to be no allowance for the element of interest. Harry also pledged to pay rent for the property that would now stand empty, though the level was set well below commercial levels. The property cannot be re-let for security reasons.

Harry is very much Action Man. In 2011, he walked with injured war veterans on their way to the North Pole, and in 2013 he undertook a 200-mile trek to the South Pole. His commitment to supporting wounded veterans is undoubtedly genuine, and all the more admirable for that. He also clearly feels an affinity for Africa and became president of African Parks and of the Queen's Commonwealth Trust. He and Meghan went to Botswana in both 2016 and 2017. It was rumoured that they were minded to spend a lengthy period on the continent, perhaps helping to track wildlife poachers, which would also have conveniently got them away from the stuffiness of the Buckingham Palace regime.

If Harry is Action Man, William comes across as a sort of posh solicitor from Rickmansworth: studiously reliable if much less spirited and, well, rather dull. He is expected, as a future king, to behave more carefully than Harry, and some of his activities, such as the weeks he spent on an attachment to MI5, MI6 and GCHQ, inevitably keep him out of the headlines.

There is a sense that Harry feels vulnerable in some way. One national newspaper editor told me: 'Harry wants to be both celebrity and victim.' It was a perceptive observation. When the Prince was asked how he felt about being moved down the succession list when one of William's offspring was born, he enthusiastically pronounced it great news, but was there a bit of him, like Prince Andrew before him, that felt he was moving inexorably to the outer zone of the radar screen? He had been third in line to the throne and is now sixth. The prominent publication of a photograph in January 2020 which captured the Queen, Charles, William and George – but not Harry – can only have reinforced this relegation in status and is said to have caused Harry and Meghan hurt feelings.

It was noticeable that just ahead of the release of pictures marking the first birthday of Prince Louis, Harry released seven previously unseen wildlife photos he had taken. Was this just clumsy timing, or a Fergie-type attempt to steal the headlines? Certainly, on another occasion, photographs of the brothers and their wives were edited to remove William and Kate before they were released on the Sussexes' Instagram account.

On the flip side, of course, a spare can feel liberated – reckless, even. When he was just six, Harry said to William: 'You'll be king, I won't, so I can do what I want.'

But it was another seed, also latent in Act One, that grew into a poisonous plant and perhaps did the most damage: the relationship with the media.

This had been an issue for both William and Harry long before their prospective wives appeared on the scene. Both harboured a visceral dislike of the fourth estate as a result of what happened to their mother, holding the press to a degree responsible for her death. Speaking of his mother's experience, William said, 'I don't believe being chased by thirty guys on motorbikes who block your path, who spit at you to get a reaction … and make a woman cry in public to get a photograph, I don't believe that is appropriate.' While he is totally right to condemn this sort of behaviour, this seems to have evolved into an unwise general hostility to the media, and suspicion towards every journalist. 'William needs to be careful,' one royal correspondent told me. 'Ultimately he is just another bald bloke in a suit.'

Diana's independence of mind and increasing willingness to speak out came as a shock to the system, for it was not just the Palace who were comfortable with the traditional subservient role of the royal wife. The media connived at this, and still do, regularly commenting on what royal women are wearing, while paying no attention to what the men are decked out in (except occasionally and with justification to comment disparagingly on the number of medals individuals seem to have collected). It is a 1960s Miss World mentality of beautiful but essentially brainless females that has by and large been consigned to the dustbin in other walks of life.

In late 2019, we were given a brief respite from the normal diet of dresses and disputes by an even better story for the media: a royal birth. The scale of interest can be measured by the fact that even before their wedding, Google had recorded almost five million hits for 'Meghan Markle baby'. There was no respite for Meghan, however. Even before the child was conceived, a vast array of highly personal articles appeared assessing her chances of fertility at thirty-seven, and the odds of complications arising. After the announcement that she was expecting, more such stories followed. Meghan was described as 'approaching forty' and one sneeringly referred to her 'geriatric pregnancy'.

When her pregnancy was visible for all to see, the *Daily Express* then ran a story suggesting she was using 'sneaky tricks' to 'flaunt' her baby bump. This 'trick' was to wear a coat that opened to reveal the bump. Perhaps someone at this most useless of papers had decided that she should instead be wearing some sort of ghastly 1950s floral dress for pregnant mums, or even better keeping out of the public limelight altogether in the latter stages of her pregnancy. But why should she conform to some outdated stereotype just because someone on a newspaper thinks she should?

The same papers that tut-tutted about the fact that Meghan was not hidden away somewhere as a matter of decorum are often those that choose to demean women, written by loutish lads who prefer women to be obscene and not heard. Indeed, early on in their liaison, *The Sun* ran a story headed 'Harry's Girl On Pornhub' (girl?). Those readers who will have been prompted to buy the paper for extracts will have been disappointed, for what was on the site were merely some clips from the series *Suits*.

But then there is the happy birth for them all to pore over and hostilities are temporarily halted. Producing a child is, after all, what royal wives are there for, is it not? A moment of happiness on the steps of the hospital, a slew of ecstatic, almost deranged stories in the press, including this time the unlikely enthusiasm for pictures of the baby's feet, and then the women are expected to retreat again to the sidelines and let the men take the spotlight.

Two months before Archie was born, the Sussexes had appointed Sara Latham as their new communications director, or 'spin doctor' as some papers labelled her. So at that point we had separate media teams for the Queen, Charles, William and Harry, plus the random activities of Andrew. Naturally, nobody in royal circles worried about how many support teams the public was expected to pay for.

Ms Latham came with a strong track record, including working for Bill Clinton and Tony Blair, and clearly knows what she is doing, though her leftish leanings and her vaguely new-age mission statement were seen as likely to further widen the gap between the Sussexes and the rest of the family. Ms Latham, in her previous role, laid a particular emphasis on 'executive thought leadership and purpose-led campaigns'.

To head this off, the Palace required that she needed to report to the Queen's new communications secretary as her line manager. Donal McCabe, a more traditional figure, spent six years as head of media relations for the basket case that was Railtrack, or Failtrack as it was known in the trade, and most recently worked for Ladbrokes. As it happens, Ms Latham undertook her role with some skill and tact, and when Harry and Meghan decided to relocate across the Atlantic, she was transferred to a post in the Queen's private office.

She seemed powerless, however, to stop Harry and Meghan increasingly and unwisely waging war on the tabloid press. Harry, like his brother, had not hidden his dislike of the press, but his good works, his admirable military service and his sense of fun and humour meant that despite this he generally received positive coverage. That changed when Meghan came on the scene, for the press were not universally prepared to give her the near-free pass Harry had had. A crunch point was reached with the release of a calm but hard-hitting statement challenging the press, issued by the Palace on Harry's behalf on 8 November 2016. This was seen as an unprecedented move, but actually William had previously made a strong intervention following the appearance in the papers of a picture of Kate, then his girlfriend, looking slightly harried on her way to work. The alternative pictures William released showed her being hounded by huge numbers of paparazzi shoving long lenses in her face.

Harry's statement followed a run of stories about Meghan's racial background, her sex life, her previous marriage, in fact anything salacious that could be dug up. He had never been comfortable with the 'significant curiosity' about his private life, the statement said, but he had tried to develop 'a professional relationship' with the media – but now a line had been crossed. Meghan, the statement read, 'has been subject to a wave of abuse and harassment. Some of this has been very public – the smear on the front page of a national newspaper; the racial undertones of comment pieces; and the outright sexism and racism of social media trolls...'

It went on to catalogue the harassment of her mother, her ex-boyfriend and friends and co-workers, and to say that Harry was worried about her safety. To the suggestion that this is 'all part of the game', the statement responded: 'He strongly disagrees. This is not a game – it is her life and his.' He concluded by asking the press to reflect and back off.

Some of the papers have been sympathetic, though by and large the broadsheets rather than the tabloids. 'The press pack has found its perfect prey,' wrote Ian Burrell in the *i*. 'Tormenting Meghan Markle has become a national sport that shames us,' wrote Catherine Bennett in *The Guardian*. An analysis by *The Guardian* concluded that Meghan received twice as many negative headlines as positive ones between May 2018 and January 2020. The proportion will only have worsened thereafter.

It is deeply frustrating to be at the wrong end of unfair press coverage, where prejudice and a wider hidden agenda are dressed up as news. It is an experience that many of us who have been involved in national politics have often had to endure. Individual complaints about particularly inaccurate pieces can be pursued with the relevant media outlet, though if done at all are best taken forward calmly and rationally, but generally speaking, the best response is to shrug shoulders and move on. That, however, has not been the response from Harry and Meghan. The pair have increasingly resorted to social media to get their message across unvarnished, without having to go through the prism of the traditional media, but while they can get their version of a story up first, they cannot of course control the follow-up, or the appearance of stories which are original and not helpful to them.

Harry seems to have begun to see any negative story in the press as automatically unfair, but some, while obviously negative, are perfectly fair. These have included ones detailing Harry's extravagant and carefree use of public money, or his somewhat inconsistent – some would say hypocritical – actions relating to climate change and the protection of animals. The hypocrisy, as this book catalogues, can be seen in Harry's powerful statements on climate change juxtaposed with his gratuitous use of private jets and helicopters, and his plea to protect some animals while he goes around shooting others.

The pair have also decided that a central plank of their response is to invoke legal action. This has always been a tool in the royal armoury, but they have moved it up a level. In September 2019, proceedings were issued on Harry's behalf against the owners of *The Sun* and the *Mirror* over alleged phone hacking and an associated huge cover-up over a period of more than twenty years. The actual hacking is alleged to have taken place over the period from 1994 to 2011, and the timing of the Duke's legal action seems related not to any new developments in the case but to a new determination to stick it to the papers.

In what looked very much like a piece of coordinated action, Meghan initiated a case against the *Mail on Sunday*, claiming that the paper breached both her copyright and her privacy by publishing a letter she had written to her father, Thomas Markle. It was a very personal letter and doubtless very embarrassing to see it splashed across the paper for all to see, but, while technically the law says the copyright remains with Meghan as the writer, many would take the view that it was up to her father to do what he wanted with the letter he had received and that she would be better pointing the finger at him than at the newspaper. The letter, when published, also provided an opportunity for some self-appointed specialists to weigh in. 'Handwriting expert' Ruth Myers in the *Daily Mirror* concluded that her writing showed she was 'emotionally insecure and self-pitying', with 'an inability to forgive'. Emma Bache asserted that she was a 'narcissist', and Tracy Trussell detected vulnerability. This – all from women, incidentally – was simply bullying dressed up as science.

There could, however, be no doubting the anger of the Sussexes, and their legal representatives threw everything at the *Mail on Sunday*, perhaps unwisely as a number of lines or arguments were ruled out by the judge at the first hearing. The paper made clear its intention to contest the case vigorously, and they have the money to do so. They will also have made the calculation that to throw in the towel on this one would lead to further lawsuits in the future. This is a high-stakes game, and both Harry and Meghan have opened up the possibility that they may be called to give evidence in court in their respective cases, as indeed could Meghan's father in the *Mail on Sunday* case, with all the unpredictability that entails.

Part of Meghan's case is that her letter was quoted selectively, something that the paper denies. Interestingly, Harry had a similar accusation levelled at him by the same paper, which generated a complaint from the Prince to IPSO, the voluntary body that deals with press complaints. The article in question was headed 'Drugged and tethered... what Harry didn't tell you about these awe-inspiring wildlife photos'. The paper suggested that the photographs which Harry posted on his Instagram account had been edited to obscure the fact that the animals pictured – a lion, a rhino and an elephant – had been drugged, and also that the elephant had been tethered, a fact clearly visible from the unedited photograph. Harry objected to the paper's implication that he had deliberately misled those who accessed his Instagram account. His complaint was not upheld.

The initiation of legal action by Meghan also coincided with a bitter attack on the media by Harry. In a 570-word piece published on a website created for the purpose, sussexofficial.uk, he accused them of 'waging campaigns against individuals with no thought to the consequences', and compared what Meghan was going through with what his mother had had to endure. The irony is that the statement was issued at the end of an African tour which had seen much favourable reporting for the pair. The timing of this statement therefore both annoyed the press unnecessarily and undermined the success of the tour.

There is no doubt that Harry is genuine in his fear that history might somehow repeat itself, but his response to the perceived threat is not one that is likely to bear fruit. By this point, in the autumn of 2019, the Sussexes were in essence self-detached from the royal family, but it is still surprising that their flurry of legal activity left the Palace blindsided. Moreover, the royal family's normal legal firm, Harbottle and Lewis, were bypassed. Not only had the Sussexes declared war on the fourth estate; they had also put the royal family offside.

It was gradually becoming clear that the pair wanted more space, and specifically to spend much of their time out of the country. This was a radical and indeed unique development for which there was no royal template. The pair were immediately open to the accusations that they were abandoning their duties, embarking on an ego trip and, worst of all, letting down the Queen. At such a time some friends in the media would have been useful to allow them to explain their thinking and their intentions, but by this point, a great many boats had been burnt.

Even with goodwill on all sides, the matter was not simple. What would happen with Frogmore Cottage? What were the security implications? What about all the charities where they were patrons? Could – indeed, should – Harry hold on to his military appointments? Would they still receive public money? And, most pertinently, how could the public positions they now wanted to take be reconciled with membership of the royal family?

An emergency family summit at Sandringham in early January 2020 achieved very little, largely because Meghan had decided to fly back to Canada instead. The option of a conference call was rejected for fear that the conversation might be taped at the Canadian end.

A devastating statement from the Sussexes followed in which the pair announced formally that they intended to 'step back as "senior" members of the Royal Family and work to become financially independent'. They talked of 'starting to carve out a progressive new role within this institution'. This latter idea was interpreted, not unreasonably, as them wanting to have their cake and eat it. While the decision to step back was not a surprise to the rest of the royals, the premature release of a statement and its contents were. Once again, there was no prior consultation with the Queen or the Palace, and the statement left many questions unanswered. The Queen demanded that Charles, William and Harry come up with a coherent plan in a matter of days.

The news hit the headlines around the world, and not the sort of coverage Buckingham Palace was looking for. The *New York Post* used the headline 'The Great British Break Off!', while the sardonic *West Australian* offered up 'The Royal Formerly Known As Prince'.

Worse, one of the loose ends in the statement led to a public row over the use of the 'Sussex Royal' brand the pair had been patiently building up since the previous March, when it had been registered without informing the Palace. Could they really continue to use the word 'royal' for their own commercial purposes and when they were no longer working royals? As referred to earlier in this book, the word 'royal' is heavily protected and cannot just be annexed for personal gain.

The Palace let it be known that the Queen regarded their intended use of Sussex Royal as untenable and would not allow them to use it after they ended their royal duties on 31 March, dubbed Megxit Day by the press. By that point, their Sussex Royal Instagram page had attracted over eleven million followers.

And then the pair made the grave tactical error of appearing to take a swipe at the 93-year-old monarch. The Queen cannot stop us using the Sussex Royal brand outside Britain, Meghan reportedly told friends. And in an official statement from the pair in February – yes, another one – they rubbed this in: 'While there is not any jurisdiction by The Monarchy or Cabinet Office over the use of the word "Royal" overseas, The Duke and Duchess of Sussex do not intend to use [it].' If this was intended to mollify the Palace, the press and the public, it had the opposite effect.

Their move to a £10.7 million mansion on Canada's Vancouver Island had also raised the question of security, and specifically who would pay for it. It seems nobody wanted to be left standing when the music stopped. As part of the exit deal negotiated, Harry and Meghan kept their HRH titles but would not use them. This is actually significant as HRH status provides a mechanism for support, including financial support from the taxpayer, to be provided to them, including for protection.

The pair's stated intention was to move towards financial independence, and most people agree that if they are not undertaking royal duties, they should not be supported from public funds. A poll for ITV in March 2020 produced a figure of over 90 per cent of respondents against providing financial cover for their protection abroad. The public was not in the mood for multimillion-pound bailouts for multimillionaires to play at philanthropy when travel by private jet is their norm, and when Meghan is swanning round the world for events like baby showers, swimming in expensive jewellery.

Moreover, if the Metropolitan Police were to continue to provide security while they were abroad, the cost to the public purse would actually increase significantly. In the event, Metropolitan Police officers were indeed sent to Canada and were captured on camera meeting Harry off a flight at Victoria International Airport. Of course, this was Canadian soil, so the Mounties also had to be involved, pushing the cost of security up even further, as did the fact that Harry, Meghan and Archie each qualified for protection, which meant three teams if they were in three separate locations. Or four, in fact, as there still needed to be cover for the now empty Frogmore Cottage. Ken Wharfe, the former royal protection officer, has estimated that that last element alone would amount to some £5 million annually, for security officers to patrol the extensive premises, and for a full security entourage including motorcycle outriders any time Harry needed to get to London. The bill for the ongoing security falls to Thames Valley Police, a force which has seen large cuts to its budget.

The cost of cover had already increased substantially as a result of the couple's decision to move from Kensington Palace to the more vulnerable Frogmore Cottage. Now the costs could explode and were expected to run as high as £20 million a year in total. It cannot be right that the royals can expect a blank cheque from the taxpayer to cover the costs of protection while they jet across the world. There is a need for a root-and-branch review of security, to assess who actually needs it, rather than who simply wants it as a status symbol. There should then be a ceiling established to set a sensible maximum amount to be allocated for each person protected, and any extra costs that arise as a result of decisions the protected persons themselves make should be met either from their own resources or from those of the wider royal family.

The Canadian government said in a terse statement, 'As the Duke and Duchess are currently recognised as Internationally Protected Persons, Canada has an obligation to provide security assistance on an as-needed basis.' But if the royal pair thought that it would be uncontroversial for Canada, as a Commonwealth country, to pick up the tab, they were soon to be disillusioned. A poll revealed that almost three-quarters of Canadians objected to the idea, even though the same poll showed that Harry was personally popular. It might in any case be thought somewhat rude to arrive in a country uninvited and announce you want to stay, cause a friendly government a headache and then ask them to pick up a big bill and responsibility for security. Justin Trudeau's government found itself in a difficult spot, needing to reflect public opinion but not wishing to cause offence to the royals. In the end, they smudged over the costs involved and announced that the protection provided at the expense of the Canadian taxpayer would end when the Sussexes stopped being working royals on 31 March. The *Globe and Mail*, one of the country's most prominent papers, ran a critical editorial which went further: 'You are welcome to visit but so long as you are senior royals, Canada cannot allow you to come to stay ... Canada is not a halfway house for anyone looking to get out of Britain while remaining a royal.'

Of course, Canada turned out to be exactly that, for before long, the couple were off again, this time to the United States. Kensington Palace, Frogmore Cottage, Vancouver Island – each one a step further removed from the royal family, all planned to be permanent locations, and all abandoned almost before the paint on the door was dry. The couple took a private flight – what else? – from Vancouver to California the week before the border was closed as part of the coronavirus measures. They were greeted by a tweet from Donald Trump that read: 'The US will not pay for their security protection. They must pay!' It probably did not help that Meghan, pledging support for Hillary Clinton, had previously described the notoriously thin-skinned President as being 'misogynistic' and 'divisive'. Trump's response had been to say, 'I didn't know that she was nasty.' Nor would it have helped that Harry, duped on the phone by Russian hoaxers pretending to be Greta Thunberg and her father, volunteered the view that Trump 'has blood on his hands' for increasing coal production in the US.

Inevitably, in the end, Harry and Meghan accepted that they would have to pay towards their own security, at least for private and commercial trips where there was no royal connection. That still left an estimated £5 million annual bill to look after the empty Frogmore Cottage, and who would pay for their static protection at their new home in California, an $18 million mansion equipped with twelve bathrooms and sitting in twenty-two acres?

That suggested that the line in the Palace press statement announcing the terms of their departure – 'They will no longer receive public funds for royal duties' – was, in the best traditions of Whitehall, both entirely accurate and quite misleading. Besides the security costs, it was made known that they could still expect over £2 million a year from Charles, at least in year one. However, money for Harry had up until that point come from the Duchy of Cornwall and Charles would classify this as a legitimate expense which would then reduce the amount of tax he has to pay to the Exchequer. Clarence House briefed the media that after 31 March 2020, the money for Harry would come from Charles's private funds. We should, however, reserve judgement, given that the Prince misleadingly calls the Duchy of Cornwall a 'private estate'.

The expectation is that Harry and Meghan, freed from the restrictions of the royal family, will become hot property and will not find it difficult to make many millions to add to the tens of millions they already have. Indeed, Harry's first private engagement in his new liberated role, which actually took place in February while he was still a working royal in receipt of public funds, was a speech to bankers and other rich Americans at a private JP Morgan event in Miami. Naturally, he was flown there by private jet. It is not known what Harry was paid, but the month before, JP Morgan announced an annual profit of around $28 billion, the biggest in US history. Speculation said it was likely Harry had been paid hundreds of thousands of dollars, so probably worth the public relations hit that he took.

By May 2020, they had already lined up a bewildering range of activities, some charitable, from a TV show for Apple about mental health featuring Harry and Oprah Winfrey, to Harry reading *Thomas the Tank Engine* (though he was not a patch on Ringo, it has to be said), to Meghan writing a children's book about dogs, launching a new line in clothing, and voicing a tale about elephants for Disney, the contract for which incidentally was signed before the release of the bombshell announcement from the couple in early January. Meghan also made it known that she would like to play a Hollywood superhero.

They still had time, however, to continue their war against the tabloids. With a hubris that grated, Harry chose a time in the middle of the coronavirus crisis that was sweeping Britain, with the NHS hugely stretched, thousands dying and the rest of the country in lockdown, to issue an open letter to various tabloid editors to lay down their 'new media relations policy'. 'The Duke and Duchess of Sussex will not be engaging with your outlet,' they sniffed grandly. There would be 'zero engagement', they added – though as they had not been engaging anyway, there seemed to be little point to this open letter, other than ironically to get it reported in the papers. The consequence of the letter, its contents and its timing, was to erode to almost zero whatever sympathy was left in what used to be called Fleet Street. Their circle of support now appears to be largely a celebrity one, and one to be found near their new base in Los Angeles, with the likes of Oprah Winfrey and Elton John.

And so the saga which began with Meghan being integrated into the ways of the British royal family has changed into one where Harry is integrated into the ways of Meghan's home environment. It is a plot twist worthy of Shakespeare.

Meghan is back in the city and the country where she grew up, and where her mum Doria Ragland still lives. She is back amongst the glitterati and her actor friends. She is back in her comfort zone.

She had applied to become a British citizen, but to complete the process requires the applicant to remain in the country for three years, a condition clearly not met. Still, we can at least be assured that as an American citizen, Meghan must still pay tax to the US Internal Revenue Service, though, in an astute move, in 2019 she moved her business interests to the state of Delaware, known as the US corporate haven for the wealthy. She will still, however, have to declare the monetary value of income in kind, such as free royal accommodation. It is a policy it would be good to see Her Majesty's Revenue and Customs follow for the royals over here.

That Harry is very much in love with Meghan cannot be doubted. We might even say smitten. In February 2019, for example, he chartered a jet at a cost of some £20,000 to get him home from Norway so he could be with Meghan on Valentine's Day, which may be wonderfully romantic but did suggest a surplus of cash to splurge as well as a cavalier disregard for the environment.

The Palace establishment no doubt hoped that Harry would help turn Meghan into what they would regard as an appropriate royal wife, as Kate was now regarded, but as matters have turned out, it has been Meghan who has changed Harry, not the other way round. The Duke, it seems, has been persuaded to give up hunting and shooting and has even sold off his two prize hunting rifles, for which he recouped £50,000. Meghan has also weaned him off his twenty-a-day habit.

In personal terms, Harry has bet the farm on his relationship with Meghan, and we can only hope it works out for them. The price Harry is paying is a high one, including estrangement from his friends, his family and his country. Friends say Harry has been left bewildered by the turn and pace of events and is missing in particular the camaraderie of colleagues in the armed forces.

It was a picture of William and Kate with Harry and Meghan

captured when they appeared as a quartet at a Sandringham church service at Christmas 2017 that led some enterprising journalist to dub them the 'fab four'. The analogy, of course, was to the Beatles, whose reputation and recognition factor hardly wanes even now, more than fifty years after their demise. Perhaps it was an even more apposite analogy that the journalist had in mind, for the Beatles ended their relationship in bitter acrimony and never played together again – indeed, were never all in the same room as each other again. Their last album to be released was *Let It Be*. That may also prove to be an appropriate piece of advice for those hoping for a reconciliation of the royal fab four.

On Your Bike

There are ten monarchies left in Europe: in Britain, Spain, the Benelux and Scandinavian countries, and the tiny territories of Liechtenstein and Monaco. As in Britain, many of these are long-standing. There has been a King of Norway since 872, while the Dutch monarchy can be traced back to William I, who became Prince of Orange in 1544.

All call themselves constitutional monarchies, but some are more constitutional than others. Under Article 19 of the Norwegian constitution, the King, to accede the throne, has to intone the following: 'I promise and swear that I will govern the Kingdom of Norway in accordance with the Constitution.' Article 32 of the Dutch constitution requires that 'the King shall swear or promise allegiance to the Constitution and that he will faithfully discharge his duties'.

These constitutions cement the democratic structures that govern the countries, and make clear the monarch is subservient to them. In Britain, our concept of a constitutional monarchy is rather different, not least as we famously only have an unwritten constitution, which in some respects is not worth the paper it is not written on.

Here there is no question of the monarch pledging to uphold

democratic values. The coronation vows require the new monarch to respect God and the church, but there is not a single reference to anything even vaguely connected to democracy. It is as if the last few hundred years had never happened.

Instead we, the subjects, find from time to time that we have to pledge to succumb to the unelected head of state, most ironically if we find ourselves elected to Parliament. For while other monarchies in Europe have genuinely modernised to become a seamless and inherent part of a modern democracy, ours sits uncomfortably alongside our democratic institutions, a vestige from the past, Europe's last imperial monarchy.

This is not simply a dry academic point. The imperial nature of our monarchy is reflected in how its members see themselves, and how they behave. There are the historic privileges that underpin a sense of superiority and entitlement. As catalogued in this book, this shows up in the tax breaks, the special and numerous unique legal entitlements and exemptions, and most of all, the cavalier and extravagant use of public money.

A 2016 comparison of European monarchies put the British to the top of the league for the receipt of public money, at £40 million. As we have seen, the Sovereign Grant has more than doubled since then to £82 million, and of course even that figure is a gross underestimate, failing as it does to take account of many other hidden costs, especially those concerned with security. Here, then, are the rounded comparative figures for the public money given to European monarchies:

- Britain: £82 million (2020)
- Netherlands: £39 million (2020)
- Norway: £34 million (2019)
- Belgium: £12 million (2018)
- Denmark: £10 million (2018)

- Luxembourg: £9 million (2019)
- Spain: £7 million (2018)
- Sweden: £6 million (2019)
- Liechtenstein: zero (2020)

In Spain, King Felipe has even renounced his personal inheritance from his father, Juan Carlos, who abdicated in favour of his son, and ended his annual grant after it was revealed that the former king was about to receive millions from a secret offshore fund. Revelations in Britain that the Queen was benefiting from an offshore fund raised barely an eyebrow.

Then there are the palaces. Spain, Holland, Denmark – they all manage with just two apiece. Our royal family manages to occupy fifteen state residences, and that is without counting those owned privately like Balmoral or Sandringham, or those owned by the Duchy of Cornwall, all of which we also pay for to a degree. In terms of private wealth, none of Europe's monarchies is on the breadline, but none bar Liechtenstein has the fabulous treasure chest running into billions that the British royals have.

Our royal family continues to grow, so that there is barely room on the balcony at Buckingham Palace to hold them all. The photo on the cover of this book shows forty-four crammed in. Large numbers feature on the payroll, but just how many royals do we need to cut ribbons? In other countries, there is a core monarchy and the rest of them go out to work and have normal jobs, just like everybody else. Most, like Andrew's children, seem simply to swan around in a half-world of upmarket social gatherings.

In May 2016 Denmark announced plans to reduce royal funding by cutting out all minor royals. Others had already taken that step. When will we follow suit?

European monarchies such as those in Belgium, Holland, Luxembourg and Spain have begun creating the principle of monarchs retiring and passing the baton on to the next in line. The last three queens in the Netherlands have each stood down around the age of seventy. And we have even had a Pope standing down because of age. But there is more chance of finding Elvis on the moon than Queen Elizabeth II following suit.

Charles used to argue that monarchs should step down at seventy, but he rather went off that idea as he approached the milestone himself. He has however allegedly been giving serious consideration to limiting his reign to a short period before abdicating in favour of William. We will see. The enthusiasm for that may well fade when he is actually in pole position.

In Britain the rituals of yesteryear are fiercely adhered to, and convey not so much the dignity of the Crown as a sense of distasteful arrogance and insufferable stuffiness. Nobody can arrive at an event after a royal, nobody can look down on the Queen, the royal personage must leave an event first. The hierarchy of place is strictly enforced, with unbending rules as to which medal is more important than which, or who must curtsey to whom, even forcing Meghan to curtsey to the Queen at her own wedding. She will also have to curtsey to Camilla and Sophie, Countess of Wessex. How absurd.

This all belongs more naturally in some BBC costume drama set in Georgian times than in Britain in 2020. How long is this historical nonsense going to last? But all the pomp is good for tourism, comes the rejoinder. Leaving aside the point that it is hardly sensible to base our constitutional arrangements on what works best for the tourism industry, it is worth noting that the European royal palace that attracts the most visitors is actually to be found in Versailles, and the French abolished their monarchy in 1848.

How different it is elsewhere. On one occasion I found myself at a rather swish event in Sweden. I started chatting harmlessly to another guest, who to my considerable surprise then turned out to be a senior member of the Swedish royal family. You can never imagine a British royal just mingling in that natural way. Queen Juliana of the Netherlands used to pour drinks for her guests, go shopping at the local supermarket and sent her children to state school. Anyone seen Prince Charles down the Co-op? Or even at Waitrose, to stock up on Duchy Originals?

The present Dutch King, Willem-Alexander, personally paid for 150 dinner guests to attend his fiftieth birthday in 2017. Moreover, the 150 were ordinary citizens, chosen by ballot. In Britain, the state would have been handed the bill for such an event, and the guests would have been full of titled individuals and ones with double-barrelled names.

Even in Japan, which arguably has the oldest monarchy in the world, Prince Akishino announced that the highly religious ritual, part of the 2019 succession ceremony, should be paid for by the imperial family, rejecting the government's offer to pay. Has there ever been an occasion when the British royal family has refused an offer of public money and instead offered to meet the bill themselves?

The modern monarchies of Europe are sometimes known as bicycling monarchies, because they have scaled back the excesses of centuries past. And because members of their royal families do actually use a bike to get around. It is time our royal family learnt a thing or two. Sadly that day seems somewhat distant. For the imperial nature of the royal family, with all its puffed-up pomp and circumstance, performs a wider function in Britain that many fear to lose: it conveys the message that the comfortable past is still here, and helps us turn our eyes from the diminished status of the present.

It was the American Dean Acheson, a right-hand man to President Truman, who observed that 'Great Britain has lost an empire and has not yet found a role.' That remark was made in December 1962 but it could equally have been made almost sixty years later.

Over that intervening period, British governments have been edging the nation, often uncomfortably, towards a logical role as an important but medium-sized European power. But our politicians have not wanted to spell this out, for to do so would be to admit that the glory days are truly over. So the gap between the public rhetoric and the practical reality has become ever wider.

My current passport, in EU maroon, still grandly 'requires in the Name of Her Majesty all those whom it may concern to allow the bearer to pass freely without let or hindrance, and to allow the bearer such assistance and protection as may be necessary.' You can imagine some pompous nineteenth-century traveller pointing that statement out to some tremulous official in some distant land, to good effect. Nowadays, to do so would, I fear, be more likely to generate a contemptuous snort. But still the statement survives, like some old gnarled relative. Only the typeface has changed.

And now we are reverting to a blue passport, produced to the fury of the Brexiteers by a company in France, rather than De La Rue, the ever-so-British-sounding competitor. Their idea of free trade harks back to the empire. We are free to sell other countries what we want, and on our terms, but we will jolly well control what comes in by way of imports. Does anyone with even a modicum of common sense think that this approach will wash with other countries? But then, as the former Tory Party chairman Chris Patten observed, the nearest some of those who talk of new trade treaties have actually come to negotiating one is at the checkout at Waitrose. All a blue passport will do is to make Britons wishing to travel abroad stand out and lead to obstructions to our own free movement. Fog in channel: Britain cut off.

Another element in the self-delusion kit is the so-called special relationship with the Americans, much trumpeted by those Brexit-leaning politicians who seem to think we can carry on where Yalta left off, as if nothing has happened in the interim. Yes, there is a bond of language and history, and yes, there are genuinely valuable and unique features to the relationship, such as the considerable intelligence sharing.

But it was the Americans who in effect forced the British to abandon the empire to which Dean Acheson referred, who pulled the rug from under the British over Suez and who left us laden with an enormous debt on not very good terms from the Second World War, a debt that was not finally paid off until the early years of the twenty-first century.

The Americans do not base their dealings with this country on sentimentality. They are hard-headed and transactional in their approach, and why would they not be? A free-trade deal with the US will not be a deal of equals. It will mean abandoning legislation that protects the public in areas like the environment and food safety. It will mean bending to their will. But our obsequious approach to the United States government of the day does at least mean the Americans continue to humour us, by dutifully referring when necessary to the special relationship in a sort of pitying way. After all, the British crave the appearance of unique importance and it costs the United States very little to play along. It is certainly cheaper than providing anything meaningful in return.

I witnessed this myself when Barack Obama addressed MPs in Westminster Hall in 2011. As he intoned the phrase 'special relationship', you could almost hear some MPs purring away, and from the platform almost hear the box being ticked.

The true nature of the relationship can be gauged by the exchange of presents that took place between Gordon Brown and Barack Obama after the latter became President in 2009. The Prime Minister gave the President an ornamental pen-holder, carved from the timbers of the

Victorian anti-slave ship, HMS *Gannet*, carefully chosen to sit with the oak desk that had sat in the Oval Office since the 1880s and which was hewn from HMS *Gannet*'s sister ship, HMS *Resolute*. The Prime Minister also presented the President with a framed commission for the latter vessel, as well as a first edition of the seven-volume biography of Churchill by Sir Martin Gilbert.

Barack Obama gave Gordon Brown a box of twenty-five DVDs of American films, carefully chosen from the shelves of the nearest store down the road. They included *Singin' in the Rain*, *Psycho* and *Casablanca*.

Obama's predecessor, George W. Bush, was called George by Gordon Brown's predecessor, who in return called him Blair. And while she was Prime Minister we saw poor Theresa May torn between sucking up to the childish, bullying egomaniac in the White House, and maintaining sensible positions widely shared across the West on everything from Iran to climate change, Israel to sexual health, at the risk of having Trump throw his toys out of the pram because the UK does not love him enough. Even the most ardent anti-monarchist can feel sorry for the Queen, having had to entertain this vulgar buffoon on a state visit.

Nor is it just in the eulogising of the so-called special relationship that Britain's decline and uncertain place in the world can be hidden. The much lauded independent nuclear deterrent, a hugely expensive symbol of our macho power in the world, is far from independent, wholly relying as it does on American technology. Moreover, it is inconceivable that we could ever use this without American permission. Nuclear it is, independent it is not. And who exactly is it supposed to be deterring? Not the terrorists who are the immediate threat to this country. Nor those hostile countries who have found cyber-attacks a much cheaper and safer way to destabilise us.

At the United Nations, we retain the semblance of world-power status in that we are one of only five permanent members of the Security Council, and thus retain a veto. But this is just like the veto the Queen has on legislation passed in Parliament. It is tolerated as long as it is never used, and there would be uproar if it ever were. While the Americans, Russians and Chinese can veto with impunity, we dare not do so.

When I was in New York a few years back, I asked our ambassador when we had last used the veto alone. He did not know but came back some moments later with the answer 1973, on a Rhodesian matter. I suggested there was not much point in having a veto we could not use and would it not be more sensible if we and France relinquished our seats and instead we had an EU seat where the veto could actually be exercised. I watched with interest as the blood visibly drained from his face.

Empires wax and wane with the sweep of time: those of the Romans, the Ottomans, the Spanish, the Portuguese, the French and, yes, the British, have all gone. Yet somehow we like to pretend that, even if the map of the world is no longer covered in numerous splashes of pink, we still retain our position and power, and glory and grandeur. And now the political classes, who had been moving us surreptitiously and somewhat painfully into the position of a top-rank European power within the EU, find that, having failed to sell this vision, we are now to undo the work of the last fifty years and leave the bloc, casting ourselves adrift to bob around on the ocean waves like a champagne cork, and with no bottle.

The politicians now in the ascendancy, often the same ones who over-interpret the importance of the special relationship with the United States, assert that Britain can go it alone, when the rest of the world is huddling into regional trading associations, and that laughably the rest of the EU needs us more than we need them. We tell ourselves the world envies us, when actually they often regard us, not unfondly in fact, as a historical curiosity, a sort of royal theme park. It is hardly surprising if that is the image formed if that is the image we project.

Brexit has damaged matters further. Much of the world thinks we have gone mad. One Australian observed that Britain was now seen as a loved grandparent who has lost it. The rest of the world regards us as a laughing stock. The British always did take a long time to leave, quipped an Indian newspaper.

Central to all this tragic self-delusion is the monarchy and with it the self-inflicted infantilisation of much of British society. 'Bring back the royal yacht *Britannia*,' came the cry from the idiocracy that now runs the Tory Party, and from Prince Andrew. *Britannia* no longer rules the waves, royal yacht or not. But for those who want to pretend that the clock has stopped, or can be wound back, and the march of time defied, it is comforting to retreat into this fantasy. And if part of that is to allow the royal family to waive the rules, then that is part of the price.

Unintentionally, Brexit has brought us to a crunch point. Are we going to face up to, and accept with good grace, our much diminished but still important place in the world, or are we going to go on pretending that this is still 1954, and again put off the day when reality is looked in the eye?

If Britain is to face up to the future rather than trying to hang on to the past, it needs to give itself a cold, hard look in the mirror. That look needs to include consideration of the monarchy. Tradition has its strength and can be a good comfort blanket, but it is by definition sclerotic, a bar to progress, a stone in a flowing river.

The imperial nature of the British royal family is a delusion that sends out the message that Britain's days of past greatness still exist. It is a delusion that prevents us moving on, like an old boxer who still thinks he can somehow regain his crown from the young upstart who took it from him in the ring some time ago. Yet to date, the response has been to hype up the monarchy, to play up its imperial nature, as if by shouting louder, the truth can be drowned out. But we are fooling ourselves, not other people.

Some will argue, as some always have, that we should move to a republic. They put the intellectual case that to have the head of state determined by accident of birth is undemocratic and random, and far from guaranteed to get the best person. They will argue that, just as the case for the abolition of hereditary peers was convincingly made (if not fully carried through) so the same logic should apply to our head of state.

Others will argue that while nobody would, from a blank piece of paper, create the system we now have, it is there now and not worth disrupting. More to the point, the Queen herself is held in high regard by most people and there is a reluctance to challenge matters fundamentally out of respect for her as she nears the end of her reign. But the Queen ascended the throne in 1952 when Britain was a very different place, when our role in the world was very different. It was a time when almost nobody had a fridge or a washing machine or a television to watch the solitary black-and-white channel. It was a time even before Elvis Presley or Bill Haley, let alone the Beatles. It was a time of food rationing, of steam trains, of a country that was almost 100 per cent white.

The country has moved on but the monarchy has not. In some ways, it has gone backwards. As the constitutional importance of the monarchy has lessened, the amount of public money spent on them has mushroomed. Meanwhile their private wealth has increased immeasurably, with the gap between the royal family and their 'subjects' now wider than ever. And while the country's institutions have become more open and accountable, the shroud of secrecy surrounding the royal family has been pulled ever tighter.

The change of monarch, when it comes, will represent an important crossroads. Prince Charles has in part recognised the need for a new approach, most notably by his clear wish to narrow down the public face of the royals. It was Charles who decided that, for the jubilee flypast in 2012, only the core team would appear on the Buckingham Palace balcony: William and Kate, Harry, Camilla and himself. Similarly, Prince George's christening in 2013 was notable for the absence of the Yorks and the Wessexes. He will have an uphill struggle, though. The Queen insisted on a full balcony turnout of every inconsequential royal for the Trooping the Colour ceremony in 2018.

It is clear that the public approve of the direction of travel Charles wishes to pursue. A 2015 poll conducted by YouGov found that a majority believed the core team should continue to receive state funding, albeit not by a huge majority: 69 per cent for the Queen, with 24 per cent against, and majorities otherwise only for Charles, William and Harry. The public was against funding Andrew and Edward by about two to one, and eight to one against funding the Queen's cousins, the Dukes of Gloucester and Kent. If this were an election, this would be lost-deposit territory for those two.

Moreover, those views were expressed without a full appreciation of just how much public money goes to the royals, and just how much they have enriched themselves from public money over the decades. If the British people could see the way public money is spent on Bourbon excesses for pampered individuals, see the privileged exemptions and favours that are available only to the royals, then they might conclude that they have been sorely hoodwinked. Those shaky percentages in favour of public funding would plummet.

There is no inviolable rule that says the monarchy will always be with us. In 2015, at the time when Virginia Roberts's allegations about Andrew hit the headlines, *The Times*, of all papers, ran an editorial stating that 'no royal family is indispensable, or permanent'.

Another poll, this time carried out by MORI in 2002, asked people how long they thought the monarchy would exist: 86 per cent thought it would still exist in 2012, but only 44 per cent in 2052 and just 26 per cent in 2102. It seems the monarchy is seen as an aspect of the past, not the future.

Britain should have the self-confidence to set aside this magic-dust monarchy, just as an adult relinquishes the toys they enjoyed as a child. Letting go may come with a tinge of sadness, but it is necessary if Britain is to adjust to life in the twenty-first century. The world has moved on. We need to as well. We need to face facts: the monarchy as presently constituted is not part of the solution. It is part of the problem.

There is a strong intellectual case for moving to a republic, for enabling every person to have a say in who their head of state is, and having the power to get rid of them if they fail to pass muster. And how can it be right that in a democracy the only job you can never aspire to is that of head of state? Yet we start from where we are, and many would accept, or indeed prefer, reform to revolution. So a sensible alternative is to exchange our imperial monarchy for a modern bicycling alternative, to tread the same road as all those other European countries have who still retain a monarchy.

The British royal family would in fact be well advised in its own interests to modernise, and to grasp that the tree that does not bend must surely break. And to grasp that reform means more than simply reducing the numbers who appear on the balcony of Buckingham Palace. The huge sprawling property portfolio that we pay for needs to be slimmed down too. The whole financial package that has evolved over centuries to the great personal benefit of the royals must be recast. The Duchies of Lancaster and Cornwall should be subsumed in the Crown Estates, as should have happened in 1760, with the heir to the throne instead receiving an allowance to support his or her activities.

The convention that money for the royals can only go up, never down, must end, as must the uniquely favourable tax breaks, especially on inheritance tax as it relates to private property.

The tight rules that apply to others in the public sector in respect of the use of public money need to be applied to the royals as well. No more helicopters paid for by us to take Prince Andrew to a golf course. No more staying in swanky hotels abroad when the British ambassador's house is available, no more private jets when commercial flight alternatives exist.

The ability of the monarch and the heir to the throne to fashion proposed government legislation so it suits them personally is a democratic outrage and should be stopped forthwith. Other self-serving legal advantages, such as the ability to keep wills secret, must also be dispensed with. Crucially, the monarchy must be subject to freedom of information legislation in the same way as any other public body is, and they should be required to maintain a register of interests, detailing private gifts and hospitality received, just as others in the public sector are required to do. A clear delineation between private and public must be established, policed and enforced.

If we are to have a monarchy, let it be a modern one that reflects the Britain of today. Let it be one where the monarchy is of the people, not above them.

Let the curtain be pulled back, as it is at the end of *The Wizard of Oz*, to dispel the magic illusion and reveal the unwelcome truth. From there we can move forward.

Appendix 1

The secret instructions I was given for my induction as a Privy Counsellor.
New entrants are told to destroy these instructions.

THE PRIVY COUNCIL INDUCTION CEREMONY

The Clerk of the Privy Council will, before the Council starts, explain the order of entry into the Council Chamber, and the position you should take up once you have entered and shaken hands with The Queen.

Induction is the first item of business. When you hear the Lord President read out your name you should proceed to the first footstool (the Clerk will have explained the layout of the footstools) and kneel down on your right knee and hold up your right hand. The Clerk will then read out the short Affirmation of Allegiance. You do not repeat the Affirmation aloud, but you should mentally repeat the words, and say "I do" at the end.

After saying "I do" you should stand and move to the second footstool, which is directly in front of The Queen, and kneel (right knee). The Queen will hold out Her right hand. You should take it with your right hand, raise it to your lips, kiss it and release it. Standing up, you should take a pace or two backwards, make a neck bow (ladies may curtsey), and return to your original position in the line of Privy Counsellors (there is no need to walk backwards).

Once back in the line you should once again raise your right hand and the Clerk will read out the long Privy Counsellor's Affirmation. Once again you do not repeat the Affirmation aloud, but you should follow the words carefully and say "I do" at the end.

You then shake hands with the Lord President and the other Counsellors present (though not with The Queen).

The remainder of the business of the Council will then proceed. At the end The Queen normally engages in a short informal conversation with the Counsellors before pressing the bell. On that signal the Counsellors in turn shake hands with The Queen and leave the Chamber, with no special ceremony.

The Privy Council Office will, after the Council, send you a copy of the Order recording that you have affirmed and a copy of the Privy Counsellor's Affirmation.

Privy Counsellors may use the prefix "Right Honourable" and peers may additionally use the suffix "PC".

Privy Council Office

The Privy Council oath as administered to new entrants,
unchanged over centuries.

You do swear by Almighty God to be a true and faithful Servant unto the Queen's Majesty, as one of Her Majesty's Privy Council. You will not know or understand of any manner of thing to be attempted, done, or spoken against Her Majesty's Person, Honour, Crown, or Dignity Royal, but you will let and withstand the same to the uttermost of your Power, and either cause it to be revealed to Her Majesty Herself, or to such of her Privy Council as shall advertise Her Majesty of the same. You will, in all things to be moved, treated, and debated in Council, faithfully and truly declare your Mind and Opinion, according to your Heart and Conscience; and will keep secret all Matters committed and revealed unto you, or that shall be treated of secretly in Council. And if any of the said Treaties or Counsels shall touch any of the Counsellors, you will not reveal it unto him, but will keep the same until such time as, by the Consent of Her Majesty, or of the Council, Publication shall be made thereof. You will to your uttermost bear Faith and Allegiance unto the Queen's Majesty; and will assist and defend all Jurisdictions, Pre-eminences, and Authorities, granted to Her Majesty, and annexed to the Crown by Acts of Parliament, or otherwise, against all Foreign Princes, Persons, Prelates, States, or Potentates. And generally in all things you will do as a faithful and true Servant ought to do to Her Majesty. So help you God.

Appendix 2

Prince Harry's October 2019 statement attacking the media, released as he and the Duchess of Sussex launched legal proceedings against the *Mail on Sunday*

As a couple, we believe in media freedom and objective, truthful reporting. We regard it as a cornerstone of democracy and in the current state of the world – on every level – we have never needed responsible media more.

Unfortunately, my wife has become one of the latest victims of a British tabloid press that wages campaigns against individuals with no thought to the consequences – a ruthless campaign that has escalated over the past year, throughout her pregnancy and while raising our newborn son.

There is a human cost to this relentless propaganda, specifically when it is knowingly false and malicious, and though we have continued to put on a brave face – as so many of you can relate to – I cannot begin to describe how painful it has been. Because in today's digital age, press fabrications are repurposed as truth across the globe. One day's coverage is no longer tomorrow's chip-paper.

Up to now, we have been unable to correct the continual misrepresentations – something that these select media outlets have been aware of and have therefore exploited on a daily and sometimes hourly basis.

It is for this reason we are taking legal action, a process that has been many months in the making. The positive coverage of the past week from these same publications exposes the double standards of this specific press pack that has vilified her almost daily for the past nine months; they have been able to create lie after lie at her expense simply because she has not been visible while on maternity leave. She is the same woman she was a year ago on our wedding day, just as she is the same woman you've seen on this Africa tour.

For these select media this is a game, and one that we have been unwilling to play from the start. I have been a silent witness to her private suffering for too long. To stand back and do nothing would be contrary to everything we believe in.

This particular legal action hinges on one incident in a long and disturbing pattern of behaviour by British tabloid media. The contents of a private letter were published unlawfully in an intentionally destructive manner to manipulate you, the reader, and further the divisive agenda of the media group in question. In addition to their unlawful publication of this private document, they purposely misled you by strategically omitting select paragraphs, specific sentences, and even singular words to mask the lies they had perpetuated for over a year.

There comes a point when the only thing to do is to stand up to this behaviour, because it destroys people and destroys lives. Put simply, it is bullying, which scares and silences people. We all know this isn't acceptable, at any level. We won't and can't believe in a world where there is no accountability for this.

Though this action may not be the safe one, it is the right one.

Because my deepest fear is history repeating itself. I've seen what happens when someone I love is commoditised to the point that they are no longer treated or seen as a real person. I lost my mother and now I watch my wife falling victim to the same powerful forces.

We thank you, the public, for your continued support. It is hugely appreciated. Although it may not seem like it, we really need it.

Bibliography

Allen, Martin, *Hidden Agenda: How the Duke of Windsor Betrayed the Allies* (Macmillan, 2000)

Bates, Stephen, *Royalty Inc.: Britain's Best-Known Brand* (Aurum Press, 2015)

Bower, Tom, *Rebel Prince: The Power, Passion and Defiance of Prince Charles* (HarperCollins, 2018)

Eckert, Astrid, *The Struggle for the Files: The Western Allies and the Return of German Archives after the Second World War* (Cambridge University Press, 2012)

Hall, Phillip, *Royal Fortune: Tax, Money and the Monarchy* (Bloomsbury, 1992)

Hamilton, Willie, *My Queen and I* (Quartet Books, 1975)

Haseler, Stephen, *The Grand Delusion: Britain after Sixty Years of Elizabeth II* (I. B. Tauris, 2012)

Hocking, Jennifer, *The Dismissal Dossier: Everything You Were Never Meant to Know about November 1975* (Melbourne University Publishing, 2017)

Hurd, Douglas, *Elizabeth II: The Steadfast* (Allen Lane, 2015)

Kelley, Kitty, *The Royals* (Grand Central Publishing, 2010)

Morton, Andrew, *17 Carnations: The Windsors, The Nazis and The Cover-Up* (Michael O'Mara Books, 2015)

Morton, Andrew, *Theirs Is the Kingdom: The Wealth of the Windsors* (Michael O'Mara Books, 1989)

Petropoulos, Jonathan, *Royals and the Reich: The Princes von Hessen in Nazi Germany* (Oxford University Press, 2009)

Rogers, David, *By Royal Appointment: Tales from the Privy Council – The Unknown Arm of Government* (Biteback Publishing, 2015)

Smith, Joan, *Down with the Royals* (Biteback Publishing, 2015)

Taylor, A. J. P., *The Struggle for Mastery in Europe 1848–1918* (Clarendon Press, 1954)

Temple, Jon, *Living off the State: A Critical Guide to Royal Finance* (Progress Books, 2008)

Thomson, David, *Europe Since Napoleon* (Penguin, 1990)

Urbach, Karina, *Go-Betweens for Hitler* (Oxford University Press, 2015)

Wilson, A. N., *The Queen* (Atlantic Books, 2016)

Acknowledgements

I am immensely grateful to all the people who have given me their time, insight and encouragement to complete this book.

There have been the journalists, especially Rob Evans at *The Guardian*, Richard Kay at the *Daily Mail*, Kevin Maguire at the *Daily Mirror*, Dave Wooding at *The Sun* and the former BBC royal correspondent Michael Cole, as well as freelancers Miles Goslett and Marie Woolf. I wish to especially thank Sharon Churcher, whose enthusiasm has been wonderful, and Ian Hislop and his team at *Private Eye* for allowing me access to their records.

Other authors have been generous with their time, especially Andrew Morton, Tom Bower and Jon Temple, but also Jennifer Hocking, Karina Urbach and Astrid Eckert.

Amongst many others who have helped are academics including Professor Rory Cormac and Dr Piers Brendon, the historian John Kirkhope, parliamentarians Margaret Hodge MP, Norman Lamb MP and Lord Berkeley, and Graham Smith from Republic.

A special thanks go to the ever helpful staff at the British Library, at Balliol College, Oxford, and at the Royal Archives in Windsor.

Thanks also to my agent, Charlie Viney, to all at Biteback, particularly

Stephanie Carey, and to my friends Guy Earl and Paul Myles, who helped me with the proofreading and fact-checking. And of course to those with government or Palace connections who wanted to remain anonymous. You know who you are.

Lastly, a reverse acknowledgement of thanks to the Lord Chamberlain, the Cabinet Office, the Privy Council and Prince Charles, all of whom have given every possible assistance short of actual help.

About the Author

Norman Baker was the Lib Dem MP for Lewes from 1997 to 2015 and established a reputation as one of the most dogged and persistent parliamentary interrogators the modern House of Commons has known. Following the 2010 general election, he was appointed Parliamentary Under-Secretary of State for Transport, then Minister of State for Crime Prevention at the Home Office. He is the author of the acclaimed *The Strange Death of David Kelly* and a political memoir, *Against the Grain*. He is an established singer-songwriter and has released three albums and also hosts three weekly music shows on his local FM station.

Index

Members of royal family are indexed by their first names, other nobility are indexed by their title.